Step Forward
Language for Everyday Life

Step-By-Step Lesson Plans

SERIES DIRECTOR
Jayme Adelson-Goldstein

Jenni Currie Santamaria

OXFORD
UNIVERSITY PRESS

OXFORD
UNIVERSITY PRESS

198 Madison Avenue
New York, NY 10016 USA

Great Clarendon Street, Oxford OX2 6DP UK

Oxford University Press is a department of the University of Oxford.
It furthers the University's objective of excellence in research,
scholarship, and education by publishing worldwide in

Oxford New York

Auckland Cape Town Dar es Salaam Hong Kong Karachi
Kuala Lumpur Madrid Melbourne Mexico City Nairobi
New Delhi Shanghai Taipei Toronto

With offices in

Argentina Austria Brazil Chile Czech Republic France Greece
Guatemala Hungary Italy Japan Poland Portugal Singapore
South Korea Switzerland Thailand Turkey Ukraine Vietnam

OXFORD and OXFORD ENGLISH are registered trademarks of
Oxford University Press

© Oxford University Press 2007

Database right Oxford University Press (maker)

No unauthorized photocopying

Executive Publisher: Janet Aitchison

Editorial Manager: Stephanie Karras

Senior Editor: Sharon Sargent

Art Director: Maj-Britt Hagsted

Senior Designer: Claudia Carlson

Layout Artist: Colleen Ho

Production Manager: Shanta Persaud

Production Controller: Eve Wong

Printed in Hong Kong

10 9 8 7 6 5 4
ISBN: 978 0 19 439230 3 STEP-BY-STEP LESSON PLANS
ISBN: 978 0 19 439839 8 STEP-BY-STEP LESSON PLANS WITH CD-ROM (PACK)
ISBN: 978 0 19 439840 4 CD-ROM

Many thanks to Sharon Sargent for her guidance
and encouragement; Jayme Adelson-Goldstein
for her insight and leadership; and Stacey Hunter
and Meg Araneo, who made my writing look
good. I am also grateful to Jean Rose and my
colleagues and students at ABC Adult School for
their constant inspiration.

Special thanks to Tony and Amaya, whose love
and laughter keep me going.

Jenni Currie Santamaria

I gratefully acknowledge the dedication and
expertise of Jenni Santamaria, Jane Spigarelli,
Stephanie Karras, Sharon Sargent, Stacey Hunter,
Meg Araneo, Niki Barolini, Colleen Ho, Maj-Britt
Hagsted, Shanta Persaud, and Eve Wong. Special
thanks to Jenni for bringing her exceptional
"multilevel" talents to all four books.

For Norma, who always taught that the best
lessons come from the learner.

Jayme Adelson-Goldstein

Acknowledgments

The publishers would also like to thank the following for their permission to adapt copyrighted material:

p. 28 "Parks and Recreation: The Benefits are Endless…" used with permission of the National Recreation and Park Association

p. 56-57 "Job Outlook 2005: Good News for College Graduates" used with permission of Job Outlook and the National Association of Colleges and Employers

p. 70 "History of Earth Day" used with permission of www.earthday.net

p. 112 "'Attitudes and Beliefs about the Use of Over-the-Counter Medicines: A Dose of Reality' A National Survey of Consumers and Health Professionals" used with permission of National Council on Patient Information and Education © 2002-2006

p. 126-127 "State Lemon Law Criteria" used with permission of the Center for Auto Safety

p. 139, "Loveland Police Department Public Safety Survey 2003" used with permission of Loveland, Colorado Police Department

Cover photograph: Corbis/Punchstock
Back cover photograph: Brian Rose

Illustrations: Laurie Conley, p.2, p.6, p.18, p.32, p.45, p.73, p.118, p.143, p.157; Geo Parkin, p.4, p.19, p.25, p.78, 83, 94, 106, 123, p.150, p.158; Claudia Carlson, p.5; Gary Ciccarelli, p.10, p.13 (two illustrations top right), p.59, p.120; Jane Spencer, p.11, p.22, p.41, p. 101, p.151; Annie Bissett, p.13, p.27, p.50, p.69, p.148, p.162; Jay Montgomery, p.17, p.31 (four illustrations); Arlene Boehm, p.20, p.167; Barb Bastian, p.31 (poster), p. 36 (two ads), p.37 (ad), p.47, p.51, p.61, p.103, p.112, p.139, p.146, p.147, p.159; John Batten, p.33, p.34, p.39, p.48, p.67, p.87, p.104, p.111; p.115, p.137, p.160, p.163; Terry Paczko, p.36 (two laptops), p.60, p.75, p.84, p.88 (document call-outs), p.117, p.132; Guy Holt, p.37 (three cameras); Karen Prichett, p.88; Mark Hannon, p.38, p.64, p.79, p.90, p.95, p.125, p.139; Mark Collins, p.45; Tom Newscom, p.46, p.74, p.130, p.131; Bill Dickson, p.81, p.92, p.98, p.122, p.126, p.135; Karen Minot, p.89, p.145; Matt Zang, p.102; Uldis Klavins, p.116; Angelo Tillery, p.144.

Photographs: Grant Heilman: p.5 (elementary school); Superstock: p.5 (middle school); Photo Edit Inc.: David Young-Wolff, p.5 (high school); Photo Edit Inc.: David Young-Wolff, p.5 (university); The Image Works: p.5 (community college); Photo Edit Inc.: Davis Barber, p.5 (adult school); Superstock: p.14; Masterfile: p.24; The Image Works: p.28; Robertstock: Jack Hollingsworth, p. 38 (business woman); Punch Stock: p.47; Photo Edit Inc.: Jeff Greenberg, p.52 (shipping clerk); The Image Works: p.61 (community clinic); The Image Works: p.61 (senior center); Punch Stock: p.61 (pet adoption); The Image Works: p.61 (city hall); The Image Works: p.66; Masterfile: p.69 (recycling symbol); Photo Edit Inc.: Tony Freeman, p.70; Painet Photos: Cheryl & Leo Meyer, p.108; Grant Heilman: p.129; Age Fotostock: p.134; Photographers Direct: Vincent Abbey, p.139 (woman reporting a crime); Photo Edit Inc.: Michael Newman, p.139 (policeman); Photo Edit Inc.: Eric Fowke, p.140; Stockbyte/Superstock: p.145; Photo Edit Inc.: Dana White, p.154; Punch Stock: p.159 (tax form); Susan and Neil Silverman: p.159 (no littering sign); Superstock: p.159 (group); Getty Images: p.159 (jury); Photo Edit Inc.: David Young-Wolff, p.150 (woman reading); Corbis: p.168;

Contents

Introduction to *Step Forward Step-By-Step Lesson Plans*

Welcome to *Step Forward Step-by-Step Lesson Plans.* These lesson plans are your guide to *Step Forward,* the adult English language course designed to work in single-level and multilevel classes. In addition to being a step-by-step lesson-planning tool, this book is also a rich collection of tips, strategies, and activities that complement the lessons in the *Step Forward Student Book.* In keeping with current, scientifically based research on language acquisition and instruction, these lesson plans provide a variety of instructional strategies and techniques that work across methodologies and learner populations.

What is *Step Forward?*

The *Step Forward* series is

- the instructional backbone for any standards-based, integrated skills, English language course;
- a program that teaches the skills needed for everyday life, the workplace, the community, and academic pursuits;

- a ready-made framework for learner-centered instruction within a single-level or multilevel environment; and
- a four-skills program that develops students' listening, speaking, reading, and writing skills, as well as their grammar, pronunciation, math, cooperative, and critical-thinking skills.

Step Forward's communication objectives are authentic and taught in conjunction with contextualized language forms. Research shows that when lessons are based on authentic communication and there is a focus on form within that context, learners incorporate new and correct structures into their language use.[1]

What's in this book?

The *Step Forward Step-By-Step Lesson Plans,* a comprehensive instructional planning resource, contains detailed lesson plans interleaved with *Step Forward Student Book* pages.

Each unit in the *Step-By-Step Lesson Plans* follows this format.

Student Book pages are next to lesson plan pages for easy reference.

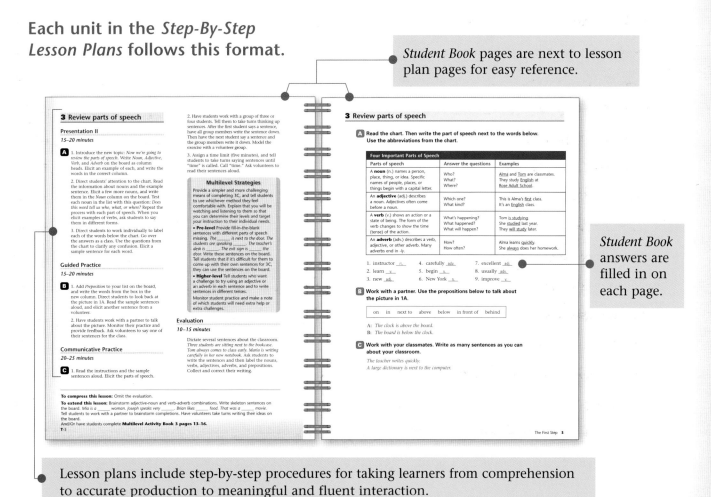

Student Book answers are filled in on each page.

Lesson plans include step-by-step procedures for taking learners from comprehension to accurate production to meaningful and fluent interaction.

---

[1] Rod Ellis, et al., "Doing focus on form," *Systems,* 30 (2002): 419-432.

Each lesson references related *Oxford Picture Dictionary* topics for vocabulary support.

Every lesson in *Step Forward* is correlated to CASAS competencies, Florida's Standardized Student Syllabi (LCPs), Equipped for the Future (EFF) standards, and the Secretary's Commission on Achieving Necessary Skills (SCANS).

A general lesson information chart provides multilevel objectives, support-skill focus, and correlations.

Unit 1 Lesson 5

Objectives	Grammar	Vocabulary	Correlations
On-, Pre-, and Higher-level: Read about and discuss library services	Simple-present tense and simple-past tense (*I read the newspaper every day. I read the newspaper yesterday.*)	*Check out, librarian, reserve* For vocabulary support, see this **Oxford Picture Dictionary** topic: A Library	**CASAS:** 0.1.2, 2.5.6 **LCPs:** 39.04, 46.01, 49.02, 49.04, 49.16 **SCANS:** Listening, Participates as member of a team, Reading, Writing **EFF:** Convey ideas in writing, Cooperate with others, Listen actively, Read with understanding

Warm-up and Review

10–15 minutes (books closed)

Make an idea map on the board with *library* in the central circle. Add branching circles with *library services, what you find at the library,* and *what you can do at the library.* Have the class brainstorm words and phrases to go with each of the branches. Leave this on the board.

Introduction

5 minutes

1. Read the words on the board aloud and answer any questions. Say: *You can find more than books at your library.*

2. State the objective: *Today we're going to read and talk about some of the things you can find and do at the library.*

1 Get ready to read

Presentation

10–20 minutes

A Read the questions aloud. Ask volunteers to share their answers.

B Read the words and definitions. Elicit sample sentences using the words.

Pre-Reading

C 1. Read the questions aloud. Ask students to signal to you (raise their hands, cross their arms) when they know the answers to the questions. Call on a volunteer to share the answers.

2. Direct students to find the names of the students who wrote the letters to Alison. Tell

them that it is customary for the writers of these kinds of letters to use nicknames so that their real names don't appear in the paper.

2 Read and respond

Guided Practice I

25–30 minutes

A 1. Ask students to read the letters silently.

2. Direct students to underline unfamiliar words they would like to know. Elicit the words and encourage other students to provide definitions or examples.

3. Check students' comprehension. Ask: *What is Sad Student's problem?* [He's bored in the car.] *What's Looking in Laredo's problem?* [He needs to research career choices.] *What's Frustrated Father's problem?* [His son's homework is difficult.] Ask students if Alison mentions any library services, items, or activities that were missed during the warm-up. Add them to the idea map on the board.

Multilevel Strategies

For 2A, adapt your comprehension questions to the level of your students.

• **Pre-level** Ask these students short-answer information questions. *What does Sad Student have in his car?* [a cassette player]

• **On-level** Ask these students information questions that will elicit longer responses. *Why does Looking in Laredo need a computer?* [He needs to research career choices.]

• **Higher-level** Ask these students inference questions. *Why do you think Frustrated Father dislikes computers?*

T-14

Lesson plans are organized into seven stages.

Multilevel Strategies help meet the varying needs of all learners in the classroom.

Guided Practice II

15–20 minutes

B 1. Play the audio. Have students read along silently.

2. Elicit and discuss any additional questions about the reading.

C Have students work individually to mark the sentences T (true), F (false), or NI (no information). Elicit the answers and write them on the board. Ask students to correct the false sentences.

D 1. Read the information in the chart aloud. Elicit and discuss any questions the students have about the meanings of the words or the prefix *dis-*. Say the words and have students repeat them.

2. Direct students to work individually to circle the correct word that completes each sentence. Ask volunteers to read the completed sentences aloud.

Multilevel Strategies

After 1D, give on- and pre-level students more time to work with the words in 1D while you challenge higher-level students.

• **Pre- and On-level** Have these students work together to write sentences for some of the words in the chart. Provide skeleton structures. *My _____ (family member) and I agree about _____. I like _____. I dislike _____. _____ (famous person) is honest. _____ (famous person) is dishonest.* Ask volunteers to complete the sentences on the board.

• **Higher-level** Have these students look in their dictionaries for words beginning with *dis-*. Ask them to look for words that have a base word that they already know. Tell them to write sentences with the words they find.

3 Talk it over

Communicative Practice

10–20 minutes

A Read the questions aloud. Set a time limit (three minutes). Have students work independently to think about the questions and then write their answers in note form.

B Ask volunteers to share their answers to the questions from 3A with the class. Ask: *What are the most popular kinds of things people read every day? Why do you think some people don't like to read?* Discuss the barriers to reading that students sometimes face. Brainstorm solutions. *How can you make time for reading? How can you make reading more fun and interesting? Why is it important to read?*

Application

5–10 minutes

BRING IT TO LIFE

Read the instructions aloud. Write the name, address, and directions to the local library on the board. If transportation is a problem, help students make arrangements for a car pool.

TIP If you have access to computers, have your students check out the local library's website. Ask them to find the library hours and the list of services. Provide students with the name of a book, and demonstrate how to search for the book in the online catalog.

To compress this lesson: Conduct the word study in 2D as a whole-class activity.

To extend this lesson: Have students write letters asking for and giving advice.
1. Put students in groups, and provide them with a large sheet of paper. Fold the paper in half. Tell the groups to use the top of the paper to write an "Ask Alison" letter about a problem with studying English or with reading. Encourage them to sign the letter with a nickname.
2. When each group finishes the letter, pass it to a new group. Have the new group write "Alison's" advice letter in response.
3. Post the letters and the answers in the front of the room. Have two reporters from each group come to the front to read the letter they received and the advice they wrote.

And/Or have students complete **Workbook 3 page 7** and **Multilevel Activity Book 3 pages 24–25**.

Unit 1 Learning Log for _____ (name) **Date:** _____

I can

❏ use words for study skills, study habits, and types of schools.
❏ write a journal entry about school.
❏ use present- and past-tense verbs. (*I learn. I'm learning. I learned.*)
❏ answer questions about my career interests.
❏ use adjectives and adverbs to talk about careers.
❏ understand information about library services.

My favorite exercise was _____

I need to practice _____

I want to learn more about _____

Unit 2 Learning Log for _____ (name) **Date:** _____

I can

❏ use words for recreational places, events, and activities.
❏ write an email invitation.
❏ use the future with *will* and *be going to.* (*I'll be home at 4:00. I'm going to study.*)
❏ talk about my preferences.
❏ understand an article about outdoor activities and health.
❏ use the suffix *-ful* to describe people and places. (*The trees are colorful now.*)

My favorite exercise was _____

I need to practice _____

I want to learn more about _____

Unit 3 Learning Log for _____ (name) **Date:** _____

I can

❏ use words for computer parts and office workers.
❏ write a memo about classroom policies.
❏ use comparisons. (*The $80 laptop is less expensive than the 680.*)
❏ give and respond to feedback.
❏ use the superlative. (*He is the most efficient worker I know.*)
❏ understand an article about workplace training.

My favorite exercise was _____

I need to practice _____

I want to learn more about _____

○   Name: _____
Unit 5
Exercise 32   Date: _____

Complete the conversations with *ever*, *already*, or *yet*.

Miles: Have you (1) ___*already*___ assigned our homework?

Ms. Ortiz: Yes, I've (2) _____ assigned it. You need to read Chapter 4.

Miles: OK. Have you given the test (3)_____?

Ms. Ortiz: No, I haven't given the test (4)_____. It's next week.

Diana: Have you (5)_____ had your job interview?

Wen: Yes, I've (6)_____ had my interview. I was almost late!

Diana: Have you (7)_____ been late for an interview before?

Wen: No, I haven't (8)_____ been late before.

Alison: CompTime is having a sale. Have you (9)_____ bought your new computer?

Alma: Yes, I've (10)_____ bought my new computer. I bought a laptop yesterday.

Alison: Have you used it (11)_____?

Alma: No, I haven't used it (12)_____. I'll use it tomorrow. Have you (13)_____ used a laptop before?

Alison: No, I haven't (14)_____ used a laptop. Maybe I can try yours!

How does *Step Forward* meet learners' needs?

Step Forward's framework supports the creation of effective, learner-centered classes. Researchers and teachers alike know that learners have a variety of learning styles and preferences; therefore the activities in th*e Step Forward* program derive from a number of approaches and techniques.[2] Each lesson includes the visual and aural material, practice exercises, communication tasks, and evaluation activities that are key elements of an effective lesson. No matter what your teaching style, *Step Forward* will make it easier to respond to your learners' language needs.

The Step Forward Framework

Step Forward Student Book 3 has 12 thematic units based on these life-skill topics:

1. Study habits	7. Money
2. Recreation	8. Health
3. Workplace	9. Cars
4. Job Interviews	10. Justice System
5. Community	11. Life Events
6. Food	12. Civic Rights

Each unit is divided into six lessons. The first five lessons focus on objectives related to the unit theme and develop specific language skills within the context of the topic. The sixth lesson provides opportunities to review and expand upon the previous lessons' language and information.

In addition to its main objective, each lesson works with the support skills students will need in order to achieve the objective (vocabulary, grammar, pronunciation, computation, etc.) In each of the lessons, learners accomplish the following general objectives:

Lesson 1 Vocabulary: express thoughts and opinions about a topic using thematically linked vocabulary.

Lesson 2 Real-life writing: use model letters, memos, or essays related to the unit topic as the basis for communicating needs or expressing ideas and opinions in writing.

Lesson 3 Grammar: learn and accurately use grammar in order to effectively interact and write on the lesson topic.

Lesson 4 Everyday conversation: use an authentic exchange as the basis for conversations on the lesson topic while developing listening and pronunciation skills and fluency.

2. C. Van Duzer and M. Florez Cunningham, *Adult English Language Instruction in the 21st Century* (Washington, D.C.: National Center for ESL Literacy Education/Center for Applied Linguistics, 2003):13.

Lesson 5 Real-life reading: increase comprehension of narrative reading materials while developing the vocabulary and skills required for both academic and non-academic reading.

Review and expand: integrate the language learned in the previous five lessons in order to accomplish a variety of communication tasks.

What are *Step Forward's* principles of effective lesson-plan design?

Lessons in the *Student Book* follow four principles of effective lesson-plan design:

- Successful learning is anchored to objectives that connect to learners' needs outside the classroom;
- Learners need listening, speaking, reading, and writing, plus math and critical-thinking skill development within each lesson. The lesson's skill focus always relates to the skills that support the objective;
- A staged and sequential lesson helps learners move from knowing about and understanding new language and concepts to putting the new language and concepts to use in their daily lives; and
  - A variety of processing and practice activities help learners integrate new information with their prior knowledge in order to achieve the lesson objectives.

Step-by-Step Lesson Plans employs these principles in the easy-access, detailed lesson-teaching notes and multilevel strategies for each of the 72 lessons in the *Student Book*.

The Stages of the *Step Forward* Lesson

A typical *Step Forward* lesson includes seven basic stages, as shown in the chart below. Multiple presentation and practice stages may occur in a lesson, depending on the complexity of the objectives.

Math Extension, Pronunciation Extension, and Problem Solving are self-contained mini-lessons that occur throughout the book. Each provides presentation and practice activities.

STEP FORWARD LESSON STAGES	
Warm-up and Review	Learners typically engage with the whole class and prepare for the upcoming lesson. Missing this stage does not penalize learners who have arrived late.
Introduction	The instructor focuses learners' attention on the lesson objective, relating it to their lives outside the classroom.
Presentation	New information, language, and content is presented and developed to ensure comprehension. Comprehension is carefully checked before proceeding to the next stage.
Guided Practice (controlled practice)	Learners work on developing their accuracy through various exercises and activities, which may be interactive. The activities are tightly structured to support learners' use of the lesson's grammar and vocabulary.
Communicative Practice (less-controlled practice)	Learners apply their skills to build their fluency. Team tasks, pair interviews, and role-plays are all examples of communicative practice.
Application	This stage is often merged with the communicative practice stage. In Lesson 5, however, learners "Bring It To Life" by finding print materials on the life skill or narrative reading topic outside of the classroom.
Evaluation	This stage assesses learners' achievement of the objective. Instructors use informal assessments, such as observations, and more formal evaluation tasks or tests.

How do I use this book?

Planning daily lessons with *Step Forward* and the *Step-by-Step Lesson Plans* is as easy as opening this book, making a couple of notes, and heading to class. Before you begin your daily planning though, it's wise to do a bit of "big picture" planning.

Step One

Reflect

The first step in planning effective lessons is to determine which learning objectives match the needs of your learners. Because the objectives in *Step Forward* are based on the CASAS competencies and the curriculum of some of the best adult programs across the country, it's a pretty safe bet that most of the objectives will match your students' communication needs. Nevertheless, it's important to determine what experience learners already have with the lesson topic, and what they already know. Before starting a unit, read through the topics (labeled *Focus on*) on the first *Student Book* page in the unit and ask yourself the following questions:

- What level of experience do my learners have with each of these topics?
- What is their command of the support skills needed to communicate about these topics?
- How will I determine what my learners already know about this topic? (Possible answers include using the opening exercises in each lesson, using the warm-up activity from the Lesson Plans, and using the Picture Differences activity from the *Multilevel Activity Book*.)

Step Two

Preview

Once you have an overview of the unit, preview the *Student Book* page of the first lesson and read through the lesson plan objectives. If you have a single-level class, you may choose to work from the on-level objective, or (as is so often the case) if you have an unidentified multilevel class, you may want to identify which learners will be working toward which objectives.

Step Three

Scan

Next, read through each stage of the lesson plan and the matching sections of the *Student Book* page. The lettered and numbered sections in the lesson plan correlate to the lettered and numbered exercises on the *Student Book* page.

Step Four

Gather

Be sure you have the tools you need. Ask yourself:

- Would any authentic materials help with the presentation of any of the lesson content? (For example, are coins needed for a lesson on money?)
- Will I use the audio CD or cassette tapes for the listening practice or read from the audio script (pages 172–182)?
- Which pages of *The Oxford Picture Dictionary* will be helpful in building comprehension?
- Which *Workbook* pages can learners use while waiting for other learners to complete a lesson task?

Step Five

Calculate

As you read through each stage of the lesson, be sure to notice the suggested time frames and use the compression and extension tips to adjust the lesson to your instructional time period.

Planning for Closing

Many teachers, new and experienced alike, commonly forget to provide a closing activity. Formally bringing the class back together to emphasize what has been accomplished gives learners a chance to assess what they liked and learned in the lesson. Closing activities can be as simple as a class brainstorm of all the words and ideas covered in the lesson or a chain drill that completes the sentence, "Today, I learned ...." The closing is also an opportunity for you to share your positive reflections on the lesson and send everyone out into the world a little more lighthearted.

How does *Step Forward* address the multilevel classroom?

Step Forward's multilevel framework addresses a common classroom reality that most instructors face: Even though learners share a classroom and an instructor, they may be working at different competency levels.

Two of the key concepts of successful multilevel instruction are:

1) learners need to feel that they are all part of the same class community; and
2) learners at different levels can work in the same general topic area while achieving different objectives.[3]

---

3. Jill Bell, *Teaching Multilevel Classes in ESL* (San Diego: Dominie Press, 1991): 36–38.

Using *Step Forward's* Multilevel Framework

Multilevel experts recommend that instructors begin their lesson planning by identifying a common theme for students at all levels. Instructors can then create level-specific objectives that relate to that theme. All the lessons within a *Step Forward* unit link to a common theme, with each lesson exploring a facet of that theme. In addition, each lesson plan in *Step-by-Step Lesson Plans* has a set of objectives for three sequenced levels:

Pre-level objectives are for those students who place below the level of the selected student book.

On-level objectives are for those learners who place at the level of the selected student book.

Higher-level objectives are for those learners who place above the level of the selected student book.

By planning a lesson around these three objectives, the teacher can use the *Student Book* and ancillary materials to support instruction across three sequential levels of learners.

Working with Broad Spectrum Multilevel Classes

Experts in multilevel instruction suggest that even broad spectrum classes, those with learners ranging from low-beginning to advanced and having a wide array of skill levels, can be divided into three general groups during each lesson. Because not all learners have the same proficiency level in the same skill areas, learners in multilevel classes may be placed in different groups depending on the skill focus. For example, a student may be in the beginning group in speaking but the intermediate group in writing. Also, depending on the span of levels, an instructor may want to use two levels of *Step Forward* to help meet the needs of learners at either end of the spectrum. (For more information, see the *Step Forward Professional Development Program*).

Learners may move between groups based on the type of lesson being taught. In a lesson where learners' listening and speaking skills are the focus, you might create one group of beginners, a second group of intermediate learners, and a third group of advanced learners. Of course, the formation of these groups would also depend on the number of learners at each level.

For more information, see the Multilevel Troubleshooting Chart on pg T-204 for more tips and resources for resolving multilevel instruction challenges.

How do I use the Multilevel Strategies to plan multilevel lessons?

Planning a multilevel lesson incorporates the same five steps from page T-x with three variations:

1. Base the lesson on two or three of the multilevel objectives (identified at the top of the lesson page), depending on the abilities of students in your class.
2. In preparing for the presentation stage, consider correlating materials from the *Basic Oxford Picture Dictionary* program for your pre-literacy learners.
3. Incorporate the multilevel grouping and instructional strategies in each lesson.

Grouping students in the multilevel classroom maximizes learner involvement and minimizes teacher stress. Putting learners in same-level groups during guided practice activities allows them to move at the right pace for their level. Creating different-level groups for communicative practice allows learners to increase their fluency. Assigning roles and tasks based on learners' proficiency level allows all learners to participate and succeed. The multilevel instructional strategies in this book are fairly consistent within each lesson type. Once a strategy is mastered, it can easily be applied to future lessons or activities.

How is *Step Forward* a complete program?

In addition to the *Student Book* and *Step-by-Step Lesson Plans*, the *Step Forward* program also includes ancillary materials that support communicative language instruction. Each of the following ancillary materials is correlated to the units and topics of each *Student Book*:

- *Audio Program*
- *Workbook*.
- *Multilevel Activity Book*
- *Test Generator*

In addition, the *Step Forward Professional Development Program* provides opportunities to learn about, reflect upon, and refine instructional strategies.

We created these materials with one goal in mind: to help *you* help *your learners*. Please write to us at **Stepforwardteam.us@oup.com** with your comments, questions, and ideas.

Jayme Adelson-Goldstein

Jayme Adelson-Goldstein, Series Director

TABLE OF CONTENTS

Unit	Life Skills & Civics Competencies	Vocabulary	Grammar	Critical Thinking & Math Concepts	Reading & Writing
Pre-unit **The First Step** page 2	• Greet others • Say and spell names of classmates • Alphabetize a list	• Parts of speech	• Review parts of speech • Review prepositions of location	• Alphabetize names • Recognize parts of speech	• Read and write names • Write abbreviations of parts of speech
Unit 1 **Learning Together** page 4	• Identify study skills and habits • Identify study techniques • Identify the educational system of the U.S. • Write a journal entry • Interpret library services • Express indecision	• Study skills and habits • Educational terms • Library service terms **In other words:** • Saying you're not sure	• Review present and past verb forms • Review present and past question forms • Review *Yes/No* questions and answers • Distinguish between adjectives and adverbs • The prefix *dis-*	• Reflect on personal study styles • Compare study habits and personal studying styles • Recognize library services **Real-life math:** • Determine percentages **Problem solving:** • Find ways to make new friends	• Write about personal study styles • Read and write a journal entry • Read an advice column
Unit 2 **Ready for Fun** page 18	• Identify recreational activities • Make predictions • Interpret a flyer • Read and write an email invitation • Make plans with friends • Identify the health benefits of parks	• Places in the community • Recreational activities • Meeting friends **In other words:** • Giving someone a choice **Idiom note:** • *play it by ear*	• Review *be going to* and *will* • Future predictions with *will* • Expressing preferences with *would rather* + verb • The suffix *-ful*	• Reflect on favorite recreational activities • Analyze a list of scheduled events • Compare predictions of future • Recognize the health benefits of parks **Real-life math:** • Calculate ticket costs **Problem solving:** • Resolve disagreements in preferences	• Read and write an email invitation • Write questions about future predictions • Read an article about the health benefits of parks **Writer's note:** • Use commas in letters and emails after the greeting and the closing
Unit 3 **A Job to Do** page 32	• Describe workplace and school policies • Interpret memos • Interpret computer ads • Make comparisons • Give and respond to job feedback • Identify the benefits of and sources for job training	• Computer vocabulary • Office vocabulary • Job training **In other words:** • Responding to negative feedback	• Comparisons with adjectives • Review superlatives • Answering questions with superlatives • Review superlative forms • The suffix *-tion*	• Resolve business-related conflicts • Compare features of products • Reflect on store preferences • Reflect on appropriate workplace behaviors **Real-life math:** • Calculate averages **Problem solving:** • Analyze and compare job benefits	• Read and write a memo • Read computer ads • Read an article about workplace training **Writer's note:** • Sign and print your name at the end of a formal business letter

Listening & Speaking	CASAS Life Skills Competencies	Standardized Student Syllabi/ LCPs	SCANS Competencies	EFF Content Standards
• Listen for and give personal information • Talk about the location of objects	0.1.2, 0.1.4, 0.1.5, 0.2.1	39.01, 50.03, 50.06	• Listening • Speaking • Sociability	• Listening actively • Speaking so others can understand
• Talk about personal study styles • Discuss the first day of English class • Listen for career information • Talk about career plans • Talk about reading habits **Grammar listening** • Listen for present or past verb tenses **Pronunciation:** • Differentiate between "sh", "ch", and "j" sounds	**L1:** 0.1.2, 0.1.5, 4.8.1, 7.4.1, 7.4.5 **L2:** 0.1.2, 0.1.5 **L3:** 0.1.2 **L4:** 0.1.2, 0.1.3, 0.1.5, 6.0.3, 6.0.4, 6.2.6, 7.2.5 **L5:** 0.1.2, 2.5.6 **RE:** 0.1.2, 0.1.5, 7.2.6, 7.3.1, 7.3.2, 7.4.1	**L1:** 49.02, 49.09 **L2:** 39.01, 49.03, 49.16 **L3:** 49.16, 50.02 **L4:** 49.02, 50.04, 50.05 **L5:** 39.04, 46.01, 49.02, 49.04, 49.16 **RE:** 49.01, 50.02, 50.04, 50.05, 50.08	Most SCANS are incorporated into this unit, with an emphasis on: • Knowing how to learn • Participating as a member of a team • Seeing in the mind's eye	Most EFFs are incorporated into this unit, with an emphasis on: • Conveying ideas in writing • Reading with understanding • Reflecting and evaluating
• Talk about recreational activities • Ask and answer questions about future predictions • Listen for and talk about preferences • Listen to a recorded message of community events • Discuss community parks **Grammar listening:** • Listen for predictions, plans, or promises **Pronunciation:** • "j" and "ch" sounds	**L1:** 0.1.2, 0.1.5, 2.6.1, 4.8.1, 7.5.1 **L2:** 0.1.2, 0.1.5, 0.2.3, 2.6.1 **L3:** 0.1.2, 7.2.5 **L4:** 0.1.2, 6.0.3, 6.0.4, 6.1.1, 6.1.2 **L5:** 0.1.2, 2.6.1, 2.6.3 **RE:** 0.1.2, 0.1.3, 0.1.5, 2.6.1, 7.2.6, 7.3.1, 7.3.2, 7.3.3, 7.3.4	**L1:** 39.01, 0.1.5, 2.6.1, 4.8.1 **L2:** 39.04, 49.16, 49.02, 49.03 **L3:** 49.16, 49.03, 50.02 **L4:** 49.02, 49.03, 49.16 **L5:** 39.01, 49.03, 49.04, 49.16, 49.17 **RE:** 39.01, 49.16, 50.02	Most SCANS are incorporated into this unit, with and emphasis on: • Applying technology to task • Participating as member of a team • Seeing things in the mind's eye	Most EFFs are incorporated into this unit, with an emphasis on: • Cooperating with others • Learning through research • Speaking so others can understand
• Talk about computers • Discuss problems in school • Ask and answer questions about shopping in different stores • Listen to evaluations of employees • Discuss job training **Grammar listening:** • Listen for comparatives **Pronunciation:** • "v", "b", and "f" sounds	**L1:** 0.1.2, 0.1.5, 4.1.6, 4.8.1, 7.2.3 **L2:** 0.1.2, 0.1.5, 4.4.1, 4.6.2, 7.2.5, 7.4.7 **L3:** 0.1.2, 0.2.1, 4.2.2, 7.4.7 **L4:** 0.1.2, 0.1.5, 4.4.4, 4.6.1, 6.1.1, 6.1.4, 7.2.5, 7.4.7 **L5:** 0.1.2, 2.5.5, 4.4.2 **RE:** 0.1.2, 0.1.5, 1.2.1, 7.2.5, 7.2.6, 7.2.7, 7.3.1, 7.3.2	**L1:** 35.02, 49.02 **L2:** 49.02, 49.16, 49.17 **L3:** 45.01, 49.02, 49.03, 49.16, 50.04 **L4:** 49.02, 49.03, 50.04 **L5:** 37.02, 49.02, 49.03, 49.04 **RE:** 49.01, 49.02, 49.03, 50.04	Most SCANS are incorporated into this unit, with and emphasis on: • Arithmetic/mathematics • Decision making • Interpreting and communicating iInformation	Most EFFs are incorporated into this unit, with an emphasis on: • Cooperating with others • Observing critically • Taking responsibility for learning

Listening & Speaking	CASAS Life Skills Competencies	Standardized Student Syllabi/ LCPs	SCANS Competencies	EFF Content Standards
• Talk about job interview behavior • Discuss personal strengths • Talk about life events • Listen for and talk about job information **Grammar listening:** • Listen for the present perfect **Pronunciation:** • "th"	**L1:** 0.1.2, 0.1.3, 0.1.4, 0.1.5, 4.1.5, 4.1.7, 4.4.1, 4.8.1, 7.4.5, 7.5.6 **L2:** 0.1.2, 0.1.5, 4.1.7, 4.6.2, 7.4.7 **L3:** 0.1.2, 0.1.5, 0.2.1, 7.4.7 **L4:** 0.1.5, 4.1.2, 4.1.5, 4.4.2, 6.2.1, 6.2.3 **L5:** 0.1.2, 4.1.6, 4.4.1, 4.4.2, 7.4.7, 7.5.1, 8.3.1 **RE:** 0.1.2, 0.1.5, 0.2.1, 7.3.1, 7.3.2, 7.3.3, 7.3.4	**L1:** 35.02, 35.06, 39.01, 49.02, 49.09, 49.10 **L2:** 49.02, 49.12, 49.16, 49.17 **L3:** 39.01, 49.03, 49.09, 49.16, 49.17, 50.02 **L4:** 37.01, 37.02, 37.03, 39.01, 49.02, 49.09, 50.02 **L5:** 37.01, 37.02, 38.01, 39.01, 49.01, 49.02, 49.16, 49.17 **RE:** 39.01, 49.01, 49.02, 49.16, 50.02	Most SCANS are incorporated into this unit, with and emphasis on: • Acquiring and evaluating information • Organizing and maintaining information • Problem solving	Most EFFs are incorporated into this unit, with an emphasis on: • Advocating and influencing • Conveying ideas in writing • Reading with understanding
• Talk about community resources • Discuss safety problems at school • Talk about recycling issues • Listen to a news interview • Discuss ways to reduce trash **Grammar listening:** • Listen for information using the present perfect **Pronunciation:** • "y", "w", and "j" sounds	**L1:** 0.1.2, 0.1.5, 4.1.6, 4.8.1, 7.4.5 **L2:** 0.1.2, 0.1.5, 4.9.4, 7.2.5, 7.3.1, 7.3.2 **L3:** 0.1.2, 0.2.1 **L4:** 0.1.2, 0.1.5, 2.6.2, 5.6.1 **L5:** 0.1.2, 0.1.3, 5.7.1, 7.2.5, 7.3.1, 7.3.2, 7.4.7 **RE:** 0.1.2, 0.1.5, 0.2.1, 4.8.1, 5.6.1, 7.3.1, 7.3.2	**L1:** 0.1.2, 0.1.5, 4.1.6, 4.8.1, 7.4.5 **L2:** 0.1.2, 0.1.5, 4.9.4, 7.2.5, 7.3.1, 7.3.2 **L3:** 0.1.2, 0.2.1 **L4:** 0.1.2, 0.1.5, 2.6.2, 5.6.1 **L5:** 0.1.2, 0.1.3, 5.7.1, 7.2.5, 7.3.1, 7.3.2, 7.4.7 **RE:** 0.1.2, 0.1.5, 0.2.1, 4.8.1, 5.6.1, 7.3.1, 7.3.2	Most SCANS are incorporated into this unit, with an emphasis on: • Creative thinking • Interpreting and communicating information • Reasoning	Most EFFs are incorporated into this unit, with an emphasis on: • Conveying ideas in writing • Reading with understanding • Solving problems and making decisions
• Talk about cooking and restaurants • Discuss meal preparation and favorite foods • Order a meal • Talk about restaurant bills • Discuss safe food preparation **Grammar listening:** • Listen for information using phrasal verbs **Pronunciation:** • Linking of phrasal verbs	**L1:** 0.1.2, 0.1.5, 0.2.1, 4.8.1, 7.4.5, 8.2.1 **L2:** 0.1.2, 0.2.1, 2.7.2, 8.2.1 **L3:** 0.1.2, 1.1.1 **L4:** 0.1.2, 1.6.4, 2.6.4, 6.0.3, 6.0.4, 6.2.3 **L5:** 0.1.2, 1.6.1, 3.1.1, 3.4.1, 3.4.2, 3.5.1, 3.5.3, 3.5.5, 8.2.1 **RE:** 0.1.2, 0.1.5, 0.2.1, 1.1.1, 4.8.1, 7.2.6, 7.3.1, 7.3.2	**L1:** 39.01, 49.02, 49.03, 49.10, 50.02, 50.08 **L2:** 39.01, 49.02, 49.03, 49.14, 49.16 **L3:** 49.01, 49.02, 49.09, 49.16, 49.17, 50.02 **L4:** 39.01, 45.03, 49.02, 49.09, 49.16, 49.17, 50.04 L5:39.01, 49.02, 49.03, 49.16 **RE:** 39.01, 49.02, 49.03, 49.16, 49.17, 50.01, 50.02	Most SCANS are incorporated into this unit, with an emphasis on: • Acquiring and evaluating information • Interpreting and communicating information • Writing	• Most EFFs are incorporated into this unit, with an emphasis on: • Conveying ideas in writing • Cooperating with others • Solving problems and making decisions

Listening & Speaking	CASAS Life Skills Competencies	Standardized Student Syllabi/ LCPs	SCANS Competencies	EFF Content Standards
• Talk about banking services • Discuss bank jobs and duties of employees • Discuss financial planning • Listen for automated account information **Grammar listening:** • Listen for information using real conditional sentences **Pronunciation:** • Silent "h" sounds in linked words	**L1:** 0.1.2, 0.1.5, 1.8.2, 4.8.1, 7.4.5 **L2:** 0.1.2, 0.2.1, 1.8.5, 7.4.7 **L3:** 0.1.2, 0.2.1 **L4:** 0.1.2, 1.5.3, 6.0.3, 6.0.4, 6.2.3 **L5:** 0.1.2, 5.3.7, 7.3.1, 7.4.7 **RE:** 0.1.2, 0.1.5, 0.2.1, 1.8.5, 4.8.1, 7.2.6, 7.3.1, 7.3.2, 7.3.4, 8.3.2	**L1:** 39.01, 42.04, 49.01, 49.02, 49.09, 49.10 **L2:** 39.01, 49.01, 49.02, 49.03, 49.16, 49.17 **L3:** 49.02, 49.03, 49.09, 49.16, 49.17 **L4:** 49.02, 49.03, 49.09, 49.16, 49.17 **L5:** 49.01, 49.03, 49.04, 49.16, 49.17 **RE:** 39.01, 49.01, 49.02, 49.03, 49.16, 49.17, 50.08	Most SCANS are incorporated into this unit, with an emphasis on: • Arithmetic/mathematics • Creative thinking • Seeing things in the mind's eye	Most EFFs are incorporated into this unit, with an emphasis on: • Conveying ideas in writing • Reflecting and evaluating • Solving problems and making decisions
• Talk about doctors' knowledge of the human body • Discuss ways to stay healthy • Listen for a doctor's advice • Listen to a radio program **Grammar listening:** • Listen for information using *used to* **Pronunciation:** • "v" vs "s" sounds in use	**L1:** 0.1.2, 0.1.5, 0.2.1, 2.5.1, 3.1.1, 3.1.3, 3.5.9, 4.8.1, 7.4.5 **L2:** 0.1.2, 0.2.1, 0.2.4, 3.5.2, 3.5.8, 7.1.2, 7.1.3, 7.2.7, 7.4.2 **L3:** 0.1.2, 0.1.5, 0.2.1, 7.4.7 **L4:** 0.1.2, 0.1.5, 3.5.8, 6.0.3, 6.0.4, 6.2.3 **L5:** 0.1.2, 0.1.5, 3.1.3, 3.3.1, 3.3.2, 3.3.3, 3.4.1, 3.4.2, 7.2.3, 7.4.7 **RE:** 0.1.2, 0.1.5, 0.2.1, 3.5.8, 7.2.6, 7.3.1, 7.3.2	**L1:** 39.01, 49.02, 49.09, 49.10 **L2:** 39.01, 41.06, 49.02, 49.16, 49.17 **L3:** 39.01, 41.06, 49.02, 49.09, 49.13, 49.16, 49.17 **L4:** 41.03, 41.06, 49.02, 49.09, 49.16, 50.02, 51.03 **L5:** 41.04, 49.04, 49.09, 49.16, 49.17 **RE:** 41.06, 49.02, 49.16, 50.02	Most SCANS are incorporated into this unit, with an emphasis on: • Interpreting and communicating information • Listening • Organizing and maintaining information	Most EFFs are incorporated into this unit, with an emphasis on: • Observing critically • Reading with understanding • Using math to solve problems and communicate
• Talk about car parts • Discuss trips and vacations • Listen for car terms in conversations **Grammar listening:** • Listen for the event that happened first **Pronunciation:** • The schwa sound	**L1:** 0.1.2, 0.1.5, 1.9.6, 4.8.1 **L2:** 0.1.2, 0.1.5, 0.2.1 **L3:** 0.1.2, 0.2.1, 7.4.2 **L4:** 0.1.2, 1.2.2, 17.71, 1.9.5, 1.9.6, 1.9.8, 6.0.3, 6.0.4, 6.2.3 **L5:** 0.1.2, 1.6.3, 7.4.4 **R E:** 0.1.2, 0.1.5, 2.2.3, 4.8.1, 7.2.6, 7.3.1, 7.3.2, 7.3.4	**L1:** 39.01, 49.02, 49.10 **L2:** 39.01, 49.02, 49.03, 49.13, 49.16, 49.17 **L3:** 49.02, 49.09, 49.13, 49.16, 49.17 **L4:** 45.01, 49.02, 49.09, 49.16, 51.01 **L5:** 38.01, 49.09, 49.16, 49.17 **RE:** 49.16, 49.17	Most SCANS are incorporated into this unit, with and emphasis on: • Creative thinking • Interpreting and communicating • Using computers to process information	Most EFFs are incorporated into this unit, with an emphasis on: • Conveying ideas in writing • Learning through research • Taking responsibility for learning

Unit	Life Skills & Civics Competencies	Vocabulary	Grammar	Critical Thinking & Math Concepts	Reading & Writing
Unit 10 **Crime Doesn't Pay** **page 130**	• Identify safe habits • Identify elements of the criminal justice system • Describe home and neighborhood security • Report a crime to police • Identify careers in public safety • Read a chart about careers in public safety	• Safety • Criminal justice system • Home security features **In other words:** • Sequencing events	• Gerunds as subjects • Compare gerunds and the present continuous • Gerunds and infinitives	• Speculate on ways to stay safe • Determine whether actions are safe or dangerous • Speculate reasons for not reporting crimes • Interpret a chart about careers in public safety **Real-life math:** • Interpret a survey about crime **Problem solving:** • Respond appropriately to an unsafe situation	• Read and write about home security • Read an article about careers in public safety **Writer's note:** • Use quotation marks (" ") to show a person's exact words. Use a comma before you begin the quotation.
Unit 11 **That's Life** **page 144**	• Identify life events • Identify special occasions • Read newspaper announcements • Respond to invitations • Respond to good and bad news appropriately • Interpret information about renting or buying a home	• Life events • Special occasions • Terms used for renting or buying a house **In other words:** • Responding to good news **Idiom note:** • *make it*	• The present passive • The present passive with *by* • *be able to* + verb for ability in the future and past	• Interpret announcements in a newspaper • Speculate about appropriate ways to respond to invitations • Analyze a flyer from a retirement community • Interpret statistic about income spent on rent **Real-life math:** • Calculate wedding expenses **Problem solving:** • Determine how to respond late to a wedding invitation	• Read and write responses to an invitation • Read a retirement community flyer • Write sentences in a chart about different types of parties • Read an article about moving to a new home
Unit 12 **Doing the Right Thing** **page 158**	• Identify civic rights, freedoms, and responsibilities • Describe civic involvement • Read a community volunteer form • Describe a legal problem • Interpret information about protecting civil rights • Recognize the Civil Rights contributions of Rosa Parks	• Civic terms • Community participation **In other words:** • Describing possible reasons **Idiom note:** • *stand up for*	• Verb + infinitive • Verb + gerund or infinitive • Report requests • Word stress in nouns and verbs	• Analyze a pamphlet about civic responsibilities • Draw conclusions on the importance of civic involvement • Reflect on likes and dislikes regarding community involvement • Interpret a webpage from a legal clinic **Real-life math:** • Analyze a voter poll **Problem solving:** • Determine appropriate action in a car accident	• Read and write a letter to the newspaper • Read a form for volunteers • Read an article about the Civil Rights Movement • Write a summary of the article **Writer's note:** • Using examples to help make your ideas clear

Listening & Speaking	CASAS Life Skills Competencies	Standardized Student Syllabi/ LCPs	SCANS Competencies	EFF Content Standards
• Discuss ways of staying safe • Talk about home security • Listen to someone report a crime to the police • Discuss issues connected with reporting crimes • Listen to a telephone conversation about a crime • Discuss careers in public safety **Grammar listening:** • Listen for gerunds vs. the present continuous **Pronunciation:** • Stressed words in sentences	**L1:** 0.1.2, 0.1.5, 0.2.1, 3.5.9, 5.5.3 **L2:** 0.1.2, 0.2.1, 8.1.4 **L3:** 0.1.2, 0.2.1, 8.1.4 **L4:** 0.1.2, 5.3.8, 6.7.2 **L5:** 0.1.2, 5.5.6, 7.4.4 **RE:** 0.1.2, 0.1.5, 4.8.1, 5.3.8, 5.6.1, 7.2.6, 7.3.1, 7.3.2, 7.3.4	**L1:** 39.01, 44.02, 49.02, 49.10 **L2:** 39.01, 44.02, 49.01, 49.02, 49.13, 49.16 **L3:** 44.01, 49.16 **L4:** 39.01, 44.01, 49.02, 49.09, 49.16, 51.05 **L5:** 38.01, 49.09, 49.16, 49.17 **RE:** 39.01, 44.01, 49.02, 49.17, 50.02	Most SCANS are incorporated into this unit, with and emphasis on: • Acquiring and evaluating information • Applying technology to the task • Listening	Most EFFs are incorporated into this unit, with an emphasis on: • Conveying ideas in writing • Reading with understanding • Solving problems and making decisions
• Talk about personal experiences with life events • Discuss ways to respond to invitations • Listen to a conversation about a life event • Discuss wedding traditions • Listen to a story about wedding traditions **Grammar listening:** • Listen for the same meaning of two sentences **Pronunciation:** • Show excitement through intonation	**L1:** 0.1.2, 0.1.5, 0.2.1, 1.2.5, 4.8.1 **L2:** 0.1.2, 0.2.1, 0.2.3 **L3:** 0.1.2, 0.1.5, 0.2.1, 1.4.2, 4.8.1 **L4:** 0.1.2, 0.2.1, 2.7.2, 2.7.3, 6.0.3, 6.0.4, 6.1.1, 6.1.3, 6.1.4 **L5:** 0.1.2, 0.2.1, 1.4.3 **RE:** 0.1.2, 0.1.5, 0.2.1, 2.7.1, 2.7.2, 2.7.3, 4.8.1, 7.2.6, 7.3.1, 7.3.2, 7.3.4, 7.4.7	**L1:** 49.02, 49.10 **L2:** 39.01, 39.04, 49.02, 49.03, 49.13 **L3:** 39.01, 49.02, 49.09, 49.13, 49.17 **L4:** 39.01, 49.02, 49.03, 49.09, 49.16 **L5:** 45.07, 49.01, 49.02 **RE:** 39.01, 49.02, 49.16	Most SCANS are incorporated into this unit, with an emphasis on: • Acquiring and evaluating information • Listening • Reading	Most EFFs are incorporated into this unit, with an emphasis on: • Conveying ideas in writing • Reading with understanding • Solving problems and making decisions
• Talk about rights of U.S. residents and citizens • Discuss civic activities and involvement • Listen to a conversation about a legal problem • Talk about community concerns • Listen to a town meeting • Discuss protests and boycotts • Word stress in nouns and verbs **Grammar listening:** • Listen and complete sentences with gerunds or infinitives **Pronunciation:** • Homophones	**L1:** 0.1.2, 0.1.5, 0.2.1, 5.1.1, 5.1.6, 4.8.1 **L2:** 0.1.2, 0.2.1, 0.2.3, 5.6.2, 5.6.3 **L3:** 0.1.2, 0.1.5, 0.2.1, 0.2.4, 4.8.1, 5.6.2 **L4:** 0.1.2, 0.2.1, 5.6.1 **L5:** 0.1.2, 0.2.1, 5.2.1, 5.6.3 **RE:** 0.1.2, 0.1.5, 0.2.1, 4.8.1, 5.6.3, 7.2.6, 7.3.1, 7.3.2, 7.3.3, 7.3.4	**L1:** 39.01, 49.02, 49.10 **L2:** 39.01, 49.02, 49.13, 49.16, 49.17 **L3:** 39.01, 49.02, 49.03, 49.09, 49.17 **L4:** 39.01, 49.02, 49.16, 49.17 **L5:** 39.01, 49.02, 49.03, 49.13, 49.16 **RE:** 49.02, 49.16	Most SCANS are incorporated into this unit, with an emphasis on: • Creative thinking • Interpreting and communicating information • Listening	Most EFFs are incorporated into this unit, with an emphasis on: • Advocating and influencing • Cooperating with others • Reflecting and evaluating

A Word or Two About Reading Introductions to Textbooks

Teaching professionals rarely read a book's introduction. Instead, we flip through the book's pages, using the pictures, topics, and exercises to determine whether the book matches our learners' needs and our teaching style. We scan the reading passages, conversations, writing tasks, and grammar charts to judge the authenticity and accuracy of the text. At a glance, we assess how easy it would be to manage the pair work, group activities, evaluations, and application tasks.

This Introduction, however, also offers valuable information for the teacher. Because you've read this far, I encourage you to read a little further to learn how *Step Forward's* key concepts, components, and multilevel applications will help you help your learners.

Step Forward's Key Concepts

Step Forward is...

- the instructional backbone for single-level and multilevel classrooms.
- a standards-based, performance-based, and topic-based series for low-beginning through high-intermediate learners.
- a source for ready-made, four-skill lesson plans that address the skills our learners need in their workplace, civic, personal, and academic lives.
- a collection of learner-centered, communicative English-language practice activities.

The classroom is a remarkable place. *Step Forward* respects the depth of experience and knowledge that learners bring to the learning process. At the same time, *Step Forward* recognizes that learners' varied proficiencies, goals, interests, and educational backgrounds create instructional challenges for teachers.

To ensure that our learners leave each class having made progress toward their language and life goals, *Step Forward* works from these key concepts:

- **The wide spectrum of learners' needs makes using materials that support multilevel instruction essential.** *Step Forward* works with single-level and multilevel classes.
- **Learners' prior knowledge is a valuable teaching tool.** Prior knowledge questions appear in every *Step Forward* lesson.

- **Learning objectives are the cornerstone of instruction.** Each *Step Forward* lesson focuses on an objective that derives from identified learner needs, correlates to state and federal standards, and connects to a meaningful communication task. Progress toward the objective is evaluated at the end of the lesson.
- **Vocabulary, grammar, and pronunciation skills play an essential role in language learning. They provide learners with the tools needed to achieve life skill, civics, workplace, and academic competencies.** *Step Forward* includes strong vocabulary and grammar strands and features pronunciation and math lesson extensions in each unit.
- **Effective instruction requires a variety of instructional techniques and strategies to engage learners.** Techniques such as Early Production Questioning, Focused Listening, Total Physical Response (TPR), Cooperative Learning, and Problem Solving are embedded in the *Step Forward* series, along with grouping and classroom management strategies.

The *Step Forward* Program

The *Step Forward* program has five levels:

- Intro: pre-beginning
- Book 1: low-beginning
- Book 2: high-beginning
- Book 3: low-intermediate
- Book 4: intermediate to high-intermediate

Each level of *Step Forward* correlates to *The Oxford Picture Dictionary*. For pre-literacy learners, *The Basic Oxford Picture Dictionary Literacy Program* provides a flexible, needs-based approach to literacy instruction. Once learners develop strong literacy skills, they will be able to transition seamlessly into *Step Forward Student Introductory Level*.

Each *Step Forward* level includes the following components:

Step Forward Student Book

A collection of clear, engaging, four-skill lessons based on meaningful learning objectives.

Step Forward Audio Program

The recorded vocabulary, focused listening, conversations, pronunciation, and reading materials from the *Step Forward Student Book*.

Step Forward Step-By-Step Lesson Plans with Multilevel Grammar Exercises CD-ROM

An instructional planning resource with interleaved *Step Forward Student Book* pages, detailed lesson plans featuring multilevel teaching strategies and teaching tips, and a CD-ROM of printable multilevel grammar practice for the structures presented in the *Step Forward Student Book*.

Step Forward Workbook

Practice exercises for independent work in the classroom or as homework.

Step Forward Multilevel Activity Book

More than 100 photocopiable communicative practice activities and 24 high-interest Jigsaw Readings; lesson materials that work equally well in single-level or multilevel settings.

Step Forward Test Generator CD-ROM with ExamView® Assessment Suite

Hundreds of multiple-choice and life-skill oriented test items for each *Step Forward Student Book*.

Multilevel Applications of *Step Forward*

All the *Step Forward* program components support multilevel instruction.

Step Forward is so named because it helps learners "step forward" toward their language and life goals, no matter where they start. Our learners often start from very different language abilities within the same class.

Regardless of level, all learners need materials that bolster comprehension while providing an appropriate amount of challenge. This makes multilevel materials an instructional necessity in most classrooms.

Each *Step Forward* lesson provides the following multilevel elements:

- **a general topic or competency area** that works across levels. This supports the concept that members of the class community need to feel connected, despite their differing abilities.
- **clear, colorful visuals and realia** that provide pre-level and on-level support during introduction, presentation and practice exercises, as well as prompts for higher-level questions and exercises.

In addition, *Step Forward* correlates to *The Oxford Picture Dictionary* so that teachers can use the visuals and vocabulary from *The Oxford Picture Dictionary* to support and expand upon each lesson.

- **learner-centered practice exercises** that can be used with same-level or mixed-level pairs or small groups. *Step Forward* exercises are broken down to their simplest steps. Once the exercise has been modeled, learners can usually conduct the exercises themselves.
- **pre-level, on-level, and higher-level objectives for each lesson and the multilevel strategies** necessary to carry out the lesson. These objectives are featured in the *Step-By-Step Lesson Plans*.
- **Grammar Boost pages in the Step Forward Workbook that provide excellent "wait time" activities** for learners who complete an exercise early, thus solving a real issue in the multilevel class.
- **a variety of pair, whole class, and small group activities** in the *Step Forward Multilevel Activity Book*. These activities are perfect for same-level and mixed-level grouping.
- **customizable grammar and evaluation exercises** in the *Step Forward Test Generator CD-ROM with ExamView® Assessment Suite*. These exercises make it possible to create evaluations specific to each level in the class.

Professional Development

As instructors, we need to reflect on second language acquisition in order to build a repertoire of effective instructional strategies. The *Step Forward Professional Development Program* provides research-based teaching strategies, tasks, and activities for single- and multilevel classes.

About Writing an ESL Series

It's collaborative! *Step Forward* is the product of dialogs with hundreds of teachers and learners. The dynamic quality of language instruction makes it important to keep this dialog alive. As you use this book in your classes, I invite you to contact me or any member of the *Step Forward* authorial team with your questions or comments.

Jayme Adelson-Goldstein

Jayme Adelson-Goldstein, Series Director
Stepforwardteam.us@oup.com

Step Forward: All you need to ensure your learners' success. All the *Step Forward Student Books* follow this format.

LESSON 1: VOCABULARY teaches key words and phrases relevant to the unit topic, and provides conversation practice using the target vocabulary.

> New vocabulary is introduced through vibrant art and high-interest listening texts.

> Standards-based objectives are identified at the beginning of every lesson.

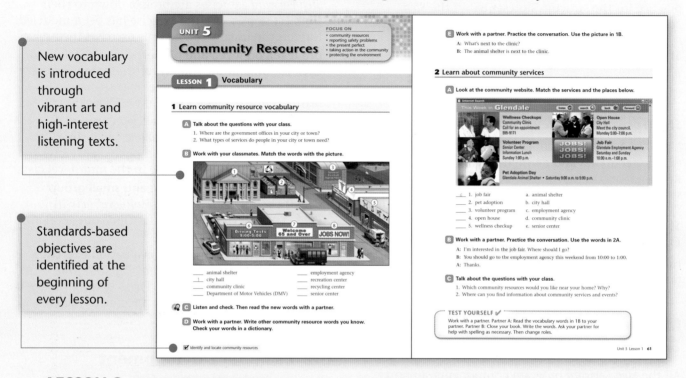

LESSON 2: REAL-LIFE WRITING expands on vocabulary learned in Lesson 1 and furthers learners' understanding through reading and writing about a life skills topic.

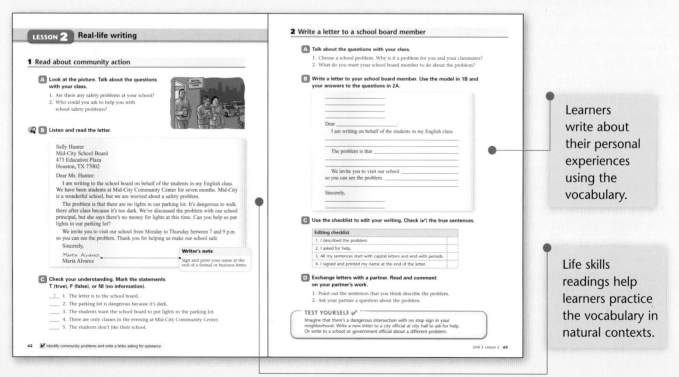

> Learners write about their personal experiences using the vocabulary.

> Life skills readings help learners practice the vocabulary in natural contexts.

LESSON 3: GRAMMAR provides clear, simple presentation of the target structure followed by thorough, meaningful practice of it.

Clear grammar charts make learning grammar easy.

LESSON 3 Grammar

1 Learn Yes/No questions with the present perfect

A Read the conversation and the project report. When will the electrician arrive?

A: Have you painted the cafeteria?
B: Yes, I have.
A: Has the electrician fixed the air-conditioning?
B: No, he hasn't.
A: When will he fix it?
B: He'll be here tomorrow.

Senior Center Project Report:

	yes	no
1. paint cafeteria	✔	
2. fix air-conditioning		✔
3. buy lunch tables	✔	
4. repair stove		✔
5. advertise programs	✔	
6. start lunch program		✔

B Study the chart. Underline the 2 present perfect questions in the conversation above.

YES/NO QUESTIONS WITH THE PRESENT PERFECT

Yes/No Questions			Answers					
Have	I you we they	repaired the stove?	Yes,	I you we they	have.	No,	I you we they	haven't.
Has	he she			he she	has.		he she	hasn't.

C Complete the questions and answers. Use the project report in 1A.

1. ___Have___ the workers ___painted___ the cafeteria?   ___Yes, they have.___
2. _____ the office manager _____ new lunch tables?
3. _____ the electrician _____ the air conditioning?
4. _____ the office manager _____ the _____ lunch program?
5. _____ the office manager _____ the center programs?
6. _____ they _____ the stove?

D Work with a partner. Talk about class activities.

A: Have you completed exercise C?
B: Yes, I have.
A: Has Maria written the answers on the board?
B: No, she hasn't.

Need help?

Class activities
done the homework
read ___
talked to ___
learned ___

2 Learn the present perfect with ever, already, and yet

A Study the chart. Circle the correct word in the sentences below.

Present perfect with ever, already, and yet	Notes
A: Have you **ever** volunteered at an animal shelter? B: No, I haven't. **or** No, I've never volunteered before.	ever = at any time (not ever = never) Use ever in Yes/No and information questions and in negative statements.
A: Have you **already** served lunch to the seniors? B: Yes, I have. They've **already** eaten.	already = some time before now Use already in questions when you expect a yes answer and in affirmative statements.
A: Have you called the clinic **yet**? B: No, I haven't. I haven't found the number **yet**. I'll call tomorrow.	yet = at any time until now Use yet in Yes/No questions and in negative statements.

1. We haven't (already / (ever)) used that new copy machine.
2. Have you (yet / ever) visited city hall?
3. I haven't signed the paper (yet / ever).
4. Has Sam (already / yet) painted the kitchen?

B Match the questions and the answers. Then practice them with a partner

__d__ 1. Has Maria been to New York yet?   a. No, I haven't ever been there.
____ 2. Has George already been to Miami?   b. Yes, he went twice last year.
____ 3. Have they ever gone to Russia?   c. No, they plan to go next year.
____ 4. Have you ever been to Mexico?   d. No, she's going next week.

C Get the form. Work with your class. Correct the sentences.

1. Marisol hasn't never volunteered.   ___Marisol hasn't ever volunteered.___
2. I haven't done my homework already. I'll do it tonight.   _____
3. Natasha went to the DMV yet. She got her license last week.   _____
4. Michael has ever been to a job fair. Maybe he'll go next week.   _____

Grammar listening exercises help learners identify the grammar point in spoken English.

3 Grammar listening

🎧 Listen and circle the correct answer.

1. (a.) Mark has been to Los Angeles.
   b. Mark has never been to Los Angeles.
2. a. He's been to the recreation center three times.
   b. He's taken three classes at the recreation center.
3. a. She has gotten a new dog.
   b. She's planning to get a new dog.
4. a. Toshi has already started working.
   b. Roberto has already started working.
5. a. She's never written a letter to the school board.
   b. She wrote three letters to the school board.
6. a. He hasn't been to the job fair.
   b. He's been to the job fair twice.

4 Practice the present perfect

A Work with a partner. Complete the questions.

1. Have you ever been to _____? (place in your state)
2. Have you ever read _____? (name of a book)
3. Have you ever visited _____? (name of a community resource)
4. Have you eaten _____ yet today? (a meal you eat every day)
5. Have you spoken* to _____ yet today? (name of a person in your class)

*speak-spoke-spoken

B Work with another pair. Ask and answer the questions in 4A. Give as much information as possible.

A: Have you ever been to Miami?
B: No, I haven't. I'd like to go there some day.
A: Have you ever read "Romeo and Juliet"?
B: Yes, I have. But, I haven't read it in English yet.

Miami

TEST YOURSELF ✓
Close your book. Write 6 sentences using the information you learned about your classmates. Use the present perfect, ever, already, and yet.
Yana hasn't ever visited city hall.

Learners work together to increase fluency and accuracy, using the grammar point to talk about themselves.

Test Yourself, at the end of every lesson, provides learners with ongoing self-assessment.

LESSON 4: **EVERYDAY CONVERSATION** provides learners with fluent, authentic conversations to increase familiarity with natural English.

Model dialogs feature authentic examples of everyday conversation.

Pronunciation activities focus on common areas of difficulty.

Listening activities build listening skills.

Real-life math exercises help learners practice language and math skills.

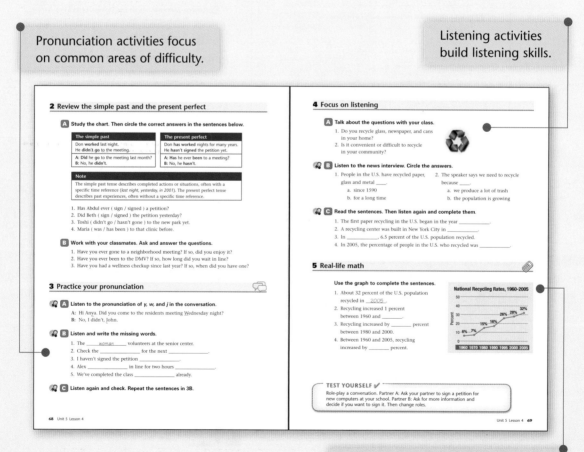

LESSON 5: **REAL-LIFE READING** develops essential reading skills and offers both life skill and pre-academic reading materials.

High-interest readings recycle vocabulary and grammar.

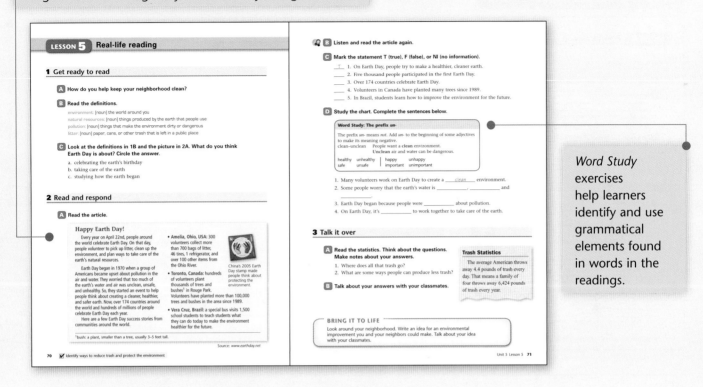

Word Study exercises help learners identify and use grammatical elements found in words in the readings.

REVIEW AND EXPAND includes additional grammar practice and communicative group tasks to ensure your learners' progress.

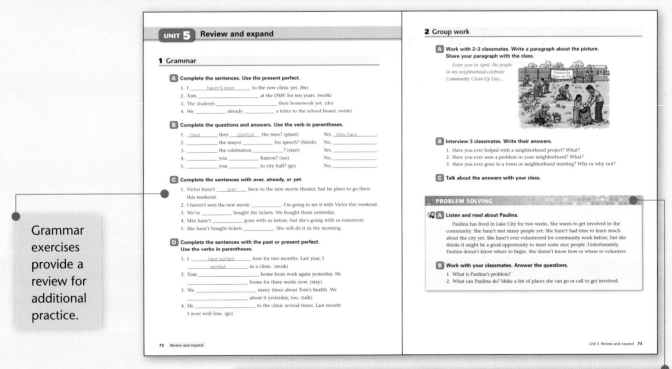

Grammar exercises provide a review for additional practice.

Problem solving tasks encourage learners to use critical thinking skills and meaningful discussion to find solutions to common problems.

Step Forward offers many different components.

Step-By-Step Lesson Plans

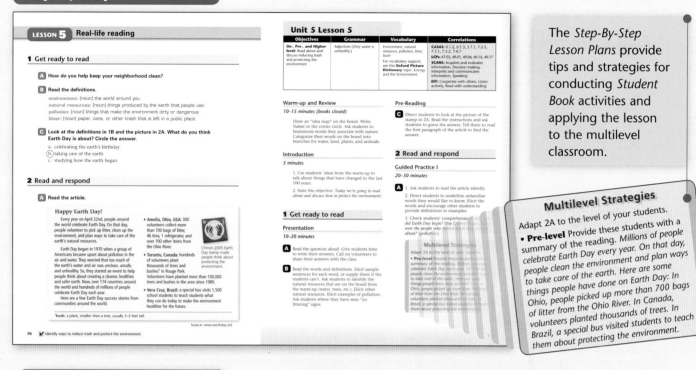

The *Step-By-Step Lesson Plans* provide tips and strategies for conducting *Student Book* activities and applying the lesson to the multilevel classroom.

Multilevel Strategies

Adapt 2A to the level of your students.

• **Pre-level** Provide these students with a summary of the reading. Millions of people celebrate Earth Day every year. On that day, people clean the environment and plan ways to take care of the earth. Here are some things people have done on Earth Day: In Ohio, people picked up more than 700 bags of litter from the Ohio River. In Canada, volunteers planted thousands of trees. In Brazil, a special bus visited students to teach them about protecting the environment.

The *Multilevel Grammar Exercises CD-ROM*, a free CD-ROM included with the *Step-By-Step Lesson Plans*, offers additional exercises for pre-level, on-level, and higher-level learners for each grammar point in the *Student Book*.

Workbook

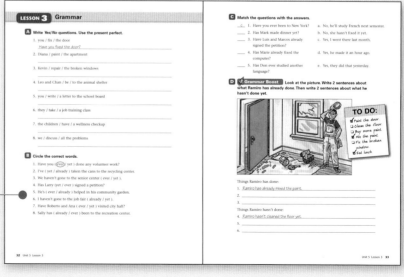

The *Workbook* offers additional exercises ideal for independent practice, homework, or review.

Multilevel Activity Book

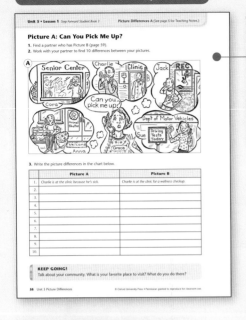

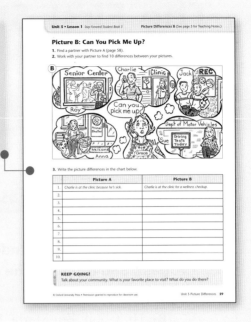

The *Multilevel Activity Book* features over 80 reproducible activities to complement the multilevel classroom through a variety of pair, small group, and whole-class activities.

Audio Program

Audio CDs and Cassettes feature the listening exercises from the *Student Book* as well as conversations, pronunciation, and readings.

Test Generator

The *Test Generator CD-ROM with ExamView® Assessment Suite* offers hundreds of test items for each *Student Book*. Teachers can print out ready-made tests or create their own tests.

Professional Development

Professional Development Task 8

Imagine you want your learners to practice listening carefully during a group task. One behavior you could demonstrate would be leaning forward. Make a list of at least three other behaviors or expressions that careful listeners use.

The *Professional Development Program* offers instructors research-based teaching strategies and activities for single- and multilevel classes, plus Professional Development Tasks like this one.

The First Step

Let's get started

1 Get to know your classmates

A Listen and repeat. Underline 1 example of the present, past, and future in the conversation.

A: Hello. I'm Chen.

B: Hi, Chen. I'm Maria. It's great to meet you. Is this your first English class?

A: No. I studied with Mr. Hopkins last year. How about you?

B: This is my first class, and I'm going to study hard. I really want to improve my pronunciation.

B Practice the conversation with 5 classmates. Use your own information.

C Write the first names of the classmates you met.

2 Alphabetize a list

A Read the names of Chen's classmates. Mark the sentences T (true) or F (false).

　F　1. All the names end with a capital letter.

　T　2. These students are all in the same class.

　T　3. The students' names are in alphabetical order.

B Work with your classmates. Make a list of all the students in your class. Put the list in alphabetical order.

Chen's Classmates

Ali	Nami
Diana	Paulina
Maki	Ramiro
Maria	Wen
Miguel	

　✔ Meet classmates; alphabetize names; review parts of speech

The First Step

Objectives	Grammar	Vocabulary	Correlations
On-, Pre-, and Higher-level: Meet classmates, alphabetize names, and review parts of speech	Parts of speech (noun, adjective, verb, adverb)	Words for introducing, parts of speech, classroom items For vocabulary support, see these **Oxford Picture Dictionary** topics: A Classroom, Personal Information	**CASAS:** 0.1.2, 0.1.4, 0.1.5, 0.2.1 **LCPs:** 39.01, 50.03, 50.06 **SCANS:** Listening, Participates as member of a team **EFF:** Listen actively, Speak so others can understand

Warm-up

10–15 minutes (books closed)

Write information about yourself on the board—for example, your name, the city you live in, the city (or state or country) where you are from, your marital status, how many children you have. Elicit the question to go with each piece of information. For example: *What's your name? Where do you live?* Have students repeat the questions. Elicit any other questions they have about you.

Introduction

5 minutes

1. Say: *Now you know something about me. It's time for us to get to know each other.*

2. State the objective: *Today we're going to get to know each other and review alphabetizing and the parts of speech.*

1 Get to know your classmates

Presentation I

15–20 minutes

A 1. Direct students to look at the picture. Ask: *Who are these people? What are they doing?*

2. Read the instructions aloud. Direct students to read the conversation silently and underline the examples of the past, present, and future. Call on volunteers for the answers.

3. Play the audio. Ask students to listen and repeat the conversation.

4. Elicit different completions for *I want to improve my _____*. Write students' ideas on the board.

Guided Communicative Practice I

15–20 minutes

B 1. Model the conversation with a volunteer. Switch roles and model with a different volunteer.

2. Direct students to walk around the room and practice the conversation with five different partners. Tell them to remember the first names of their classmates. Participate in the exercise and provide feedback.

C Ask students to write the names of the classmates they met. Encourage them to ask each other for help with spelling. Elicit and write this question on the board: *Excuse me, how do you spell your name?*

2 Alphabetize a list

Guided Communicative Practice II

15–20 minutes

A 1. Introduce the new topic: *Now we're going to practice alphabetizing.* Write *alphabetize = put in alphabetical order* on the board. Ask students why this skill is important in English class. [for organizing vocabulary lists and looking up words in the dictionary]

2. Direct students to look at the list of names and mark the sentences T (true) or F (false). Go over the answers as a class.

3. Point out that *Maki, Maria,* and *Miguel* all begin with the same letter. Elicit the process for alphabetizing words that start with the same letter.

B Have students refer to their lists and call out the name they think should come first on the list. Working together, create an alphabetized list of the students' names on the board.

3 Review parts of speech

Presentation II

15–20 minutes

 1. Introduce the new topic: *Now we're going to review the parts of speech.* Write *Noun, Adjective, Verb,* and *Adverb* on the board as column heads. Elicit an example of each, and write the words in the correct column.

2. Direct students' attention to the chart. Read the information about nouns and the example sentence. Elicit a few more nouns, and write them in the *Noun* column on the board. Test each noun in the list with this question: *Does this word tell us who, what, or where?* Repeat the process with each part of speech. When you elicit examples of verbs, ask students to say them in different forms.

3. Direct students to work individually to label each of the words below the chart. Go over the answers as a class. Use the questions from the chart to clarify any confusion. Elicit a sample sentence for each word.

Guided Practice

15–20 minutes

 1. Add *Preposition* to your list, and write the words from the box in the new column. Direct students to look back at the picture in 1A. Read the sample sentences aloud, and elicit another sentence from a volunteer.

2. Have students work with a partner to talk about the picture. Monitor their practice and provide feedback. Ask volunteers to say one of their sentences for the class.

Communicative Practice

20–25 minutes

 1. Read the instructions and the sample sentences aloud. Elicit the parts of speech.

2. Have students work with a group of three or four students. Tell them to take turns thinking up sentences. After the first student says a sentence, have all group members write the sentence down. Then have the next student say a sentence and the group members write it down. Model the exercise with a volunteer group.

3. Assign a time limit (five minutes), and tell students to take turns saying sentences until "time" is called. Call "time." Ask volunteers to read their sentences aloud.

Multilevel Strategies

Provide a simpler and more challenging means of completing 3C, and tell students to use whichever method they feel comfortable with. Explain that you will be watching and listening to them so that you can determine their levels and target your instruction to their individual needs.

- **Pre-level** Provide fill-in-the-blank sentences with different parts of speech missing. *The _____ is next to the door. The students are speaking _____. The teacher's desk is _____. The exit sign is _____ the door.* Write these sentences on the board. Tell students that if it's difficult for them to come up with their own sentences for 3C, they can use the sentences on the board.

- **Higher-level** Tell students who want a challenge to try using an adjective or an adverb in each sentence and to write sentences in different tenses.

Monitor student practice and make a note of which students will need extra help or extra challenges.

Evaluation

10–15 minutes

Dictate several sentences about the classroom. *Three students are sitting next to the bookcase. Tom always comes to class early. Maria is writing carefully in her new notebook.* Ask students to write the sentences and then label the nouns, verbs, adjectives, adverbs, and prepositions. Collect and correct their writing.

To compress this lesson: Omit the evaluation.

To extend this lesson: Brainstorm adjective-noun and verb-adverb combinations. Write skeleton sentences on the board. *Mia is a _____ woman. Joseph speaks very _____. Brian likes _____ food. That was a _____ movie.* Tell students to work with a partner to brainstorm completions. Have volunteers take turns writing their ideas on the board.

And/Or have students complete **Multilevel Activity Book 3 pages 13–16.**

3 Review parts of speech

A **Read the chart. Then write the part of speech next to the words below. Use the abbreviations from the chart.**

Four Important Parts of Speech		
Parts of speech	Answer the questions	Examples
A **noun** (n.) names a person, place, thing, or idea. Specific names of people, places, or things begin with a capital letter.	Who? What? Where?	<u>Alma</u> and <u>Tom</u> are classmates. They study <u>English</u> at <u>Rose Adult School</u>.
An **adjective** (adj.) describes a noun. Adjectives often come before a noun.	Which one? What kind?	This is Alma's <u>first</u> class. It's an <u>English</u> class.
A **verb** (v.) shows an action or a state of being. The form of the verb changes to show the time (tense) of the action.	What's happening? What happened? What will happen?	Tom <u>is studying</u>. She <u>studied</u> last year. They <u>will study</u> later.
An **adverb** (adv.) describes a verb, adjective, or other adverb. Many adverbs end in -*ly*.	How? How often?	Alma learns <u>quickly</u>. She <u>always</u> does her homework.

1. instructor <u>n.</u>   4. carefully <u>adv.</u>   7. excellent <u>adj.</u>

2. learn <u>v.</u>   5. begin <u>v.</u>   8. usually <u>adv.</u>

3. new <u>adj.</u>   6. New York <u>n.</u>   9. improve <u>v.</u>

B **Work with a partner. Use the prepositions below to talk about the picture in 1A.**

on   in   next to   above   below   in front of   behind

A: *The clock is above the board.*
B: *The board is below the clock.*

C **Work with your classmates. Write as many sentences as you can about your classroom.**

The teacher writes quickly.
A large dictionary is next to the computer.

UNIT 1
Learning Together

FOCUS ON
• study skills and habits
• writing a journal entry
• present and past verb forms
• career plans
• identifying library services

LESSON 1 Vocabulary

1 Learn study skills and habits vocabulary

A **Talk about the questions with your class.**

1. What do you do to study English?
2. Are good study skills and habits more important for children or for adults?

B **Work with your classmates. Match the words with the pictures.**

__3__ (do) research	__9__ make an outline	__5__ search online
__2__ find a quiet place	__8__ memorize words	__4__ take a break
__7__ make a study schedule	__6__ organize materials	__1__ take notes

C **Listen and check. Then read the new words with a partner.**

D **Work with a partner. Write other study words you know. Check your words in a dictionary.**

Unit 1 Lesson 1

Objectives	Grammar	Vocabulary	Correlations
On-level: Identify study skills and study habits, and describe the educational system **Pre-level:** Identify study skills, study habits, and educational-system vocabulary **Higher-level:** Talk and write about study skills and study habits, and explain the educational system	Simple-present tense (*Sometimes I make an outline.*)	Study skills and study habits, the educational system For vocabulary support, see these **Oxford Picture Dictionary** topics: Studying, Schools and Subjects	**CASAS:** 0.1.2, 0.1.5, 4.8.1, 7.4.1, 7.4.5 **LCPs:** 49.02, 49.09 **SCANS:** Knowing how to learn, Listening, Participates as a member of a team, Seeing things in the mind's eye **EFF:** Cooperate with others, Listen actively, Speak so others can understand

Warm-up and Review

10–15 minutes (books closed)

Write *in bed, at the library, at the kitchen table* on the board. Ask: *Which of these is the best place to study?* Elicit the advantages and disadvantages of each place. Use the students' ideas to come to a class consensus on the qualities of an ideal study place (quiet, comfortable, good light, materials at hand, etc.).

Introduction

5 minutes

1. Say: *We've talked about where to study; now let's talk about how to study. What should you do when you study?* Elicit students' ideas.

2. State the objective: *Today we're going to talk about study skills, study habits, and the U.S. educational system.*

1 Learn study skills and habits vocabulary

Presentation I

20–25 minutes

A 1. Write *Studying* on the board, and elicit students' answers to question 1. Ask follow-up questions. *When do you study vocabulary? Where?*

2. Elicit answers to question 2. Encourage students to think about how children's studying goals are different from adults' and also how children and adults face different challenges to studying.

B 1. Direct students to look at the pictures. Say: *This is David. Where is he studying? Do you think David is a good student?*

2. Group students and assign roles: leader, fact checker, recorder, and reporter. Explain that students work with their groups to match the words and pictures.

3. Check comprehension of the roles. *Who looks up the words in a dictionary?* [fact checker] *Who writes the numbers in the book?* [recorder] *Who tells the class your answers?* [reporter] *Who helps everyone and manages the group?* [leader]

4. Set a time limit (three minutes). As students work together, copy the wordlist onto the board.

5. Call "time." Have reporters take turns giving their answers. Write each group's answer on the board next to the word.

C 1. To prepare students for listening, say: *We're going to hear about David's study habits.* Ask students to listen and check their answers.

2. Have students check the wordlist on the board and then write the correct numbers in their books.

3. Pair students. Set a time limit (three minutes). Monitor pair practice to identify pronunciation issues.

4. Call "time" and work with the pronunciation of any troublesome words or phrases.

D 1. Ask students to work with a partner to brainstorm a list of related words.

2. Elicit words from the class. Write them on the board. Ask students to copy them into their vocabulary notes for the unit.

Guided Practice

5–10 minutes

 1. Model the conversation with a volunteer. Model it again using other information from 1B.

2. Set a time limit (three minutes). Direct students to practice with a partner. Ask volunteers to repeat one of their conversations for the class.

2 Learn about the educational system

Presentation II

15–20 minutes

 1. Direct students to look at the brochure. Introduce the new topic by asking: *What is this brochure about?*

2. Ask students to work individually to complete the brochure. Call on volunteers to read the completed sentences aloud. Write the answers on the board.

3. Check comprehension. Ask: *What school do seventh graders attend? What do you need to attend a university or community college?*

Guided Practice

10–15 minutes

 1. Model the conversation with a volunteer. Model it again using a different word from 2A.

2. Set a time limit (three minutes). Direct students to practice with a partner.

3. Call on volunteers to repeat one of their conversations for the class.

Communicative Practice and Application

10–15 minutes

 1. Give students time to make notes of their answers to the questions. Call on individuals to share their ideas with the class.

2. Elicit ways that adult students can overcome the difficulties they have with studying.

Evaluation

10–15 minutes (books closed)

TEST YOURSELF

1. Direct students to work individually to write a list of at least ten words from the lesson. Assign a time limit (three minutes). Call "time" and direct students to work with a partner to combine their lists and put the words in alphabetical order. Circulate and monitor students' progress.

2. Ask a volunteer pair to write its list on the board. Ask other students to add words to the list on the board.

> ### Multilevel Strategies
>
> Target the *Test Yourself* to the level of your students.
>
> • **Higher-level** After these students have worked with a partner to alphabetize their lists, ask them to write three to five sentences to describe study habits and explain the educational system using the words from the list.

To compress this lesson: Conduct 1B as a whole-class activity.

To extend this lesson: Explore students' questions about the U.S. school system in general or about your local school system in particular. Have students work with a partner to brainstorm two or three questions they have about the U.S. school system or about your local schools. Elicit questions and discuss them as a class. Write down any unanswered questions. Suggest where students can look for the answers, or find the answers yourself and share them with the class.

And/Or have students complete **Workbook 3 page 2** and **Multilevel Activity Book 3 pages 18–19**.

E Work with a partner. Practice the conversation. Use the pictures in 1B.

A: What do you do when you study at home?

B: Sometimes I make an outline. Sometimes I memorize words.

2 Learn about the educational system

A Look at the pictures. Then complete the brochure with the schools.

Schools in the U.S.

elementary school   adult school

middle school   community college

high school   university

In the United States, most children begin kindergarten at age five. They usually attend elementary school
1
from kindergarten to fifth grade. From grades six to eight, kids often go to

 middle school . From there, they
2
go on to high school , which is
3
usually grades nine to twelve, and receive their diploma.

Adults can attend an adult school
4
with or without a high-school diploma. Adults who attend a community college
5
or a university must have a
6
high-school diploma or a GED (general educational development certificate).

Answers 5 and 6 may be reversed.

B Work with a partner. Practice the conversation. Use the words in 2A.

A: Who can attend elementary school?

B: Children in kindergarten to fifth grade.

C Talk about the questions with your class.

1. Is it easier for adults or for children to memorize things? Why?
2. Which study skills are most difficult for adult students?

TEST YOURSELF ✔

Close your book. Work with a partner. Make a list of as many new words from the lesson as you can. Alphabetize your list.

1 Read a journal entry

A **Look at the picture. Talk about the questions with your class.**

1. What are the students doing?
2. How do they feel?

B **Listen and read the journal entry.**

> Monday, September 10
>
> The first day of English class was very interesting. Our teacher asked us to practice speaking English in groups. I was nervous at first. I usually like to work alone. I didn't want to make a mistake and feel embarrassed, but everything was fine in the end.
>
> Our first assignment was to tell the group why we were studying English. I had a lot to say, but I was worried about my pronunciation. My group had four students. Before we began, Kim whispered to me that she was nervous. I said, "Me too." I guess Maria heard us because she said, "Me three." Then Ali said, "Me four." We all laughed a lot. After that, we practiced a lot of English. I want to work in groups again tomorrow.

C **Check your understanding. Circle *a* or *b*.**

1. The teacher wanted the students to ____.
   a. work alone
   b. work in groups

2. The students were nervous because ____.
   a. it was fun and they laughed
   b. they didn't want to make a mistake

3. The students talked about ____.
   a. their reasons for studying English
   b. their first day of English class

4. In the end, the students ____.
   a. practiced a lot of English
   b. were very quiet

☑ Write a journal entry about a class experience

Unit 1 Lesson 2

Objectives	Grammar	Vocabulary	Correlations
On- and Higher-level: Analyze, write, and edit a journal entry about English class **Pre-level:** Read a journal entry, and write about the first day of class	Simple-past tense (*The students worked in groups.*)	*Journal entry, nervous, embarrassed, worried, whispered* For vocabulary support, see these **Oxford Picture Dictionary** topics: Studying, Feelings	**CASAS:** 0.1.2, 0.1.5 **LCPs:** 39.01, 49.03, 49.16 **SCANS:** Listening, Reading **EFF:** Convey ideas in writing, Cooperate with others, Listen actively, Read with understanding, Take responsibility for learning

Warm-up and Review

10–15 minutes (books closed)

Think of four to six activities that your students do in class—for example, *talk in groups, work with a partner, write new words in a notebook, read the textbook, do grammar exercises, listen to conversations,* etc. Make a sign for each activity, and post the signs around the room. Direct students to stand next to the activity they like to do most. Ask students to tell a partner what they like about the activity they chose.

Introduction

5 minutes

1. Briefly explain why all of the activities you discussed in the warm-up are important. Tell them that today they will focus on writing.

2. State the objective: *Today we'll read and write about the things we do in English class.*

1 Read a journal entry

Presentation

20–25 minutes

A 1. Direct students to look at the picture.

2. Elicit answers to questions 1 and 2. Ask students how they feel when they work in groups.

B 1. Write *journal* on the board, and elicit the meaning. Ask if any of your students keep a journal. Tell them: *Now we're going to read and listen to a journal entry about a student's first day of class.*

2. Direct students to read the journal entry silently. Check comprehension. Ask: *How did this student feel about working in groups?* [nervous] *How does he usually like to work?* [alone] *How does he feel now?* [He wants to work in groups tomorrow.]

3. Play the audio. Have students read along silently.

Guided Practice I

10 minutes

C Have students work independently to circle *a* or *b*. Go over the answers as a class. Write them on the board.

Multilevel Strategies

Seat pre-level students together for 1C.

• **Pre-level** While other students are working on 1C, ask these students *Yes/No* and *Or* questions about the reading. *Was the English class interesting? Was the writer relaxed or nervous? Did he have a lot to say or nothing to say? Did he finally relax?* Allow these students to copy the answers to 1C from the board.

• **On- and Higher-level** After these students complete 1C, ask them to share their answers with a partner. Then ask them to circle the adjectives the writer uses to describe the class and his feelings.

2 Write a journal entry

Guided Practice II

20–25 minutes

A 1. Read the questions aloud. Elicit students' answers.

2. Write the students' ideas for question 2 on the board, so they can refer to them while they write.

B 1. Direct students to look back at the model in 1B. Focus their attention on the simple-past verbs. Ask them to look through the journal entry quickly and mark the simple-past verbs. Elicit the verbs and discuss any questions.

2. Read the questions for each paragraph aloud, and call on volunteers to answer. Write vocabulary they use (adjectives, simple-past verbs, words for classroom activities) on the board to serve as a wordlist during the writing process.

3. Go over the words in the *Need Help?* box. Elicit and write any additional ideas on the board.

4. Check comprehension of the exercise. Ask: *How many paragraphs are you going to write?* [two] *Should you write the questions in your journal entry?* [no]

5. Direct students to look at the example. Elicit ideas for the first three sentences, and write them on the board to illustrate paragraph format. Remind them that sentences in a paragraph continue one after the other and that the first sentence is indented. They should not start each new sentence on a new line.

Multilevel Strategies

Adapt 2B to the level of your students.

• **Pre-level** Work with these students to brainstorm answers to each of the questions. Give students time to answer in complete sentences before moving on to the next question.

• **Higher-level** Ask these students to add a third paragraph that answers these questions: *What was another activity you did the first day of school? Did you like it more or less than the first activity? Why?*

 1. Lead students through the process of using the *Editing checklist*. Read each sentence aloud, and ask students to check their papers before moving onto the next item.

2. Allow students a few minutes to edit their writing as necessary.

Communicative Practice

10 minutes

D 1. Read the instructions aloud. Emphasize to students that they are responding to their partners' work, not correcting it.

2. Use the journal entry in 1B to model the exercise. *I think the part about the students whispering to each other is interesting. I'd like to ask this writer what else he did on the first day of class.*

3. Direct students to exchange papers with a partner and follow the instructions.

4. Call on volunteers to share what they found interesting in their partners' papers.

Application and Evaluation

15 minutes

TEST YOURSELF

1. Review the instructions aloud. Assign a time limit (ten minutes), and have students work independently.

2. Before collecting students' work, remind them to use the *Editing checklist* in 2C. Collect and correct students' writing.

Multilevel Strategies

Adapt the *Test Yourself* to the level of your students.

• **Pre-level** Write questions for these students to answer in writing. *Was today's writing assignment difficult or easy? How do you feel about writing?*

To compress this lesson: Assign the *Test Yourself* for homework.

To extend this lesson: Write a list of classroom activities on the board. Share your thoughts about the purpose of each one. Come to a class consensus about the ideal percentage of time to spend on each activity. Remind students that the percentages refer to the overall course and that on certain days they will focus more heavily on particular kinds of activities.

And/Or have students complete **Workbook 3 page 3** and **Multilevel Activity Book 3 page 20**.

2 Write a journal entry

A **Talk about the questions with your class.**

1. Do you like to study alone or with other people?
2. What are some reasons people get nervous in class?

B **Write a journal entry in your notebook. Use the model in 1B and the questions below to help you.** Answers will vary.

Paragraph 1:

What did you think about your first day of English class?

What assignments did your teacher give you?

How did you feel about that?

Paragraph 2:

What was the first assignment?

How did you feel about it?

Would you like to do this assignment again in the future?

> **Need help?**
>
> **Assignments**
> introduce ourselves
> meet our classmates
> give a presentation
> write about ourselves
> talk about our goals

> (Day), (Date)
>   The first day of English class was very exciting.
> Our teacher asked us to introduce ourselves.

C **Use the checklist to edit your writing. Check (✔) the true sentences.** Answers will vary.

Editing checklist	
1. I wrote about my first day of English class.	
2. I wrote about one class activity.	
3. I used capital letters for the first letters of the day and date.	
4. I wrote my story in the past tense.	

D **Exchange journal entries with a partner. Read and comment on your partner's work.**

1. Point out one sentence that you think is very interesting.
2. Ask your partner a question about his or her first day of class.

TEST YOURSELF ✔

Write a new journal entry in your notebook about another day of class.
What did you do? How did you feel about the activity?

1 Review present and past verb forms

A **Read the paragraph and the notebook page. What classes does this student take?** The student takes English class and computer class.

I write my assignments in a notebook. In my English class we learn five new words every day. I always write and memorize them. On Monday night I wrote my journal entry. On Tuesday night I answered the questions for my computer class. Today is Wednesday. I'm studying at the library now. I'm memorizing my new words for the day.

Homework Assignments:	
Date: Mon. 9/26	Class: English
1. Learn 5 new words	
2. Write journal entry – due Wed.	
Date: Tue. 9/27	Class: Computers
Chapter 2: questions p. 24 – due Thurs.	
Date: Wed. 9/28	Class: English
Learn 5 new words	

B **Study the charts. Underline 1 example of each verb form in the paragraph above.**
Answers will vary.

Simple present				
I learn	new words every day.		I don't learn	new words every day.
He learns			He doesn't learn	

Present continuous				
I'm learning	new words now.		I'm not learning	new words now.
He's learning			He isn't learning	

Simple past				
I learned	new words yesterday.		I didn't learn	new words yesterday.
He learned			He didn't learn	

C **Complete the sentences. Use the verbs in parentheses.**

1. Blanca _____is not taking_____ notes in her English class now. (not take)
2. Estelle __wrote_____ a journal entry yesterday. (write)
3. Jerry always __answers_____ the questions in class. (answer)
4. They __are taking_____ a test now. (take)
5. Yesterday, we __learned_____ about different kinds of schools. (learn)
6. We __didn't work_____ in groups yesterday. (not work)

Unit 1 Lesson 3

Objectives	Grammar	Vocabulary	Correlations
On- and Higher-level: Use present and past verb forms to talk about personal habits and experiences, and to listen for simple past, simple present, and present continuous **Pre-level:** Recognize present and past verb forms, and answer *Yes/No* questions in present and past tense in order to talk about personal habits and experiences	Simple-present tense (*He studies every day.*) Present-continuous tense (*He is studying.*) Simple-past tense (*He studied last night.*)	*Assignment, memorize* For vocabulary support, see this **Oxford Picture Dictionary** topic: Studying	**CASAS:** 0.1.2 **LCPs:** 49.16, 50.02 **SCANS:** Interprets and communicates information, Listening, Reading **EFF:** Convey ideas in writing, Cooperate with others, Listen actively, Read with understanding

Warm-up and Review

10–15 minutes (books closed)

Write *Yesterday, Every Day*, and *Now* as column heads on the board. Ask: *What did you do yesterday? What do you do every day? What are you doing right now?* As students answer, write the base forms of the verbs they use to the right of the columns. Leave these on the board.

Introduction

5–10 minutes

1. Elicit the names of the tenses that are represented on the board, and write *Simple Past* above *Yesterday, Present Continuous* above *Now*, and *Simple Present* above *Every Day*. Tell students: *When we are speaking and writing in English, we use these tenses all the time.*

2. State the objective: *Today we're going to review present and past tenses so that we can talk about our study habits and other activities.*

1 Review present and past verb forms

Presentation I

20–25 minutes

A 1. Direct students to look at the notebook page. Ask: *What is on the notebook page? Do you write your assignments in your notebook?*

2. Read the instructions aloud. Ask students to read the paragraph silently to find the answer to the question. Call on a volunteer for the answer.

B 1. Demonstrate how to read the grammar charts. Read the charts through sentence by sentence. Then read them again, and have students repeat after you.

2. Ask students to substitute a new verb into each chart—for example, *memorize*.

3. Direct students to underline one example of each tense in the paragraph in 1A. Go over the answers as a class.

4. Talk about the form and meaning of each verb in the paragraph. Ask: *Where is the writer right now? How do you know? How do you form the present continuous? Why does the writer use simple present for "learn new words"?*

5. Assess students' understanding of the verb tenses. Refer to the verbs from the warm-up. Elicit the correct verb forms for each "time" column (*Yesterday, Every Day, Now*) in complete sentences.

Guided Practice I

15–20 minutes

C Ask students to work individually to complete the sentences. Ask volunteers to write the answers on the board.

Guided Practice II

5–10 minutes

D 1. Read sentence number 1 aloud. Ask students to identify the "time" word in the sentence. Refer to the chart in 1B, and point out that *now* is used with the present continuous. Elicit the form of the present continuous. Read the corrected sentence aloud.

2. Read each sentence aloud, and ask students to identify the "time" word and the subject. Ask students to raise their hands when they think they have the right answer. When most of the students have raised their hands, call on a volunteer for the answer. Use the chart in 1B to demonstrate why the answer is correct. Write all of the answers on the board.

2 Review present and past Yes/No question forms

Presentation II

20–25 minutes

A 1. Introduce the new topic. *Now we're going to practice asking present and past-tense questions about studying.*

2. Read each question and short answer in the chart aloud. Ask students to identify the two parts of each verb.

3. Check comprehension. Say several different questions without time clues, and ask students to call out the time frame (right now, usually, in the past). *Are you working?* [right now] *Did you sleep well?* [in the past] *Does she work?* [usually] *Do you go to the library?* [usually]

4. Direct students to circle the correct words in the exercise below the chart. Ask volunteers to read the questions and answers aloud.

Guided Practice I

10–15 minutes

B 1. Have students work individually to write short answers to the questions. Then direct them to ask and answer the questions with a partner.

2. Elicit possible answers from the class.

TIP For more practice after 2B, dictate questions and have students write short answers. Ask questions for which students know the answers. For example: *Did it rain yesterday? Are you studying English? Does this class start at 9:00? Does our classroom have a computer?*

D **Get the form. Work with your class. Correct the sentences.**

1. Paulo doesn't taking notes now.   _Paulo isn't taking notes now._
2. Yan memorize words every day.   Yan memorizes words every day.
3. We is taking a break now.   We are taking a break now.
4. Mia search online yesterday.   Mia searched online yesterday.
5. I don't take notes yesterday.   I didn't take notes yesterday.
6. They do research now.   They are doing research now.

2 Review present and past *Yes/No* question forms

A **Study the charts. Then circle the correct words below.**

YES/NO QUESTIONS AND ANSWERS

Simple present	Present continuous	Simple past
A: Do you study every day? **B:** Yes, I do. OR No, I don't.	**A:** Are you studying now? **B:** Yes, I am. OR No, I'm not.	**A:** Did you study yesterday? **B:** Yes, I did. OR No, I didn't.
A: Does she study every day? **B:** Yes, she does. OR No, she doesn't.	**A:** Is she studying now? **B:** Yes, she is. OR No, she isn't.	**A:** Did she study yesterday? **B:** Yes, she did. OR No, she didn't.

1. **A:** (Does /(Did)) the students do their homework?
   B: Yes, they (do /(did)).
2. **A:** ((Are)/ Is) they helping each other?
   B: Yes, they ((are)/ do).
3. **A:** ((Do)/ Does) you like to work in a group?
   B: Yes, I (am /(do)).
4. **A:** ((Does)/ Is) Kim like to work alone?
   B: No, she ((doesn't)/ isn't).

B **Write your answers to the questions. Then ask and answer the questions with a partner.** Answers will vary.

1. Did you go to the library yesterday?   _____
2. Are you listening to music now?   _____
3. Do you always speak English in class?   _____
4. Did you learn any new words today?   _____
5. Are you studying in the library now?   _____
6. Do you make a study schedule?   _____

3 Grammar listening

Listen to the sentences. Check (✔) _Simple present, Present continuous,_ or _Simple past._

	Simple present	Present continuous	Simple past
1.		✔	
2.			✔
3.			✔
4.	✔		
5.		✔	
6.	✔		

4 Practice present and past verb forms

A Think about your answers to these questions.

1. What is something you did for fun ten years ago?
2. What is something you do for fun on the weekends?
3. Are you having fun right now?

B Work with a partner. Ask and answer the questions in 4A.

A: _What is something you did for fun ten years ago?_
B: _I took dance lessons._
A: _What is something you do for fun on the weekends?_
B: _I go to the movies._
A: _Are you having fun right now?_
B: _Yes, I am._

C Talk about your answers with the class.

Rita took dance lessons ten years ago.
She goes to the movies on the weekends.
She's having fun in class right now.

TEST YOURSELF ✔

Close your book. Write 3 complete sentences about yourself. Use the
simple past, the simple present, and the present continuous.
   I played baseball ten years ago.

3 Grammar listening

Guided Practice II
10–15 minutes

1. Say: *We've been talking about our study habits—what we usually do, what we did yesterday, and what we're doing right now. Now we're going to listen to sentences about different people and decide what tense the sentence is in.*

2. Direct students to look at the chart. Elicit an example sentence for each column.

3. Play the audio. Ask students to check the correct box.

4. Call on volunteers for the answers.

> ### Multilevel Strategies
> Replay *Grammar listening* to challenge on- and higher-level students while allowing pre-level students to catch up.
> - **Pre-level** Have these students listen again to complete the exercise.
> - **On- and Higher-level** Ask these students to write the verb they hear. When you elicit the answers to the *Grammar listening*, call on these students to state the verb and pre-level students to state the tense.

4 Practice present and past verb forms

Communicative Practice and Application
20–25 minutes

A 1. Direct students to look at the cartoon. Ask: *What is the teenage girl doing? Does that look fun?*

2. Direct students to read the questions and work individually to write their answers.

B 1. Put students in pairs. Direct students to take turns asking and answering the questions.

2. Check comprehension of the exercise. Ask: *How many questions do you ask?* [three]

3. Ask individuals to share with the class some interesting points that they heard.

C Call on individuals to share what they learned about their partners. Give feedback on students' use of verb forms.

Evaluation
10–15 minutes (books closed)

TEST YOURSELF

Ask students to write the sentences independently. Collect and correct their writing.

> ### Multilevel Strategies
> Target the *Test Yourself* to the level of your students.
> - **Pre-level** Provide skeleton sentences for these students to complete. 1. _____ (classmate's name) _____ (verb) ten years ago. 2. _____ (classmate's name) _____ (verb) on the weekends. 3. _____ (classmate's name) is/isn't having fun right now.
> - **Higher-level** Have these students write as many sentences as they can about their classmates.

To compress this lesson: Conduct 1C as a whole-class activity.

To extend this lesson: Have students practice speaking in the third person.
1. After 4B, direct students to stand up and find a new partner. Have them tell their new partners what they learned about their previous partners. Tell them to move on to another partner when they have finished speaking. Tell that person about their previous partner.
2. As students are talking, participate in the activity, or monitor and provide feedback.

And/Or have students complete **Workbook 3 pages 4–5, Multilevel Activity Book 3 pages 20–21,** and the corresponding **Unit 1 Exercises** on the **Multilevel Grammar Exercises CD-ROM 3.**

Unit 1 Lesson 4

Objectives	Grammar	Vocabulary	Correlations
On-, Pre-, and Higher-level: Talk about career possibilities, and listen for information about career preparation	Adjectives and adverbs (*He's a careful worker. He works carefully.*)	Career words For vocabulary support, see these **Oxford Picture Dictionary** topics: Jobs and Occupations, Describing Things	**CASAS:** 0.1.2, 0.1.3, 0.1.5, 6.0.3, 6.0.4, 6.2.6, 7.2.5 **LCPs:** 49.02, 50.04, 50.05 **SCANS:** Arithmetic/Mathematics, Decision making, Listening, Speaking **EFF:** Cooperate with others, Listen actively, Speak so others can understand, Use math to solve problems and communicate

Warm-up and Review

10–15 minutes (books closed)

Review job titles. Write the alphabet on the board, and have volunteers come up and write one job title on the board for each letter. When they have run out of ideas, help them come up with something for the missing letters or allow students to check *The Oxford Picture Dictionary* or another picture dictionary.

Introduction

5 minutes

1. Say: *There are many different careers and many different things to think about when you're choosing one. What kind of person are you? What do you like to do? What type of training do you need for different jobs? How many jobs are available? A school counselor will have the answers to many of these questions.*

2. State the objective: *Today we're going to learn how to talk about careers and career choices.*

1 Learn to talk about careers

Presentation I

10–20 minutes

A 1. Direct students to look at the pictures. Ask students to talk about who each person is and what he/she is doing. Read the questions aloud.

2. Play the audio. Give students a minute to answer the questions. Go over the answers as a class.

3. Ask additional comprehension questions. *What career does the counselor recommend for Tara?* [teacher] *Why does the counselor recommend hotel management for Carlos?* [He works at a hotel. He is doing well in his business management class.]

Guided Practice

20–25 minutes

B 1. Read the instructions aloud. Play the audio. Ask students to read along silently and listen for the answer to the question. Elicit the answer.

2. Ask students to read the conversation with a partner. Circulate and monitor pronunciation. Model and have students repeat difficult words or phrases.

3. Say and have students repeat the expressions in the *In other words* box. Elicit the placement of the expressions in the conversation. Ask volunteers to read the conversation using expressions from the box.

Communicative Practice and Application

15–20 minutes

C 1. Ask students to read the instructions silently. Check their comprehension of the exercise. Ask: *What's the situation? What are the two roles?* Elicit examples of what the student and the counselor might say.

2. Set a time limit (five minutes). Ask students to act out the role-play in both roles. Ask one to three volunteer pairs to act out their conversations for the class. Tell students who are listening to make a note of how Partner B says he/she isn't sure.

LESSON **4** Everyday conversation

1 Learn to talk about careers

🎧 **A** **Look at the pictures. Listen to the conversations. Then answer the questions below with your classmates.**

1. What did Tara do last year? She volunteered at a middle school.
2. Where does Carlos work now? He works part-time in a hotel.

🎧 **B** **Listen and read. What career does the counselor suggest?**

Counselor:	What kind of career are you thinking about?
Student:	I'm just not sure. There are so many choices.
Counselor:	What kinds of things do you like to do?
Student:	Well, I volunteered at a hospital last year and I enjoyed that. I'm studying biology now. I like my class and I'm doing well.
Counselor:	You should think about a career in health care. It's a good field and it's growing quickly.

> **In other words...**
>
> **Saying you're not sure**
> I'm just not sure.
> I really don't know.
> It's hard to say.

C **Role-play a career conversation with a partner. Use the example in 1B to make a new conversation.**

Partner A:	You're the school counselor. Ask the student about career plans and things he or she likes to do. Listen. Then suggest a career in computer arts.
Partner B:	You're a student. You are talking to your school counselor. You don't know which career is right for you. You drew some pictures for the school paper last year and you are taking a computer class now.

2 Learn about adjectives and adverbs

A Study the charts. Then circle the correct words below.

Adjectives	
quick	We took a **quick** break.
careful	He's a **careful** worker.
hard	It's **hard** work.
good	She got **good** grades in math.

Adverbs	
quickly	We finished the lesson **quickly**.
carefully	He works **carefully**.
hard	They work **hard**.
well	She did **well** in math.

Notes
• Adjectives describe nouns. We took a **quick** <u>break</u>.
• Adverbs often give more information about the verb in a sentence. We <u>finished</u> the lesson **quickly**.
• Most adverbs end in -*ly*, but some adjectives and adverbs have the same form (*hard-hard*).
• Some adjectives and adverbs are irregular (*good-well*).

1. The counselor spoke (clear /(clearly)) about careers.
2. There are so many kinds of careers. It isn't an ((easy)/ easily) choice.
3. Some people know what they want and can decide (quick /(quickly)).
4. People who do research on careers usually find ((good)/ well) jobs.

B Complete the sentences with an adjective or adverb. Answers will vary.

1. I memorize words _____quickly_____.
2. I am a _____ worker.
3. I read the assignment _____.

4. I take notes _____ in class.
5. I usually get _____ grades on my tests.

3 Practice your pronunciation

A Listen to the pronunciation of the *sh, ch,* and *j* sounds in these sentences.

1. I'm just not <u>sure</u>.
2. There are so many <u>ch</u>oices.
3. I en<u>j</u>oyed that.
4. You <u>sh</u>ould think about it.

B Listen to the words in the chart. Underline the letter(s) in each word that make the *sh, ch,* or *j* sounds.

"sh"		"ch"		"j"	
1. <u>sh</u>ow	3. <u>s</u>ugar	5. <u>ch</u>ange	7. <u>ch</u>oose	9. <u>J</u>oe	11. <u>j</u>ar
2. ca<u>sh</u>	4. <u>s</u>ure	6. cat<u>ch</u>	8. mu<u>ch</u>	10. ob<u>j</u>ect	12. en<u>j</u>oy

C Work with a partner. Partner A: Say a word from the chart. Partner B: Point to the word you hear. Then change roles.

2 Learn about adjectives and adverbs

Presentation II and Guided Practice

10–15 minutes

A 1. Introduce the new topic. Write *1. The students are quiet.* and *2. The students work quietly.* on the board. Ask: *What does* quiet *describe in sentence number 1? What kind of word is* students? *What does* quietly *describe in the second sentence? What kind of word is* worked? Say: Quiet *is an adjective. It describes the students.* Students *is a noun. Adjectives describe nouns.* Quietly *is an adverb. It describes the way students work. Adverbs describe verbs.*

2. Read the sentences in the chart aloud. Draw students' attention to the note about *well*.

3. Ask students to work individually to choose the correct form in the sentences under the chart. Call on volunteers for the answers. Elicit the noun or verb being described in each sentence.

Communicative Practice

15–20 minutes

B Have students work individually to complete the sentences. Call on volunteers for answers. Elicit other possible completions. Ask students to take turns reading their sentences with a partner.

TIP
For more practice with adverbs, provide students with other adjectives that can become *-ly* adverbs—for example, *happy, angry, slow, excited, soft, loud.* Ask volunteers to write sentences on the board with the adjective and adverb forms.

3 Practice your pronunciation

Pronunciation Extension

10–15 minutes

A 1. Write *Which job should she choose?* on the board. Say the sentence and ask students to repeat it. Underline *sh, ch,* and *j,* and repeat each sound. Say: *Now we're going to focus on pronunciation of these three sounds.*

2. Play the audio. Direct students to listen for the pronunciation of *sh, ch,* and *j.*

3. Ask: *Which letters make the* sh *sound?* [*sh* and *su*] Make a sound and ask students to read you the sentence(s) with that sound.

B Play the audio. Ask students to listen and underline the letters that make the *sh, ch,* and *j* sounds. Call on volunteers to pronounce the words.

C Model the exercise with a volunteer. Say several words and have the volunteer point to them. Then switch roles. Put students in pairs to complete the exercise.

4 Focus on Listening

Listening Extension

20–25 minutes

A Read the questions aloud, and elicit answers from volunteers. Encourage students to respond to one another's ideas. After one student speaks, ask other students for their opinions: *Do you agree or disagree with what he/she said? Why?*

B 1. Direct students to look at the pictures in 4C. Ask what the student is doing in each picture.

2. Tell students they are going to listen to two students talk about a high school with a special career-preparation program. Ask if they know of any high schools in your area that run special career-preparation programs.

3. Direct students to read the questions. Play the audio and ask them to mark the sentences T (true) or F (false) as they listen.

C 1. Direct students to read the questions in the chart before listening.

2. Replay the audio and have students work individually to check the correct column. Go over the answers as a class.

> ### Multilevel Strategies
>
> Replay the audio for 4C to challenge on- and higher-level students while allowing pre-level students to catch up.
>
> • **Pre-level** Have these students listen again to complete 4C.
>
> • **On- and Higher-level** Write additional questions on the board for these students to answer. *Can any student go to Freemont? What did Maria do last summer? When did each student graduate?*

5 Real-life math

Math Extension

5–10 minutes

1. Direct students to look at the chart and read the sentences. Ask: *What is the total number of people in the survey? How many people have the career they started in? What percentage of the total is that? How do you figure out the percentage?* Ask a volunteer to demonstrate how to solve the problem.

2. Ask students to work individually to label the rest of the chart. Ask volunteers to write the problems on the board.

Evaluation

10–15 minutes

TEST YOURSELF

1. Model the role-play with a volunteer. Then switch roles.

2. Pair students. Check comprehension of the exercise by eliciting ideas about what each partner might say.

3. Set a time limit (five minutes), and have the partners act out the role-play in both roles.

4. Circulate and monitor. Encourage pantomime and improvisation. Provide feedback.

> ### Multilevel Strategies
>
> Target the *Test Yourself* to the level of your students.
>
> • **Pre-level** Ask these students to use a skeleton conversation. *Counselor: What kind of career are you thinking about? Student: I don't know. C: What do you like to do? S: I like to _____ and _____. C: Maybe you should study _____. S: That's a good idea!*
>
> • **Higher-level** Have these students practice the role-play with more than one partner.

To compress this lesson: Conduct 2B and *Real-life math* as whole-class activities.

To extend this lesson: After 2B, provide more practice with adverbs and adjectives.
1. Write a short story on the board that lacks detail: *A man walked into the room. He sat down at a table. A woman came in. She sat down. She spoke to the man. Then the woman stood up. She left.*
2. Put students in groups. Tell the groups to rewrite the story with adjectives, adverbs, and other details.
3. Have a reporter from each group read the group's new, improved version of the story.

And/Or have students complete **Workbook 3 page 6** and **Multilevel Activity Book 3 page 23.**

4 Focus on listening

A Talk about the questions with your class.

1. Why is education important for a career?
2. In addition to education, what else is important for a career?

B Listen to the story. Mark the sentences T (true) or F (false).

__T__ 1. At Fremont, students study and prepare for their careers at the same time.

__F__ 2. Freemont students do not study the usual subjects like math and science.

__T__ 3. Both Marie and Malik found careers they love.

C Listen again. Check (✔) *Marie* or *Malik*.

	Marie	Malik
1. Who studied banking?	✔	
2. Who likes making things?		✔
3. Who came to the U.S. from Jamaica?	✔	
4. Who was offered a job at a bank?	✔	
5. Who helped build an apartment building?		✔
6. Who is taking classes in the evening?		✔

Marie

Malik

5 Real-life math

Read the information and do the math problems. Label the chart with the correct percentages. Then compare your answers with the class.

A survey asked 8,000 people about their careers. Here's what they said:

1,680 people: "I have the career I started in."

1,680 ÷ 8,000 = .21 or 21%
Have the career they started in: 21%

2,400 people: "I changed careers once."

__2,400__ ÷ __8,000__ = __.30__ or __30__ %
Changed careers once: 30%

3,920 people: "I changed careers two or more times."

__3,920__ ÷ __8,000__ = __.49__ or __49__ %
Changed careers two or more times: 49%

How many times have you changed your career?

21% have the career they started in

30% changed careers once

49% changed careers two or more times

TEST YOURSELF ✔

Role-play a conversation about career choices. Partner A: You are a school counselor. Ask your partner about his or her interests. Suggest a career. Partner B: Respond. Then change roles.

1 Get ready to read

A Is there a library in your neighborhood? How often do you go there?

B Read the definitions.

check out: (verb) to take, or borrow, for a period of time and then return

librarian: (noun) a person who works in or is in charge of a library

C Look at the title and the picture in the newspaper advice column in 2A. Answer the questions.

1. Who is the person in the picture? Alison, the person who gives advice in the newspaper
2. What does she do? She answers the questions.

2 Read and respond

A Read the advice column.

ASK ALISON

Dear Alison,
I usually listen to English on the radio in my car. Unfortunately, my car isn't running. I'm driving my brother's car. The radio is broken, so it only has a cassette player. I'm so bored in the car now! What should I do?
—Sad Student

Dear Sad Student,
Audio books are books recorded on cassettes or CDs. They're a great way to listen to English. You can check them out from the library for free.

Dear Alison,
I need to research career choices. I want to search for jobs online, but I don't have a computer. What should I do?
—Looking in Laredo

Dear Laredo,
Don't worry. Most libraries have computers. Get a library card— it's free— and you can be online in no time. Many libraries even let you sign up for the computer in advance so you don't wait in line.

Dear Alison,
My son is in high school. His homework is very difficult. I try to help him, but sometimes it's over my head.[1] Please help.
—Frustrated Father
P.S. I dislike computers. Please don't tell me to use one!

Dear Frustrated,
Don't worry! Your library can help. Many libraries have free homework help centers. Go to the library with your son and ask a librarian for advice.

[1]over (my) head: too difficult to understand

Unit 1 Lesson 5

Objectives	Grammar	Vocabulary	Correlations
On-, Pre-, and Higher-level: Read about and discuss library services	Simple-present tense and simple-past tense (*I read the newspaper every day. I read the newspaper yesterday.*)	*Check out, librarian, reserve* For vocabulary support, see this **Oxford Picture Dictionary** topic: The Library	**CASAS:** 0.1.2, 2.5.6 **LCPs:** 39.04, 46.01, 49.02, 49.04, 49.16 **SCANS:** Listening, Participates as member of a team, Reading, Writing **EFF:** Convey ideas in writing, Cooperate with others, Listen actively, Read with understanding

Warm-up and Review

10–15 minutes (books closed)

Make an idea map on the board with *library* in the central circle. Add branching circles with *library services, what you find at the library,* and *what you can do at the library.* Have the class brainstorm words and phrases to go with each of the branches. Leave this on the board.

Introduction

5 minutes

1. Read the words on the board aloud and answer any questions. Say: *You can find more than books at your library.*

2. State the objective: *Today we're going to read and talk about some of the things you can find and do at the library.*

1 Get ready to read

Presentation

10–20 minutes

A Read the questions aloud. Ask volunteers to share their answers.

B Read the words and definitions. Elicit sample sentences using the words.

Pre-Reading

C 1. Read the questions aloud. Ask students to signal to you (raise their hands, cross their arms) when they know the answers to the questions. Call on a volunteer to share the answers.

2. Direct students to find the names of the students who wrote the letters to Allison. Tell them that it is customary for the writers of these kinds of letters to use nicknames so that their real names don't appear in the paper.

2 Read and respond

Guided Practice I

25–30 minutes

A 1. Ask students to read the letters silently.

2. Direct students to underline unfamiliar words they would like to know. Elicit the words and encourage other students to provide definitions or examples.

3. Check students' comprehension. Ask: *What is Sad Student's problem?* [He's bored in the car.] *What's Looking in Laredo's problem?* [He needs to research career choices.] *What's Frustrated Father's problem?* [His son's homework is difficult.] Ask students if Alison mentions any library services, items, or activities that were missed during the warm-up. Add them to the idea map on the board.

Multilevel Strategies

For 2A, adapt your comprehension questions to the level of your students.

• **Pre-level** Ask these students short-answer information questions. *What does Sad Student have in his car?* [a cassette player]

• **On-level** Ask these students information questions that will elicit longer responses. *Why does Looking in Laredo need a computer?* [He needs to research career choices.]

• **Higher-level** Ask these students inference questions. *Why do you think Frustrated Father dislikes computers?*

Guided Practice II

15–20 minutes

B 1. Play the audio. Have students read along silently.

2. Elicit and discuss any additional questions about the reading.

C Have students work individually to mark the sentences T (true), F (false), or NI (no information). Elicit the answers and write them on the board. Ask students to correct the false sentences.

D 1. Read the information in the chart aloud. Elicit and discuss any questions the students have about the meanings of the words or the prefix *dis-*. Say the words and have students repeat them.

2. Direct students to work individually to circle the correct word that completes each sentence. Ask volunteers to read the completed sentences aloud.

Multilevel Strategies

After 1D, give on- and pre-level students more time to work with the words in 1D while you challenge higher-level students.

• **Pre- and On-level** Have these students work together to write sentences for some of the words in the chart. Provide skeleton structures. *My _____ (family member) and I agree about _____. I like _____. I dislike _____. _____ (famous person) is honest. _____ (famous person) is dishonest.* Ask volunteers to complete the sentences on the board.

• **Higher-level** Have these students look in their dictionaries for words beginning with *dis-*. Ask them to look for words that have a base word that they already know. Tell them to write sentences with the words they find.

---

3 Talk it over

Communicative Practice

10–20 minutes

A Read the questions aloud. Set a time limit (three minutes). Have students work independently to think about the questions and then write their answers in note form.

B Ask volunteers to share their answers to the questions from 3A with the class. Ask: *What are the most popular kinds of things people read every day? Why do you think some people don't like to read?* Discuss the barriers to reading that students sometimes face. Brainstorm solutions. *How can you make time for reading? How can you make reading more fun and interesting? Why is it important to read?*

Application

5–10 minutes

BRING IT TO LIFE

Read the instructions aloud. Write the name, address, and directions to the local library on the board. If transportation is a problem, help students make arrangements for a car pool.

TIP If you have access to computers, have your students check out the local library's website. Ask them to find the library hours and the list of services. Provide students with the name of a book, and demonstrate how to search for the book in the online catalog.

To compress this lesson: Conduct the word study in 2D as a whole-class activity.

To extend this lesson: Have students write letters asking for and giving advice.
1. Put students in groups, and provide them with a large sheet of paper. Fold the paper in half. Tell the groups to use the top of the paper to write an "Ask Allison" letter about a problem with studying English or with reading. Encourage them to sign the letter with a nickname.
2. When each group finishes the letter, pass it to a new group. Have the new group write "Allison's" advice letter in response.
3. Post the letters and the answers in the front of the room. Have two reporters from each group come to the front to read the letter they received and the advice they wrote.

And/Or have students complete **Workbook 3 page 7** and **Multilevel Activity Book 3 pages 24–25**.

B Listen and read the advice column again.

C Mark the sentences T (true), F (false), or NI (no information).

   _T_ 1. You can listen to audio books with a cassette player.

   _T_ 2. Sometimes you can sign up for a computer at the library.

   _T_ 3. Library cards don't cost any money.

   _T_ 4. You can go online at the library.

   _F_ 5. You can pay for help with homework at the library.

   _T_ 6. A librarian can help you do homework.

D Study the chart. Circle the correct words below.

Word Study: The prefix -dis

The prefix *dis-* means "not." Add *dis-* to the beginning of some verbs and adjectives to change their meaning.

dis + like = dislike   Sam **likes** books but he **dislikes** computers.

organized	disorganized	obey	disobey
agree	disagree	honest	dishonest

---

1. A person who lies, or doesn't tell the truth is ((dishonest) / disorganized).
2. Jack and I have different opinions. We (agree / (disagree)).
3. The librarian keeps the books in order. She's very ((organized) / disorganized).
4. Mark and Bill talk loudly in the library. They (obey / (disobey)) the rules.
5. Ben said that he broke the window. He's a very ((honest) / dishonest) boy.
6. Mel (likes / (dislikes)) tests because he gets very nervous.

3 Talk it over

A Think about the questions. Make notes about your answers.

1. What kinds of things do people read every day? Name at least five.
2. What was the last thing you read outside of class? What do you like to read?
3. Should libraries buy more computers or more books? Why?

B Talk about the answers with your classmates.

BRING IT TO LIFE

Visit a local library. Check out a book or an audio book and bring it to class.
If you don't have a library card, get an application form and bring it to class.

1 Grammar

A Complete the sentences with the correct forms of the verbs in parentheses.

1. (work) Sometimes in class, we _____ work _____ in pairs. Right now,
   I'm working _____ alone. Last week, we _worked_____ in groups.

2. (listen) Sam _is listening_____ to the radio right now. He usually
   _listens_____ to music in the car,
   but yesterday he _listened_____ to the news.

3. (memorize) Ivan always _memorizes_____ new words in English. Last night,
   Ivan _memorized_____ five new words. Now, he 's memorizing_____
   three more words.

B Unscramble the questions. Write short answers with your own information.

1. do / Did / night / you / research / last
   A: _Did you do research last night?_____
   B: _Yes, I did. (or No, I didn't.)_____

2. computers / you / studying / Are
   A: _Are you studying computers?_____
   B: _Yes, I am. or (No, I'm not.)_____

3. take / you / notes / in / Do / class
   A: _Do you take notes in class?_____
   B: _Yes, I do. or (No, I don't.)_____

4. make / a study schedule / you / Do
   A: _Do you make a study schedule?_____
   B: _Yes, I do. or (No, I don't.)_____

C Complete the sentences. Use the correct adjective or adverb.

1. We answered the questions <u>easily</u>. The answers were ____easy____.
2. Mike is <u>careful</u>. He works _carefully____.
3. It's a <u>good</u> picture. You draw _well_____.
4. Your answer was _clear_____. You speak <u>clearly</u>.

D Complete the paragraph with the correct form of the verbs in parentheses.

Right now, I _'m listening_____ (listen) to the radio and
I _am ('m) writing_____ (write) in my journal. Today was my second class.
We _didn't work_____ (not work) in groups today. We _worked_____ (work)
in pairs. I _practiced_____ (practice) with Maria today and we
_had_____ (have) a lot of fun. Maria always _speaks_____ (speak)
slowly and clearly. It's easy to understand her. We _learned_____ (learn) a lot
together today.

Unit 1 Review and expand

Objectives	Grammar	Vocabulary	Correlations
On-, Pre-, and Higher-level: Expand upon and review unit grammar and life skills	Contrast simple-present tense, present-continuous tense, and simple-past tense statements, *Yes/No* questions and answers (*He studies all the time. Does he study on Saturdays? Yes, he does. Did he study yesterday? Yes, he did. Is he studying now? No, he isn't.*)	Classroom activities For vocabulary support, see these **Oxford Picture Dictionary** topics: Studying, Feelings	**CASAS:** 0.1.2, 0.1.5, 7.2.6, 7.3.1, 7.3.2, 7.4.1, 7.4.7 **LCPs:** 49.01, 50.02, 50.04, 50.05, 50.08 **SCANS:** Listening, Participates as member of a team, Reading, Seeing things in the mind's eye, Speaking **EFF:** Convey ideas in writing, Read with understanding, Solve problems and make decisions

Warm-up and Review

10–15 minutes (books closed)

1. Review the *Bring It to Life* assignment from Lesson 5.

2. Have students who did the exercise discuss what they learned. Tell students who didn't do the assignment to ask their classmates questions about what they got or learned at the library.

Introduction and Presentation

5 minutes

1. Ask students *Yes/No* questions about the library. *Did you go to the library yesterday (last week)? Do you usually study in the library? Are you studying in the library now?* Write your questions and students' answers (both in short answer and statement form) on the board.

2. Ask students to identify both parts of the verb in each sentence and question. Elicit the tense.

3. State the objective: *Today we're going to review how to talk about learning together.*

1 Grammar

Guided Practice

40–45 minutes

A Read the sentences in number 1 aloud. Ask students to identify the "time" words. Point out the verb forms in the sentences on the board. Elicit the missing verb form in number 1. Have students work individually to complete the exercise. Go over the answers as a class.

B Ask students to work individually to unscramble the questions and write their short answers. When they finish, have them read the questions and answers with a partner.

C 1. Write *My computer is slow.* and *She speaks slowly.* on the board. Ask: *What does* slow *describe? What does* slowly *describe?* Ask students to identify which one is the adjective and which is the adverb.

2. Have students work individually to complete the sentences. Go over the answers as a class. Elicit the noun or verb described in each sentence.

D 1. Read the first two sentences of the paragraph aloud. Draw students' attention to the simple verb in parentheses. Say: *This paragraph has past, present, and continuous verbs.* Encourage students to read the entire paragraph before they fill in the blanks.

2. Have students work individually to complete the paragraph. Go over the answers as a class, and write them on the board. As you put up each verb, elicit the time frame.

Multilevel Strategies

Pair pre-level students with on- and higher-level students for 1D.

• **Pre, On-, and Higher-level** Ask the on- and higher-level students to tell their partners the missing words, and then ask them to read the paragraph aloud to their partners.

Go over the answers as a class. Call on pre-level students for the answers. Call on other students to explain the time frame of the verbs.

2 Group work

Communicative Practice

25–30 minutes

A 1. Direct students, in groups of three to four, to focus on the picture. Ask students to describe what some of the people in the picture are doing.

2. Group students and assign roles: leader, recorder, reporter, and timekeeper. Explain that students work with their groups to write the paragraph.

3. Check comprehension of the roles. Ask: *Who writes the paragraph?* [recorder] *Who will read the paragraph to the class?* [reporter] *Who helps everyone and manages the group?* [leader] *Who tells the group how much time has passed?* [timekeeper] *Who creates the paragraph?* [everyone]

4. Set a time limit (five minutes) to complete the exercise. Circulate and answer any questions.

5. Have a reporter from each group read the group's paragraph to the class.

Multilevel Strategies

For 2A, use mixed-level groups.

• **Pre-level** Assign these students the role of timekeeper.

• **On-level** Assign these students the role of recorder or reporter.

• **Higher-level** Assign these students the role of leader.

B 1. Have students walk around the room to conduct the interviews. To get students moving, tell them to interview three people who were not in their groups for 2A.

2. Set a time limit (five minutes) to complete the exercise.

3. Tell students to make a note of their classmates' answers but not to worry about writing complete sentences.

Multilevel Strategies

Adapt the mixer in 2B to the level of your students.

• **Pre-level** Allow these students to ask and answer the questions without writing.

• **Higher-level** Have these students ask two additional questions and write all answers.

C Call on individuals to report what they learned about their classmates. Encourage students to make generalizations. *Three out of four students like to study in their bedrooms.*

PROBLEM SOLVING

10–15 minutes

A 1. Ask: *Did you ever join a class after it had already started? How did you feel?* Tell students they will read a story about a new student. Direct students to read Teresa's story silently.

2. Ask: *When did the class start? Does Teresa like the class? Why is she worried?*

3. Play the audio and have students read along silently.

B 1. Elicit answers to question 1. Have volunteers write answers to question 2 on the board. Continue until all of the class ideas have been put up.

2. Discuss the pros and cons of each solution.

Evaluation

30–35 minutes

To test students' understanding of the unit grammar and life skills, have them take the Unit 1 Test in the *Step Forward Test Generator CD-ROM* with *ExamView® Assessment Suite*.

Learning Log

To help students record and discuss their progress, use the *Learning Log* on page T-200.

To extend this review: Have students complete **Workbook 3 page 8, Multilevel Activity Book 3 page 26**, and the **Unit 1 Exercises** on the **Multilevel Grammar Exercises CD-ROM 3.**

2 Group work

A Work with 2–3 classmates. Write a paragraph about the picture. Share your paragraph with the class.

Annie is searching online. Tomas is talking to Ms. Carlson...

B Interview 3 classmates. Write their answers.

1. Where do you like to study? Why?
2. Are you taking other classes in school?
3. Where did you learn English before?

Mei
1. the library—likes quiet places
2. yes—a computer class
3. In China

C Talk about the answers with your class.

PROBLEM SOLVING

A Listen and read about Teresa.

    Teresa is a new student in an English class at Mid-City School. The class started three weeks ago, but today is Teresa's first day. She likes the class and the teacher very much, but she's a little worried about making friends. The students in the class already know each other very well. Some even studied together last year. Teresa doesn't like being the only new student in the class. All the other students are having fun together. Teresa feels alone.

B Work with your classmates. Answer the questions.

1. What is Teresa's problem? Teresa feels lonely because she is new and doesn't know anyone.
2. What should Teresa do? Think of 2 or 3 solutions to her problem.

UNIT **2**

FOCUS ON
- recreation
- email invitations
- the future
- making plans with friends
- health benefits of parks

Ready for Fun

1 Learn recreation vocabulary

A **Talk about the questions with your class.**

1. Where do you go to have fun?
2. What are some of your favorite recreational activities?

B **Work with your classmates. Match the words with the picture.**

_3_	amusement park	_5_	gym	_9_	swimming pool
_7_	bowling alley	_4_	nightclub	_2_	theater
_1_	farmers' market	_8_	playground	_6_	zoo

C **Listen and check. Then read the new words with a partner.**

D **Work with a partner. Write other recreation words you know. Check your words in a dictionary.**

Unit 2 Lesson 1

Objectives	Grammar	Vocabulary	Correlations
On-level: Identify and describe recreational activities, places, and events **Pre-level:** Identify recreational activities, places, and events **Higher-level:** Talk and write about recreational activities, places, and events	*Like* + gerund (*I like bowling.*)	Recreational places and activities For vocabulary support, see this **Oxford Picture Dictionary** topic: Places to Go	**CASAS:** 0.1.2, 0.1.5, 2.6.1, 4.8.1, 7.5.1 **LCPs:** 39.01, 39.04, 49.02, 49.03, 50.04 **SCANS:** Listening, Participates as member of a team, Seeing things in the mind's eye, Speaking **EFF:** Cooperate with others, Listen actively, Reflect and evaluate, Speak so others can understand

Warm-up and Review

10–15 minutes (books closed)

Bring in items from games, sports, and free-time activities, and pass them around the room. Elicit the name of an activity, sport, or game with which the item may belong. Write the words on the board. Items could include dice, sports equipment, entertainment listings, etc.

Introduction

5 minutes

1. Write *recreation* on the board. Say: *All of the words on the board refer to recreation. Recreation means an activity you do for fun or relaxation.*

2. State the objective: *Today we're going to learn ways to talk about recreation.*

1 Learn recreation vocabulary

Presentation I

20–25 minutes

A Elicit students' answers to question 1. Add their ideas to the board if they are not already there. Do the same with activities they mention for question 2.

B 1. Direct students to look at the pictures. Ask: *Are any of these pictures of your favorite recreational activity?*

2. Group students and assign roles: leader, fact checker, recorder, and reporter. Explain that students work with their groups to match the words and pictures.

3. Check comprehension of the roles. Ask: *Who looks up the words in a dictionary?* [fact checker] *Who writes the numbers in the book?* [recorder] *Who tells the class your answers?* [reporter] *Who helps everyone and manages the group?* [leader]

4. Set a time limit (three minutes). As students work together, copy the wordlist onto the board.

5. Call "time." Have reporters take turns giving their answers. Write each group's answer on the board next to the word.

C 1. To prepare students for listening, say: *We're going to listen to a guide showing some people around a recreation center. She's going to talk about the places and activities in the picture.* Ask students to listen and check their answers.

2. Have students check the wordlist on the board and then write the correct numbers in their books.

3. Pair students. Set a time limit (three minutes). Monitor pair practice to identify pronunciation issues.

4. Call "time" and work with the pronunciation of any troublesome words or phrases.

D 1. Ask students to work with a partner to brainstorm a list of related words.

2. Elicit words from the class. Write them on the board in two columns labeled *Places* and *Activities*. Ask students to copy the words into their vocabulary notes for the unit.

Guided Practice

5–10 minutes

 1. Model the conversations with a volunteer. Model them again using other information from 1B. Encourage students to use words from the warm-up and their own ideas.

2. Set a time limit (three minutes). Direct students to practice with a partner. Ask volunteers to repeat one of their conversations for the class.

2 Learn to describe places and events

Presentation II

15–20 minutes

 1. Direct students to look at the pictures. Introduce the new topic: *We've talked about places and activities. Now we're going to learn how to describe those places and activities.*

2. Say and have students repeat the places and activities in the pictures.

3. Ask students to work individually to match the adjectives to the activities they describe. Write the number-letter match on the board. Call on volunteers to read the matching activities and adjectives aloud.

4. Check comprehension. Ask: *Is going to the dentist exciting? Is taking a hot shower relaxing? Is washing the dishes entertaining?*

> ### Multilevel Strategies
>
> Provide a challenge for higher-level students.
>
> • **Higher-level** After these students finish 2A, direct them to look up synonyms for *exciting, entertaining,* and *boring.* Help them with pronunciation and example sentences.

Guided Practice

10–15 minutes

 1. Model the conversation with a volunteer. Model it again using a different word from 2A.

2. Set a time limit (three minutes). Direct students to practice with a partner. Call on volunteers to say one of their conversations for the class.

Communicative Practice and Application

10–15 minutes

 Give students a minute to make notes of their answers to the questions. Call on individuals to share their ideas with the class. Encourage students to make generalizations about the class. *Most of us prefer exciting/relaxing activities. Four out of twenty people think _____ is boring.*

Evaluation

10–15 minutes (books closed)

TEST YOURSELF

1. Direct students to work individually to write a list of ten words from the lesson. Assign a time limit (three minutes). Call "time" and direct students to work with a partner to combine their lists and put the words in alphabetical order. Circulate and monitor students' progress.

2. Ask a volunteer pair to write their list on the board. Ask other students to add words.

> ### Multilevel Strategies
>
> Target the *Test Yourself* to the level of your students.
>
> • **Higher-level** After these students have worked with a partner to alphabetize their lists, ask them to write three to five sentences using words from the list.

To compress this lesson: Conduct 1B as a whole-class activity.

To extend this lesson: Play a "round-table" game using the adjectives from this unit. Put students in mixed-level groups, and give each group a piece of paper. Write an adjective on the board. Have each student write one place or activity on the paper that can be described by that adjective. After the first student writes, he/she passes the paper to the person to the left. Members of the group can help each other with ideas, but everyone must write. Call "time" after two minutes. Ask groups how many places/activities they have written. Ask a reporter from the group with the most ideas to read the group's paper aloud. Play again with a different adjective.

And/Or have students complete **Workbook 3 page 9** and **Multilevel Activity Book 3 pages 28–29**.

E **Work with a partner. Practice the conversation. Use the picture in 1B.**

A: Do you go to the farmers' market? A: Do you go to the zoo?

B: Yes, I go there once a month. B: No, I never go there.

2 Learn to describe places and events

A **Look at the pictures. Match the places and the adjectives below.**

It's **exciting**!

It's **loud**!

It's **entertaining**.

It's **crowded**.

It's **relaxing**.

It's **boring**.

<u> e </u> 1. bowling at the bowling alley   a. exciting

<u> f </u> 2. exercising at the gym   b. relaxing

<u> a </u> 3. riding a roller coaster   c. entertaining

<u> c </u> 4. seeing a play   d. crowded

<u> d </u> 5. dancing in a nightclub   e. loud

<u> b </u> 6. people watching at the park   f. boring

B **Work with a partner. Practice the conversation. Use the words in 2A.**

A: *What are they doing?* A: *Is it fun?*

B: *They're riding a roller coaster.* B: *Yes. It's exciting.*

C **Talk about the questions with your class.**

1. Do you prefer relaxing or exciting activities? Why?
2. Which activities do you think are entertaining? Which are boring?

TEST YOURSELF ✔

Close your book. Work with a partner. Make a list of as many new words from the lesson as you can. Alphabetize your list.

1 Read an email invitation

A Look at the flyer. Talk about the questions with your class.

1. What are some fun and inexpensive places to visit in your community?
2. Do you like to go places with a group of friends, just one friend, or alone?

B Listen and read the email.

Writer's note

In a letter or email, use a comma (,) after the greeting and the closing.

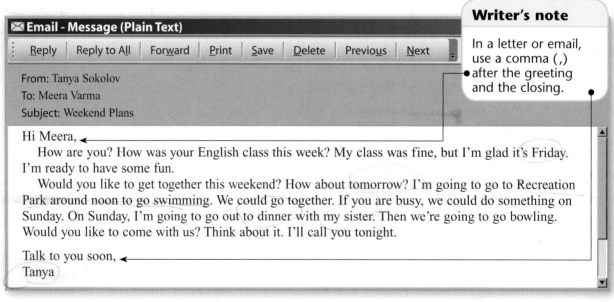

From: Tanya Sokolov
To: Meera Varma
Subject: Weekend Plans

Hi Meera,

How are you? How was your English class this week? My class was fine, but I'm glad it's Friday. I'm ready to have some fun.

Would you like to get together this weekend? How about tomorrow? I'm going to go to Recreation Park around noon to go swimming. We could go together. If you are busy, we could do something on Sunday. On Sunday, I'm going to go out to dinner with my sister. Then we're going to go bowling. Would you like to come with us? Think about it. I'll call you tonight.

Talk to you soon,
Tanya

C Check your understanding. Mark the statements T (true), F (false), or NI (no information).

  F   1. Tanya and Meera are in the same English class.

 NI 2. Tanya had a test in class today.

  T   3. Tanya wants to go swimming at 12:00 on Saturday.

  F   4. She also wants to go bowling on Saturday.

Unit 2 Lesson 2

Objectives	Grammar	Vocabulary	Correlations
On- and Higher-level: Analyze, write, and edit an email invitation **Pre-level:** Read and write an email invitation	*Would like* for invitations (*Would you like to go bowling?*) *Be going to* for future (*I'm going to go swimming.*)	Recreational activities For vocabulary support, see this **Oxford Picture Dictionary** topic: Places to Go	**CASAS:** 0.1.2, 0.1.5, 0.2.3, 2.6.1, 4.6.2 **LCPs:** 39.04, 49.16, 49.02, 49.03 **SCANS:** Applies technology to task, Listening, Speaking, Writing **EFF:** Cooperate with others, Convey ideas in writing, Read with understanding, Reflect and evaluate, Speak so others can understand

Warm-up and Review

10–15 minutes (books closed)

Review *be going to* for future. Ask individuals: *What are you going to do for fun next weekend? Next month? Next summer?* Write their future activities on the board. After you have a list of eight to ten activities, challenge other students to remember who said which activity. *Who is going to go dancing next weekend? Who is going to go shopping?* Write a first-person and a third-person example sentence on the board.

Introduction

5 minutes

1. Ask students how many of them use email to communicate with their friends. Point out that many of the activities on the board are things they might want to do with friends.

2. State the objective: *Today we're going to learn how to write an email invitation.*

1 Read an email invitation

Presentation

20–25 minutes

A 1. Direct students to look at the flyer. Ask: *What place is this flyer for? What activities do they offer? Which activity would you choose to do?*

2. Elicit answers to questions 1 and 2. Write a list of places to go in your community on the board. Encourage students to ask for more information about the places if they are interested.

TIP Check your city's website for flyers or announcements about upcoming or ongoing events. Bring the information to class. Discuss activities students have done, places they have visited, and which activities and events interest them the most.

B 1. Say: *Now we're going to read an email invitation. Tanya is inviting her friend out this weekend.* Direct students to read the email silently. Check comprehension. Ask: *What is Tanya doing on Saturday? What is she doing on Sunday?*

2. Play the audio. Have students read along silently. Draw students' attention to the *Writer's note.* Ask students to identify the greeting and the closing. Elicit other greetings and closings. Talk about the level of formality of each greeting. Point out that when friends email each other, they often do not use a closing.

Guided Practice I

10 minutes

C Have students work independently to mark the statements T (true), F (false), or NI (no information). Go over the answers as a class. Write them on the board.

Multilevel Strategies

Seat pre-level students together for 1C.

• **Pre-level** While other students are working on 1C, ask these students *Yes/No* and *Or* questions about the reading. *Is Tanya going swimming? Is Tanya going out to dinner on Saturday? Is Tanya going bowling with her mother? Does Tanya want Meera to come with them to dinner and bowling?* Allow these students to copy the answers to 1C from the board.

2 Write an email invitation

Guided Practice II
20–25 minutes

A Read the questions. Elicit students' answers. Write their ideas on the board.

B 1. Direct students to look back at the model in 1B. Focus their attention on the use of the future. Ask them to look through the email quickly and mark the two sentences that tell what Tanya is going to do this weekend. Elicit the sentences. Some of them use *going to* for the future, and some use the present continuous. Point out that both are correct for talking about plans.

2. Go through the email template step by step. Elicit possible completions for each of the blanks.

3. Go over the expressions in the *Need help?* box. Point out that *hang out* is more informal than the other expressions.

4. Check comprehension of the exercise. Ask: *What are you writing?* [an email] *What's the purpose of the email? Do you need to put your friend's name at the top? Do you need to put your name at the bottom?*

Multilevel Strategies

Adapt 2B to the level of your students.

• **Pre-level** Work with these students to write a group letter. Read the email template. At each blank, stop and elicit completions. Decide as a group what to write.

• **Higher-level** Ask these students to include plans for both Saturday and Sunday, and to include whom they are going with and what they will do in each place.

C 1. Lead students through the process of using the *Editing checklist*. Read each sentence aloud, and ask students to check their papers before moving onto the next item.

2. Allow students a few minutes to edit their writing as necessary.

Communicative Practice
10 minutes

D 1. Read the instructions aloud. Emphasize to students that they are responding to their partners' work, not correcting it.

2. Use the email in 1B to model the exercise. *I think the part about going bowling is interesting. I'd like to ask Tanya where they are going out to dinner.*

3. Direct students to exchange papers with a partner and follow the instructions.

4. Call on volunteers to share something interesting they read in their partners' papers.

Application and Evaluation
15 minutes

 If students are using computers for the *Test Yourself*, have them send the emails to you. Insert your corrections/comments, and email them back to the students.

TEST YOURSELF

1. Review the instructions aloud. Assign a time limit (ten minutes), and have students work independently.

2. Before collecting students' work, remind them to use the *Editing checklist*. Collect and correct students' writing.

Multilevel Strategies

Adapt the *Test Yourself* to the level of your students.

• **Pre-level** Write a skeleton email for these students to complete. *Hi _____, I'm going to _____ at _____ on _____. Would you like to _____?*

To compress this lesson: Assign the *Test Yourself* for homework.

To extend this lesson: Have students practice oral invitations. Write expressions for accepting and rejecting invitations on the board. *I'd love to. That sounds fun. I'm sorry, I can't. I have to _____. Can we do it another day/weekend?* Have students repeat the expressions, and elicit possible completions for *I have to _____.* Have students walk around the room telling people about their weekend plans and inviting them to come. Direct students to accept or politely reject their partners' invitations. Participate in the activity, and provide feedback to the students you talk to.

And/Or have students complete **Workbook 3 page 10** and **Multilevel Activity Book 3 page 30.**

2 Write an email invitation

A **Talk about the questions with your class.**

1. Where would you like to go this weekend?
2. Who could you invite to go with you?

B **Write an email. Invite someone to go out with you. Use the model in 1B and the questions in 2A to help you.** Answers will vary.

✉ Email - Message (Plain Text)

Reply | Reply to All | For<u>w</u>ard | Print | Save | Delete | Previous | Next

From: _____
To: _____
Subject: _____

Hi _____

　　How are you? How was _____ this week? My _____ was fine,
but I'm glad it's Friday. I'm ready to _____.
　　Would you like to _____ this weekend? How about _____?
I'm going to go to _____
_____ Think about it. I'll call
you _____.

_____

Need Help?

Would you like to...
get together?
go out?
do something?
hang out?

C **Use the checklist to edit your writing. Check (✔) the true sentences.** Answers will vary.

Editing checklist	
1. I wrote a subject line to tell the person what the email is about.	
2. I wrote the name of the place that I'm going to and the time.	
3. I invited someone to go out with me this weekend.	
4. I used a comma after the greeting and closing in my email.	

D **Exchange emails with a partner. Read and comment on your partner's work.**

1. Point out one sentence that you think is very interesting.
2. Ask your partner a question about his or her weekend plans.

TEST YOURSELF ✔

Write a new email. Use a computer if possible. Invite a classmate to go out with you this weekend. Give information about the time, the day, and the place you want to go.

1 Review *be going to* and *will*

A **Read the conversation. Where are they going to go?**

Sam: What are you going to do tomorrow?

Ken: I'm going to study all day.

Sam: Let's go to the pool. We'll be home
by 3:00. We won't stay late. I promise!

Ken: Well, I guess I can study tomorrow
night. OK, I'll go.

Sam: Great! I'll see you tomorrow.

B **Study the chart. Underline the 4 examples of *will* and circle
the 2 examples of *be going to* in the conversation above.** Answers will vary.

The future with *be going to* and *will*	Notes
I**'m going to** study all day. I**'m not going to** go out.	• Use *be going to* to talk about future plans.
We**'ll** be home by 3:00. We **won't** stay late.	• Use *will* for promises.

C **Complete the conversations with the correct forms of *be going to* or
will. Use the words in parentheses to help you.**

1. **A:** When _____ are _____ we _____ going to _____ go shopping this weekend? (plan)

   B: I don't know. I __'ll_____ call you when I get up. (promise)

   A: What time _are_____ you _going to_____ get up? (plan)

   B: I _am ('m), going to_____ get up early tomorrow. (plan)

   I _will ('ll)_____ call you at 9:15. (promise)

2. **A:** When _are_____ you _going to_____ clean the garage? (plan)

   B: I _am ('m) going to_____ clean it soon. (plan)

   A: When?

   B: I _will ('ll)_____ clean it before I go out tonight. (promise)

   A: Are you sure?

   B: Yes, I won't forget. I _will ('ll)_____ clean it before I go out. (promise)

3. **A:** _Are_____ you _going to_____ go to work tomorrow? (plan)

   B: No, I'm not. I _am ('m) going to_____ go to an amusement park. (plan)

   A: Have fun. I _will_____ talk to you next week. (promise)

Unit 2 Lesson 3

Objectives	Grammar	Vocabulary	Correlations
On- and Higher-level: Use *be going to* and *will* to make plans, promises, and predictions, and listen for plans, promises, and predictions. **Pre-level:** Recognize *be going to* and *will* for plans, promises, and predictions	*Be going to (I'm going to go bowling.)* *Will (I'll call you.)*	Recreational activities; *plan, promise, prediction* For vocabulary support, see this **Oxford Picture Dictionary** topic: Places to Go	**CASAS:** 0.1.2, 7.2.5 **LCPs:** 49.16, 49.03, 50.02 **SCANS:** Creative thinking, Listening, Organizes and maintains information, Reading, Writing **EFF:** Cooperate with others, Convey ideas in writing, Listen actively, Read with understanding, Reflect and evaluate

Warm-up and Review

10–15 minutes (books closed)

Review the differences in form between *will* and *be going to*. Write first-person sentences on the board. *I'm going to call my mother tonight. I'll call you around 6:00. I'm going to go to the mall this weekend. I'll buy something for you.* Say and have students repeat the sentences. Ask volunteers to change the sentences to third person. Point out that the verb *be* changes in *be going to* but that the *will* form is the same for all subjects. Leave the sentences on the board.

Introduction

5–10 minutes

1. Tell students that all of the sentences on the board refer to future time but that *will* and *be going to* are not used in exactly the same way.

2. State the objective: *Today we're going to learn the difference between* be going to *and* will.

1 Review *be going to* and *will*

Presentation I

20–25 minutes

 1. Direct students to look at the picture. Ask: *What do you think the men are saying?*

2. Read the question. Ask students to read the conversation silently to find the answer. Call on a volunteer for the answer.

B 1. Read the chart aloud.

2. Direct students to underline the examples of *will* and circle the examples of *be going to* in 1A. Go over the answers as a class.

3. Ask: *When Ken says* I'm going to study, *is it his plan or a promise? Why does he say* I'll go *when he agrees to go to the pool?*

4. Read the chart through sentence by sentence. Then read it again, and have students repeat after you.

5. Assess students' understanding of the charts. Ask: *Which sentences on the board from the warm-up are plans and which are promises? Why?*

Guided Practice I

15–20 minutes

C Ask students to work individually to complete the conversation. Ask volunteers to write the answers on the board.

Multilevel Strategies

For 1C, seat same-level students together.

• **Pre-level** While other students are completing 1C, provide these students with skeleton sentences to copy and complete. *I'm going to _____ tonight. I'm going to _____ tomorrow. I promise I'll _____.*

• **On- and Higher-level** Have these students write an additional two-sentence exchange using *be going to* and *will*.

Guided Practice II

5–10 minutes

D Have students work individually to rewrite the sentences. While they are writing, copy the exercise onto the board. Have volunteers write the new sentences on the board.

2 Learn about future predictions

Presentation II

20–25 minutes

TIP Students may ask about making predictions with *be going to* (as in *It's going to rain*). We often use *be going to* for predictions that are strongly connected to the present. (*It's cloudy. Therefore, it's going to rain*).

A 1. Introduce the new topic. *Now we're going to talk about predictions. A prediction is something we think will happen in the future. Someday we'll drive flying cars. I think it's true, but it's not my plan!*

2. Read the chart aloud.

3. Ask students to work individually to complete the sentences. Have volunteers read the completed sentences aloud.

TIP After 2A, provide more practice with predictions. Make a list or show pictures of items for students to make predictions about—for example, a computer, a car, a hospital, a TV, a house, etc. Put students in groups. Write the names of the items on large sheets of paper, and give a different one to each group. Tell the students in each group to write one prediction about its group's item and then pass the paper to another group. Direct that group to make a different prediction. Continue passing the papers until every group has had a chance to make a prediction about each item. Go over their ideas as a class.

Alternatively, show a video clip from a futuristic movie, and have students make predictions based on what they saw.

Guided Practice I

10–15 minutes

B Have students work individually to write answers to the questions. Ask them to read the questions and answers with a partner.

Multilevel Strategies

For 2B, seat same-level students together.

• **Pre-level** Work with these students with their books closed. Read the questions aloud, and elicit answers from volunteers. Write the answers on the board. Have the group open their books and write the answers.

• **On- and Higher-level** After these students finish reading the questions and answers in 2B with a partner, ask them to work with their partners to write one additional question and answer. Have volunteers put their original questions and answers on the board.

TIP For more prediction practice, have students write and read fortunes. Write *fortune cookie* on the board, and ask a student to explain what it is (or bring a fortune cookie to class). Tell students that everyone in the class has a fantastic future ahead of them, and you want them to write predictions for each other. The predictions can be wild or funny, but they must be happy predictions (no bad news!). Give students small slips of paper, and have them write one prediction each. Collect all of the predictions, and put them in a hat. Have students pull their "fortune" out of the hat and read it to the class.

D **Get the form. Work with your class. Correct the sentences.**

1. I will to call you later today. _____I will call you later today._____
2. We going to go to class next week. _____We are ('re) going to class next week._____
3. She are going to work tomorrow. _____She is ('s) going to work tomorrow._____
4. They're study tonight. _____They are ('re) going to study tonight._____

2 Learn about future predictions

A **Study the chart. Then complete the predictions below with *will*. Use the verbs in parentheses.**

Predictions with *will*
Ten years from now, our city **will have** better parks and community centers. There **will be** more playgrounds and swimming pools in the future.

Note

Use *think* or *probably* with *will* to make predictions about the future.
   I **think** they'**ll build** a new baseball stadium next to the park.
   They'**ll probably start** next year.

1. There _____will be_____ many positive changes in our city next year. (be)
2. The city _will build_____ a new park in our neighborhood. (build)
3. The new park _will_____ probably _be_____ nice. (be)
4. I think my neighbors and I _will enjoy_____ the new park very much. (enjoy)
5. The city _will buy_____ new buses. (buy)
6. The new buses _will cause_____ less pollution. (cause)

B **Answer the questions. Use your own information. Then ask and answer the questions with a partner.** Answers will vary.

1. What will you do for fun next weekend?

   _____

2. What do you think the weather will be like next week?

   _____

3. Will you take a vacation next year?

   _____

4. Where do you think you will work five years from now?

   _____

5. Where will you live ten years from now?

   _____

3 Grammar listening

🎧 **Listen to the sentences. Check (✔) *Plan, Promise,* or *Prediction*.**

	Plan	Promise	Prediction
1.	✔		
2.		✔	
3.	✔		
4.			✔
5.		✔	
6.			✔

4 Practice future predictions

A **Think about the year 2075. Think about your answers to these questions.**

1. Do you think the president of the United States will be a man or a woman?
2. What kind of recreation do you think will be popular?
3. Do you think people will stay home more or go out more?
4. Do you think most people will live in houses or apartments?

B **Work with a partner. Ask and answer the questions in 4A.**

A: *Do you think the president will be a man or a woman in 2075?*
B: *I think the president will be a woman.*

C **Write 3 more questions about the future with your partner. Ask and answer the questions with another pair of students.**

A: *What do you think will be the biggest city in the world in 50 years?*
B: *I think the biggest city will be Beijing.*

TEST YOURSELF ✔

Close your book. Write about your future. Write 2 sentences about your plans, 2 prediction sentences, and 2 promises. Use *will* or *be going to.*

---

3 Grammar listening

Guided Practice II

10–15 minutes

1. Read the chart headings, and elicit an example of a plan, a promise, and a prediction.

2. Direct students to listen and check the correct column in the chart.

3. Replay the audio and ask students to check their answers. Go over the answers as a class.

> After *Grammar listening,* try an "auxiliaries dictation." Read sentences with contracted forms of *will* and *be going to.* Ask students to write the subject + verb out in full form. Tell them to write the entire sentence if they can. 1. *I'll see you after school.* 2. *He's gonna visit his mom tonight.* 3. *We're gonna do our homework in the evening.* 4. *They'll take the test tomorrow.*

4 Practice future predictions

Communicative Practice and Application

20–25 minutes

A 1. Direct students to look at the picture. Ask: *Do you think our city will look like this someday?*

2. Read the questions aloud and check comprehension. Ask: *What does* popular *mean?* Have students work individually to write their answers.

B 1. Put students in pairs. Direct students to take turns asking and answering the questions in 4A.

2. Check comprehension of the exercise. Ask: *How many questions are you going to ask?* [three] *Do you need to write your partner's answers?* [no]

C 1. Direct students to write three more questions with their partners.

2. Put the pairs together in groups of four, and have students change partners. Tell them to ask their new partners the questions in 4A and the new questions they wrote with their former partners.

3. Check comprehension of the exercise. Ask: *How many questions are you going to ask?* [seven] *Do you need to write?* [no]

4. Ask individuals to share some interesting predictions that they heard with the class.

Evaluation

10–15 minutes (books closed)

TEST YOURSELF

Ask students to write the sentences independently. Collect and correct their writing.

> ### Multilevel Strategies
>
> Target the *Test Yourself* to the level of your students.
>
> • **Pre-level** Provide skeleton sentences for these students to complete. 1. *After school today, I'm going to _____.* 2. *Next weekend, I'm going to _____.* 3. *I think people will _____ in the year 2099.*
>
> • **Higher-level** Have these students write a paragraph in response to this prompt: *Write a paragraph about your future plans. Include one prediction and one promise.*

To compress this lesson: Conduct 2A as a whole-class discussion.

To extend this lesson: Have students share the plans, predictions, and promises from the *Test Yourself* with a partner.

And/Or have students complete **Workbook 3 pages 11–12, Multilevel Activity Book 3 pages 31–32,** and the corresponding **Unit 2 Exercises** on the **Multilevel Grammar Exercises CD-ROM 3.**

Unit 2 Lesson 4

Objectives	Grammar	Vocabulary	Correlations
On-, Pre-, and Higher-level: Ask about and express preferences, and listen for information about an event	*Would rather* + simple verb (*I'd rather go to the park.*)	Free time activities, *event* For vocabulary support, see this **Oxford Picture Dictionary** topic: Entertainment	**CASAS:** 0.1.2, 6.0.3, 6.0.4, 6.1.1, 6.1.2 **LCPs:** 49.02, 49.03, 49.16 **SCANS:** Interprets and communicates information, Listening, Reading, Seeing things in the mind's eye **EFF:** Cooperate with others, Listen actively, Read with understanding, Reflect and evaluate

Warm-up and Review

10–15 minutes (books closed)

Write these newspaper categories on the board: *arts, nightlife, family events, festivals, concerts*. Ask students if they can name any recent examples of these in your area.

Introduction

5 minutes

1. Ask students which kind of event they would like to attend. Say: *Most people like to do some things more than other things. They have preferences.*

2. State the objective: *Today we're going to learn how to talk about our preferences.*

1 Learn to talk about preferences

Presentation I

15–20 minutes

A 1. Direct students to look at the pictures. Ask: *What is the man doing in the two pictures? What is the woman doing?*

2. Play the audio. Give students a minute to answer the two questions. Go over the answers as a class.

Guided Practice

20–25 minutes

B 1. Read the instructions aloud. Ask students to read along silently and listen for the answer to the question. Elicit the answer.

2. Ask students to read the conversation with a partner. Circulate and monitor pronunciation. Model and have students repeat difficult words or phrases.

3. Say and have students repeat the expressions in the *In other words* box. Elicit the placement of the expressions in the conversation. Ask volunteers to read the conversation using expressions from the box.

Communicative Practice and Application

15–20 minutes

C 1. Ask students to read the instructions silently. Check their comprehension of the exercise. Ask: *What does Partner A want? What does Partner B want?* Elicit examples of what each partner might say.

2. Set a time limit (five minutes). Ask students to act out the role-play in both roles. Ask one to three volunteer pairs to act out their conversations for the class. Tell students who are listening to note the words Partner A uses to offer Partner B a choice.

Multilevel Strategies

For 1C, adapt the role-play to the level of your students.

• **Pre-level** Provide a simplified conversation for these students to use for the role-play. *A: Would you like to get together this weekend? B: Sure. What do you want to do? A: There's a new movie on Saturday or there's a party on Sunday. B: I'd rather go to the party. I'll pick you up at 2:00. A: See you then.*

1 Learn to talk about preferences

A Look at the pictures. Listen to the conversations. Then answer the questions below with your classmates.

1. What are the man and woman going to do on Wednesday night? They are going to watch a movie on Wednesday night.
2. When will they decide what to do on Friday night? They will decide on Thursday night.

B Listen and read. What are the people going to do on Saturday?

A: Would you like to get together this Saturday?

B: Sure. What would you like to do?

A: Well, on Saturday night there's a soccer match at the stadium or there's a free concert in the park. Take your pick.

B: I think I'd rather go to the concert. Should I pick you up at 7:00?

A: Let's play it by ear*. I'll call you on Friday night.

B: Sounds good.

*Idiom note: play it by ear = to wait and decide later

In other words...

Giving someone a choice
Take your pick.
It's up to you.
Your choice.

C Role-play a conversation about preferences with a partner. Use the example in 1B to make a new conversation.

Partner A: Ask your friend to get together on Saturday. There's a new movie opening on Saturday or a party at the community center.

Partner B: Your friend asks you to get together on Saturday. Listen to your friend's ideas. You'd rather go to the party. You can pick your friend up at 2:00.

2 Learn to ask about and express preferences

A Study the chart. Complete the sentences below with *would rather*.

Expressing preferences with *would rather* + verb
A: **Would** you **rather see** a movie or a play?   B: I **would rather see** a movie.
A: **Would** they **rather stay home** or **go out**?   B: I think they'**d rather go out**.

Note
Use *would rather* + verb to talk about preferences, or what you want to do.

1. **A:** _Would_ you _rather_ buy a car or a motorcycle?

   B: I _would rather_ buy a car.

2. **A:** _Would_ Sara _rather_ study or go dancing?

   B: She _would rather_ study because she has a big test tomorrow.

B Work with a partner. Ask and answer the questions in the chart. Write your partner's preferences. Answers will vary.

Would you rather...	My partner's preference
watch a movie or a sports event?	
stay home or go dancing?	
read a book or watch TV?	
eat Chinese food or Italian food?	

C Take a class poll. Talk about the answers with the class.

Twenty-five students would rather watch a movie. Four would rather watch a sports event.

3 Practice your pronunciation

A Listen to the pronunciation of the *j* and *ch* sounds in these sentences.

"j"
1. Would <u>^</u> you like to get together?

"ch"
2. I'll meet <u>^</u> you in the park.

B Listen to the sentences. Underline the letters that combine to make the *j* or *ch* sounds.

1. Coul<u>d y</u>ou call me tomorrow?
2. I'll ge<u>t y</u>ou two tickets for the game.
3. Woul<u>d y</u>ou like to go out?
4. What di<u>d you</u> do last Saturday night?
5. What shoul<u>d y</u>ou do when you're sick?
6. I bough<u>t y</u>ou a present.

C Read the sentences with a partner. Then listen again and check.

2 Learn to ask about and express preferences

Presentation II

10–15 minutes

 A 1. Introduce the new topic. Now we're going to look at questions and answers with *would rather*.

2. Read the conversations in the chart aloud. Ask students to identify the verbs. Ask what form they're in.

3. Draw students' attention to the note about *would rather*. Point out that *would* is pronounced clearly in the question but is usually contracted in the statement.

4. Have students work individually to complete the conversations in 1 and 2. Ask volunteers to read the conversations aloud.

Guided Practice

15–20 minutes

 B 1. Model the questions and answers with a volunteer.

2. Set a time limit (five minutes). Have students take turns asking and answering the questions with a partner. Tell them to note their partners' answers in the chart.

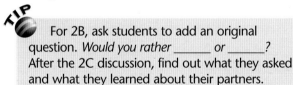
> For 2B, ask students to add an original question. *Would you rather _____ or _____?* After the 2C discussion, find out what they asked and what they learned about their partners.

Communicative Practice and Application

5–10 minutes

C Ask for a show of hands about each question, and have a volunteer count the "votes" for you and tell you the total. Elicit sentences to summarize the results using *would rather*. *Fifteen students would rather watch a movie.* Write the sentences on the board.

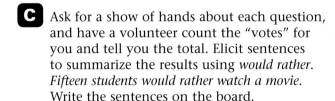
> Have students "vote with their feet." Put up one choice on each side of the room, and have students go to the side of their choice. This makes counting easy and forces everyone to vote.

3 Practice your pronunciation

Pronunciation Extension

10–15 minutes

A 1. Write *Would you like to eat your lunch in the park?* on the board. Say the sentence with relaxed pronunciation, and ask students to repeat it. Draw a line to connect the final *d* in *would* and the final *t* in *eat* with the *y* in *you* and *your*. Say: *Now we're going to focus on the "j" and "ch" sounds that we make when we connect these sounds.*

2. Play the audio. Direct students to listen for the linking sound made in *would + you* and in *meet + you.* Ask several students to say the two sentences, pronouncing the linking sound.

 B 1. Play the audio. Have students work individually to underline the letters.

2. Call on volunteers to read the sentences aloud and say what letters they underlined. Ask: *What letters make the "j" sound? What letters make the "ch" sound?*

C Ask students to take turns reading the sentences in 3B with a partner. Monitor and provide feedback.

4 Focus on listening

Listening Extension

20–25 minutes

A Read the questions aloud, and elicit answers from volunteers. For question 2, encourage students to respond to each other's ideas. After one student speaks, ask other students for their opinions: *Do you agree or disagree with what he/she said? Why?*

B 1. Tell students they are going to listen to a recorded message from the Greenville Parks and Recreation Department. Direct them to read the questions before they listen.

2. Play the audio. Have students write the answers to the questions as they listen. Go over the answers as a class.

C 1. Direct students to read the flyer before listening.

2. Replay the audio and have students work individually to fill in the blanks on the flyer. Go over the answers as a class.

Multilevel Strategies

Replay the audio to challenge on- and higher-level students while allowing pre-level students to catch up.

• **Pre-level** Have these students listen again to fill in the blanks in 4B.

• **On- and Higher-level** Write questions on the board for these students to answer. *What can you do at A Taste of Greenville? What ages must children be to play soccer?*

5 Real-life math

Math Extension

5–10 minutes

1. Direct students to read the word problem. Ask: *How many adult tickets do they need to buy?* Write *3 x $9.00* on the board. Ask: *How many children's tickets do they need to buy?* Write: *1 x $5.00.*

2. Ask students to work individually to figure out the problem. Ask a volunteer to write the final math problem and the answer on the board.

Evaluation

10–15 minutes

TEST YOURSELF

1. Model the role-play with a volunteer. Then switch roles.

2. Pair students. Check comprehension of the exercise by eliciting what Partner A and Partner B might say.

3. Set a time limit (five minutes), and have the partners act out the role-play in both roles.

4. Circulate and monitor. Encourage pantomime and improvisation.

5. Provide feedback.

Multilevel Strategies

Target the *Test Yourself* to the level of your students.

• **Pre-level** Ask these students to use this skeleton conversation: *A: Would you like to get together this weekend? B: Sure. What do you want to do? A: There's _____ on Wednesday and _____ on Saturday. B: I'd rather go to _____. I'll pick you up at _____. A: See you then.*

• **Higher-level** Have these students practice the role-play with several partners.

To compress this lesson: Conduct 2A as a whole-class activity.

To extend this lesson: Have students make a flyer of fun events.
1. Put students in groups. Tell each group to make a flyer for their city, which has three wonderful events planned this weekend. Direct students to include the day, time, price of the events, who can attend, and a short description.
2. Have a reporter from each group share his/her group's flyer. Have the class decide which event they'd rather attend.

And/Or have students complete **Workbook 3 page 13** and **Multilevel Activity Book 3 page 33**.

4 Focus on listening

A **Talk about the questions with your class.**

1. Is there a park or stadium in your community where large public events take place?
2. Would you rather go to a large public event or have a quiet evening at home?

B **Read the questions. Listen to the recorded message. Then write the answers.**

1. What holiday will Greenville celebrate this weekend? <u>Independence Day</u>
2. How many events are happening this weekend? <u>three</u>
3. Are there more events in the evening or during the day? <u>in the evening</u>

C **Listen again and complete the flyer.**

GREENVILLE ☀ STADIUM   *Summer Events!*

4th of July Weekend Events

JACKIE "FUNNY MAN" NELSON

Friday at <u>7:00</u> p.m.
        1

Comedy and laughs for the whole

<u>family</u> .
  2

Adults: $ <u>9:00</u> Children: $ <u>5:00</u>
      3   4

A TASTE OF GREENVILLE

Saturday
<u>evening</u> , 5:00 - <u>10:00</u> p.m.
   5   6

Adults: $ <u>9.00</u> Children: $ <u>5.00</u>
      7   8

Summer Soccer

Sunday, <u>July 6th</u> - Sunday,
        9
August 19th

8 weeks of soccer

$ <u>30.00</u> per <u>child</u>
   10   11

5 Real-life math

Read about the Adams family and answer the question.

The Adams family is going to the *Taste of Greenville* festival at the stadium. Mr. and Mrs. Adams have a teenage daughter, a seven-year-old son, and a four-year-old daughter. Mrs. Adams gives the woman at the ticket counter $40.00 for tickets for all the family members. How much change will she receive? <u>$8.00 change</u>
[(3 adults) $27.00 + (1 child) $5.00 + (1 free child) = $32.00
$40.00 - $32.00 = $8.00]

> **TASTE OF GREENVILLE WELCOMES YOU**
>
> Adults: $9.00
> Children 6 - 12: $5.00
> Children under 5: free

┌ **TEST YOURSELF** ✔ ┐

Role-play a conversation about an event. Look at the flyer in 4C. Partner A: Invite a friend to their choice of two events at Greenville Stadium this week. Partner B: Say which event you'd rather go to. Then change roles.

1 Get ready to read

A **Why are neighborhood parks important?**

B **Read the definitions.**

immune system: (noun) the parts of the body that fight or prevent illness

outdoors: (noun) outside, for example, a park or a beach

strengthen: (verb) to make something stronger

stress: (noun) worry caused by difficulties in life

C **Scan* the article in 2A for numbers. Complete the sentences.**

1. Every mile you walk or run can add __21__ minutes to your life.

2. __89__ % of Americans often have a high stress level.

3. In Cincinnati, Ohio, teenage crime went down by __24__ %.

*scan = to look at something quickly to find specific information

2 Read and respond

A **Read the article.**

The Good Life: A Walk in the Park

Studies show that people are happier and healthier when they spend time outdoors. For example, if you're getting a cold, take a walk in the park. It can help strengthen your immune system for 48 hours. Some studies show that when you exercise, you add 21 minutes to your life for every mile you walk or run. Parks are an excellent place to get healthy and stay healthy for free.

Parks are important for more than just physical health. They can also lower stress. Jobs, money, and other things cause stress. 89% of Americans say their lives are too stressful. Spending time outdoors lowers stress and makes people feel good.

Parks are also great places for kids. After-school programs[1] help kids and working parents. These programs teach kids to share and work in teams. Parks also have helpful programs that keep teenagers out of trouble. For example, when the parks in Cincinnati, Ohio started a basketball program late at night on Friday and Saturday, teenage crime went down by 24%.

So if you're ready for better health, less stress, happier kids, and a safer neighborhood, take a walk in the park. The good life is waiting for you.

[1]after-school programs: sports, arts and crafts, or other classes after school

Source: *National Recreation and Park Association*

☑ Identify the health benefits of parks

Unit 2 Lesson 5

Objectives	Grammar	Vocabulary	Correlations
Pre-, On-, and Higher-level: Read about and discuss parks and good health	Simple present (*The park offers exercise classes.*)	*Immune system, outdoors, stress* For vocabulary support, see this **Oxford Picture Dictionary** topic: The Park and Playground	**CASAS:** 0.1.2, 2.6.1, 2.6.3 **LCPs:** 39.01, 49.03, 49.04, 49.16, 49.17 **SCANS:** Acquires and evaluates information, Listening, Reading **EFF:** Learn through research, Listen actively, Read with understanding

Warm-up and Review

10–15 minutes (books closed)

Make a transparency of a local map. Ask students to identify the parks on the map. Ask them if they ever go to the parks, how big the various parks are, and what you can find there.

Introduction

5 minutes

1. Ask how much people usually pay for activities at the park. Say: *Parks have a lot to offer, and their services are usually either free or very low priced.*

2. State the objective: *Today we're going to talk about how parks help people and communities stay healthy.*

1 Get ready to read

Presentation

15–20 minutes

A Read the question aloud. Call on volunteers to share their ideas.

B Read the words and definitions. Elicit sample sentences from students using *stress* and *outdoors*. Talk about the immune system. *When you are sick, your immune system fights the illness.*

Pre-Reading

C 1. Write the word *scan* on the board. Say: *Scan means look through the article very quickly. Focus only on what you are looking for.*

2. Instruct students to read the sentences first and then scan the article for numbers to complete the sentences. Go over the answers as a class.

3. Ask students to predict what the article is going to say about parks. *What benefits do you think it will mention?*

2 Read and respond

Guided Practice I

25–30 minutes

A 1. Ask students to read the article silently.

2. Direct students to underline unfamiliar words they would like to know. Elicit the words and encourage other students to provide definitions or examples.

3. Check students' comprehension. Ask: *How do parks help your physical health?* [Being outside helps your immune system; exercise is healthy.] *How do parks help mental health?* [Spending time outdoors lowers stress.] *How do parks help the community?* [They provide healthy activities for children and teenagers.]

Multilevel Strategies

Adapt 2A to the level of your students.

• **Pre-level** Provide these students with an outline of the ideas in the reading. *1. Exercise helps you stay healthy. Parks are a good, free place to exercise. 2. Stress is bad for you. Relaxing outdoors lowers stress. 3. Many parks have after-school programs for children and teenagers. These programs teach kids to share and work in teams.* Direct them to read the outline while other students are reading 1B.

Guided Practice II

15–20 minutes

B 1. Play the audio. Have students read along silently.

2. Elicit and discuss any additional questions about the reading.

C 1. Read the words in the box aloud. Direct students to work individually to complete the sentences.

2. Call on volunteers to read the completed sentences aloud.

Multilevel Strategies

For 2C, work with pre-level students.

• **Pre-level** Ask these students *Yes/No* and *Either/Or* questions about their outlines while other students are completing 2C. *Is walking in the park healthy or unhealthy?* [healthy] *Does relaxing outdoors raise your stress or lower your stress?* [lower] *Do some parks have programs for teenagers?* [yes]

D 1. Read the information in the chart aloud. Elicit and discuss any questions the students have about the meanings of the words or the suffix *-ful*. Say the words and have students repeat them.

2. Direct students to work individually to write the correct word to complete each sentence. Ask volunteers to write the answers on the board.

Multilevel Strategies

Give pre-level students time to work with the words in 2D while you challenge on- and higher-level students.

• **Pre-level** Direct these students to write sentences with three to five adjectives from the chart.

• **On- and Higher-level** Have these students correct their answers to 2D using the answers on the board. Then ask them to write sentences with the words from the chart. Tell them to use at least one of the verbs, one of the nouns, and one of the adjectives. Have volunteers write their sentences on the board.

3 Talk it over

Communicative Practice

15–20 minutes

A Read the questions aloud. Set a time limit (three minutes). Have students work independently to think about the questions and write their answers in note form.

B Call on individuals to share their ideas from 3A with the class. Ask students where they can find out about the parks programs.

Application

5–10 minutes

BRING IT TO LIFE

Have students tell the class where they are going to look for information. Try to vary the information students will find by having different students go to different places or look in different sources.

To compress this lesson: Conduct the word study in 2D as a whole-class activity.

To extend this lesson: Write a letter to the city.
1. Use student responses from 3A as the basis for writing a letter to the city. Elicit their suggestions for new programs that they would like to see offered by the parks. Help them articulate arguments for the new programs. Ask: *How would this program benefit the community?*
2. As a class, choose one idea and compose a letter to the city on the board. The letter should include a greeting and a closing, a suggestion for the new program, and at least one argument in favor of the program. Have a student recorder copy the letter neatly or type it on the computer.
3. Send the letter to the city. Read the students the reply when you get it.

And/Or have students complete **Workbook 3 page 14** and **Multilevel Activity Book 3 pages 34–35**.

B Listen and read the article again.

C Complete the sentences. Use the words in the box.

immune system   programs   park   stress   ~~outdoors~~   crime

1. People who spend time _____outdoors_____ are usually happier and healthier.
2. A walk in the park can strengthen your __immune system_____.
3. You can get healthy and stay healthy for free at the __park_____.
4. Sports and arts and crafts classes are examples of after-school __programs_____.
5. Some park programs at night help stop teenage __crime_____.
6. Many people say they have too much __stress_____ in their lives.

D Study the chart. Then write the adjectives.
Use the nouns in parentheses.

> **Word Study: The suffix -ful**
>
> Add -ful to the end of some nouns to make an adjective.
> stress + ful = stressful   Too much **stress** is not good for you. My job is **stressful**.
>
> | stress | stressful | beauty | beautiful | help | helpful |
> |---|---|---|---|---|---|
> | care | careful | color | colorful | thank | thankful |

1. Our new neighborhood park is _____beautiful_____. (beauty)
2. The park's trees are very __colorful_____ right now. (color)
3. A walk in the park makes life less __stressful_____. (stress)
4. The park is very __helpful_____ for bringing families together. (help)

3 Talk it over

A Think about the questions. Make notes about your answers.

1. What programs do the parks in your community offer?
2. At the park, would you rather spend time alone, or in a class or program? Why?

B Talk about your answers with your classmates.

> **BRING IT TO LIFE**
>
> Look in the newspaper, look online, or stop by a local park or community center. Find a flyer or other information about programs in your neighborhood. Bring the information to class.

1 Grammar

A Complete the answers. Use the correct forms of *be going to* or *will*.

1. **A:** What are you going to do tomorrow?

   B: I _'m going to_ go to the park.

2. **A:** What do you think the park will be like in five years?

   B: It _will ('ll)_ be bigger and cleaner.

3. **A:** What are you going to do next summer?

   B: I _am ('m) going to_ work at the recreation center.

4. **A:** Will you help me get a job at the recreation center?

   B: Sure, I _will ('ll)_ talk to the boss for you.

B Complete the sentences. Use *will, think,* or *probably*.

1. It _will_ _probably_ be hot tomorrow.

2. The park _will probably_ not be open on Sunday.

3. Do you _think_ the kids _will_ like the rides at the park?

4. I _think_ the play _will_ start in five minutes.

5. Paul _will_ _probably_ go to Montreal next weekend.

6. How long do you _think_ the art show _will_ be in town?

C Write the answers to the questions. Use your own information.

1. Would you rather play soccer or watch a soccer game on the weekend?

   _____

2. Would you rather watch TV or watch a movie?

   _____

3. Would you rather go bowling or go dancing?

   _____

4. Would you rather go to an amusement park or go to the theater?

   _____

5. Would you rather go to a nightclub or go to the theater?

   _____

Unit 2 Review and expand

Objectives	Grammar	Vocabulary	Correlations
On-, Pre-, and Higher-level: Expand upon and review unit grammar and life skills	*Be going to (We're going to go to the park.)* *Will (I think I'll take a vacation this summer.)* *Would rather (I'd rather go dancing than stay at home.)*	Recreation center, workshop, yoga For vocabulary support, see this **Oxford Picture Dictionary** topic: Recreation	**CASAS:** 0.1.2, 0.1.3, 0.1.5, 2.6.1, 7.2.6, 7.3.1, 7.3.2, 7.3.3, 7.3.4 **LCPs:** 39.01, 49.16, 50.02 **SCANS:** Listening, Participates as member of a team, Problem solving, Seeing things in the mind's eye **EFF:** Cooperate with others, Guide others, Solve problems and make decisions

Warm-up and Review

10–15 minutes (books closed)

1. Review the *Bring It to Life* assignment from Lesson 5.

2. Have students who did the exercise discuss what they learned. Direct students who didn't collect any information to ask questions of those who did. Write questions on the board for them to ask. *Who is the class/program for? Where is it? When does it start? How much does it cost? Do I need to register? How?*

3. Find out what your students still want to learn about local programs, and direct them to resources where they can find the answers.

Introduction and Presentation

5 minutes

1. Write *Prediction, Promise,* and *Plan* on the board. Elicit a sample sentence for each word, and write it on the board under the correct heading.

2. Ask students to identify all parts of the verb in the sentences on the board.

3. State the objective: *Today we're going to review making promises and predictions with* will *and talking about our plans with* be going to.

1 Grammar

Guided Practice

40–45 minutes

A Read the question and answer in number 1. Ask: *Is* I'm going to go to the park *a plan or a prediction?* Direct students to work individually to complete the sentences. Ask volunteers to write the answers on the board.

B Read the instructions aloud. Check comprehension of the exercise. Ask: *What words can you put in the blanks?* [*will, think,* and *probably*] Ask students to work individually to complete the sentences. Ask volunteers to write the answers on the board.

> ### Multilevel Strategies
>
> For 1A and 1B, seat same-level students together.
>
> • **Pre-level** While other students are completing 1A and 1B, work with these students on 1A. Read each question aloud, and elicit the answer. After you complete the exercise orally, go over 1A and 1B with the whole class.

C Ask students to work independently to answer the questions. Have them read the questions and answers with a partner.

2 Group work

Communicative Practice

20–35 minutes

 1. Direct students, in groups of three to four, to focus on the brochure. Ask: *What programs and classes does the recreation center offer?*

2. Group students and assign roles: leader, recorder, reporter, and timekeeper. Explain that students work with their groups to write the questions.

3. Check comprehension of the exercise. Ask: *Who writes the questions?* [recorder] *Who will read the questions to the class?* [reporter] *Who helps everyone and manages the group?* [leader] *Who tells the group how much time has passed?* [timekeeper] *Who creates the questions?* [everyone]

4. Set a time limit (five minutes) to complete the questions. Circulate and answer any questions.

5. Have a reporter from each group read the group's questions to the class. Provide feedback on the questions.

> ### Multilevel Strategies
>
> For 2A, use mixed-level groups.
> - **Pre-level** Assign these students the role of timekeeper.
> - **On-level** Assign these students the role of recorder or reporter.
> - **Higher-level** Assign these students the role of leader.

B 1. Have students walk around the room to conduct the interviews. To get students moving, tell them to interview three other people not in their groups for 2A.

2. Set a time limit (five minutes) to complete the exercise.

3. Tell students to make a note of their classmates' answers but not to worry about writing complete sentences.

> ### Multilevel Strategies
>
> Adapt the mixer in 2B to the level of your students.
> - **Pre-level** Allow these students to ask and answer the questions without writing.
> - **Higher-level** Have these students ask two additional questions and write all answers.

 Call on individuals to report what they learned about their classmates. Encourage students to make generalizations. *Four out of five students are going to go shopping this weekend.*

PROBLEM SOLVING

15–25 minutes

A 1. Ask: *Do you ever disagree with your friends about where to go for fun?* Tell students they will read a story about two friends who disagree about where to go. Direct students to read Juanita and Anna's story silently.

2. Ask: *What does Juanita want to do? Why? What does Anna want to do? Why?*

3. Play the audio and have the students read along silently.

B 1. Elicit answers to question 1. Have volunteers write answers to question 2 on the board until all of the class ideas have been put up.

2. Discuss the pros and cons of each solution.

Evaluation

10–15 minutes

To test students' understanding of the unit grammar and life skills, have them take the Unit 2 Test in the *Step Forward Test Generator CD-ROM* with *ExamView® Assessment Suite*.

> ### Learning Log
>
> To help students record and discuss their progress, use the *Learning Log* on page T-200.

To extend this review: Have students complete **Workbook 3 page 15, Multilevel Activity Book 3 page 36,** and the **Unit 2 Exercises** on the **Multilevel Grammar Exercises CD-ROM 3.**

2 Group work

A Work with 2–3 classmates. Write 6 questions about the recreation center. Share your questions with the class.

POND STREET RECREATION CENTER

Sign up now for summer programs and classes! There's something for everyone!
Programs start June 24th. All classes and trips are at the Pond Street Rec center. See you there!

ART WORKSHOP
Tuesdays and Thursdays
Kids: 3:30-5:00 p.m.
Adults: 6:00–8:30 p.m.
Fee: $20/session

MOUNTAIN BIKE TRIPS
6 Saturdays starting June 24th
8:30–4:30
Fee: $30/trip

YOGA CLASS
Exercise and relax at the same time.
Bring a blanket or a mat.
Wednesdays, 7:00–8:00 p.m.
Fee: $10/class

VIDEO CLASS
Let's make a video!
Learn the basics!
Mondays, 7:00–9:00 p.m.
6-week program
Fee: $60

What time will the video class begin?

B Interview 3 classmates. Write their answers.

1. What are you going to do this weekend?
2. Would you rather go to a concert or go to the library?
3. How do you think this neighborhood will change in ten years?

C Talk about the answers with your class.

PROBLEM SOLVING

A Listen and read about Juanita and Anna.

Juanita and Anna are friends. They want to go out together this weekend. Juanita wants to go to an amusement park. Tickets are expensive, but they can have fun there all day. Anna doesn't have much money. She would rather stay home and watch TV during the day and go dancing in the evening. They want to spend the day together, but they can't agree about what to do.

B Work with your classmates. Answer the questions.

1. What is the problem? Juanita and Anna cannot agree on what to do this weekend.
2. What should Juanita and Anna do? Think of 2 or 3 solutions to their problem.

A Job to Do

FOCUS ON
- computers and jobs
- writing memos
- making comparisons
- job feedback
- job skills

LESSON 1 **Vocabulary**

1 Learn computer and office vocabulary

A **Talk about the questions with your class.**

1. What computer equipment is in your school's office?
2. What are some ways people use computers at work?

B **Work with your classmates. Match the words with the picture.**

_9_	computer technician	_1_	graphic designer	_7_	monitor
_8_	CPU	_6_	headset	_3_	office manager
_4_	digital camera	_2_	keyboard	_5_	photographer

C **Listen and check. Then read the new words with a partner.**

D **Work with a partner. Write other computer and office words you know. Check your words in a dictionary.**

Unit 3 Lesson 1

Objectives	Grammar	Vocabulary	Correlations
On-level: Identify and describe computer equipment, problems, and jobs **Pre-level:** Identify computer equipment, problems, and jobs **Higher-level:** Talk and write about computer equipment, problems, and jobs	Simple-present tense sentences with *when* (*When computers crash, documents are lost.*)	Computer and office vocabulary For vocabulary support, see these **Oxford Picture Dictionary** topics: Computers, An Office	**CASAS:** 0.1.2, 0.1.5, 4.1.6, 4.8.1, 7.2.3 **LCPs:** 35.02, 49.02 **SCANS:** Knowing how to learn, Listening, Participates as a member of a team, Seeing things in the mind's eye, Speaking **EFF:** Cooperate with others, Listen actively, Observe critically, Reflect and evaluate, Speak so others can understand

Warm-up and Review

10–15 minutes (books closed)

Put up one sign on each wall: *I don't know anything; I know a little; I know an average amount; I know a lot.* Tell students the topic is computers. Ask them to stand next to the sign that best represents their knowledge of computers.

Introduction

5 minutes

1. Call on individuals to talk about their experience with computers. Elicit the names of some jobs in which people use computers.

2. State the objective: *Today we're going to learn some computer and office vocabulary.*

Learn computer and office vocabulary

Presentation I

20–25 minutes

A Write *computers* on the board, and elicit students' answers to the questions. As students mention equipment or uses, ask if they can find them in the picture in 1B.

B 1. Direct students to look at the pictures. Ask: *What is this place?*

2. Group students and assign roles: leader, fact checker, recorder, and reporter. Explain that students work with their groups to match the words and pictures.

3. Check comprehension of the roles. Ask: *Who looks up the words in a dictionary?* [fact checker] *Who writes the numbers in the book?* [recorder] *Who tells the class your answers?* [reporter] *Who helps everyone and manages the group?* [leader]

4. Set a time limit (three minutes). As students work together, copy the wordlist onto the board.

5. Call "time." Have reporters take turns giving their answers. Write each group's answer on the board next to the word.

C 1. To prepare students for listening, say: *You're going to hear sentences about the people in this office. As you listen, look at the picture and check your answers.*

2. Have students check the wordlist on the board and then write the correct numbers in their books.

3. Pair students. Set a time limit (three minutes). Monitor pair practice to identify pronunciation issues.

4. Call "time" and work with the pronunciation of any troublesome words or phrases.

5. Replay the audio and challenge students to listen for additional information about each item. Call on volunteers to share what they heard.

D 1. Ask students to work with a partner to brainstorm a list of related words.

2. Elicit words from the class. Write them on the board in two columns labeled *Computer* and *Office*. Ask students to copy the words into their vocabulary notes for the unit.

Guided Practice

5–10 minutes

 1. Model the conversations with a volunteer. Model them again using other information from 1B.

2. Set a time limit (three minutes). Direct students to practice with a partner.

3. Ask volunteers to repeat one of their conversations for the class.

2 Learn more computer vocabulary

Presentation II

15–20 minutes

 1. Direct students to look at the pictures. Introduce the new topic: *Now we're going to learn more computer words. All of these words have a computer and a "non-computer" meaning.*

2. Ask students to work individually to check the words they know.

3. Go through the words. Ask students to give examples of the "non-computer" and the computer meaning. *The flu is a dangerous virus. It makes people sick. Computer viruses cause computers not to work properly.* Provide examples for the words students don't know.

4. Say and have students repeat the words.

5. Check comprehension. Ask: *What do you call a secret program that makes your computer not work properly?* [a virus]

Guided Practice

10–15 minutes

 Have students work individually to complete the sentences. Go over the answers as a class.

Communicative Practice and Application

10–15 minutes

 1. Give students time to make notes of their answers to the questions. Call on individuals to share their ideas with the class.

2. Write any new vocabulary that students use on the board, and elicit sentences to illustrate the meaning.

 Before students answer the questions in 2C, demonstrate note taking. Call on a volunteer to answer question 1. Then ask other students to rephrase the ideas in note form. Write the notes on the board.

Evaluation

10–15 minutes (books closed)

TEST YOURSELF

1. Make a three-column chart on the board with the headings *Computer Parts and Equipment*, *Computer Problems*, and *Jobs*. Have students close their books and give you an example for each column.

2. Have students copy the chart into their notebooks.

3. Give students five to ten minutes to test themselves by writing the words they recall from the lesson.

4. Call "time" and have students check their spelling in a dictionary. Circulate and monitor.

5. Direct students to share their work with a partner and add additional words to their charts.

Multilevel Strategies

Target the *Test Yourself* to the level of your students.

• **Higher-level** Have these students complete the chart and then write a sentence with one word from each column. Challenge them to write sentences that illustrate the meaning of the words.

To compress this lesson: Conduct 1B as a whole-class activity.

To extend this lesson: Have groups practice or extend their computer vocabulary. Put students in groups of three or four. Direct them to draw a picture of a computer and label its parts. For the class discussion, have each group member name a part of the computer. If some of the students are knowledgeable about computers, ask them to talk about what the various parts do or are used for.

And/Or have students complete **Workbook 3 page 16** and **Multilevel Activity Book 3 pages 38–39**.

E Work with a partner. Practice the conversation. Use the picture in 1B.

    A: *Is the keyboard on the desk?*
    B: *Yes, it is. It's in front of the monitor.*

2 Learn more computer vocabulary

A Look at the pictures. Check (✔) the words you know. Answers will vary.

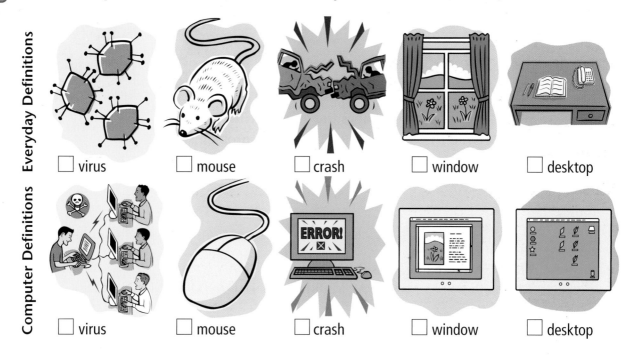

Everyday Definitions

☐ virus   ☐ mouse   ☐ crash   ☐ window   ☐ desktop

Computer Definitions

☐ virus   ☐ mouse   ☐ crash   ☐ window   ☐ desktop

B Complete the sentences. Use the words in 2A.

1. When computers ____crash____, files and documents are often lost.
2. When you move the __mouse__ with your hand, things on the screen move.
3. When you turn on the computer, the first thing you see is the __desktop__.
4. A __virus__ is a "secret" computer program that causes computer problems.
5. You might need to close a __window__ to see the files on your desktop.

C Talk about the questions with your class.

1. Which computer words are easy to remember? Why?
2. What are two or more computer problems?
3. What are three or more jobs that use computer equipment?

TEST YOURSELF ✔

Close your book. Categorize the new words in 3 lists: *Computer Parts and Equipment, Computer Problems,* and *Jobs.* Check your spelling in a dictionary. Compare your lists with a partner.

1 Read a memo

A Look at the pictures. Talk about the questions with your class.

1. What kinds of problems does the company have?
2. What should the company do about these problems?

B Listen and read the memo.

MEMO

TO: All Employees
FROM: Miles Baine, President
RE: EMPLOYEES MUST PAY MORE ATTENTION TO COMPANY POLICIES

Many office managers are noticing the following problems:
1. Employees are not coming to work on time.
2. Some employees are taking longer and longer breaks.
3. Coffee and water spills are hurting computer keyboards.

Please follow these company policies:
- All employees must be at work by 9:00 a.m.
- Break times are from 10:00–10:15 and 3:00–3:15 daily.
- Employees may not eat or drink near computers.

If you have questions or comments, please see your office manager.

C Check your understanding. Mark the statements T (true), F (false), or NI (no information).

  _T_   1. The memo is from the company president.

  _F_   2. The subject of the memo is company managers.

  _T_   3. Office managers are noticing some problems.

  _NI_   4. Some employees are taking 30-minute breaks.

  _T_   5. Employees have two breaks every day.

  _F_   6. Employees should only drink water near the computers.

Unit 3 Lesson 2

Objectives	Grammar	Vocabulary	Correlations
On- and Higher-level: Analyze, write, and edit a memo about problems and solutions **Pre-level:** Read and write a memo about problems and solutions	Present-continuous tense (*Employees are taking longer breaks.*)	*Policies, memo* For vocabulary support, see this **Oxford Picture Dictionary** topic: An Office	**CASAS:** 0.1.2, 0.1.5, 4.4.1, 4.6.2, 7.2.5, 7.4.7 **LCPs:** 49.02, 49.16, 49.17 **SCANS:** Interprets and communicates information, Listening, Reading **EFF:** Convey ideas in writing, Listen actively, Observe critically, Read with understanding, Reflect and evaluate, Speak so others can understand

Warm-up and Review

10–15 minutes (books closed)

Write *Home, School,* and *Work* on the board. Ask: *What are some things children do when they're not following their parents' rules?* Write their ideas under *Home.* Ask the same question about students and employees, and write their ideas in the correct columns.

Introduction

5 minutes

1. Say: *When people don't follow the rules, there may be problems, at home, at work, or at school.*

2. State the objective: *Today we're going to read and write a memo about some employees who aren't following the rules.*

1 Read a memo

Presentation

20–25 minutes

 1. Direct students to look at the pictures. Ask: *Would you like to work at this company?*

2. Elicit answers to questions 1 and 2. Have a class discussion about the answers.

 1. Introduce the reading: *You're going to read a Sun Company memo explaining the problems at the company and providing solutions.*

2. Direct students to read the memo silently. Check students' comprehension. Ask: *How many problems does the memo explain?* [three] *Is there a policy for every problem?* [yes]

3. Play the audio. Have students read along silently.

Guided Practice I

10 minutes

 Have students work independently to mark the statements T (true), F (false), or NI (no information). Ask volunteers to write the answers on the board.

Multilevel Strategies

For 1C, challenge on- and higher-level students while working with pre-level students.

• **Pre-level** While other students are working on 1C, ask these students *Yes/No* and *Or* questions about the reading. *Are the employees coming to work on time or late? Are they taking long breaks or short breaks? Is there one break every day?* Give students time to write the answers to 1C.

• **Higher-level** Write questions on the board for these students to answer after they finish 1C: *Do you think this memo will be effective? Why or why not?* After allowing students to work individually to answer the questions, ask volunteers to share their opinions with the class.

2 Write a memo

Guided Practice II

20–25 minutes

 A 1. Read the questions aloud. Write *Problems, Policies,* and *Who to talk to* on the board.

2. Elicit students' answers to the questions. Write their ideas in the correct columns. Leave this on the board for students to refer to during the 2B writing assignment.

B 1. Direct students to look back at the model memo in 1B. Focus their attention on the present-continuous verbs in the "problems" section of the memo. Ask them to look through the memo quickly and mark the present-continuous verbs. Ask: *When are these problems happening?* Point out that the use of present continuous emphasizes the fact that the problems are happening now. They may not have happened in the past, and hopefully they'll stop happening soon!

2. Go over the memo template with your students. Elicit appropriate entries for *To:, From:,* and *Re:.*

3. Check comprehension of the exercise. Ask: *What is the first part of your memo going to list?* [problems at school] *What is the second part going to list?* [policies]

4. Direct students to work individually to write their memos.

> ### Multilevel Strategies
>
> Adapt 2B to the level of your students.
>
> • **Pre-level** Work with these students to write a group memo. Go through the template together. Decide as a group what to write.
>
> • **Higher-level** Ask these students to include an additional problem and an additional policy.

C Lead students through the process of using the *Editing checklist.* Read each sentence aloud, and ask students to check their papers before moving onto the next item. Allow students a few minutes to edit their writing as necessary.

Communicative Practice

10 minutes

D 1. Read the instructions aloud. Emphasize to students that they are responding to their partners' work, not correcting it.

2. Use the memo in 1B to model the exercise. *I think the sentence* Coffee and water spills are hurting the computer keyboards *is interesting. I'd like to ask this writer what time the employees are coming to work.*

3. Direct students to exchange papers with a partner and follow the instructions. Call on volunteers to share what they found interesting in their partners' memos.

Application and Evaluation

15 minutes

TEST YOURSELF

1. Review the instructions aloud. Assign a time limit (ten minutes), and have students work independently.

2. Before collecting students' work, remind them to use the *Editing checklist.* Collect and correct students' writing.

> ### Multilevel Strategies
>
> Adapt the *Test Yourself* to the level of your students.
>
> • **Pre-level** Provide these students with a skeleton memo to complete.
>
> To: _____
>
> From: _____
>
> Re: _____
>
> I am noticing the following problem: _____.
>
> Please follow this policy: _____.

To compress this lesson: Assign the *Test Yourself* for homework.

To extend this lesson: Have some fun with problems and policies. Tell students that even though we don't write memos in our personal lives, sometimes we might want to. Have students work in pairs or groups and brainstorm problems and policies for "A Memo to My Children/Husband/Wife/Boyfriend/Girlfriend/Friend." Have pairs come to the board and write one problem and its corresponding policy.

And/Or have students complete **Workbook 3 page 17** and **Multilevel Activity Book 3 page 40**.

2 Write a memo

A **Talk about the questions with your class.**

1. What kind of problems do you notice at your school?
2. Which school or classroom policies focus on these problems?
3. Who should students see when they want to talk about problems at school?

B **Write a memo to your classmates about school policies. Use the model in 1B and your answers to the questions in 2A to help you.** Answers will vary.

TO: _____

FROM: _____

RE: _____

Many students and teachers are noticing the following problems:

1. _____
2. _____
3. _____

Please follow these school policies:

1. _____
2. _____
3. _____

Please see _____ for more information.

C **Use the checklist to edit your writing. Check (✔) the true sentences.** Answers will vary.

Editing checklist	
1. I wrote about three problems in my school or classroom.	
2. I explained three school or classroom policies.	
3. The *To, From,* and *Subject (RE)* lines are complete.	
4. All sentences end with a period.	

D **Exchange memos with a partner. Read and comment on your partner's work.**

1. Point out one problem or policy that you think is interesting.
2. Ask your partner a question about one of the problems or policies.

TEST YOURSELF ✔

Write a new memo about something you want to change at home, at work, or at school. Share your memo with your classmates.

1 Learn comparisons

A Read the ads and the paragraph. Which computer would you buy?

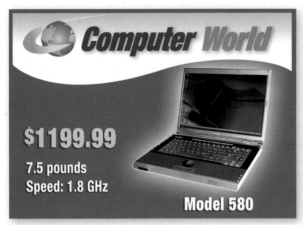

I can't decide which computer to buy. The 580 laptop is less expensive than the 680. The 580 is as heavy as the 680, but it's not as fast as the 680. The 680 is faster than the 580, but it's more expensive than the 580. I also need to decide where to buy it. Other technicians aren't as experienced as the technicians at Computer World.

B Study the chart. Underline 1 example of each comparison with *as...as,* *(not) as...as, -er than, less...than,* and *more...than* in the paragraph above. Answers will vary.

Comparisons with adjectives	
as...as	The 580 is **as** heavy **as** the 680.
not as...as	The 580 is **not as** fast **as** the 680.
-er than	The 680 is fast**er than** the 580.
less...than	The 580 is **less** expensive **than** the 680.
more...than	The 680 is **more** expensive **than** the 580.

Notes

- Add *-er than* to most adjectives with one syllable. (*fast-faster than*)
- For adjectives ending in *-y*, change the *y* to *i* and add *-er than*. (*friendly-friendlier than*)

C Complete the sentences with the comparisons and the adjectives in parentheses.

(NOT) AS...AS

1. The 580 laptop is _____ not as powerful as _____ the 680 laptop. (powerful)

2. The 580 laptop is __ as heavy as _____ the 680 laptop. (heavy)

-ER THAN/ LESS...THAN / MORE...THAN

3. The 580 laptop is __ cheaper than _____ the 680 laptop. (cheap)

4. The 680 laptop is __ more expensive than _____ the 580 laptop. (expensive)

5. Computer World's technicians are __ more experienced than _____ CheapTech's technicians. (experienced)

Unit 3 Lesson 3

Objectives	Grammar	Vocabulary	Correlations
On- and Higher-level: Use comparatives and superlatives to talk about shopping, and listen for comparisons **Pre-level:** Use adjectives and comparatives, and recognize superlatives in conversations about shopping	Comparisons (*The 580 laptop is more expensive than the 480 laptop.*) Superlatives (*The 250Z laptop is the most expensive.*)	Adjectives For vocabulary support, see these **Oxford Picture Dictionary** topics: Describing Things, Computers	**CASAS**: 0.1.2, 0.2.1, 1.2.1, 4.2.2 **LCPs**: 45.01, 49.02, 49.03, 49.16, 50.04 **SCANS**: Decision making, Interprets and communicates information, Listening, Reading, Writing **EFF**: Convey ideas in writing, Cooperate with others, Listen actively, Read with understanding, Reflect and evaluate, Speak so others can understand

Warm-up and Review

10–15 minutes (books closed)

Review the comparative form. Put up a series of nouns on one side of the board: *sofa, refrigerator, camera, cell phone, printer, car*. Put up adjectives on the other side: *small, modern, expensive, comfortable, attractive, durable*. Ask volunteers to match adjectives with nouns (accept any logical combination). Ask more advanced students to use a comparative form of the adjective. *Cell phones are smaller than cameras. Sofas are more comfortable than cars.* Call on volunteers to write their sentences on the board.

Introduction

5–10 minutes

1. Ask: *When you shop for expensive items, do you compare stores and brands?*

2. State the objective: *Today we're going to learn how to compare items and stores, and how to talk about which ones are best.*

1 Learn comparisons

Presentation I

20–25 minutes

A 1. Direct students to look at the ad. Ask: *Are these ads for the same laptop? Are they for the same store?*

2. Read the instructions aloud. Ask students to read the paragraph silently and think about their answers to the question. Call on individuals to share their ideas.

B 1. Demonstrate how to read the grammar chart. Read each sentence and check for comprehension. Say: *The 580 is as heavy as the 680.* Ask: *Does that mean they are the same or different?*

2. Direct students to underline the examples of comparisons in the paragraph in 1A. Go over the answers as a class.

3. Ask questions about the paragraph in 1A. *Is the 580 laptop the same price as the 680 laptop? Is the 580 laptop or the 680 laptop heavier?*

4. Draw students' attention to the form. *Use as with as. Use less and more with than.*

5. Assess students' understanding of the chart. Read the *Notes*. Elicit comparisons for the words on the board from the warm-up. Use this exercise to demonstrate that *as...as* can be used with all adjectives, but *more/less than* are not used with one-syllable adjectives.

Guided Practice I

15–20 minutes

C Ask students to work individually to complete the sentences. Ask volunteers to write the answers on the board.

Multilevel Strategies

For 1C, seat same-level students together.

• **Pre-level** While other students are completing 1C, assist these students with the *as...as* form. Write *tall, short, big, small, difficult* on the board. Elicit sentences from students about items or people in the room. *Miguel is not as tall as Antonio.*

Guided Practice II

5–10 minutes

D Read the instructions and the first example aloud. Read the rest of the sentences aloud, and direct students to hold up one finger for *a* and two for *b* to indicate which sentence has the same meaning. Discuss any sentences that they find difficult to understand.

TIP After 1D, provide more practice with understanding comparisons. Say sentences about items or people in the room or on campus. Direct students to hold up one finger if the sentence is true and two if it's false. *The window isn't as large as the board. Amaya is as tall as Violeta. Room 2 is less crowded than Room 3.*

2 Review superlatives

Presentation II

20–25 minutes

A 1. Put the same adjectives and nouns on the board that you used during the warm-up. Say a couple of example sentences using the basic superlative form. *Cell phones are the smallest of these items. Cars are the most expensive.*

2. Introduce the new topic. *When you use comparisons, you are talking about two things. But when we want to talk about one thing in a group, we use a superlative form.*

3. Direct students to look at the pictures in the ads and read the captions.

4. Check comprehension. Ask: *What is the superlative form of more?* [most] *What is the superlative form of less?* [least] *Can I use these with one-syllable adjectives?* [no]

Multilevel Strategies

While on- and higher-level students do 2B, review the basic superlative forms with pre-level students.

- **Pre-level** Provide these students with a list of adjectives: *big, small, happy, tall, comfortable, expensive, difficult, easy.* Write three categories on the board: *-est, -iest,* and *most.* Help students put the words in the correct categories and pronounce the superlative forms. Together write a sentence for each adjective.

- **Higher-level** After these students write their answers to 2B on the board, provide them with magazines, and ask them to cut out pictures and write original comparative and superlative sentences (using all of the different forms) about the pictures. Have volunteers share their sentences and pictures with the class.

Guided Practice I

10–15 minutes

B Have students work individually to answer the questions. Ask volunteers to write their answers on the board.

TIP For more practice with comparatives and superlatives, have students compare information from ads.

1. Put students in groups. Give each group sales flyers from several different stores that sell the same products—for example, grocery stores, clothing stores, or furniture stores. Or print out pages from online stores selling similar items.

2. Tell the groups to look through the ads and write three comparative or superlative sentences based on the information they find. Have a reporter from each group read the group's sentences to the class.

D **Get the meaning. Work with your class. Which sentence has the same meaning? Circle _a_ or _b_.**

1. The salespeople are as helpful as the technicians.
   a. Some salespeople are more helpful than the technicians.
   (b.) Both the salespeople and the technicians are helpful.

2. Other salespeople are not as experienced as Computer World's salespeople.
   a. Other salespeople are more experienced than Computer World's salespeople.
   (b.) Other salespeople are less experienced than Computer World's salespeople.

3. Computer World's computers are less expensive than CheapTech's computers.
   (a.) Computer World isn't as expensive as CheapTech.
   b. CheapTech is as expensive as Computer World.

2 Review superlatives

A **Study the ads. Then read the sentences in the chart with a partner.**

Superlatives: _-est, least, most_
The 100X is the **cheapest** camera.
The 100X is the **least** expensive camera.
The 250Z is the **most** expensive camera.

B **Write the answers to the questions.**

1. Which camera is the most expensive?
   The 250Z is the most expensive.

2. Which camera is the most popular?
   The 180X is the most popular.

3. Which camera is the newest?
   The 250Z is the newest.

4. Which camera is the smallest?
   The 100X is the smallest.

5. Which camera is the largest?
   The 250Z is the largest.

3 Grammar listening

Listen to the story. Write the comparison words you hear.

My name is Lin. I'm an office manager for a large insurance company. I usually order all of our office supplies from Office Star or Business Max. For everyday items like paper and file folders, Office Star is usually _____ less expensive _____
1
than Business Max. For special items like printer ink, Office Star is __the most expensive_____ . But, I've noticed that the people
2
who work at Business Max are __not as helpful_____ as
3
the people who work at Office Star. The salespeople at Office Star are __more professional_____ than the salespeople at
4
Business Max. Oh, and I almost forgot! When I order from Office Star, my orders arrive

__faster than_____ than my orders from Business Max. They arrive in 48 hours or
5
less, or they're free!

4 Practice comparisons

A **Think about your answers to these questions.**

1. What are three stores you like?
2. Which store has the most helpful salespeople?
3. Which store is usually the least crowded?
4. Which store is the least expensive?

B **Work with a partner. Ask and answer the questions in 4A.**

C **Talk about your answers with another pair. Does the other pair agree or disagree? Why or why not?**

TEST YOURSELF ✔

Close your book. Write 5 sentences about the stores you discussed in section 4.
Use *(not) as...as, -er than, less, more, -est, least,* or *most* in each sentence.

3 Grammar listening

Guided Practice II
10–15 minutes

1. Write *office supplies* on the board, and elicit examples. Ask students where people go in your area to buy office supplies. Say: *Now we're going to listen to an office manager talk about his favorite office-supply store.*

2. Play the audio. Direct students to read along silently without writing.

3. Replay the audio. Ask students to write in the correct words.

4. Call on volunteers for the answers. Write them on the board.

> ### Multilevel Strategies
>
> Replay the *Grammar listening* to allow pre-level students to catch up. Provide an additional challenge for on- and higher-level students.
>
> • **Pre-level** Direct these students to listen again to complete the sentences.
>
> • **On- and Higher-level** Ask these students to close their books and write the adjectives they hear.

4 Practice comparisons

Communicative Practice and Application
20–25 minutes

A 1. Direct students to look at the picture. Ask: *Where is she? Does she like this store?*

2. Read the questions aloud. Ask students to think about or write their answers.

B Direct students to ask and answer the questions with a partner.

C 1. Have each pair join another pair to form a group of four. Tell them to discuss their answers to the questions and be ready to explain why they agree or disagree.

2. Discuss the students' ideas as a class. Ask: *Which stores are popular with our class?*

Evaluation
10–15 minutes (books closed)

TEST YOURSELF

Ask students to write the sentences independently. Collect and correct their writing.

> ### Multilevel Strategies
>
> Target the *Test Yourself* to the level of your students.
>
> • **Pre-level** Provide skeleton sentences for these students to complete. *1. _____ is not as expensive as _____. 2. _____ is more crowded than _____. 3. _____ is the most expensive store in this area. 4. _____ is the least expensive store in this area.*
>
> • **Higher-level** Have these students write a paragraph in response to these questions: *Where do you usually shop? Why? Compare your favorite store to other stores.*

To compress this lesson: Conduct 4C as a whole-class discussion.

To extend this lesson: Have students create a short TV ad for a store they like.
1. Put students in groups. Ask each group to choose a store (or invent one) and write a short "ad" for it.
2. Have a reporter from each group read the ad to the class. Have the class decide which group had the most convincing ad.

And/Or have students complete **Workbook 3 pages 18–19, Multilevel Activity Book 3 pages 41–42,** and the corresponding **Unit 3 Exercises** on the **Multilevel Grammar Exercises CD-ROM 3.**

Unit 3 Lesson 4

Objectives	Grammar	Vocabulary	Correlations
On- and Higher-level: Learn how to give and respond to feedback, and listen for information in a job evaluation **Pre-level:** Identify ways to give and respond to feedback, and listen for information in a job evaluation	Superlative (*She's the friendliest person in the office.*)	*Experienced, friendly, kind, careful* For vocabulary support, see this **Oxford Picture Dictionary** topic: Office Skills	**CASAS:** 0.1.2, 0.1.5, 4.4.4, 4.6.1, 6.1.1, 6.1.4, 7.2.5, 7.4.7 **LCPs:** 49.02, 49.03, 50.04 **SCANS:** Arithmetic/Mathematics, Listening, Reading, Speaking **EFF:** Cooperate with others, Listen actively, Read with understanding, Speak so others can understand, Use math to solve problems and communicate

Warm-up and Review

10–15 minutes (books closed)

Review adjectives for describing people. Say: *My best friend is friendly, helpful, and talkative.* Write the adjectives on the board, and ask: *How would you describe your best friend?* Write students' ideas on the board.

Introduction

5 minutes

1. Ask students which of the adjectives on the board are important for an employee.

2. State the objective: *Today we're going to learn how to describe people's qualities and how to give feedback and accept correction.*

1 Learn to give and respond to feedback

Presentation I

15–20 minutes

A 1. Direct students to look at the pictures. Ask: *Which workers have a problem?*

2. Tell students that they're going to listen to a boss talking to each of these workers. Point out that he has positive feedback for them, but he also wants them to correct certain behaviors. Play the audio. Give students time to match the adjectives to the workers. Go over the answers as a class.

Guided Practice

20–25 minutes

B 1. Play the audio. Ask students to read along silently and listen for the answer to this question: *What behavior does Vicki need to correct?* Elicit the answer.

2. Ask students to read the conversation with a partner. Circulate and monitor pronunciation. Model and have students repeat words or phrases that they are having difficulty pronouncing.

3. Say and have students repeat the expressions in the *In other words* box. Elicit the placement of the expressions in the conversation. Ask volunteers to read the conversation using expressions from the box.

Communicative Practice and Application

15–20 minutes

C 1. Ask students to read the instructions silently. Check their comprehension of the exercise. Elicit examples of what the principal and the office manager might say.

2. Set a time limit (five minutes). Ask students to act out the role-play in both roles. Ask one to three volunteer pairs to act out their conversation for the class.

Multilevel Strategies

Adapt 1C to the level of your students.

• **Pre-level** Provide a simplified conversation for these students to use for their role-play. *A: Can I see you for a moment? B: Yes, of course. A: You are our most experienced person. B: Thank you. A: But you _____. B: I'm sorry. I promise I'll stop making personal phone calls at work.*

1 Learn to give and respond to feedback

A Look at the pictures. Listen to the conversations. Then complete the sentences below with your classmates.

1. The supervisor, Ms. Clark, wants Bill to _be more organized_____.
2. Ms. Clark wants Sue to _be more professional_____.

B Listen and read. What does Ms. Clark want Vicki to do?

A: Vicki, can I see you for a moment?

B: Yes, Ms. Clark? What is it?

A: You're a good worker, Vicki. You're the most organized person in the office.

B: Thanks, Ms. Clark.

A: But Vicki, you're always late. You have to come to work on time.

B: I'm sorry, Ms. Clark. I'll try to do better.

A: Thank you, Vicki.

In other words...

Responding to negative feedback

I'll try to do better.
You won't have to tell me again.
Thanks for letting me know.

C Role-play giving and responding to feedback with a partner. Use the example in 1B to make a new conversation.

Partner A: You're a school principal. Ask to see your office manager. Your office manager is the most experienced person at school, but he or she makes too many phone calls to friends. Tell him or her to spend less time on the phone.

Partner B: You are the office manager at a school. Listen to your principal's positive and negative feedback. Promise to change your behavior.

☑ Give and respond to positive and negative feedback   **39**

2 Review superlative forms

A Study the chart. Write the superlative forms of the words below in the correct columns.

> angry   ~~big~~   efficient   fast   friendly   great
> ~~happy~~   hot   ~~kind~~   organized   ~~patient~~   thin

adjectives + -est	adjectives ending in y + -est	adjectives + -est (double the final consonant)	most/least + adjectives
kindest	happiest	biggest	most patient
fastest	angriest	hottest	most efficient
greatest	friendliest	thinnest	most organized

B Complete the sentences with the superlative form of the words in parentheses.

1. Al doesn't work quickly or carefully. He's the ____least efficient____ worker I know. (efficient)
2. Paulo is nice to everyone. He's is the __kindest_____ person I know. (kind)
3. Lee isn't friendly. He's the __least friendliest_____ person I know. (friendly)
4. Don is very happy. He's the __happiest_____ person I know. (happy)
5. Rosa never gets angry. She's the __most patient_____ person I know. (patient)

C Work with a partner. Ask and answer the questions.

1. Who is the friendliest student in class?
2. Who is the most organized person you know?

3 Practice your pronunciation

A Listen to the pronunciation of *v, b,* and *f* in these sentences.

1. **V**icki, can I see you for a moment?   3. You're the **f**riendliest student.
2. I'll try to do **b**etter.

B Listen to the names. Circle the sound you hear.

1. (v) f   2. (b) v   3. (f) b   4. v (b)   5. b (f)   6. f (v)

C Listen again. Repeat the names.

2 Review superlative forms

Presentation II
10–15 minutes

 1. Introduce the new topic. *Now we're going to focus on how to give feedback using the superlative.*

2. Read the top row of the chart aloud (the adjectives and their superlative forms). Elicit the rules. *How many syllables does* kind *have? How do you form the superlative? Why is the g in* biggest *doubled? Why does* happiest *end in –iest? When do I use* most/least?

3. Ask students to work individually to write the superlative forms of the adjectives in the correct columns. Go over the answers as a class.

Guided Practice
15–20 minutes

 Have students work individually to complete the sentences. Go over the answers as a class.

Communicative Practice and Application
15–20 minutes

 1. Model the questions and answers with a volunteer.

2. Set a time limit (five minutes). Ask students to ask and answer the questions with several partners.

3. Call on individuals to share their answers with the class.

3 Practice your pronunciation

Pronunciation Extension
10–15 minutes

A 1. Write *Vince is a terrific boss* on the board. Say the sentence and ask students to repeat it. Underline *V*, *f*, and *b*, and repeat each sound. Say: *Now we're going to focus on pronunciation of these three sounds.*

2. Play the audio. Direct students to listen for the pronunciation of *v*, *b*, and *f*.

3. Say the words with the bolded sounds, and direct students to look at your mouth. Ask them which sound uses a different mouth position. [/b/]

B Direct students to listen to the sentences and circle the sound they hear. Go over the answers as a class.

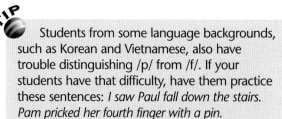

TIP Students from some language backgrounds, such as Korean and Vietnamese, also have trouble distinguishing /p/ from /f/. If your students have that difficulty, have them practice these sentences: *I saw Paul fall down the stairs. Pam pricked her fourth finger with a pin.*

If your students are having difficulty with the difference between the /b/ and /v/ lip positions, encourage them to look in a mirror as they practice. (Ask them to bring small mirrors to class for pronunciation practice.)

C Replay the audio. Ask students to repeat the names.

TIP For more practice with these sounds after 3C, write these tongue twisters on the board, and have students practice saying them with a partner. *1. Becky and Brandon are the best bosses in the business. 2. Farrah finally found five file folders for her efficient friend.*

4 Focus on listening

Listening Extension

20–25 minutes

A 1. Direct students to look at the cartoons. Ask: *What is the student looking at?*

2. Read the questions aloud, and elicit answers from volunteers.

B 1. Introduce the audio. *You are going to listen to a supervisor talk to three employees. He has positive feedback for them, but there are also things he wants them to do better.* Direct students to listen to the audio and circle what each employee needs to do better.

2. Play the audio. Go over the answers as a class.

C 1. Direct students to read the adjectives in 4B before listening.

2. Replay the audio and have students work individually to write the correct adjectives in the blanks. Go over the answers as a class.

> ### Multilevel Strategies
>
> Replay the audio to challenge on- and higher-level students while allowing pre-level students to catch up.
>
> • **Pre-level** Have these students listen again to complete 4C.
>
> • **On- and Higher-level** Write questions on the board, and ask these students to write short answers. *Which workers does he describe with superlatives? What does he say?* Ask volunteers to share their answers after you have gone over the answers to 4C.

5 Real-life math

Math Extension

5–10 minutes

1. Direct students to look at the report card. Ask: *What are the subjects on this report card?*

2. Read the footnote for *average* aloud.

3. Have students work individually to write the answers to the questions.

4. Ask a volunteer to write the problem and solution for question 3 on the board.

Evaluation

10–15 minutes

TEST YOURSELF

1. Model the role-play with a volunteer. Then switch roles.

2. Pair students. Check comprehension of the exercise by asking for examples of what the supervisor and the delivery driver might say.

3. Set a time limit (five minutes), and have the partners act out the role-play in both roles.

4. Circulate and monitor. Encourage pantomime and improvisation.

5. Provide feedback.

> ### Multilevel Strategies
>
> Target the *Test Yourself* to the level of your students.
>
> • **Pre-level** Ask these students to use this conversation: *A: Can I see you for a moment? B: Yes, of course. A: You are a good worker. B: Thank you. A: But you _____. B: I'm sorry. I promise I'll do better.*
>
> • **Higher-level** Tell these students to give two positive comments and suggest two areas of improvement.

To compress this lesson: Have students practice the questions and answers in 2C with only one partner.

To extend this lesson: Have students conduct self-evaluations.

1. Tell students that supervisors often ask employees to evaluate themselves. Ask them to choose one of their roles in life (worker, parent, student, etc.) and write a self-evaluation for that role. Tell them they must include at least one piece of positive feedback and one area in which they could improve. Write your own self-evaluation (in one of your life roles) on the board as a model.

2. Don't require students to share their self-evaluations. Allow them to read them with a partner or turn them in only if they want to.

And/Or have students complete **Workbook 3 page 20** and **Multilevel Activity Book 3 page 43**.

4 Focus on listening

A Talk about the questions with your class.

1. What kinds of evaluations do students get?
2. What kinds of evaluations do workers get?
3. Do you ever have to evaluate other people?

B Listen to the conversations. Check the positive feedback for each worker.

1. Elizabeth is	2. Ben is	3. Habib is
☐ organized.	☐ careful.	☐ careful.
☐ kind.	☐ helpful.	☑ helpful.
☐ creative.	☑ organized.	☐ kind.
☑ on-time.	☐ reliable.	☐ confident.

C Listen again. Write what each worker needs to improve.

1. Elizabeth needs to __be on time__.
2. Ben needs to __be more organized__.
3. Habib needs to __be more helpful__.

5 Real-life math

**Look at the student report card. Answer the questions.
Talk about your answers with the class.**

1. What is this student's best subject? __Math__
2. What is this student's worst subject? __Science__
3. What is this student's average* grade, or grade point
   average (GPA)? __3.0__

English	B	(3.0)
Math	A	(4.0)
History	B	(3.0)
Science	C	(2.0)
Art	B	(3.0)

*To get the average, add the points for each grade.
 Then divide the total points by the number of grades.

TEST YOURSELF ✔

Role-play an evaluation. Partner A: You are the supervisor in a large factory.
Your partner is a delivery driver at the factory. Give your partner positive and
negative feedback. Partner B: Respond. Then change roles.

1 Get ready to read

A How do workers learn to use new machines at work?

B Read the definitions.

flexible: (adj.) able to change

production: (noun) the amount of products or services that a company makes or offers

train: (verb) to teach or educate

C Scan the article in 2A for percentages.

1. Production increased up to __20__ % in companies with training programs.

2. Workers with a college degree earn __77__ % more than workers with only a high school diploma.

2 Read and respond

A Read the article.

Workplace Training Spells Success

How do people describe the 21st century? "The digital age," "the information age," and "the technology[1] age" are popular descriptions. Whatever the name, one thing is sure; employees in the 21st century need to have more education and be more flexible than ever before. New technology means new machines, new ideas, and different jobs. Employees must learn new skills to prepare for new jobs.

More and more companies in the U.S. are providing training classes for their workers. The facts show that businesses with education programs are more successful. Here are some facts about worker education:

- Companies with training programs see production increase by 15 to 20%.
- Workers who learn more, earn more money. On average, college graduates' salaries are 77% higher than salaries for workers with only a high school degree.
- More than 57% of companies increased their worker education programs.
- Only two percent said they decreased their programs.

Today's workers need to be smarter, more creative, and more skilled than workers from the past. With the help of workplace training, they can be.

[1]technology: machines, computers

Source: *A Report of the U.S. Department of Commerce, U.S. Department of Education, U.S. Department of Labor, National Institute of Literacy, and the Small Business Administration*

☑ Identify the benefits of and sources for job training

Unit 3 Lesson 5

Objectives	Grammar	Vocabulary	Correlations
Pre-, On-, and Higher-level: Read about and discuss workplace training	Simple present (*Workplace training helps employees and companies.*)	*Production, flexible, train, union, technology* For vocabulary support, see this **Oxford Picture Dictionary** topic: Job Skills	**CASAS:** 0.1.2, 2.5.5, 4.4.2 **LCPs:** 37.02, 49.02, 49.03, 49.04 **SCANS:** Acquires and evaluates information, Interprets and communicates information, Listening, Reading **EFF:** Listen actively, Read with understanding, Speak so others can understand, Take responsibility for learning

Warm-up and Review

10–15 minutes (books closed)

Write *Hospital, Factory,* and *Office* on the board. Ask students to brainstorm names of items people use in those work locations. Then ask which items have changed in the last twenty years.

Introduction

5 minutes

1. Say: *Did you ever learn to use a new technology or do a new job? Who taught you? How did you feel about it?* Call on volunteers to share their experiences.

2. State the objective: *Today we're going to read and talk about ways that companies help their workers learn new skills.*

1 Get ready to read

Presentation

15–20 minutes

A Read the question aloud. Call on volunteers to share their answers.

B Read the words and definitions. Elicit sample sentences from students using the words. Students may have difficulty using *production* (the process of making something) versus *product* (the item made). Tell them we often talk about rates of production: *The production slowed down/sped up/increased/decreased/stopped.*

Pre-Reading

C 1. Read the instructions aloud. Remind students that *scan* means to look quickly for something

specific. Tell students to look very quickly for a number plus the percent symbol (%) and to complete sentences 1 and 2. Instruct them to put their pencils down when they've finished so that you can see how well they are scanning. Go over the answers as a class.

2. Ask students to predict what the article will be about based on the title. Ask: *Is workplace training good for companies?*

2 Read and respond

Guided Practice I

25–30 minutes

A 1. Ask students to read the article silently. Direct students to underline unfamiliar words they would like to know. Elicit the words and encourage other students to provide definitions or examples.

2. Check students' comprehension. Ask: *Why do workers need more education now? Are companies more successful when they provide their own training programs? Do employees with more education make more money or less money?*

Multilevel Strategies

Adapt 2A to the level of your students.

- **Pre-level** Provide these students with a summary of the reading. *1. There is a lot of new technology, so employees need more education. 2. Many companies have classes for employees. 3. Employees with more education make more money. 4. Companies that educate their employees are more successful.* Direct them to read the outline while other students are reading 2A.

Guided Practice II

15–20 minutes

B 1. Play the audio. Have students read along silently.

2. Elicit and discuss any additional questions about the reading.

C Ask students to work individually to circle the correct words. Call on volunteers to read the completed sentences aloud.

Multilevel Strategies

For 2C, work with pre-level students.

• **Pre-level** Ask these students *Yes/No* and *Either/Or* questions about their summaries while other students are completing 2C. *Nowadays, is there more technology or less technology?* [more] *Do employees need more education or less education?* [more] *Are companies offering classes for employees?* [yes]

As volunteers are reading the sentences in 2C aloud, write the answers on the board, and direct pre-level students to circle the correct words in their books.

D 1. Read the information in the chart aloud. Elicit and discuss any questions the students have about the meanings of the words or the suffix *–tion*. Say the words and have students repeat them.

2. Direct students to work individually to circle the correct word to complete each sentence. Ask volunteers to write the answers on the board.

Multilevel Strategies

For 2D, seat same-level students together.

• **Pre-level** Direct these students to write sentences with three of the nouns from the chart.

• **On- and Higher-level** Have these students correct 2D using the answers on the board. Then ask them to write sentences with the words from the chart. Tell them to use as many of the verbs and nouns as they can. Have volunteers write their sentences on the board.

3 Talk it over

Communicative Practice

15–20 minutes

A Read the questions aloud. Set a time limit (three minutes). Have students work independently to think about the questions and then write their answers in note form.

B Call on volunteers to share their ideas from 3A with the class.

Application

5–10 minutes

BRING IT TO LIFE

Have students decide where they are going to look for the information. Provide URLs or locations of career-counseling offices.

To compress this lesson: Conduct the word study in 2D as a whole-class activity.

To extend this lesson: Extend your discussion of technology.
1. Put students in mixed-level groups. Ask them to brainstorm ways in which the world is different now from 30 years ago because of technology. Give them several examples to help them get started. *People talk on the phone everywhere because of cell phones. Young children do their homework on computers.*
2. Have a reporter from each group share the group's ideas. When possible, use their ideas to make a comparative statement, and write it on the board. *People are busier now than they were then because now they can work all of the time. Children's handwriting isn't as good now as it was then because they use computers a lot.*

And/Or have students complete **Workbook 3 page 21** and **Multilevel Activity Book 3 pages 44–45**.

B **Listen and read the article again.**

C **Circle the correct words.**

1. Companies see (employees /(production)) increase when they train their workers.
2. Workers need to learn new (salaries /(skills)).
3. Employees need to be ((more)/ less) flexible in the 21st century.
4. When employees have training, their pay usually ((increases)/ decreases).
5. High-school graduates earn 77% (more /(less)) than college graduates.

D **Study the chart. Circle the correct words below.**

> **Word Study: The suffix -tion**
>
> Add *tion* to the end of some verbs to change them to nouns.
> produce — production   The company **produces** a lot. They have a high **production** rate.
> Note: The spelling may change when adding -*tion*.
>
> | describe | description | educate | education | dictate | dictation |
> | --- | --- | --- | --- | --- | --- |
> | add | addition | invite | invitation | | |

1. People need more (educate /(education)) for new technology.
2. Computer World ((produces)/ production) excellent computers.
3. My job (describes /(description)) is very clear.
4. (Add /(Addition)) and subtraction are not difficult.
5. Office managers ((dictate)/ dictation) memos to their staff.

3 Talk it over

A **Think about the questions. Make notes about your answers.**

1. How do you think workers feel when they get good job training?
2. What are some reasons that a company might not give job training?

B **Talk about the answers with your classmates.**

┌ **BRING IT TO LIFE** ─────────────

Search the Internet, your local library, or your school office to find
information on job training in your area. Bring the information to class.

1 Grammar

A **Complete the sentences with the comparative form of the words in parentheses.**

1. My sister is a graphic designer. She is _____ more creative _____ than most people are. (creative)

2. Heather is _as friendly_____ as Tracy. (friendly)

3. Today the technicians aren't _as busy_____ as they were yesterday. (busy)

4. Digital cameras are usually _less expensive than_____ computers. (expensive)

B **Read the sentences. Write a new sentence with the same idea. Use the words in parentheses.**

1. Sue is not patient. Marta is patient.

   (not as...as)   _Sue is not as patient as Marta._____

2. Mark and Fernando are both reliable.

   (as...as)   _Mark is as reliable as Fernando._____

3. Ken is more efficient than Jack.

   (less)   _Jack is less efficient than Ken._____

4. Ellen is not helpful. Tom is very helpful.

   (more)   _Tom is more helpful than Ellen._____

5. Yanna is always creative. Jean isn't creative.

   (not as...as)   _Jean is not as creative as Yanna._____

C **Complete the sentences with the superlative form of the words in parentheses.**

1. Bill has his papers everywhere. He's _____ the least organized _____ person at work. (organized)

2. Sheila doesn't talk much. She's _the quietest_____ student in class. (quiet)

3. Olga is not very organized. She's _the most disorganized_____ person I know. (disorganized)

4. Yesterday it was 100 degrees outside. It was _the hottest_____ day of the year. (hot)

5. Megan works very slowly. She's _the least efficient_____ person in the office. (efficient)

Unit 3 Review and expand

Objectives	Grammar	Vocabulary	Correlations
On-, Pre-, and Higher-level: Expand upon and review unit grammar and life skills	Comparative with *as...as* and *less/more than* (*Mark is as friendly as Tracy. He is more creative than I am.*) Superlative (*She's the friendliest person in the office.*)	Adjectives For vocabulary support, see this **Oxford Picture Dictionary** topic: Describing Things	**CASAS**: 0.1.2, 0.1.5, 1.2.1, 7.2.5, 7.2.6, 7.2.7, 7.3.1, 7.3.2 **LCPs:** 49.01, 49.02, 49.03, 50.04 **SCANS:** Listening, Participates as a member of a team, Problem solving, Reading, Speaking, Seeing things in the mind's eye, Writing **EFF:** Read with understanding, Solve problems and make decisions

Warm-up and Review

10–15 minutes (books closed)

1. Review the *Bring It to Life* assignment from Lesson 5.

2. Have students who did the exercise discuss what they learned. Direct students who didn't collect any information to ask questions of those who did. If necessary, write questions on the board for them to ask. *Where can I go for job training? How much does it cost? Can anyone use the service?*

3. Discuss the information that your students are most interested in. Find out what questions they still have, and direct them to resources where they can find the answers.

Introduction and Presentation

5 minutes

1. Write *difficult* and *easy* on the board. Ask: *Was this unit more or less difficult than the last one? Or was it the same?* Write students' conclusions on the board as comparative sentences. Use the same adjectives to write more example sentences. Then ask what part of English class is the most difficult, and have them write a superlative sentence.

2. State the objective: *Today we're going to review the comparative and superlative to describe people at work.*

1 Grammar

Guided Practice

40–45 minutes

A Ask students to work individually to complete the sentences. Have them take turns reading the completed sentences with a partner. Write the answers on the board.

B Ask students to work with their partners from 1A to write the sentences. Have them take turns reading the sentences aloud when they've finished. Write the answers on the board.

Multilevel Strategies

For 1A and 1B, seat same-level students together.

• **Pre-level** While on-level and high-level pairs work together for 1A and 1B, work with these students. Elicit each answer before students write it in their books.

C Direct students to work individually to complete the sentences. Ask volunteers to write their sentences on the board. Go over the answers as a class.

2 Group work

Communicative Practice

20–35 minutes

A 1. Direct students, in groups of three to four, to focus on the pictures. Ask: *Which chair do you like the best?*

2. Group students and assign roles: leader, recorder, reporter, and timekeeper. Explain that students work with their groups to write the sentences.

3. Check comprehension of the roles. Ask: *Who writes the sentences?* [recorder] *Who will read the sentences to the class?* [reporter] *Who helps everyone and manages the group?* [leader] *Who tells the group how much time has passed?* [timekeeper] *Who creates the sentences?* [everyone]

4. Set a time limit (five minutes) to complete the exercise. Circulate and answer any questions.

5. Have a reporter from each group read the group's sentences to the class.

Multilevel Strategies

For 2A, use mixed-level groups.

- **Pre-level** Assign these students the role of timekeeper.
- **On-level** Assign these students the role of recorder or reporter.
- **Higher-level** Assign these students the role of leader.

B 1. Have students walk around the room to conduct the interviews. To get students moving, tell them to interview three other people not in their groups for 2A.

2. Set a time limit (five minutes) to complete the exercise.

3. Tell students to make a note of their classmates' answers but not to worry about writing complete sentences.

C Call on individuals to report what they learned about their classmates. Encourage students to make generalizations. *Three out of five students think vocabulary is the least difficult thing about English.*

PROBLEM SOLVING

15–25 minutes

A 1. Ask: *Did you ever have to decide between two jobs?* Tell students they will read a story about a man who is trying to make that decision. Direct students to read Omar's story silently.

2. Ask: *Why can't Omar decide between the two jobs?*

3. Play the audio and have students read along silently.

B 1. Elicit answers to question 1. Write *Value Comp* and *Tech Time* on the board. Assign one volunteer to be the recorder for the *Value Comp* job and another for the *Tech Time* job. Elicit the positive and negative things about each job from the class. Have the recorders write them on the board.

2. Ask: *Which job is better for Omar?* Ask for a show of hands, or have the class divide to show who prefers which job. Have volunteers explain their reasons.

Evaluation

10–15 minutes

To test students' understanding of the unit grammar and life skills, have them take the Unit 3 Test on the *Step Forward Test Generator CD-ROM* with *ExamView® Assessment Suite.*

Learning Log

To help students record and discuss their progress, use the *Learning Log* on page T-200.

To extend this review: Have students complete **Workbook 3 page 22, Multilevel Activity Book 3 page 46,** and the **Unit 3 Exercises** on the **Multilevel Grammar Exercises CD-ROM 3.**

2 Group work

A Work with 2–3 classmates. Write 6 sentences about the chairs. Use comparatives and superlatives. Share your sentences with the class.

The first chair is not as expensive as the third chair.
The second chair is more comfortable than the first one.

B Interview 3 classmates. Write their answers.

1. What's the most difficult thing about English? Why?
2. Which is the least difficult for you to learn—vocabulary, grammar, or pronunciation?
3. Is speaking English as easy as speaking other languages? Why or why not?

C Talk about the answers with the class.

PROBLEM SOLVING

A Listen and read about Omar.

Omar is looking for a job. He has two job offers. The first job is at Value Comp Computers. The second job is at Tech Time Electronics. The pay is a lot better at Value Comp, but the drive to work is longer. The medical benefits at Value Comp are not as good as the benefits at Tech Time, but the hours are more flexible. Omar can't decide what to do. Money, benefits, and travel time are all important to him.

B Work with your classmates. Answer the questions.

1. What is Omar's problem? Omar has to decide which job is better for him.
2. Which job is better for Omar? Make a list of the positive and negative things about each job.

Good Work

FOCUS ON
- job interviews
- follow-up thank-you letters
- the present perfect
- job promotions
- employee skills

LESSON **1** Vocabulary

1 Learn job interview vocabulary

A Talk about the questions with your class.

1. What kinds of questions does an employer ask at an interview?
2. What kinds of questions can you ask the employer?

B Work with your classmates. Match the words with the pictures.

Interview Do not's

Interview Do's

_5_	arrive on time	_6_	greet the interviewer	_3_	(don't) dress inappropriately
_9_	bring your resume	_7_	look confident	_2_	(don't) look nervous
_8_	dress professionally	_1_	(don't) be late	_4_	(don't) use your cell phone

C Listen and check. Then read the new words with a partner.

D Work with a partner. Write other job interview do's and do not's you know. Check your words in a dictionary.

Unit 4 Lesson 1

Objectives	Grammar	Vocabulary	Correlations
On-level: Identify job interview *do's* and *do not's,* and describe personal strengths **Pre-level:** Identify job interview and personal strength vocabulary **Higher-level:** Talk and write about work using job interview and personal strength vocabulary	Simple-present tense (*A team player works well with other people.*)	Job interview and personal strength vocabulary For vocabulary support, see this **Oxford Picture Dictionary** topic: Job Search	**CASAS:** 0.1.2, 0.1.3, 0.1.4, 0.1.5, 0.2.1, 4.1.5, 4.1.7, 4.4.1, 4.8.1, 7.4.5, 7.5.6 **LCPs:** 35.02, 35.06, 39.01, 49.02, 49.09, 49.10 **SCANS:** Organizes and maintains information, Participates as member of a team **EFF:** Cooperate with others, Listen actively, Reflect and evaluate

Warm-up

10–15 minutes (books closed)

Find out how many of your students have been on a job interview. Ask them to share their experiences. For students who have not had a job interview, ask about other interviewing experiences. Elicit details. *How long did it take? How did you feel? Did you have to wait a long time for the results?*

Introduction

5 minutes

1. Say: *If your friend is going for an interview, what advice would you give him/her? How can he/she make the job interview successful?* Call on volunteers to share their ideas.

2. State the objective: *Today we're going to learn about what to do and say at job interviews.*

1 Learn job interview vocabulary

Presentation I

20–25 minutes

A 1. Write *Employer* and *Job Applicant* on the board. Elicit students' answers to question 1, and write their ideas under *Employer.* Write their ideas for question 2 under *Job Applicant.*

2. Tell students to copy the questions from the board into their notebooks for use later in the unit (Lesson 4).

B 1. Direct students to look at the pictures. Ask: *Who is going to have a successful interview: Applicant #1 or Applicant #2?*

2. Group students and assign roles: leader, fact checker, recorder, and reporter. Explain that students work with their groups to match the words and pictures.

3. Check comprehension of the roles. Ask: *Who looks up the words in a dictionary?* [fact checker] *Who writes the numbers in the book?* [recorder] *Who tells the class your answers?* [reporter] *Who helps everyone and manages the group?* [leader]

4. Set a time limit (three minutes). As students work together, copy the wordlist onto the board.

5. Call "time." Have reporters take turns giving their answers. Write each group's answer on the board next to the word.

C 1. To prepare students for the listening, say: *We're going to listen to some advice about what to do and what not to do at job interviews. As you listen, look at the pictures and check your answers.*

2. Have students check the wordlist on the board and then write the correct numbers in their books.

3. Pair students. Set a time limit (three minutes). Monitor pair practice to identify pronunciation issues.

4. Call "time" and work with the pronunciation of any troublesome words or phrases.

D 1. Ask students to work with a partner to brainstorm a list of other interview *do's* and *do not's.*

2. Elicit ideas from the class. Write them on the board. Ask students to copy them into their vocabulary notes for the unit.

Guided Practice

5–10 minutes

 1. Model the conversation with a volunteer. Model it again using other information from 1B.

2. Set a time limit (three minutes). Direct students to practice with a partner. Encourage them to use ideas from their 1D lists as well as from 1B.

3. Ask volunteers to repeat one of their conversations for the class.

2 Learn to describe your personal strengths

Presentation II

15–20 minutes

 1. Introduce the new topic: *We've been talking about things to do and not to do at an interview. Now we're going to discuss the personal strengths that you can talk about during an interview.*

2. Discuss the meaning of each word in column 1. Elicit examples of classroom behaviors that demonstrate each type of worker. For example, a problem solver could be a student who figures out a better way to distribute classroom materials or arrange the seating; a team player could be a student who is always helpful in the group without dominating it. Apply the words to your students: *Maria always gets her books out and starts reviewing yesterday's work before the class begins. Which word could describe her?* [*self-starter* or *go-getter*]. *Hong always helps the other students at his table. How could we describe him?* [a team player].

3. Ask students to work individually to check the strengths they have.

4. Call on volunteers to say which strengths they checked and why.

5. Check comprehension. Ask: *What type of worker is someone with great ideas?* [a creative thinker]

Guided Practice

10–15 minutes

 1. Model the conversation. Model it again using different words from 2A.

2. Set a time limit (three minutes). Direct students to practice with a partner. Call on volunteers to say one of their conversations for the class.

Communicative Practice and Application

10–15 minutes

 1. Give students time to make notes of their answers to the questions. Call on individuals to share their ideas with the class.

2. Try to reach a class consensus on the answers to the questions. Ask students to consider which interview behaviors and which personal strengths would be important in most jobs.

Evaluation

10–15 minutes (books closed)

TEST YOURSELF

1. Make a three-column chart on the board with the headings *Interview Do's, Interview Do not's,* and *Personal Strengths.* Have students close their books and give you an example for each column.

2. Have students copy the chart into their notebooks.

3. Give students five to ten minutes to test themselves by writing the words they recall from the lesson.

4. Call "time" and have students check their spelling in a dictionary. Circulate and monitor students' progress.

5. Direct students to share their work with a partner and add additional words to their charts.

To compress this lesson: Conduct 1B as a whole-class activity.

To extend this lesson: Have students act out interviews. Group students and have the groups write a short job interview with two or three question-answer exchanges. Have two members from each group perform their interview for the class. After each pair has performed, ask the class to say what good interview behaviors they saw.

And/Or have students complete **Workbook 3 page 23** and **Multilevel Activity Book 3 pages 48–49**.

E Work with a partner. Practice the conversation. Use the pictures in 1B.

A: What should you do at a job interview?

B: You should dress professionally.

A: What shouldn't you do at a job interview?

B: You shouldn't look nervous.

2 Learn to describe your personal strengths

A Read about different types of workers and their strengths. Check (✔) the strength(s) you have. Answers will vary.

This type of worker:	has this strength:	Is this you? (✔)
A problem-solver	is good at fixing problems.	☐
A team player	works well with other people.	☐
A self-starter	works well without much supervision.	☐
A creative thinker	has great ideas.	☐
A go-getter	sees what things need to be done and does them.	☐
A good leader	is good at supervising and showing people what to do.	☐

B Work with a partner. Practice the conversation. Use the words in 2A.

A: *Are you a problem-solver?*

B: *Yes, I am. I'm good at fixing problems.*

A: *Are you a team player?*

B: *Yes, I work well with other people.*

C Talk about the questions with your class.

1. What do you think are the three most important things to do at a job interview? Why?

2. What do you think are the three most important personal strengths to have? Why?

TEST YOURSELF ✔

Close your book. Categorize the new words in 3 lists: *Interview Do's, Interview Do not's,* and *Personal Strengths.* Check your spelling in a dictionary. Compare your lists with a partner.

1 Read an interview thank-you letter

A **Look at the picture. Talk about the questions with your class.**

1. When do you usually write thank-you letters?
2. Why is it important to write a thank-you letter after a job interview?

Thank you so much...

B **Listen and read about thank-you letters.**

Congratulations! You have finished the job interview. But, your work isn't finished yet. It's important to write a thank-you letter to the interviewer. Write the letter after your interview and send it by mail or email the next day. Here's a sample letter:

> Ms. Paulina Reyes, Personnel Manager
> Sherman's Auto Sales
> 1212 Willow Lane
> Richmond, VA 23230
>
> Dear Ms. Reyes: ◄
>
> Thank you for the opportunity to interview for the position of sales manager at Sherman's Auto Sales. I enjoyed learning more about your company.
>
> I hope to have the chance to use my communication skills and sales experience at Sherman's.
>
> If you have any questions, or need more information, please contact me at: tling@abc.us.
>
> Sincerely,
> *Tom Ling*
> Tom Ling

Writer's note

Use a colon (:) after the greeting in a formal business letter.

C **Check your understanding. Circle a or b.**

1. What does the writer say in the first paragraph?
   a. Thank you.
   b. Please contact me.

2. Why does the writer talk about his skills in the letter?
   a. To show that he has other job offers.
   b. To show the employer that he's perfect for the job.

Unit 4 Lesson 2

Objectives	Grammar	Vocabulary	Correlations
On- and Higher-level: Analyze, write, and edit a thank-you letter. **Pre-level:** Read and write a thank-you letter	Verb + gerund or infinitive (*I hope to have the chance to use my computer skills. I enjoyed learning more about your company.*)	Business-letter vocabulary, job-skills vocabulary, *colon* For vocabulary support, see this **Oxford Picture Dictionary** topic: Job Search, Interview Skills	**CASAS:** 0.1.2, 0.1.5, 4.1.7, 4.6.2, 7.4.7 **LCPs:** 49.02, 49.12, 49.16, 49.17 **SCANS:** Interprets and communicates information **EFF:** Advocate and influence, Convey ideas in writing, Cooperate with others, Read with understanding, Reflect and evaluate

Warm-up and Review

10–15 minutes (books closed)

Review job titles. Elicit places that students have worked, and write the words on the board—for example, *restaurant, factory, hospital,* and *office.* Ask volunteers to come to the board and write job titles of people who work in those places.

Introduction

5 minutes

1. Ask who has ever interviewed for any of the jobs on the board. Say: *One final step in the job-interview process is to write a thank-you letter after the interview.*

2. State the objective: *Today we're going to read and write a thank-you letter.*

1 Read an interview thank-you letter

Presentation

20–25 minutes

A 1. Direct students to look at the picture. Ask: *What's she doing?*

2. Elicit answers to questions 1 and 2. Encourage students to respond to each other's ideas. After one student speaks, ask other students their opinions. *Do you agree or disagree with what he/she just said? Why?*

B 1. Introduce the reading. Ask: *Is an interview thank-you letter a formal letter or an informal letter?* Point out the formal letter convention of writing the address above the greeting.

2. Ask students to read the letter silently. Check comprehension. Ask: *Who was the interviewer?* [Ms. Reyes] *Who applied for the job?* [Tam Ling] *What was the job?* [a sales manager]

3. Play the audio. Have students read along silently.

4. Draw students' attention to the *Writer's note.* Say: *For letters to friends, use a comma after the greeting. For business letters, use a colon after the greeting.* Point out that thank-you letters can be emailed.

Guided Practice I

10 minutes

C Have students work independently to circle the answers. Go over the answers as a class.

TIP After you go over 1C, have the class brainstorm additional sentences using *I enjoyed* and *I hope to. I enjoyed talking with you. I enjoyed visiting your company. I hope to hear from you soon. I hope to speak with you again soon.* Write the ideas on the board, and have students copy them for possible use in a writing assignment for 2B.

2 Write a thank-you letter

Guided Practice II

20–25 minutes

 A 1. Read the questions. Elicit students' answers. Write the job titles students mention on the board. After students answer question 3, elicit some skills and personal strengths that would be required for those positions.

2. Tell students that they are going to write a thank-you letter for a job interview. Tell the class to use the ideas on the board to help complete their letters.

> **TIP**
> Students may be interested in more information about available jobs at your school. Ask your personnel office for job descriptions, requirements, and starting salaries. You can use this kind of information to demonstrate to students how continuing education can improve economic prospects.

B 1. Direct students to look at the letter template. Elicit the information for each section of the letter (school address, interviewer's name, etc.). Have them refer to the model letter in 1B to see how each sentence was completed.

2. Check comprehension of the exercise by eliciting sample completions for the sentences. Have students work independently to complete their letters using their answers from 2A.

Multilevel Strategies

Adapt 2B to the level of your students.

• **Pre-level** Work with these students to go through the letter template sentence by sentence. Elicit students' ideas and write them on the board. Have students complete the letter with the ideas from the board.

• **Higher-level** Ask these students to include one additional sentence to remind the interviewer of why they are a perfect match for the job.

 C Lead students through the process of using the *Editing checklist*. Read each sentence aloud, and ask students to check their papers before moving onto the next item. Allow students a few minutes to edit their writing as necessary.

Communicative Practice

10 minutes

D 1. Read the instructions aloud. Emphasize to students that they are responding to their partners' work, not correcting it.

2. Use the letter in 1B to model the exercise. *I think the sentence about her communication skills and sales experience might help Ellen get the job. I'd like to ask her where she got her sales experience.*

3. Direct students to exchange papers with a partner and follow the instructions. Call on volunteers to share what they liked about their partners' letters.

Application and Evaluation

15 minutes

TEST YOURSELF

1. Review the instructions aloud. Assign a time limit (ten minutes), and have students work independently.

2. Before collecting students' work, remind them to use the *Editing checklist*. Collect and correct students' writing.

To compress this lesson: Assign the *Test Yourself* for homework.

To extend this lesson: Have students write a different kind of thank-you letter. Brainstorm a list of other situations in which students might want to write a thank-you note (after receiving a gift, after being a guest at someone's house, after someone helps them, etc.). As a class, come up with appropriate expressions for these kinds of thank-you notes. Point out that *Thank you for...* is followed by either a noun phrase or a gerund. *Thank you for the lovely gift. Thank you for being so patient.* Have students compose a short thank-you note. Ask volunteers to read their notes to the class.

And/Or have students complete **Workbook 3 page 24** and **Multilevel Activity Book 3 page 50**.

2 Write a thank-you letter

A **Talk about the questions with your class.**

1. What kinds of jobs do people have at your school?
2. Who do you think interviews people for jobs at your school?
3. Which of those jobs might be right for you? Why?

B **Imagine that you had a job interview at your school. Write a thank-you letter. Use the model in 1B and your answers to the questions in 2A.** Answers will vary.

To start: What's your contact information? Who are you writing to?
             What is the interviewer's title and address?
Paragraph 1: What are you thanking the interviewer for?
Paragraph 2: What do you hope to have the chance to do?
Paragraph 3: What should the interviewer do if he or she has any questions?

> (your contact information)
>
> (interviewer's name, title)
>
> (interviewer's address)
>
>
> Dear _____:
>
> Thank you for the opportunity to interview for the position of...

C **Use the checklist to edit your writing. Check (✔) the true sentences.**
Answers will vary.

Editing checklist	
1. I wrote the name of the position I interviewed for.	
2. I talked about my skills for the job.	
3. I used a colon after the greeting.	
4. My phone number or email address is written clearly and correctly.	

D **Exchange letters with a partner. Read and comment on your partner's work.**

1. Point out one sentence that you think may help your partner get the job.
2. Ask your partner a question about his or her job skills.

TEST YOURSELF ✔

Congratulations! You had a job interview for the position of sales clerk at GBG Sportsmart with Ms. Vera Mills. The store is in your city, state, and zip code. The address of the store is 1320 Oak St. Write a new thank-you letter.

1 Learn the present perfect

A **Read the paragraph and the job application. How many jobs did Jafar have before his current job?** He had two jobs before his current job.

Jafar is a messenger, but he wants a new job. Last year, he worked part-time in an office, and he has also worked as a sales representative. He has completed high school, but he hasn't finished college. He applied for the position of assistant manager at an automotive supply store last week. He had an interview this morning, but the manager hasn't called him back yet.

Job Application Form

Name: Jafar Fayez

Employment History:
List all jobs held starting with current or most recent.

Company	Position	FT or PT
Quicksilver Messengers	Messenger	Full-time
A1 Insurance Offices	Office Staff	Part-time
Joe's Men's Stores	Sales Representative	Full-time

B **Study the chart. Circle the 4 examples of the present perfect in the paragraph above.** Answers will vary.

THE PRESENT PERFECT

Affirmative and negative statements				Notes
Subject	*have/has*	**past participle**		• Use the present perfect to describe an event at a non-specific time in the past.
I You We They	have have not	worked	in an office.	• To form the present perfect, use *have/has* and a past participle.
He She	has has not			• Past participles of regular verbs have the same forms as the simple past (verb + -*d*/-*ed*).

C **Complete the sentences with the present perfect. Use the words in parentheses.**

1. Jafar _____has completed_____ his resume. (complete)

2. Mr. Baker __has interviewed__ Jafar. (interview)

3. Jafar __has written__ a thank-you letter. (write)

4. Mr. Baker __has not (hasn't) read__ the letter. (not read)

5. Jafar __has had__ three other interviews. (have)

Need help?

Some irregular verbs

Base form	Simple past	Past participle
be	was/were	been
do	did	done
go	went	gone
have	had	had
hear	heard	heard
read	read	read
write	wrote	written

Unit 4 Lesson 3

Objectives	Grammar	Vocabulary	Correlations
On- and Higher-level: Use the present perfect to talk about work experience and listen for information about work experience **Pre-level:** Recognize the present perfect in sentences about work experience	Present perfect (*He has worked in an office.*)	Past participles, *Apply for, supply* For vocabulary support, see this **Oxford Picture Dictionary** topic: Job Search, Interview Skills	**CASAS:** 0.1.2, 0.1.5, 0.2.1, 7.4.7 **LCPs:** 39.01, 49.03, 49.09, 49.16, 49.17, 50.02 **SCANS:** Organizes and maintains information, Reading, Writing **EFF:** Convey in writing, Listen actively, Read with understanding, Reflect and evaluate, Speak so others can understand

Warm-up and Review

10–15 minutes (books closed)

Write a list of job titles on butcher paper: *chef, hairdresser, carpenter.* Ask students to take turns writing what a person in each occupation does—for example, cooks, cuts hair, repairs fences. Save this paper for use later in the lesson.

Introduction

5–10 minutes

1. Point out to students that many of them have done the activities they wrote down (cook, cut hair, etc.) even if they have not done them professionally.

2. State the objective: *Today we're going to use the present perfect to describe our job experience.*

1 Learn the present perfect

Presentation I

20–25 minutes

A 1. Direct students to look at Jafar's job application. Ask: *What is Jafar's most recent job?*

2. Read the question aloud. Ask students to read the job application silently to find the answer. Call on a volunteer for the answer.

B 1. Write a sentence about yourself on the board. *I have worked in an office.* Ask: *Do I work in an office now?* [no] *So I'm talking about the past. Do you know when I worked in an office?*

[no] Write another sentence on the board using the simple past and a date. *I worked in an office from 1995–1998.* Ask: *Now do you know when I worked in an office?* Ask students to identify the verb and the tense in the simple-past sentence. Underline the verb. Draw students' attention back to the present-perfect sentence. Ask students to identify the verb and underline both parts. Elicit the difference between the two sentences. Say: *The sentence without the date uses a present-perfect verb form. We use the present perfect when we talk about events in the past but don't say when they happened.*

2. Read the *Notes* aloud. Point out that the past participle of *worked* is the same as the simple past. Read and have students repeat the irregular verbs in the *Need help?* box in 1C.

3. Demonstrate how to read the grammar chart.

4. Direct students to circle the examples of the present perfect in 1A. Go over the answers as a class.

5. Assess students' understanding of the chart. Write these sentences on the board: *1. I _____ to college. 2. I _____ to college from 1990–1994.* Tell students to hold up one or two fingers to indicate which sentence the verb belongs in. Say: *have gone.* Repeat with different sample sentences.

Guided Practice I

15–20 minutes

C Ask students to work individually to complete the sentences. Ask volunteers to write the answers on the board.

TIP

Before moving on to 2A, play "concentration" on the overhead projector to help students learn the past perfect. Write the following words in random order in a 4 x 4 grid on a transparency: *read, had read, did, had done, went, had gone, called, had called, heard, had heard, gave, had given, wrote, had written, knew, had known.* Cover each word with a slip of paper. Divide the class into two teams. Ask a student from Team 1 to uncover two words. Have the students repeat both words. Ask: *Do they match?* If they don't match, cover them up again. When students get a match, give the team a point, and leave the words uncovered. Ask a student from Team 2 to uncover two words. Continue until all of the words are uncovered. Then say the pairs and have students repeat them.

2 Learn the present perfect with *for* and *since*

Presentation II

20–25 minutes

A 1. To introduce the new topic, draw a timeline on the board with *today* at the far right end. Write: *She has gone to college.* Mark *gone to college* as a point on the timeline labeled *2005.* Ask: *Is she still going to college?* [no] Write: *She has gone to college since 2005. She has gone to college for _____ years.* Mark the time period on the timeline, showing that it continues to the present. Ask: *Is she still going college?* [yes] Say: *Using* for + *period of time or* since + *a date with the present perfect tells us that an action is continuing.*

2. Read and have students repeat the sentences in the chart. Use the timeline to illustrate the sentences.

3. Direct students to look at the timeline and read Carlos's life events. Have students work individually to mark the statements T (true) or F (false). Go over the answers as a class.

Guided Practice I

10–15 minutes

B 1. Write *Monday, three weeks, last month, January, July 4, 1991, last summer,* and *ten days* on the board. Write *For* and *Since* as column heads, and have students tell you which words belong in which column. Write an incomplete sentence: *I have had my car _____.* Call on students to complete the sentence with the expressions on the board, using *for* or *since* appropriately.

2. Have students work individually to complete the sentences. Go over the answers as a class.

C Read the instructions aloud. Read the sentences aloud, and ask for a show of hands for true or false. Discuss the answers.

Multilevel Strategies

After 2C, provide pre-level students with more practice with participles while you challenge on- and higher-level students.

• **Pre-level** Direct these students to "test" their partners on the participles in the *Need help?* box on page 50. Tell one partner to work with the book closed while the other partner reads aloud the base form. The partner whose book is closed should respond with the simple-past and past-participle forms. When they feel confident with saying the forms, tell them to try writing the forms rather than saying them.

• **On- and Higher-level** Write a timeline of your important life events on the board (when you started teaching, got married, had children, began working at this school, etc.). Have these students work in groups to write simple-past and present-perfect sentences about you. Have volunteers write their sentences on the board. Correct them together.

2 Learn the present perfect with *for* and *since*

A Study the chart and the time line. Then mark the statements below the time line T (true) or F (false).

The present perfect with *for* and *since*	
┌Present perfect┐ ┌*for* + period of time┐	┌ Present perfect┐ ┌ *since* + time activity began┐
I have studied English **for six months.**	I have been sick **since Monday.**
He hasn't lived in Korea **for a long time.**	Miguel has lived in Texas **since 1994.**
They have worked here **for many years.**	We haven't had a vacation **since May.**

Note
Use the present perfect to describe activities that began in the past and continue to the present.
I have been sick for 4 days. = I got sick four days ago and I'm still sick now.
I have been sick since Monday. = I got sick on Monday and I'm still sick today.

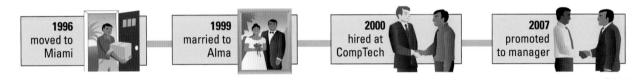

1996 moved to Miami   **1999** married to Alma   **2000** hired at CompTech   **2007** promoted to manager

  _F_ 1. Carlos has been a manager since 2004.

  _T_ 2. He has worked at CompTech since 2000.

  _F_ 3. He has lived in Miami for only two years.

  _T_ 4. He has been married for more than five years.

B Complete the sentences with *for* or *since*.

1. He has worked here _____*for*_____ eight months.

2. Mrs. Min has been a teacher __*since*_____ 1994.

3. They have studied every day __*since*_____ Tuesday.

4. Sheila has been married __*since*_____ 2001.

5. Rick has lived here __*for*_____ nine months.

6. We haven't seen our neighbors __*for*_____ a few weeks.

C Get the meaning. Work with your class. Read the sentences. Then mark the sentences T (true) or F (false).

1. They have been sick for a week.

   They're not sick now.   _F_

2. Carlos has worked in an office for three years.

   Carlos works in an office now.   _T_

3. Sheila has been married since 2001.

   Sheila got married in 2001.   _T_

3 Grammar listening

Listen to the story. Write the present perfect forms you hear.

My name is Sasha. I work for J & J Shipping Company.

I ___haven't worked___ here for very long, but
         1

I _have ('ve) made_ some great friends. My
        2

best friends at work are named Julie and Jenna. Both Julie

and Jenna _have worked_ here for 12 years.
                3

They _have ('ve) been_ in the same department since
            4

they started. Jenna helped me learn the company's computer

programs and Julie _has helped_ me with all
                       5

kinds of things. I _haven't had_ a chance to
                    6

transfer to their department, but I hope I will someday.

4 Practice the present perfect

A **Look at the time line. When did you do these things or start to do these things? Write the correct date for each event.**

moved to this city	moved to my current address	studied English	attended this class
_____	_____	_____	_____

B **Work with a partner. Ask and answer the questions. Use *for* or *since*.**

1. How long have you lived in this city?
2. How long have you lived at your current address?
3. How long have you studied English?
4. How long have you attended this class?

C **Talk about your answers with the class.**

I've lived in this city for 10 years. Elena has lived here since 2003.

TEST YOURSELF ✔

Close your book. Write 6 sentences about what you learned about people in your class. Use the present perfect.

Kemi has studied English since September.

---

3 Grammar listening

Guided Practice II
10–15 minutes

1. Ask students if they are friends with their co-workers. Ask: *Are good co-workers an important part of a job? Why or why not?* Say: *Now we're going to listen to a woman talk about her job at a shipping company. She's going to tell us about her co-workers.*

2. Play the audio. Direct students to read along silently without writing.

3. Replay the audio. Ask students to complete the sentences with the present-perfect verbs they hear.

4. Ask volunteers to read the completed sentences aloud. Write the answers on the board.

4 Practice the present perfect

Communicative Practice and Application
20–25 minutes

A 1. Direct students to look at the timeline. Ask a few volunteers: *When did you move to this city? Move to your current address?*

2. Ask students to write the appropriate dates on their timelines.

B 1. Put students in pairs. Read and have students repeat the questions.

2. Direct students to ask their partners the questions. Tell them to make notes of each other's answers. Model the exercise by asking a volunteer the first question. Have the class tell you how to write the answer in note form.

3. Check comprehension of the exercise. Ask: *Should you write complete sentences?* [no]

C Call on individuals to share information about themselves and their partners.

Evaluation
10–15 minutes

TEST YOURSELF

Ask students to write the sentences independently. Collect and correct their writing.

Multilevel Strategies

Target the *Test Yourself* to the level of your students.

• **Pre-level** Provide four skeleton sentences for these students to complete. *1. _____ has lived in this city for _____. 2. _____ has lived at his/her current address since _____. 3. _____ has studied English since _____. 4. _____ has attended this class for _____.*

• **Higher-level** Have these students write a paragraph in response to this prompt: *Contrast your own information with your partner's. I have lived in this city for _____, but Flor has lived here for _____.*

To compress this lesson: Conduct 1C as a whole-class activity.

To extend this lesson: Play the "liar" game.
1. Direct students to write three sentences about themselves using the present perfect. Two sentences should be true and one should be false. Encourage students to include at least one sentence with *since* or *for*.
2. Put students in mixed-level groups. Direct each student to read his/her sentences to the group. Encourage the group to ask follow-up questions to help them decide if a statement is true or false. Have group members guess which statements are false. Have each group tell the class which person fooled the most people.

And/Or have students complete **Workbook 3 pages 25–26, Multilevel Activity Book 3 pages 51–52**, and the corresponding **Unit 3 Exercises** on the **Multilevel Grammar Exercises CD-ROM 3**.

Unit 4 Lesson 4

Objectives	Grammar	Vocabulary	Correlations
On- and Higher-level: Interview for a promotion, and listen for information in a job history **Pre-level:** Answer basic interview questions, and listen for information in a job history	Present perfect (*I've been a salesperson for five years.*)	Occupations, past participles For vocabulary support, see this **Oxford Picture Dictionary** topic: Food Service, Interview Skills	**CASAS:** 0.1.5, 4.1.2, 4.1.5, 4.4.2, 6.2.1, 6.2.3 **LCPs:** 37.01, 37.02, 37.03, 39.01, 49.02, 49.09, 50.02 **SCANS:** Arithmetic/Mathematics, Problem solving, Speaking **EFF:** Listen actively, Read with understanding, Reflect and evaluate, Use math to solve problems and communicate

Warm-up and Review

10–15 minutes (books closed)

Write the following skeleton sentences on the board: *I have gone to _____. I have had _____. I have studied _____. I have worked _____.* Use the sentences to tell students about yourself. Then call on volunteers to complete the sentences about themselves.

Introduction

5 minutes

1. Say: *We often use these present-perfect forms in a job interview when we talk about our experience.*

2. State the objective: *Today we're going to learn how to interview for jobs and promotions.*

1 Learn to interview for a promotion

Presentation I

15–20 minutes

A 1. Direct students to look at the pictures. Ask: *What jobs has she had?*

2. Play the audio. Give students time to complete sentences 1 and 2. Go over the answers as a class.

Guided Practice

20–25 minutes

B 1. Read the instructions aloud. Ask students to read along silently and listen for the answer to the question. Elicit the answer.

2. Ask students to read the conversation with a partner. Circulate and monitor pronunciation. Model the conversation and have students repeat difficult words or phrases.

3. Say and have students repeat the expressions in the *In other words* box. Elicit the placement of the expressions in the conversation. Ask volunteers to read the conversation using expressions from the box.

Communicative Practice and Application

15–20 minutes

C 1. Ask students to read the instructions silently. Check their comprehension of the exercise. Ask: *What are the two roles?* Elicit samples of what the manager and the salesperson might say.

2. Set a time limit (five minutes). Ask students to act out the role-play in both roles. Ask a few volunteer pairs to act out their conversations for the class. Tell students who are listening to make a note of the sentence(s) Partner B uses to try to persuade Partner A to give him/her the job.

Multilevel Strategies

For 1C, adapt the role-play to the level of your students.

• **Pre-level** Provide a simplified conversation for these students to practice. *A: How long have you been salesperson? B: I've been a salesperson for five years. A: Why should you be the assistant manager? B: I want to teach other employees what I have learned.*

1 Learn to interview for a promotion

🎧 **A** **Look at the pictures. Listen to the conversation. Then answer the questions below with your classmates.**

2003–2005   2005–present *assistant chef*

1. What job does Beatriz have? server
2. What job does she interview for? assistant chef

🎧 **B** **Listen and read. What job does Ms. Ortiz want?** Ms. Ortiz wants to be head chef.

A: How long have you been an assistant chef at Henri's Restaurant, Ms. Ortiz?

B: I've been an assistant chef here since 2005.

A: Why do you think you should be the new head chef?

B: I'm creative. I want to create delicious new dishes for Henri's customers.

A: Have you been a head chef before?

B: No, but I'm a fast learner.

A: That's terrific, Ms. Ortiz.

> **In other words...**
>
> **Ways to ask**
> Why do you think...?
> What makes you think...?
>
> **Ways to persuade**
> I'm creative.
> I'm a fast learner.
> I'm hard-working.
> I know I can do it.

C **Role-play a promotion interview with a partner. Use the example in 1B to make a new conversation.**

Partner A: You are a manager at Discount Mart. Interview your best salesperson for the job of assistant manager.

Partner B: You are the best salesperson at Discount Mart. You've been a salesperson for five years. You're hard-working. You want to teach other employees what you've learned. You know you can do it.

2 Learn contractions with the present perfect

A Study the chart. Who has learned a lot? Sue and I have learned a lot.

Contractions with the present perfect
I have learned a lot. = I**'ve** learned a lot.
Sue has learned a lot. = She**'s*** learned a lot.
Al has not learned a lot. = He hasn**'t** learned a lot.
They have not learned a lot. = They haven**'t** learned a lot.

Note
*In this example, *'s* means *has*. *'s* can also mean *is* in the present tense.
She's been to the doctor. =
She **has** been to the doctor.
She's a doctor. = She **is** a doctor.

B Underline the subjects and verb contractions. Read the sentences. Then write the subjects, the full form of the verbs, and any past participles.

1. <u>They've</u> worked at the hospital since 2004.   *They have worked*

2. <u>She's</u> a good student.   *She is*

3. <u>He's</u> studied computers since June.   He has studied

4. <u>We've</u> done our homework.   We have done

5. <u>It's</u> hot today.   It is

6. It <u>hasn't</u> rained all month.   It has not rained

C Work with a partner. Follow the directions.

1. Tell your partner three places you've gone this week. Use contractions.
2. Tell your partner three things you've done at home since Sunday.

3 Practice your pronunciation

A Listen to the pronunciation of *th* in these sentences. Underline the *th* sounds you hear.

1. How long have you been a salesperson at <u>th</u>is store?
2. I want to teach o<u>th</u>er employees what I've learned.
3. <u>Th</u>at's terrific!

B Listen. Do you hear *th* in any of these sentences? Circle *yes* or *no*.

1. yes (no)   3. yes (no)   5. (yes) no
2. (yes) no   4. yes (no)   6. (yes) no

C Ask and answer the questions with a partner. Then listen to the questions and repeat.

1. Is the weather better this week than it was on the weekend?
2. Is this the only clothing that you thought about wearing today?

2 Learn contractions with the present perfect

Presentation II

10–15 minutes

 1. Introduce the new topic: *In everyday speech, we usually use contractions with the present perfect. Now we're going to work on present-perfect contractions.*

2. Read the sentences in the chart and go over the *Note*.

3. Check comprehension of the chart. Ask: *How do you contract* she has? *How do you contract* they have not?

4. Read the sentences again, and have students repeat them. Then have them read the sentences with a partner.

Guided Practice

15–20 minutes

 Read number 1 and the example answer. Have students work independently to write the subject and full form of the verb for each sentence. Ask volunteers to write the answers on the board.

 For additional practice with contractions, dictate a few sentences. Pronounce the contracted form, but ask students to write the sentence with the full form of the verb. *She's worked here for a long time. She's a good employee. He's read that book three times. He's a very creative thinker.* Have volunteers write the sentences on the board.

Communicative Practice and Application

15–20 minutes

C 1. Model the exercise. *I've gone to the bank, I've gone to the supermarket, and I've gone to the gym.*

2. Set a time limit (three minutes). Ask students to talk to several partners. Remind them to use a complete sentence for each action so that they practice saying the contractions.

3 Practice your pronunciation

Pronunciation Extension

10–15 minutes

 1. Write *They've always wanted to work at this company.* on the board. Say the sentence and ask students to repeat it. Underline *th*, and repeat *they've* and *this*. Say: *Now we're going to focus on* th *sounds.*

2. Play the audio. Direct students to listen for the pronunciation of *th*.

3. Say and have students repeat *this, other,* and *that.*

 Change the sentence on the board to read: *They've always wanted to work at this theater.* Say the sentence and underline the *th* in *theater*. Ask students if it sounds the same as the other *th* sounds. Elicit more examples of the unvoiced *th* sound—for example, *think, with, fifth, birthday*. Show students that the mouth position is the same in both sounds, but they need to use their voices to produce the sound in *this*, whereas the sound in *think* is produced with air.

B 1. Tell students they will hear a sentence and they need to listen for words with *th* and circle *Yes* if they hear it or *No* if they don't. Play the first sentence, and elicit the answer.

2. Play the rest of the sentences. Have students listen and circle *Yes* or *No*. Go over the answers by asking for a show of hands for each number or having students hold up a *Yes/No* card (see page T-199). If students have any difficulties, replay the sentences and discuss the answers.

C Say and have students repeat the questions. Have students ask and answer the questions with a partner. Monitor and make a note of pronunciation challenges. Write problem words on the board, and have students repeat them.

4 Focus on listening

Listening Extension

20–25 minutes

A Read the questions aloud, and elicit answers from volunteers. Encourage students to respond to each other's ideas. After one student speaks, ask other students for their opinions. *Do you agree or disagree with what he/she said? Why?*

B Have students read questions 1 and 2 silently. Play the audio. Direct students to listen and circle the answers. Go over the answers as a class.

C 1. Direct students to read the job application before listening.

2. Replay the audio and have students work individually to complete the application. Go over the answers as a class.

Multilevel Strategies

Replay 4C to challenge on- and higher-level students while allowing pre-level students to catch up.

• **Pre-level** Have these students listen again to complete the application.

• **On- and Higher-level** Write questions on the board for these students to answer. *Was Miguel a good student? What did he study besides accounting? What department does he work in?* Have volunteers write the answers on the board.

5 Real-life math

Math Extension

5–10 minutes

Read the problem aloud, and give students time to work out the answer. Ask a volunteer to share how he/she figured out the problem and write it on the board: *number of hours per day x hourly pay x number of days*. Have another student write the final problem and solution on the board.

Evaluation

10–15 minutes

TEST YOURSELF

1. Model the role-play with a volunteer. Then switch roles.

2. Pair students. Check comprehension of the exercise. Ask: *Who is Partner A?* [manager] *What does Partner B want?* [promotion to night manager] Ask for examples of what each person might say.

3. Set a time limit (five minutes), and have the partners act out the role-play in both roles. Circulate and monitor. Encourage pantomime and improvisation. Provide feedback.

Multilevel Strategies

Target the *Test Yourself* to the level of your students.

• **Pre-level** Ask these students to use this skeleton conversation: *A: How long have you been a/an _____? B: I've been a/an _____*
(job)   (job)
for two years. A: Why should you be the new _____? B: I'm very _____. A: Good. We need
(job)   (adjective)
more _____ employees!
(adjective)

• **Higher-level** Tell these students to practice the restaurant role-play and then create an original role-play set in a different workplace.

To compress this lesson: Have students practice 2C with only one partner.

To extend this lesson: Have students practice writing and speaking about job experiences. Put students in groups of three or four, and give them a large sheet of paper. Tell them a night manager position at a restaurant is open, and each group needs to describe a candidate for that job. Direct them to give their candidates names and write four or five sentences about their job experience. Post the descriptions on the board. Correct the sentences and have a class discussion about which candidate should get the job.

And/Or have students complete **Workbook 3 page 27** and **Multilevel Activity Book 3 page 53**.

4 Focus on listening

A **Talk about the questions with your class.**

1. What kind of information do job applications usually ask for?
2. Do you think most people like to complete job applications? Why or why not?

B **Read the questions. Then listen to the conversation and circle *a* or *b*.**

1. Where does Miguel work now?
   - (a.) Center Street Hospital
   - b. Springfield General Hospital

2. Why does he want a new job?
   - a. He wants to work at a better hospital.
   - (b.) He wants to work closer to home.

C **Listen again and complete Miguel's job application.**

Application for Employment

Personal Information

First Name: *Miguel*
Last Name: *Lopez*

Education

High School: *Central High School*
College: *City College*
Course of Study: *accounting*
Years Completed: ___*four*___
₁
Did You Graduate?
Yes: ___✔___ No: _____   Degree: *BA*
₂

Employment History

Company Name:

___Center Street Hospital___
₃

Employed (Month and Year)

From: ___February, 2005___
₄

To: ___present___
₅

Position: *Assistant Accounts Manager*

Position Desired: *Accounts Manager*

5 Real-life math

Read about Miguel's job and answer the question.

The Springfield General Hospital manager has offered Miguel a job. The hours for the job are Tuesday through Saturday from 8:30 to 3:30. The pay will be $23.50 per hour. What is the gross pay* for one week? ___$822.50 per week___

*gross pay = the money you make before taxes

TEST YOURSELF ✓

Role-play a workplace conversation. Partner A: You're the manager at a restaurant. Interview your best server for a promotion to night manager. Partner B: You're the best server in the restaurant. Tell the manager why you should get the promotion. Then change roles.

1 Get ready to read

A Has someone you know received a promotion at work? Why?

B Read the definitions.

honest: (adj.) truthful

interpersonal skills: (noun) the ability to work and communicate well with other people

market: (verb) to sell or promote

network: (verb) to talk, or communicate, with other people at work

C Scan the bold print in the article in 2A for three things you need to do to get a promotion.

1. _Improve your skills_
2. _Market yourself and your skills_
3. _Know your personal strengths_

2 Read and respond

A Read the article.

Getting the Promotion You Want

Do you like the company you work for? Are you ready for more responsibility? If you answered "yes," you might be ready for a promotion. To get a promotion, you need a plan. First, you need to make sure you have the job skills to get the promotion you want. Then you need to market yourself and your skills to your supervisor.

Improve Your Skills
- Take classes or study at home.
- Accept extra work with a smile. Employees who do this often learn new skills and make their supervisors happy. Think about what you are learning while you are working.

Market Yourself and Your Skills
- Dress for success. Clothing, shoes, and haircut can make a big difference in how your supervisor sees you. Conservative[1] choices are usually best.
- Network, or communicate, with people in other departments. Eat lunch with other employees. Attend company events. You'll be surprised how much you learn and how much people learn about you.

[1]conservative: traditional

✔ Identify ways to get a promotion

Unit 4 Lesson 5

Objectives	Grammar	Vocabulary	Correlations
Pre-, On- and Higher-level: Read about and discuss getting a promotion	*Should (You should wear conservative clothes.)*	*Honest, interpersonal, market, network, flexibility, quality* For vocabulary support, see this **Oxford Picture Dictionary** topic: Career Planning	**CASAS:** 0.1.2, 4.1.6, 4.4.1, 4.4.2, 7.4.7, 7.5.1, 8.3.1 **LCPs:** 37.01, 37.02, 38.01, 39.01, 49.01, 49.02, 49.16, 49.17 **SCANS:** Acquires and evaluates information, Interprets and communicates information **EFF:** Learn through research, Read with understanding, Take responsibility for learning

Warm-up and Review

10–15 minutes (books closed)

Write the words *Description* and *Behavior* on the board. Elicit words that describe a good employee—for example, *self-starter, go-getter,* etc. Write them under *Description*. Elicit what a person who fits that description does, and write it under *Behavior*. *He/She works without supervision; He/She comes to work on time.*

Introduction

5 minutes

1. Ask: *Which of these behaviors do you think are most important to help you get a promotion?*

2. State the objective: *Today we're going to read about getting a promotion.*

1 Get ready to read

Presentation

15–20 minutes

A Read the question aloud. Ask volunteers to share their stories.

B Read the words and definitions. Elicit sample sentences from students using the words. Students may use the more common noun form of *market* and *network*. Show them how these words can be used as verbs. *He put up a website to market his skills. She likes to network with other employees at the staff party because meeting new people might help her find a better job.*

Pre-Reading

C 1. Read the title of the article and 2A, and direct students to look quickly through the article for the items in bold print. Go over the answers as a class.

2. Before students read the article, have them brainstorm ideas about how people might improve their skills and market themselves.

2 Read and respond

Guided Practice I

25–30 minutes

A 1. Ask students to read the article silently.

2. Direct students to underline unfamiliar words they would like to know. Elicit the words and encourage other students to provide definitions or examples.

3. Check students' comprehension. Ask: *What kind of clothing should you wear? How can you improve your skills?*

Multilevel Strategies

Adapt 2A to the level of your students.

• **Pre-level** Provide these students with a summary of the reading. There are three important ways to get a promotion. *1. Take classes or do extra jobs at work to learn new skills. 2. Market yourself. Dress nicely to work, so you look serious. Try to meet other employees. 3. Know your strengths. Some important strengths are: speak and write well, be honest, be friendly, work well in teams, and be flexible.*

Direct these students to read the outline while other students are reading 2A.

Guided Practice II

5–10 minutes

B 1. Play the audio. Have students read along silently.

2. Elicit and discuss any additional questions about the reading.

C Have students work individually to mark the statements T (true), F (false), or NI (no information). Go over the answers as a class.

Multilevel Strategies

For 2C, work with pre-level students.

• **Pre-level** Ask these students *Yes/No* and short-answer information questions about their summaries while other students are completing 2C. *What do you need to learn to get a promotion?* [new skills] *How should you dress?* [nicely] *Is flexibility a strength?* [yes]

As volunteers are reading the sentences in 2C aloud, write the answers on the board, and direct pre-level students to write them in their books.

3 Talk it over

Communicative Practice

15–20 minutes

A Read the questions. Set a time limit (three minutes). Allow students to think about the questions and write their answers in note form individually.

B Elicit students' answers to the questions from 3A. Make notes about their ideas on the board. Encourage students to respond to each other's ideas.

TIP

Take this opportunity to clarify how the activities that students do in your class help develop their workplace skills. Ask: *How do you demonstrate your flexibility and your interpersonal, teamwork, and communication skills in this classroom?* For example: Flexibility—students do different kinds of activities and work with different people. Interpersonal skills—they learn and practice social language. Teamwork—they work in small groups and pairs to complete exercises. Written or spoken communication skills—of course, everything they do in English class helps with that!

Some workplace expectations are culturally influenced. Ask students how they feel about making decisions with teams, about supervisors asking workers for input, and about marketing themselves.

Application

5–10 minutes

BRING IT TO LIFE

Help make the assignment more concrete by asking students whom they will talk to. Have everyone write down the name of the person they plan on asking.

To compress this lesson: Conduct 2C as a whole-class activity.

To extend this lesson: Have students write examples of behaviors that demonstrate the "Top Qualities" from the article in 2A.
1. Put students in pairs or small groups. Have each pair come up with a specific example of a behavior that demonstrates each quality. Tell them to use their own actions or the actions of people they know as an example. *Good communication skills: I have successfully taught my co-workers how to use the cash register.*
2. Have volunteers read their sentences aloud. Congratulate correct usage of the present perfect. As a class, decide which examples would be most persuasive for an employer.

And/Or have students complete **Workbook 3 page 28** and the **Multilevel Activity Book 3 pages 54–55**.

Know your Personal Strengths
- What are your top qualities? What makes you the best person for the promotion?
- Look at the Top Qualities list. Be sure that these qualities describe you. Be sure you know your personal strengths and job skills. Be ready to talk confidently about them.

> **Top 5 Qualities Supervisors look for:**
> 1. Good communication skills
> 2. Honesty
> 3. Strong interpersonal skills
> 4. Good teamwork skills
> 5. Flexibility
>
> Source: *Job Outlook and The National Association of Colleges and Employers*

B Listen and read the article again.

C Mark the sentences T (true), F (false), or NI (no information).

  __T__   1. To get a promotion, you need to have job skills.

  __F__   2. You shouldn't network with other people if you want a promotion.

  __NI__   3. Honest employees get promoted 50% of the time.

  __F__   4. A good way to market yourself is to study at home.

  __F__   5. Flexibility isn't a quality that supervisors look for.

  __T__   6. Conservative clothing is usually best for work.

  __F__   7. Don't worry about qualities supervisors look for.

  __T__   8. It's important to know your personal strengths.

3 Talk it over

A Think about the questions. Make notes about your answers.

1. Do you think it's easier to get a promotion or to get a new job at a different company? Why?
2. Look at the Top Qualities list in the article. What other qualities are important to have at work or at school?

B Talk about the answers with your classmates.

BRING IT TO LIFE

Talk to a neighbor or family member who has a job. Ask the question:
What do you think the top 3 employee qualities are for your job? Write the answers. Bring the information to class.

1 Grammar

A **Complete the sentences. Use past participles.**

1. Don hasn't ____made____ his bed yet.
2. Suki has __seen_____ several movies this summer.
3. We haven't __taken_____ a vacation since July.
4. We've never __eaten_____ at that restaurant.
5. Leo has __drunk_____ two cups of coffee since this morning.

> **Need help?**
>
> **More irregular verbs**
>
> | Base form | Simple past | Past participle |
> |---|---|---|
> | drink | drank | drunk |
> | eat | ate | eaten |
> | get | got | gotten |
> | make | made | made |
> | see | saw | seen |
> | take | took | taken |

B **Complete the sentences. Use the present perfect of the verbs in parentheses.**

1. Adela _____has lived_____ here for a long time. (live)
2. She __has worked_____ at a hospital since 2003. (work)
3. Her brothers __have completed_____ high school. (complete)
4. They __have not (n't) gotten_____ jobs this month. (not get)
5. She __has had_____ a headache all day. (have)

C **Complete the sentences with *for* or *since*.**

1. We've been here _____for_____ 20 minutes.
2. Have you talked to Marta __since_____ yesterday?
3. Khan hasn't visited Mexico __since_____ 2001.
4. I haven't used my car _for_____ two weeks.
5. Antonio and Esteban haven't lived here __since_____ last May.

D **Look at the underlined subjects and verb contractions. Write the subject and the full forms of the contracted verbs *is* or *has*.**

1. <u>Mark's</u> the new assistant manager. _____Mark is_____
2. <u>He's</u> worked in this office since last year. __He has_____
3. <u>Mark's</u> not here right now. __Mark is_____
4. <u>He's</u> at a meeting in Toronto. __He is_____
5. <u>He's</u> been to other meetings in Canada before. __He has_____

Unit 4 Review and expand

Objectives	Grammar	Vocabulary	Correlations
On-, Pre-, and Higher-level: Expand upon and review unit grammar and life skills	Present perfect (*We've been here for 20 minutes.*)	Past participles For vocabulary support, see this **Oxford Picture Dictionary** topic: Interview Skills, Office Skills	**CASAS:** 0.1.2, 0.1.5, 0.2.1, 7.3.1, 7.3.2, 7.3.3, 7.3.4 **LCPs:** 39.01, 49.01, 49.02, 49.16, 50.02 **SCANS:** Acquires and evaluates information, Creative thinking, Participates as member of a team **EFF:** Convey ideas in writing, Read with understanding, Speak so others can understand

Warm-up and Review

10–15 minutes (books closed)

1. Review the *Bring It to Life* assignment from Lesson 5.

2. Have students who did the exercise share what they learned. Have students who didn't do the exercise determine whether the answers are the same as or different from the "Top Qualities" mentioned in the article in Lesson 5, 2A.

3. Use the students' ideas to write a new list of "Top Qualities" on the board.

Introduction and Presentation

5 minutes

1. Ask students a few questions using the present perfect. *Anna, how long have you studied English? Kyung Hee, have you been to Kansas?* Write their answers on the board in the third person. *Anna has studied English for four years. Kyung Hee hasn't been to Kansas.*

2. Ask volunteers to underline the verb in each sentence. Pointing to the sentences to make your meaning clear, ask other volunteers to tell you the name of the form, the auxiliary used, and the form of the main verb.

3. Discuss the meaning of each sentence on the board. *Is Anna still studying English? When did Kyung Hee go to Kansas? Is it possible she'll go in the future?*

4. State the objective: *Today we're going to learn more irregular past participles and review using the present perfect to talk about our experience.*

1 Grammar

Guided Practice

40–45 minutes

A 1. Say and have students repeat the irregular verbs in the *Need help?* box. Then say the base forms, and call on individuals to say the simple-past and past-participle forms.

2. Have students work individually to complete the sentences. Point out that the auxiliary is provided. Students only need to write in the correct participle. Ask volunteers to read the completed sentences aloud. Help with pronunciation of the participles.

B Have students work individually to complete the sentences. Ask volunteers to write the answers on the board. Go over the answers as a class.

C Have students work individually to complete the sentences. Ask volunteers to read the completed sentences aloud.

D Have students work individually to write the full forms. Go over the answers as a class. Write the answers on the board.

Multilevel Strategies

For 1B, 1C, and 1D, seat same-level students together.

• **Pre-level** Assist these students individually as necessary with 1B and 1C. Go through 1D with them as a group. Pronounce each sentence in full form before students write.

• **On- and Higher-Level** Ask these students to write four more sentences with contracted verbs—two with *is* and two with *has*. Have volunteers write their sentences on the board and ask students to tell you the full forms of the contracted verbs.

2 Group work

Communicative Practice

20–35 minutes

 1. Direct students, in groups of three to four, to focus on the picture. Ask: *Where are these people? Who is applying for a job? Who is interviewing?*

2. Group students and assign roles: leader, recorder, reporter, and timekeeper. Explain that students work with their groups to write the conversation.

3. Check comprehension of the roles. Ask: *Who writes the conversation?* [recorder] *Who will read the conversation to the class?* [reporter] *Who helps everyone and manages the group?* [leader] *Who tells the group how much time has passed?* [timekeeper] *Who creates the conversation?* [everyone]

4. Set a time limit (five minutes) to complete the conversation. Circulate and answer any questions.

5. Have a reporter from each group read the group's conversation to the class. Provide feedback on the questions and answers.

> ### Multilevel Strategies
>
> For 2A, use mixed-level groups.
> - **Pre-level** Assign these students the role of timekeeper.
> - **On-level** Assign these students the role of recorder or reporter.
> - **Higher-level** Assign these students the role of leader.

B 1. Have students walk around the room to conduct the interviews. To get students moving, tell them to interview three new people not in their groups for 2A.

2. Set a time limit (five minutes) to complete the exercise. Tell students to make a note of their classmates' answers but not to worry about writing complete sentences.

> ### Multilevel Strategies
>
> Adapt the mixer in 2B to the level of your students.
> - **Pre-level** Allow these students to ask and answer the questions without writing.
> - **Higher-level** Have these students ask two additional questions in the present perfect and write all answers.

 Call on individuals to report what they learned about their classmates. Encourage students to make generalizations. *Most of us are/aren't working. Most of us have had _____ jobs.*

PROBLEM SOLVING

15–25 minutes

A 1. Ask: *What can make a job interview go badly?* Tell students they will read a story about a man who has a job interview tomorrow and isn't ready. Direct students to read Hector's story silently.

2. Ask: *What hasn't Hector done? Do you think he should be nervous?*

3. Play the audio. Have students read along silently.

B 1. Elicit answers to question 1. Have volunteers write answers to question 2 on the board until all of the class ideas have been put up.

2. As a class, rank the best three ideas from one to three.

Evaluation

10–15 minutes

To test students' understanding of the unit grammar and life skills, have them take the Unit 4 Test in the *Step Forward Test Generator CD-ROM* with *ExamView® Assessment Suite*

> ### Learning Log
>
> To help students record and discuss their progress, use the *Learning Log* on page T-201.

To extend this review: Have students complete **Workbook 3 page 29, Multilevel Activity Book 3 page 56**, and the **Unit 4 Exercises** on the **Multilevel Grammar Exercises CD-ROM 4**.

2 Group work

A Work with 2–3 classmates. Write a conversation between the people in the picture. Share your conversation with the class.

A: *Tell me about your personal strengths.*
B: *I am a team player...*

B Interview 3 classmates. Write their answers.

1. Do you have a job now? What do you do?
2. How long have you been a _____?
3. How many jobs have you had?
4. How long have you been at this school?

C Talk about the answers with your class.

PROBLEM SOLVING

A Listen and read about Hector.

It's 10 p.m. Hector has a job interview in the morning. He's been at work all day. He hasn't had time to prepare for the interview. He hasn't learned much about the company. He hasn't written a list of questions to ask the interviewer, and he hasn't decided what to wear. He needs to go to bed by 11:30. Hector is worried that he is unprepared. He's getting nervous about tomorrow.

B Work with your classmates. Answer the questions.

1. What is Hector's problem? Hector hasn't prepared for his interview in the morning.
2. What is the best way for Hector to spend his time tonight? Make a list of the top 3 things he should do.

UNIT **5**

FOCUS ON
- community resources
- reporting safety problems
- the present perfect
- taking action in the community
- protecting the environment

Community Resources

LESSON **1** Vocabulary

1 Learn community resource vocabulary

A **Talk about the questions with your class.**

1. Where are the government offices in your city or town?
2. What types of services do people in your city or town need?

B **Work with your classmates. Match the words with the picture.**

_5_	animal shelter	_8_	employment agency
_1_	city hall	_3_	recreation center
_4_	community clinic	_2_	recycling center
_6_	Department of Motor Vehicles (DMV)	_7_	senior center

C **Listen and check. Then read the new words with a partner.**

D **Work with a partner. Write other community resource words you know. Check your words in a dictionary.**

Unit 5 Lesson 1

Objectives	Grammar	Vocabulary	Correlations
On-level: Identify community resources and describe services **Pre-level:** Identify community resources and services **Higher-level:** Talk and write about community resources and services	*Should (You should go to the job fair.)*	Community Resources and Services For vocabulary support, see this **Oxford Picture Dictionary** topic: City Streets	**CASAS:** 0.1.2, 0.1.5, 4.1.6, 4.8.1, 7.4.5 **LCPs:** 46.01, 49.02 **SCANS:** Listening, Participates as member of a team, Speaking **EFF:** Listen actively, Reflect and evaluate, Speak so others can understand

Warm-up and Review

10–15 minutes (books closed)

Draw a dollar sign ($) on the board, and ask students to guess what community place it represents. [a bank] Direct students to come up with a quick drawing that represents a community place. Ask volunteers to come up and draw their pictures on the board. Have the class guess what the pictures represent.

Introduction

5 minutes

1. Ask: *Which are places where we buy things? Which are places for recreation? Which are places that provide help?*

2. State the objective: *Today we're going to learn more vocabulary for community places and community services.*

1 Learn community resource vocabulary

Presentation I

20–25 minutes

A Write *Our Community* on the board, and elicit students' answers to questions 1 and 2. Make a list on the board of the services your students identify.

B 1. Direct students to look at the picture. Ask: *Is this a nice neighborhood?*

2. Group students and assign roles: leader, fact checker, recorder, and reporter. Explain that students work with their groups to match the words and pictures.

3. Check comprehension of the roles. Ask: *Who looks up the words in a dictionary?* [fact checker] *Who writes the numbers in the book?* [recorder] *Who tells the class your answers?* [reporter] *Who helps everyone and manages the group?* [leader]

4. Set a time limit (three minutes). As students work together, copy the wordlist onto the board.

5. Call "time." Have reporters take turns giving their answers. Write each group's answer on the board next to the word.

C 1. To prepare students for listening, say: *Now we're going to hear about what you can do at each of these places.* Ask students to listen and check their answers.

2. Have students check the wordlist on the board and then write the correct numbers in their books.

3. Pair students. Set a time limit (two minutes). Monitor pair practice to identify pronunciation issues.

4. Call "time" and work with the pronunciation of any troublesome words or phrases.

D 1. Ask students to work with a partner to brainstorm a list of related words.

2. Elicit words from the class. Write them on the board. Ask students to copy them into their vocabulary notes for the unit.

Guided Practice

5–10 minutes

 1. Model the conversation with a volunteer.

2. Set a time limit (three minutes). Direct students to talk with a partner.

3. Ask volunteers to repeat one of their conversations for the class.

2 Learn about community services

Presentation II

10–20 minutes

 1. Direct students to look at the website. Introduce the new topic: *We've talked about places. Now we're going to talk about services those places provide.*

2. Elicit the names of the places students see on the website.

3. Ask students to work individually to match the places to the services. Go over the answers as a class.

4. Check comprehension. Ask: *Where can I adopt a pet?* [at the animal shelter] *Where can I get a wellness checkup?* [at the community clinic]

Guided Practice

10–15 minutes

 1. Model the conversation with a volunteer. Model it again using other information from 2A.

2. Set a time limit (three minutes). Direct students to practice with a partner.

3. Call on volunteers to say one of their conversations for the class.

> ## Multilevel Strategies
> Seat same-level students together for 2B.
>
> • **Pre-level** Practice the conversation with these students. Ask the questions, and have students take turns answering.
>
> • **On- and Higher-level** After these students practice the conversation in 2B, have them write three or four sentences connecting the places and services in 2A. *I went to a job fair at the employment agency.*

Communicative Practice and Application

10–15 minutes

 1. Give students time to make notes of their answers to the questions. Call on individuals to share their ideas with the class.

2. Write the community-service information students come up with on the board.

Evaluation

10–15 minutes

TEST YOURSELF

1. Pair students. Direct Partner B to close the book and listen to Partner A dictate five words from 1B on page 60. Ask students to switch roles when they finish. Then have Partner A dictate five words from 2A on page 61.

2. Direct both partners to open their books and check their spelling when they finish.

To compress this lesson: Conduct 1B as a whole-class activity.

To extend this lesson: Have students write a conversation about community services.
1. Put students in pairs. Instruct them to write a short conversation between someone who needs a community service and someone who can give him/her the information he/she needs.
2. Provide this structure on the board for pairs to follow:
    A: *Explain your problem/need to B.*
    B: *Tell what service will help.*
    A: *Ask where to go for that service.*
    B: *Tell A where and when to go.*
And/Or have students complete **Workbook 3 page 30** and **Multilevel Activity Book 3 pages 58–59.**

E **Work with a partner. Practice the conversation. Use the picture in 1B.**

A: What's next to the clinic?

B: The animal shelter is next to the clinic.

2 Learn about community services

A **Look at the community website. Match the services and the places below.**

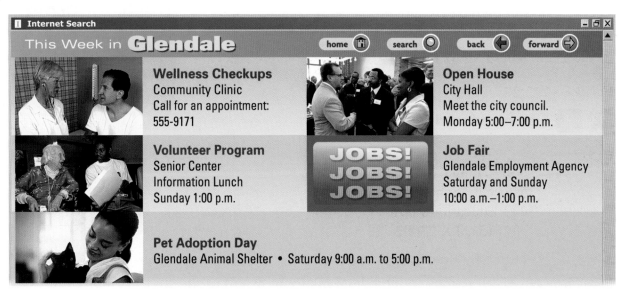

___c___ 1. job fair   a. animal shelter

___a___ 2. pet adoption   b. city hall

___e___ 3. volunteer program   c. employment agency

___b___ 4. open house   d. community clinic

___d___ 5. wellness checkup   e. senior center

B **Work with a partner. Practice the conversation. Use the words in 2A.**

A: I'm interested in the job fair. Where should I go?

B: You should go to the employment agency this weekend from 10:00 to 1:00.

A: Thanks.

C **Talk about the questions with your class.**

1. Which community resources would you like near your home? Why?

2. Where can you find information about community services and events?

TEST YOURSELF ✓

Work with a partner. Partner A: Read the vocabulary words in 1B to your partner.
Partner B: Close your book. Write the words. Ask your partner for help with
spelling as necessary. Then change roles. Partner B: Use the words in 2A.

1 Read about community action

A Look at the picture. Talk about the questions with your class.

1. Are there any safety problems at your school?
2. Who could you ask to help you with school safety problems?

B Listen and read the letter.

> Sally Hunter
> Mid-City School Board
> 473 Education Plaza
> Houston, TX 77002
>
> Dear Ms. Hunter:
>
> I am writing to the school board on behalf of the students in my English class. We have been students at Mid-City Community Center for seven months. Mid-City is a wonderful school, but we are worried about a safety problem.
>
> The problem is that there are no lights in our parking lot. It's dangerous to walk there after class because it's too dark. We've discussed the problem with our school principal, but she says there's no money for lights at this time. Can you help us put lights in our parking lot?
>
> We invite you to visit our school from Monday to Thursday between 7 and 9 p.m. so you can see the problem. Thank you for helping us make our school safe.
>
> Sincerely,
>
> *Marta Alvarez*
> Marta Alvarez

Writer's note

Sign and print your name at the end of a formal or business letter.

C Check your understanding. Mark the statements T (true), F (false), or NI (no information).

  T   1. The letter is to the school board.

  T   2. The parking lot is dangerous because it's dark.

  T   3. The students want the school board to put lights in the parking lot.

  NI   4. There are only classes in the evening at Mid-City Community Center.

  F   5. The students don't like their school.

Unit 5 Lesson 2

Objectives	Grammar	Vocabulary	Correlations
On- and Higher-level: Analyze, write, and edit a letter about a community problem **Pre-level:** Read and write a letter about a community problem	Adjectives (*The parking lot is dangerous.*)	*On behalf of, sincerely* For vocabulary support, see this **Oxford Picture Dictionary** topic: An Intersection, Public Safety	**CASAS:** 0.1.2, 0.1.5, 4.9.4, 7.2.5, 7.3.1, 7.3.2 **LCPs:** 49.01, 49.02, 49.03, 49.16, 49.17 **SCANS:** Interprets and communicates information, Problem solving **EFF:** Convey ideas in writing, Listen actively, Read with understanding, Reflect and evaluate, Solve problems and make decisions

Warm-up and Review

10–15 minutes (books closed)

Write *Safety* on the board. Tell students that all communities have some safety problems. Give them an example from your neighborhood—for example, uneven sidewalks, trees with branches that get knocked down in the wind, blind corners, etc. Ask them to brainstorm other safety problems that they have encountered. Write their ideas on the board.

Introduction

5 minutes

1. Refer to the problems on the board from the warm-up, and ask: *What do you do when you encounter these problems? Where can you go for help?*

2. State the objective: *Today we're going to read and write about seeing a problem in the community and asking for a solution.*

1 Read about community action

Presentation

20–25 minutes

A 1. Direct students to look at the picture. Ask: *Who are these people?*

2. Elicit answers to questions 1 and 2. Find out if students know where your school board meets.

B 1. Introduce the reading: *You're going to read a letter from a student to a school board member.* Ask students to read the letter silently.

2. Check comprehension. Ask: *How long have these students been at the school?* [seven months] *What's the problem?* [no lights in the parking lot] *What do the students want the school board to do?* [help them put lights in the parking lot]

3. Play the audio. Have students read along silently.

Guided Practice I

10 minutes

C Have students work independently to mark the statements T (true), F (false), or NI (no information). Go over the answers as a class.

Multilevel Strategies

For 1C, seat pre-level students together.

• **Pre-level** While other students are working on 1C, ask these students *Yes/No* and *Or* questions about the reading. *Do the students like their school? Is the parking lot safe or dangerous? Do they want the school board to visit the school?*

2 Write a letter to a school board member

Guided Practice II

20–25 minutes

 A 1. Read the questions. Elicit students' answers.

2. Write their ideas for problems and solutions on the board.

> **TIP**
> For 2B, if you don't know the name of a school board member, make one up as a place holder. Another option is to use *To Whom It May Concern* rather than an actual person.

B 1. Direct students to look back at the model letter in 1B. Elicit the main idea of each paragraph.

2. Read through the letter template. Elicit ideas that could go in each paragraph. Have students write their letters individually.

> **Multilevel Strategies**
>
> Adapt 2B to the level of your students.
>
> • **Pre-level** Work with these students to write a group letter. Read through the template. At each blank, stop and elicit completions. Decide as a group what to write.
>
> • **Higher-level** Encourage these students to include an example of something specific that happened or might happen because of the safety problem.

C 1. Lead students through the process of using the *Editing checklist*. Read each sentence aloud, and ask students to check their papers before moving onto the next item.

2. Allow students a few minutes to edit their writing as necessary.

Communicative Practice

10 minutes

 D 1. Read the instructions aloud. Emphasize to students that they are responding to their partners' work, not correcting it.

2. Use the letter in 1B to model the exercise. *I think the sentence that says,* It's dangerous to walk there after class because it's too dark *describes the problem clearly. I'd like to ask Maria if the students are going out to the parking lot in groups to stay safe.*

3. Direct students to exchange papers with a partner and follow the instructions.

4. Call on volunteers to share something interesting they found in their partners' letters.

> **TIP**
> After completing 2D, hold a "school board meeting" in class. Ask for volunteers to come to the front of the room and explain their problems and proposed solutions. All non-volunteers are "board members." Ask the board members to listen and take notes. Tell them they need to prioritize the problems. Have the board come to a consensus about which problem they should deal with first.

Application and Evaluation

15 minutes

TEST YOURSELF

1. Review the instructions aloud. Assign a time limit (ten minutes), and have students work independently.

2. Before collecting student work, remind them to use the *Editing checklist*. Collect and correct students' writing.

To compress this lesson: Assign the *Test Yourself* for homework.

To extend this lesson: Role-play a conversation with a school board member.
1. Put students in pairs. Partner A is the school board member, and Partner B is the concerned student.
2. Put a structure on the board for the pairs to follow:
   A: *What's the problem?*
   B: *At our school, [describe problem].*
   A: *Do you want us to [describe solution]?*
   B: *That would be great.*
   A: *OK. We'll talk about it at the next meeting.*

And/Or have students complete **Workbook 3 page 31** and **Multilevel Activity Book 3 page 60.**

2 Write a letter to a school board member

A **Talk about the questions with your class.**

1. Choose a school problem. Why is it a problem for you and your classmates?
2. What do you want your school board member to do about the problem?

B **Write a letter to your school board member. Use the model in 1B and your answers to the questions in 2A.**

_____
_____
_____
_____

Dear _____:
    I am writing on behalf of the students in my English class.
_____
_____

    The problem is that _____
_____
_____

    We invite you to visit our school _____
so you can see the problem. _____
_____

Sincerely,

_____
_____

C **Use the checklist to edit your writing. Check (✔) the true sentences.**

Editing checklist	
1. I described the problem.	
2. I asked for help.	
3. All my sentences start with capital letters and end with periods.	
4. I signed and printed my name at the end of the letter.	

D **Exchange letters with a partner. Read and comment on your partner's work.**

1. Point out the sentences that you think describe the problem.
2. Ask your partner a question about the problem.

TEST YOURSELF ✔

Imagine that there's a dangerous intersection with no stop sign in your neighborhood. Write a new letter to a city official at city hall to ask for help. Or write to a school or government official about a different problem.

1 Learn *Yes/No* questions with the present perfect

A Read the conversation and the project report. When will the electrician arrive?

tomorrow
A: <u>Have you painted</u>
   <u>the cafeteria?</u>
B: Yes, I have.
A: <u>Has the electrician fixed</u>
   <u>the air-conditioning?</u>
B: No, he hasn't.
A: When will he fix it?
B: He'll be here tomorrow.

Senior Center Project Report:

	yes	no
1. paint cafeteria	✔	
2. fix air-conditioning		✔
3. buy lunch tables	✔	
4. repair stove		✔
5. advertise programs	✔	
6. start lunch program		✔

B Study the chart. Underline the 2 present perfect questions in the conversation above.

YES/NO QUESTIONS WITH THE PRESENT PERFECT

Yes/No Questions		
Have	I you we they	repaired the stove?
Has	he she	

Answers					
Yes,	I you we they	have.	No,	I you we they	haven't.
	he she	has.		he she	hasn't.

C Complete the questions and answers. Use the project report in 1A.

1. <u>Have</u> the workers <u>painted</u> the cafeteria? <u>Yes, they have.</u>

2. <u>Has</u> the office manager <u>bought</u> new
   lunch tables? <u>Yes, she has.</u>

3. <u>Has</u> the electrician <u>fixed</u> the
   air-conditioning? <u>No, he hasn't.</u>

4. <u>Has</u> the office manager <u>started</u>
   the lunch program? <u>No, she hasn't.</u>

5. <u>Has</u> the office manager <u>advertised</u> the
   center programs? <u>Yes, she has.</u>

6. <u>Have</u> they <u>repaired</u> the stove? <u>No, they haven't.</u>

Unit 5 Lesson 3

Objectives	Grammar	Vocabulary	Correlations
On- and Higher-level: Use the present perfect to ask questions about community services, and listen for information about community involvement **Pre-level:** Recognize the present perfect in questions about community services	Present-perfect questions (*Have you painted the cafeteria?*)	*Ever, yet, already* For vocabulary support, see these **Oxford Picture Dictionary** topics: Daily Routines, Housework	**CASAS:** 0.1.2, 0.2.1 **LCPs:** 39.01, 49.02, 49.09, 49.16, 49.17, 50.02 **SCANS:** Listening, Writing **EFF:** Convey ideas in writing, Listen actively, Reflect and evaluate

Warm-up and Review

10–15 minutes (books closed)

Ask students to brainstorm jobs or errands they do every week or every day—for example, make dinner, go grocery shopping, go to work. Write their ideas on the board.

Introduction

5–10 minutes

1. Tell students which of the jobs on the board you have already done or haven't done yet this week (or today). *I haven't made dinner today. I'm going to make it tonight. I've already taken the kids to school. I took them at 8:00 this morning.*

2. State the objective: *Today we're going to learn how to ask questions in the present perfect and how to use* already, ever, *and* yet *to talk about being involved in the community.*

1 Learn *Yes/No* questions with the present perfect

Presentation I

20–25 minutes

 1. Direct students to look at the project report. Ask: *What place is this project report for?*

2. Read the instructions aloud. Ask students to read the conversation silently to find the answer to the question. Call on a volunteer for the answer.

B 1. Demonstrate how to read the grammar chart.

2. Direct students to underline the present-perfect questions in the conversation in 1A. Write the questions on the board.

3. Ask: *Are these questions about the past? Do they state a specific time?* Say: *We use the present perfect to mean before now. We don't use it to say when something happened.*

4. Ask students to identify the two parts of the verb in the questions.

5. Read the chart through sentence by sentence. Then read it again, and have students repeat after you.

6. Assess students' understanding of the chart. Elicit the past participles of the verbs from the warm-up. Then elicit questions with those verbs in the present perfect. Provide your own short answers.

Guided Practice I

15–20 minutes

C Ask students to work individually to complete the questions and answers. Ask volunteers to write the answers on the board.

Multilevel Strategies

For 1C, seat same-level students together.

• **Pre-level** While other students are completing 1C, ask these students to use the chart in 1B to write two questions and two answers. Give them time to copy the answers to 1C after they are written on the board.

Guided Practice II

5–10 minutes

 1. Model the questions and answers with a volunteer. Go over the words in the *Need help?* box.

2. Ask students to practice the questions and answers with their partners using words from the *Need help?* box and their own ideas.

3. Ask volunteers to repeat one of their conversations for the class.

2 Learn present perfect with *ever, already,* and *yet*

Presentation II

20–25 minutes

 1. Introduce the new topic. Now we're going to learn some words that we often use with the present perfect: *ever, yet,* and *already.*

2. Read the question with *ever* in the chart aloud, and write it on the board. Underline *ever.* Say: *When I use* ever, *it means at any time before now—maybe yesterday, maybe last year, maybe twenty years ago. We usually use* ever *in questions. Sometimes we use* ever *in negative statements.* Read the sentence with *haven't ever* aloud, and write it on the board. Ask: *Can you tell me another way to say this sentence?* Write the answer on the board [I have never volunteered before.].

3. Read the question with *already* aloud, and write it on the board. Say: Already *also means before now, but we use it to talk about recent events. When I say* He's already repaired the stove, *I'm referring to a recent event.*

4. Write the question with *yet* on the board. Say: *When I ask a question with* yet, *I want to know if something I expected has happened. When I say* Have you finished yet? *I expect you to have finished or to be finished soon. When I use* yet *with a negative, it means something I expected hasn't happened, but I expect it to.* Write: *I haven't finished yet, but I will soon.*

5. Draw students' attention to the positions of *ever, already,* and *yet* in the sentences and questions.

6. Use the verbs from the warm-up to check comprehension. Write *Have you washed the dishes?* on the board. Ask students whether they would use *ever, already,* or *yet* in this question and where they would put it. [*Ever* isn't likely because almost everyone has washed the dishes at some point in life; *already* and *yet* are both possible, but they take different positions in the sentence.] Practice with more verbs and phrases from the warm-up.

7. Direct students to circle the correct words to complete the sentences. Ask volunteers to read the completed sentences aloud.

Guided Practice I

10–15 minutes

 Ask students to work individually to match the questions and answers. Ask volunteers to read the matching questions and answers aloud. Write the letter-number match on the board.

Multilevel Strategies

Seat same-level students together for 2B.

- **Pre-level** Work with these students to help them recognize the difference between simple past and present perfect. Read each question aloud, and call on a volunteer for the answer. Discuss the tense of each answer.

- **On- and Higher-level** Direct these students to complete 2B and then ask and answer the questions with a partner. Have them write two or three original questions and answers with *ever, already,* and *yet.* Ask volunteers to read their questions and answers to the class.

C Ask students to work individually to rewrite the sentences. Go over the answers as a class.

D Work with a partner. Talk about class activities.

A: *Have you completed exercise C?*
B: *Yes, I have.*
A: *Has Maria written the answers on the board?*
B: *No, she hasn't.*

2 Learn the present perfect with *ever, already,* and *yet*

A Study the chart. Circle the correct word in the sentences below.

Present perfect with *ever, already,* and *yet*	Notes
A: Have you **ever** volunteered at an animal shelter? B: No, I haven't. OR No, I've never volunteered before.	ever = at any time (not ever = never) Use *ever* in Yes/No and information questions and in negative statements.
A: Have you **already** served lunch to the seniors? B: Yes, I have. They've **already** eaten.	already = some time before now Use *already* in questions when you expect a *yes* answer and in affirmative statements.
A: Have you called the clinic **yet**? B: No, I haven't. I haven't found the number **yet**. I'll call tomorrow.	yet = at any time until now Use *yet* in Yes/No questions and in negative statements.

1. We haven't (already /(ever)) used that new copy machine.
2. Have you (yet /(ever)) visited city hall?
3. I haven't signed the paper ((yet)/ ever).
4. Has Sam ((already)/ yet) painted the kitchen?

B Match the questions and the answers. Then practice them with a partner

___d___ 1. Has Maria been to New York yet?   a. No, I haven't ever been there.

___b___ 2. Has George already been to Miami?   b. Yes, he went twice last year.

___c___ 3. Have they ever gone to Russia?   c. No, they plan to go next year.

___a___ 4. Have you ever been to Mexico?   d. No, she's going next week.

C Get the form. Work with your class. Correct the sentences.

1. Marisol hasn't never volunteered.   <u>Marisol hasn't ever volunteered.</u>
2. I haven't done my homework already. I'll do it tonight.   <u>I haven't done my homework yet.</u>
3. Natasha went to the DMV yet. She got her license last week.   <u>Natasha went to the DMV already.</u>
4. Michael has ever been to a job fair. Maybe he'll go next week.   <u>Michael has never been to a job fair. *or* Michael hasn't ever been to a job fair.</u>

3 Grammar listening

Listen and circle the correct answer.

1. **a.** Mark has been to Los Angeles.
   b. Mark has never been to Los Angeles.
2. **a.** He's been to the recreation center three times.
   b. He's taken three classes at the recreation center.
3. a. She has gotten a new dog.
   b. She's planning to get a new dog.
4. a. Toshi has already started working.
   b. Roberto has already started working.
5. **a.** She's never written a letter to the school board.
   b. She wrote three letters to the school board.
6. a. He hasn't been to the job fair.
   b. He's been to the job fair twice.

4 Practice the present perfect

A **Work with a partner. Complete the questions.**

1. Have you ever been to _____? (place in your state)
2. Have you ever read _____? (name of a book)
3. Have you ever visited _____? (name of a community resource)
4. Have you eaten _____ yet today? (a meal you eat every day)
5. Have you spoken* to _____ yet today? (name of a person in your class)

*speak-spoke-spoken

B **Work with another pair. Ask and answer the questions in 4A. Give as much information as possible.**

A: *Have you ever been to Miami?*
B: *No, I haven't. I'd like to go there some day.*
A: *Have you ever read "Romeo and Juliet"?*
B: *Yes, I have. But, I haven't read it in English yet.*

Miami

TEST YOURSELF ✔

Close your book. Write 6 sentences using the information you learned about your classmates. Use the present perfect, *ever*, *already*, and *yet*.
   Yana hasn't ever visited city hall.

3 Grammar listening

Guided Practice II
10–15 minutes

1. Say: *Now we're going to listen to questions and answers in the present perfect. You will hear six different conversations about volunteering and community involvement. Circle the sentence that means the same as what you hear.*

2. Play the audio. Direct students to read along silently without writing.

3. Replay the audio. Ask students to circle the correct answers.

4. Elicit the answer to number 1, and replay the first conversation. Call on volunteers to say the present-perfect sentences they heard. Repeat for numbers 2–6.

4 Practice the present perfect

Communicative Practice and Application
20–25 minutes

A Direct students to work with a partner to complete the questions with their own ideas. Brainstorm several places for number 1 as an example.

B Direct students to ask and answer the questions with a partner. Model the exercise by "joining" one of the pairs and each pair takes a turn asking and answering questions while the class listens.

2. Check comprehension of the exercise. Ask: *Who asks questions?* [everyone] *Who answers questions?* [everyone]

3. Ask volunteers to share something interesting they learned about their classmates.

Multilevel Strategies

After 4B, provide more practice with *ever, yet,* and *already* for all levels.

- **Pre-level** Have these students write two versions of each of these skeleton sentences: *I have already _____ today. I haven't _____ yet this week. Have you ever _____?*

- **On-level** Have these students write one question with *ever, already,* and *yet.* Direct them to ask each other their questions and write their partners' short answers.

- **Higher-level** Have these students write one question with *ever, already,* and *yet.* Direct them to ask one follow-up question for each *Yes/No* question. *When? Where? Why?* Direct them to take notes of their partners' answers.

Have volunteers from each group share their work with the class.

Evaluation
10–15 minutes

TEST YOURSELF

Ask students to write the sentences independently. Collect and correct their writing.

Multilevel Strategies

Target the *Test Yourself* to the level of your students.

- **Pre-level** Provide skeleton sentences for these students to complete. *1. _____ (name) hasn't ever read _____ (book). 2. _____ (name) has been to _____. 3. _____ (name) has visited _____. (name) 4. _____ (name) hasn't _____ yet today.*

- **Higher-level** Have these students write eight sentences about their classmates.

To compress this lesson: Conduct 2A and 2B as whole-class activities.

To extend this lesson: Have students talk about a community event calendar.
1. Provide students with a copy of a current community event calendar—for example, from the local library or from your community's parks and recreation department.
2. Seat students in mixed-level groups. Have the highest-level student in the group ask the rest questions about the calendar using *already* and *yet. Have the pre-school classes started yet?* Direct the rest of the group to answer with short answers.
3. Discuss any events of interest on the calendar.

And/Or have students complete **Workbook 3 pages 32–33, Multilevel Activity Book 3 pages 61–62,** and the corresponding **Unit 5 Exercises** on the **Multilevel Grammar Exercises CD-ROM 3.**

Unit 5 Lesson 4

Objectives	Grammar	Vocabulary	Correlations
On-, Pre-, and Higher-level: Talk about improving the community, and listen for information about recycling	Present perfect versus simple past (*He worked last night. He has worked here for two years.*)	*Petition* For vocabulary support, see this **Oxford Picture Dictionary** topic: Apartments	**CASAS:** 0.1.2, 0.1.5, 2.6.2, 5.6.1, 5.7.1, 6.7.1 **LCPs:** 47.03, 49.02, 49.03, 50.02 **SCANS:** Arithmetic/Mathematics, Listening, Speaking **EFF:** Cooperate with others, Listen actively, Read with understanding, Reflect and evaluate, Speak so others can understand

Warm-up and Review

10–15 minutes (books closed)

Elicit some of the problems in the school and the community that the class talked about in Lesson 2. Write them on the board under the headings *Community* and *School*.

Introduction

5 minutes

1. Say: *In Lesson 2, we practiced writing letters to the school board. Whom do you write to if the problem is in your neighborhood? What if it's in your apartment building?* Tell students that when you write out your request for a change and then ask a lot of other people to sign it, you made a petition.

2. State the objective: *Today we're going to talk about how to improve our community using petitions.*

1 Learn to improve your community

Presentation I

10–20 minutes

 1. Direct students to look at the pictures. Ask: *Is this a school petition?*

2. Play the audio. Give students a minute to answer questions 1 and 2. Go over the answers as a class.

Guided Practice

20–25 minutes

 1. Read the instructions aloud. Play the audio. Ask students to read along silently and listen for the answer to the question. Elicit the answer.

2. Ask students to read the conversation with a partner. Circulate and monitor pronunciation. Model and have students repeat difficult words or phrases.

3. Say and have students repeat the expressions in the *In other words* box. Elicit the placement of the expressions in the conversation. Ask volunteers to read the conversation using expressions from the box.

Communicative Practice and Application

15–20 minutes

 1. Ask students to read the instructions silently. Check their comprehension of the exercise. Ask: *What are the two roles?* Elicit examples of what each neighbor might say.

2. Set a time limit (five minutes). Ask students to act out the role-play in both roles. Ask volunteer pairs to act out their conversations for the class. Tell students who are listening to note whether Partner B signs the petition and why or why not.

Multilevel Strategies

For 1C, adapt the role-play to the level of your students.

• **Pre-level** Provide these students with a simplified role-play. A: *Have you signed the petition for the traffic light yet?* A: *No, I haven't.* B: *We need a traffic light by the school to improve safety.* B: *That's a good idea. Where do I sign?*

1 Learn to improve your community

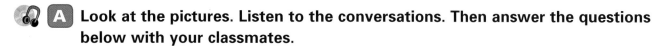

A Look at the pictures. Listen to the conversations. Then answer the questions below with your classmates.

1. What are the apartment residents doing?
2. Do you think the woman will sign the petition?

B Listen and read. **What do the residents want?** They want a security camera in the garage.

A: Hi Anya. Did you go to the residents' meeting Wednesday night? I didn't see you there.

B: No, I didn't, John. I'm sorry. I forgot all about it!

A: That's OK. By the way, have you signed the petition for a security camera yet?

B: No, I haven't. What's it about?

A: The parking garage is dark. We're asking the building owners to put in a security camera.

B: A security camera in the parking garage? That's a great idea. Where do I sign?

> **In other words...**
>
> **Apologizing**
> I'm sorry.
> I'm so sorry.
> I apologize.

C Role-play a conversation between two neighbors with a partner. Use the example in 1B to make a new conversation.

Partner A: Ask your neighbor about the neighborhood meeting last night. Ask if he or she has signed a petition for a traffic light. Explain that the intersection by the school is dangerous. You are asking the city council to put in a traffic light.

Partner B: You had to go to work and didn't go to the neighborhood meeting last night. Ask your neighbor what the petition is about. Say you will or won't sign it, and say why.

☑ Give an opinion on a community or local issue   **67**

2 Review the simple past and the present perfect

A Study the chart. Then circle the correct answers in the sentences below.

The simple past
Don **worked** last night.   He **didn't go** to the meeting.
A: **Did** he **go** to the meeting last month?   B: No, he **didn't**.

The present perfect
Don **has worked** nights for many years.   He **hasn't signed** the petition yet.
A: **Has** he ever **been** to a meeting?   B: No, he **hasn't**.

Note
The simple past tense describes completed actions or situations, often with a specific time reference (*last night, yesterday, in 2001*). The present perfect tense describes past experiences, often without a specific time reference.

1. Has Abdul ever (sign /(signed)) a petition?
2. Did Beth ((sign)/ signed) the petition yesterday?
3. Toshi (didn't go /(hasn't gone)) to the new park yet.
4. Maria (was /(has been)) to that clinic before.

B Work with your classmates. Ask and answer the questions.

1. Have you ever gone to a neighborhood meeting? If so, did you enjoy it?
2. Have you ever been to the DMV? If so, how long did you wait in line?
3. Have you had a wellness checkup since last year? If so, when did you have one?

3 Practice your pronunciation

A Listen to the pronunciation of *y, w,* and *j* in the conversation.

A: Hi Anya. Did you come to the residents meeting Wednesday night?
B: No, I didn't, John.

B Listen and write the missing words.

1. The _____woman_____ volunteers at the senior center.
2. Check the _website_____ for the next _job fair_____.
3. I haven't signed the petition _yet_____.
4. Alex _waited_____ in line for two hours _yesterday_____.
5. We've completed the class _project_____ already.

C Listen again and check. Repeat the sentences in 3B.

2 Review the simple past and the present perfect

Presentation II and Guided Practice

10–15 minutes

A 1. Introduce the new topic. Write a present-perfect and a simple-past sentence on the board. *1. He has signed a lot of petitions. 2. He signed the petition last week.* Ask students to identify the verb, and elicit the tense of each sentence. Ask: *Why is sentence number 2 past tense? In sentence number 1, do we know when he signed petitions?*

2. Read the information and the sample sentences in the chart aloud. Check comprehension of the grammar in the chart. Elicit a question and a short answer for each of the situations written on the board. *Has he signed a lot of petitions? Yes, he has. Did he sign the petition last week? Yes, he did.*

3. Have students work individually to circle the verbs in the sentences below the chart. Go over the answers as a class.

TIP After 2A, have students practice listening for auxiliaries by playing the "flyswatter" game. Write short answers on the board in a large grid. *Yes, he is. Yes, he was. Yes, he does. Yes, he has. Yes, he did. Yes, they have. Yes, they do. Yes, they are. Yes, they were.* Divide the class into two teams, and have them line up at the board. Give the first person in each team a flyswatter. Ask a *Yes/No* question using *he* or *they* as the subject. *Does he live here?* The first person to whack the correct answer earns a point for his/her team. Have the first students on each team pass the flyswatter to the person behind him/her and move to the back of the line. Halfway through the game, erase the board and write up negative short answers in a different order.

Communicative Practice and Application

15–20 minutes

B 1. Model the questions and answers with volunteers.

2. Set a time limit (five minutes). Ask students to practice the questions and answers with several partners. Call on individuals to share their answers with the class.

Multilevel Strategies

Seat mixed-level students together for 2B.

• **Pre-level** Allow these students to focus on answering the questions with short answers rather than asking them.

• **Higher-level** Direct these students to read the questions aloud for their partners and provide complete answers.

3 Practice your pronunciation

Pronunciation Extension

10–15 minutes

1. Write: *Would you like to get some job experience?* on the board. Say the question and ask students to repeat it. Underline *W, y,* and *j.* Say: *Now we're going to focus on the* w, y, *and* j *sounds.*

2. Play the audio. Direct students to listen for the *w, y,* and *j* sounds.

B Play the audio. Have students work individually to write the missing words.

C 1. Play the audio again. Have students check their answers to 3B. Call on volunteers to read the completed sentences aloud.

2. Ask students to take turns reading the sentences in 3B with a partner. Monitor and provide feedback.

4 Focus on listening

Listening Extension

20–25 minutes

A Read the questions aloud, and elicit answers from volunteers. Encourage students to respond to each other's ideas. After one student speaks, ask other students for their opinions. *Do you agree or disagree with what Maria said? Why?*

B 1. Direct students to read the questions and answer choices before they listen to the interview.

2. Play the audio. Ask students to listen and circle the correct answers. Go over the answers as a class.

C 1. Direct students to read the statements before listening. Ask what kind of information they'll be writing in the blanks.

2. Replay the audio and have students work individually to complete the sentences. Go over the answers as a class.

5 Real-life math

Math Extension

5–10 minutes

1. Direct students to look at the graph. Ask what the numbers on the horizontal axis represent. Ask what the numbers on the vertical axis represent.

2. Ask students to work individually to complete the answers. While they are working, copy the graph onto the board.

3. Have volunteers read the completed sentences aloud. Ask them to come to the board and demonstrate the answer using the graph on the board.

Evaluation

10–15 minutes

TEST YOURSELF

1. Model the role-play with a volunteer. Then switch roles.

2. Pair students. Check comprehension of the exercise. Ask: *What does Partner A want? What does Partner B need to do?*

3. Set a time limit (five minutes), and have the partners act out the role-play in both roles.

4. Circulate and monitor. Encourage pantomime and improvisation. Provide feedback.

Multilevel Strategies

Target the *Test Yourself* to the level of your students.

• **Pre-level** Ask students to use this skeleton conversation: *A: Hi. Have you signed the petition for the computers yet? A: No, I haven't. B: We need them so that we can _____. B: That's a good idea. Where do I sign?*

• **Higher-level** Ask these students to practice accepting and rejecting the petition and to practice the role-play with a different idea for a petition.

To compress this lesson: Conduct *Real-life math* as a whole class activity.

To extend this lesson: Have students come up with a petition.
1. Put the students in groups. Tell them to come up with a petition to change something at the school. Ask them to describe what they want in three or four sentences. Direct every group member to copy the sentences at the top of a sheet of notebook paper.
2. When they finish, tell them it's time to collect signatures. Write useful expressions on the board. Direct students to walk around the room telling classmates about their petitions and collecting signatures. Say: *Don't sign the same petition twice!* Assign a time limit (five minutes).
3. Have students return to their groups and add up their signatures. Find out which group got the most signatures.

And/Or have students complete **Workbook 3 page 34** and **Multilevel Activity Book 3 page 63**.

4 Focus on listening

A **Talk about the questions with your class.**

1. Do you recycle glass, newspaper, and cans in your home?
2. Is it convenient or difficult to recycle in your community?

B **Listen to the news interview. Circle the answers.**

1. People in the U.S. have recycled paper, glass, and metal __b__ .
   a. since 1590
   b. for a long time

2. The speaker says we need to recycle because __a__ .
   a. we produce a lot of trash
   b. the population is growing

C **Read the sentences. Then listen again and complete them.**

1. The first paper recycling in the U.S. began in the year ____1690____ .
2. A recycling center was built in New York City in __1897__ .
3. In __1970__ , 6.5 percent of the U.S. population recycled.
4. In 2005, the percentage of people in the U.S. who recycled was __32__ .

5 Real-life math

Use the graph to complete the sentences.

1. About 32 percent of the U.S. population recycled in __2005__ .
2. Recycling increased by 1 percent between 1960 and __1970__ .
3. Recycling increased by __13__ percent between 1980 and 2000.
4. Between 1960 and 2005, recycling increased by __26__ percent.

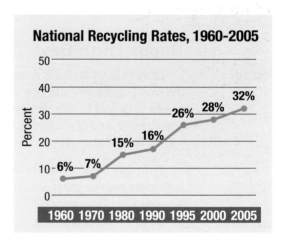

National Recycling Rates, 1960-2005

TEST YOURSELF ✔

Role-play a conversation. Partner A: Ask your partner to sign a petition for new computers at your school. Partner B: Ask for more information and decide if you want to sign it. Then change roles.

1 Get ready to read

A How do you help keep your neighborhood clean?

B Read the definitions.

environment: (noun) the world around you

natural resources: (noun) things produced by the earth that people use

pollution: (noun) things that make the environment dirty or dangerous

litter: (noun) paper, cans, or other trash that is left in a public place

C Look at the definitions in 1B and the picture in 2A. What do you think Earth Day is about? Circle the answer.

a. celebrating the earth's birthday

b. taking care of the earth

c. studying how the earth began

2 Read and respond

A Read the article.

Happy Earth Day!

Every year on April 22nd, people around the world celebrate Earth Day. On that day, people volunteer to pick up litter, clean up the environment, and plan ways to take care of the earth's natural resources.

Earth Day began in 1970 when a group of Americans became upset about pollution in the air and water. They worried that too much of the earth's water and air was unclean, unsafe, and unhealthy. So, they started an event to help people think about creating a cleaner, healthier, and safer earth. Now, over 174 countries around the world and hundreds of millions of people celebrate Earth Day each year.

Here are a few Earth Day success stories from communities around the world.

- **Amelia, Ohio, USA:** 300 volunteers collect more than 700 bags of litter, 46 tires, 1 refrigerator, and over 100 other items from the Ohio River.

- **Toronto, Canada:** hundreds of volunteers plant thousands of trees and bushes[1] in Rouge Park. Volunteers have planted more than 100,000 trees and bushes in the area since 1989.

- **Vera Cruz, Brazil:** a special bus visits 1,500 school students to teach students what they can do today to make the environment healthier for the future.

China's 2005 Earth Day stamp made people think about protecting the environment.

---

[1]**bush:** a plant, smaller than a tree, usually 3–5 feet tall.

Source: *www.earthday.net*

Unit 5 Lesson 5

Objectives	Grammar	Vocabulary	Correlations
On-, Pre-, and Higher-level: Read about and discuss reducing trash and protecting the environment	Adjectives (*Dirty water is unhealthy.*)	*Environment, natural resources, pollution, litter, bush* For vocabulary support, see this **Oxford Picture Dictionary** topic: Energy and Conservation	**CASAS:** 0.1.2, 0.1.3, 5.7.1, 7.2.5, 7.3.1, 7.3.2, 7.4.7 **LCPs:** 47.03, 49.01, 49.04, 49.16, 49.17 **SCANS:** Acquires and evaluates information, Decision making, Interprets and communicates information, Speaking **EFF:** Cooperate with others, Listen actively, Read with understanding

Warm-up and Review

10–15 minutes (books closed)

Draw an "idea map" on the board. Write *Nature* in the center circle. Ask students to brainstorm words they associate with nature. Categorize their words on the board into branches for water, land, plants, and animals.

Introduction

5 minutes

1. Use students' ideas from the warm-up to talk about things that have changed in the last one hundred years.

2. State the objective: *Today we're going to read about and discuss how to protect the environment.*

1 Get ready to read

Presentation

10–20 minutes

A Read the question aloud. Give students time to write their answers. Call on volunteers to share their answers with the class.

B Read the words and definitions. Elicit sample sentences for each word, or supply them if the students can't. Ask students to identify the natural resources that are on the board from the warm-up (water, trees, etc.). Elicit other natural resources. Elicit examples of pollution. Ask students where they have seen "no littering" signs.

Pre-Reading

C Direct students to look at the picture of the stamp in 2A. Read the instructions and ask students to guess the answer. Tell them to read the first paragraph of the article to find the answer.

2 Read and respond

Guided Practice I

20–30 minutes

A 1. Ask students to read the article silently.

2. Direct students to underline unfamiliar words they would like to know. Elicit the words and encourage other students to provide definitions or examples.

3. Check comprehension. Ask: *Where did Earth Day begin?* [the United States] *What were the people who started Earth Day worried about?* [pollution]

Multilevel Strategies

Adapt 2A to the level of your students.

• **Pre-level** Provide these students with a summary of the reading. *Millions of people celebrate Earth Day every year. On that day, people clean the environment and plan ways to take care of the earth. Here are some things people have done on Earth Day: In Ohio, people picked up more than 700 bags of litter from the Ohio River. In Canada, volunteers planted thousands of trees. In Brazil, a special bus visited students to teach them about protecting the environment.*

Direct students to read the summary while other students are reading 2A.

Guided Practice II

10–20 minutes

B 1. Play the audio. Have students read along silently.

2. Elicit and discuss any additional questions about the reading.

> **TIP** Go online or call your community's city hall to find out about Earth Day activities in your area. Share the information with your students.

C Have students work individually to mark the answers T (true), F (false), and NI (no information). Write the answers on the board.

> ### Multilevel Strategies
>
> For 2C, work with pre-level students.
>
> • **Pre-level** Ask these students *Yes/No* and short-answer information questions about their summaries while other students are completing 2C. *How many people celebrate Earth Day?* [millions] *Where did people pick up 700 bags of litter?* [the Ohio River] *Did they plant hundreds of trees in Canada?* [no—thousands] Have these students copy the answers to 2C from the board.

D 1. Read the information in the chart aloud. Elicit and discuss any questions the students have about the meanings of the words or the prefix *un-*. Say the words and have students repeat them.

2. Direct students to work individually to circle the correct word to complete each sentence. Ask volunteers to write the answers on the board.

> **TIP** After 2D, have students look up words beginning with *un-* in their dictionaries. Direct them to scan through the words to find one they already know. Elicit the words and write them on the board. Have the student who supplies the word explain what it means. Elicit a sample sentence for each word, and write it on the board.

3 Talk it over

Communicative Practice

15–20 minutes

A Read the statistics and the questions aloud. Set a time limit (three minutes). Allow students to think about the questions and then write their answers in note form

B Ask volunteers to share their ideas with the class.

Application

5–10 minutes

BRING IT TO LIFE

Ask students to brainstorm about improvements they could make in their neighborhoods. Ask volunteers to share their ideas. Tell everyone to look around their neighborhoods on their way home and come back to class with specific ideas.

To compress this lesson: Conduct the word study in 2D as a whole-class activity.

To extend this lesson: Have students make predictions about the environment.
1. Write several topics related to the environment on the board: *water, air, food production, energy.*
2. Put students into groups. Remind students that during the warm-up they talked about how the environment is today compared to 100 years ago. Tell them that now they're going to think about 100 years in the future. Ask the groups to come up with predictions for each of the topics. Tell them to write sentences with *will. Water in the future will be cleaner/dirtier because [_____].*
3. Have a reporter from each group share the group's ideas with the class.

And/Or have students complete **Workbook 3 page 35** and **Multilevel Activity Book 3 pages 64–65.**

C Mark the statement T (true), F (false), or NI (no information).

__T__ 1. On Earth Day, people try to make a healthier, cleaner earth.

__NI__ 2. Five thousand people participated in the first Earth Day.

__T__ 3. Over 174 countries celebrate Earth Day.

__T__ 4. Volunteers in Canada have planted many trees since 1989.

__T__ 5. In Brazil, students learn how to improve the environment for the future.

D Study the chart. Complete the sentences below.

> **Word Study: The prefix _un-_**
>
> The prefix _un-_ means _not_. Add _un-_ to the beginning of some adjectives to make its meaning negative.
>
> clean–unclean   People want a **clean** environment.
>   **Unclean** air and water can be dangerous.
>
> | healthy | unhealthy | happy | unhappy |
> | safe | unsafe | important | unimportant |

1. Many volunteers work on Earth Day to create a _____clean_____ environment.

2. Some people worry that the earth's water is _unhealthy_ , _unsafe_ and _unclean_ .

3. Earth Day began because people were _unhappy_ about pollution.

4. On Earth Day, it's _important_ to work together to take care of the earth.

3 Talk it over

A Read the statistics. Think about the questions. Make notes about your answers.

1. Where does all that trash go?
2. What are some ways people can produce less trash?

B Talk about your answers with your classmates.

Trash Statistics

The average American throws away 4.4 pounds of trash every day. That means a family of four throws away 6,424 pounds of trash every year.

> **BRING IT TO LIFE**
>
> Look around your neighborhood. Write an idea for an environmental improvement you and your neighbors could make. Talk about your idea with your classmates.

1 Grammar

A **Complete the sentences. Use the present perfect.**

1. I _____haven't been_____ to the new clinic yet. (be)
2. Tom _has worked_____ at the DMV for ten years. (work)
3. The students _haven't done_____ their homework yet. (do)
4. We _have_____ already _written_____ a letter to the school board. (write)

B **Complete the questions and answers. Use the verbs in parentheses.**

1. _Have_____ they ___planted___ the trees? (plant)   Yes, _they have_____.
2. _Has_____ the mayor _finished_____ his speech? (finish)   No, _he, hasn't_____.
3. _Has_____ the celebration _started_____? (start)   Yes, _it has_____.
4. _Have_____ you _seen_____ Ramon? (see)   No, _I haven't_____.
5. _Have_____ you _gone_____ to city hall? (go)   No, _I haven't_____.

C **Complete the sentences with *ever, already,* or *yet*.**

1. Victor hasn't _____ever_____ been to the new movie theater, but he plans to go there this weekend.
2. I haven't seen the new movie _yet_____. I'm going to see it with Victor this weekend.
3. We've _already_____ bought the tickets. We bought them yesterday.
4. Min hasn't _ever_____ gone with us before, but she's going with us tomorrow.
5. She hasn't bought tickets _yet_____. She will buy them in the morning.

D **Complete the sentences with the past or present perfect. Use the verbs in parentheses.**

1. I _____have worked_____ here for two months. Last year, I _____worked_____ in a clinic. (work)
2. Tom _stayed_____ home from work again yesterday. He _has stayed_____ home for three weeks now. (stay)
3. We _have talked_____ many times about Tom's health. We _talked_____ about it yesterday, too. (talk)
4. He _has gone_____ to the clinic several times. Last month I went with him. (go)

Unit 5 Review and expand

Objectives	Grammar	Vocabulary	Correlations
On-, Pre-, and Higher-level: Expand upon and review unit grammar and life skills	Present-perfect questions and answers (*Have they called her yet? No, they haven't.*)	Community and environment For vocabulary support, see this **Oxford Picture Dictionary** topic: Community	**CASAS:** 0.1.2, 0.1.5, 0.2.1, 4.8.1, 5.6.1, 7.3.1, 7.3.2 **LCPs:** 39.01, 47.03, 49.02, 49.03, 49.16, 50.02 **SCANS:** Creative thinking, Participates as member of a team, Reasoning **EFF:** Convey ideas in writing, Listen actively, Read with understanding, Solve problems and make decisions

Warm-up and Review

10–15 minutes (books closed)

1. Review the *Bring It to Life* assignment from Lesson 5.

2. Have students who did the exercise discuss their ideas for community involvement. Have students who didn't come up with an idea decide which is the most urgently needed.

3. Have the class choose one of the ideas and brainstorm a plan for putting it into action.

Introduction and Presentation

5 minutes

1. Write verbs on the board, and elicit the participles: *write, be, start, see, go, meet.*

2. Call on volunteers to say a present-perfect sentence with each of the verbs.

3. Write *ever, yet,* and *already* on the board. Call on volunteers to ask a question with *ever* and make statements with *yet* and *already.* Write those sentences on the board.

4. State the objective: *Today we're going to review the present perfect with ever, yet and already.*

1 Grammar

Guided Practice

40–45 minutes

A Ask students to work individually to complete the sentences. Have them read the answers with a partner when they finish. Write the answers on the board.

B Have students work with their partners to complete the questions and answers. Direct them to read the questions and answers aloud to each other. Go over answers with the class.

C Have students work individually to complete the sentences with *ever, already,* or *yet.* Have volunteers write the answers on the board. Go over the answers with the class.

D Direct students to work individually to complete the sentences with the verbs in the correct tense. Ask volunteers to write the completed sentences on the board. Go over the answers with the class.

Multilevel Strategies

For 1C and 1D, seat same-level students together.

• **Pre-level** Go through exercise 1C with these students. Read each sentence aloud, and elicit an answer from the group. Allow them to copy the answers from 1D into their books after they are written on the board.

• **On- and Higher-level** While you are working with pre-level students, ask these students to complete 1C and 1D, and write an additional sentence pair like the ones in 1D—one in the simple past and one in the present perfect. Ask volunteers to write their sentences on the board. Correct them together.

2 Group work

Communicative Practice

25–30 minutes

 1. Direct students, in groups of three to four, to focus on the picture. Ask where the people are and what each person is doing.

2. Group students and assign roles: leader, recorder, reporter, and timekeeper. Explain that students work with their groups to write the paragraph.

3. Check comprehension of the roles. Ask: *Who writes the paragraph?* [recorder] *Who will read the paragraph to the class?* [reporter] *Who helps everyone and manages the group?* [leader] *Who tells the group how much time has passed?* [timekeeper] *Who creates the paragraph?* [everyone]

4. Set a time limit (five minutes) to complete the exercise. Circulate and answer any questions.

5. Have a reporter from each group read the group's paragraph to the class.

Multilevel Strategies

For 2A, use mixed-level groups.

- **Pre-level** Assign these students the role of timekeeper.
- **On-level** Assign these students the role of recorder or reporter.
- **Higher-level** Assign these students the role of leader.

B 1. Have students walk around the room to conduct the interviews. To get students moving, tell them to interview four people who were not in their group for 2A.

2. Set a time limit (five minutes) to complete the exercise.

3. Tell students to make a note of their classmates' answers but not to worry about writing complete sentences.

Multilevel Strategies

Adapt the mixer in 2B to the level of your students.

- **Pre-level** Allow these students to skip the *Why?* column.
- **Higher-level** Have these students ask an additional question and write all answers.

C Call on individuals to report what they learned about their classmates. Encourage students to make generalizations. *Most people have helped some neighbors. No one has met the mayor.*

PROBLEM SOLVING

10–15 minutes

A 1. Ask: *Have you ever volunteered somewhere?* Tell students they will read a story about a woman who just moved into a new neighborhood and wants to volunteer. Direct students to read Paulina's story silently.

2. Ask: How long has Paulina lived in Lake City? Why does she want to volunteer?

3. Play the audio and have students read along silently.

B 1. Elicit answers to question 1. Come to a class consensus on the answer.

2. As a class, brainstorm places Paulina might go to answer question 2. Ask students if they know where to find these places in your area.

Evaluation

10–15 minutes

To test students' understanding of the unit grammar and life skills, have them take the Unit 5 Test in the Step Forward Test Generator CD-ROM with ExamView® Assessment Suite.

Learning Log

To help students record and discuss their progress, use the *Learning Log* on page T–201.

To extend this review: Have students complete **Workbook 3 page 36, Multilevel Activity Book 3 page 66,** and the **Unit 5 Exercises** on the **Multilevel Grammar Exercises CD-ROM 3.**

2 Group work

A Work with 2–3 classmates. Write a paragraph about the picture. Share your paragraph with the class.

Every year in April, the people in my neighborhood celebrate Community Clean-Up Day…

B Interview 3 classmates. Write their answers.

1. Have you ever helped with a neighborhood project? What was it?
2. Have you ever seen a problem in your neighborhood? What did you see?
3. Have you ever gone to a town or neighborhood meeting? Why or why not?

C Talk about the answers with your class.

PROBLEM SOLVING

A Listen and read about Paulina.

    Paulina has lived in Lake City for two weeks. She wants to get involved in the community. She hasn't met many people yet. She hasn't had time to learn much about the city yet. She hasn't ever volunteered for community work before, but she thinks it might be a good opportunity to meet some nice people. Unfortunately, Paulina doesn't know where to begin. She doesn't know how or where to volunteer.

B Work with your classmates. Answer the questions.

1. What is Paulina's problem? Paulina wants to get involved in the community, but she doesn't know how.
2. What can Paulina do? Make a list of places she can go or call to get involved.
   Answers will vary.

UNIT 6

FOCUS ON
• food preparation
• recipes
• phrasal verbs
• restaurant service and tipping
• food safety

What's Cooking?

LESSON 1 | **Vocabulary**

1 Learn kitchen vocabulary

A Talk about the questions with your class.

1. Do you like to cook? Why or why not?
2. Has anyone in your family ever worked in a restaurant kitchen?

B Work with your classmates. Match the words with the picture.

_6_	boil	_11_	fork	_4_	pan	_2_	pour
_7_	bowl	_9_	glass	_8_	plate	_12_	spoon
_1_	chop	_10_	knife	_5_	pot	_3_	stir

C Listen and check. Then read the new words with a partner.

D Work with a partner. Write other kitchen words you know. Check your words in a dictionary.

☑ Identify kitchen items and actions

Unit 6 Lesson 1

Objectives	Grammar	Vocabulary	Correlations
On-level: Identify things in the kitchen, and describe kitchen activities **Pre-level:** Identify things in the kitchen and kitchen activities **Higher-level:** Talk and write about the kitchen using words for utensils, foods, and cooking	Imperative (*Peel the vegetables.*)	Kitchen utensils, food items, and cooking For vocabulary support, see these **Oxford Picture Dictionary** topics: Food Preparation and Safety	**CASAS:** 0.1.2, 0.1.5, 0.2.1, 4.8.1, 7.4.5, 8.2.1 **LCPs:** 39.01, 49.02, 49.03, 49.10, 50.02, 50.08 **SCANS:** Participates as member of a team, Seeing things in the mind's eye **EFF:** Cooperate with others, Listen actively, Read with understanding, Reflect and evaluate, Speak so others can understand

Warm-up and Review

10–15 minutes (books closed)

Write *Vegetables* on the board. Have students come to the board and take turns writing the name of a vegetable. Allow them to help each other, but have a different student write each word. When the class runs out of ideas or you have at least ten words on the board, pronounce the words together and elicit any questions.

Introduction

5 minutes

1. Call on individuals and ask if they eat one of the foods on the board. Ask how often they eat it and whether or not they cook it.

2. State the objective: *Today we're going to learn words for cooking.*

1 Learn kitchen vocabulary

Presentation I

20–25 minutes

A Write *Cooking* on the board, and elicit students' answers to questions 1 and 2. Ask follow-up questions. *Does everyone in your family cook, or does one person do all the cooking? Do you cook breakfast and lunch, or just dinner?*

B 1. Direct students to look at the picture. Ask: *Where is this kitchen?*

2. Group students and assign roles: leader, fact checker, recorder, and reporter. Explain that students work with their groups to match the words and pictures.

3. Check comprehension of the roles. Ask: *Who looks up the words in a dictionary?* [fact checker] *Who writes the numbers in the book?* [recorder] *Who tells the class your answers?* [reporter] *Who helps everyone and manages the group?* [leader]

4. Set a time limit (three minutes). As students work together, copy the wordlist onto the board.

5. Call "time." Have reporters take turns giving their answers. Write each group's answer on the board next to the word.

C 1. To prepare students for listening, say: *Now we're going to hear sentences using the words from 1B. As you listen, look at the picture and check your answers.*

2. Have students check the wordlist on the board and then write the correct numbers in their books.

3. Pair students. Set a time limit (three minutes). Monitor pair practice to identify pronunciation issues.

4. Call "time" and work with the pronunciation of any troublesome words or phrases.

D 1. Ask students to work with a partner to brainstorm a list of related words.

2. Elicit words from the class. Write them on the board. Ask students to copy them into their vocabulary notes for the unit.

Guided Practice II

5–10 minutes

 E 1. Model the conversation with a volunteer. Model it again using other information from 1B.

2. Set a time limit (three minutes). Direct students to practice with a partner.

3. Ask volunteers to repeat one of their conversations for the class.

2 Learn more kitchen vocabulary

Presentation II

15–20 minutes

 A 1. Direct students to look at the pictures. Introduce the new topic. *Now we're going to learn more words for cooking.*

2. Say and have students repeat each of the words. After each word, elicit other foods or items that one can peel, steam, grate, etc.

3. Ask students about their cooking habits. *How do you cook broccoli?*

Guided Practice

10–15 minutes

 B 1. Read the information in the *Need help?* box aloud. Provide this example, being sure to stress the *–er* ending: *I teach, so I am a teacher.* Hold up a stapler. *What's this? What does it do?* [staple] *Point to the pencil sharpener. What does that do?* [sharpen] *What is it?*

2. Have students work individually to complete the sentences. Ask volunteers to read the completed sentences aloud.

Communicative Practice and Application

10–15 minutes

 C 1. Give students time to make notes of their answers to the questions. Call on individuals to share their ideas with the class.

2. Write their "best tools" on the board. Have the class vote on the top five and then rank them in order of usefulness.

Evaluation

10–15 minutes (books closed)

TEST YOURSELF

1. Make a two-column chart on the board with the headings *Kitchen Activities* and *Things in the Kitchen*. Have students close their books and give you an example for each column. Tell them that *Things in the Kitchen* can be food items or utensils.

2. Have students copy the chart into their notebooks.

3. Give students five to ten minutes to test themselves by writing the words they recall from the lesson.

4. Call "time" and have students check their spelling in a dictionary. Circulate and monitor students' progress.

5. Direct students to share their work with a partner and add additional words to their charts.

> ### Multilevel Strategies
>
> Target the *Test Yourself* to the level of your students.
>
> • **Higher-level** Have these students complete the chart and then write sentences with three words from each column.

To compress this lesson: Conduct 1B as a whole-class activity.

To extend this lesson: Learn more words for utensils.
1. Direct students to look at pictures of kitchen utensils in *The Oxford Picture Dictionary* or another picture dictionary. Ask them to make one list of utensils they have and another of utensils they don't have but want.
2. Elicit items from their "don't have but want" list. Ask students if there are any utensils in their kitchens that they never use.

And/Or have students complete **Workbook 3 page 37** and **Multilevel Activity Book 3 pages 68–69**.

E **Work with a partner. Practice the conversation. Use the picture in 1B.**

A: *Where are the plates?*
B: *They're in the sink.*

2 Learn more kitchen vocabulary

A **Look at the pictures. Name the foods and actions you see.**

peel   carrot

steam   broccoli / vegetables

beat   eggs

grate   cheese

mix   milk and sugar

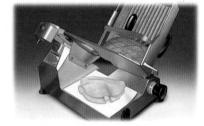
slice   ham

B **Underline the verbs in the sentences below. Then change the verbs to nouns and complete the sentences.**

1. <u>Peel</u> the carrots with a vegetable ___peeler___.
2. Steam the vegetables in a ___steamer___.
3. Beat the eggs with a ___beater___.
4. Grate the cheese with a cheese ___grater___.
5. Mix the ingredients with a ___mixer___.
6. Slice the ham with a knife or a ___slicer___.

> **Need help?**
>
> Add -r or -er to the end of some verbs to change them to nouns.
> *Peel + er = peeler*
> Use the peeler to peel the carrots.

C **Talk about the questions with your class.**

1. Which foods do you slice? Which foods do you peel?
2. How do you prepare vegetables at home?
3. What is the most useful tool in the kitchen? Why?

TEST YOURSELF ✔

Close your book. Categorize the new words in 2 lists: *Kitchen Activities* and *Things in the Kitchen*. Check your spelling in a dictionary. Compare your lists with a partner.

1 Read about a family recipe

A **Look at the picture. Talk about the questions with your class.**

1. Who usually prepares meals in your family?
2. What are some of your family's favorite foods?

B **Listen and read the story about a family recipe.**

> **My Favorite Dish**
>
> When I was a child in El Salvador, my grandfather was the best cook in the family. On Sundays, he cooked a big meal for everyone. I usually helped him. In the morning, we picked up ingredients from the market. At home, Papi cooked and I put away the groceries and cleaned up the kitchen.
>
> Papi's chicken and rice was my favorite dish. It was sweet, sour, and spicy all at the same time. First, he cooked the chicken with onions, garlic, and a few chilies to make the chicken spicy. Then he chopped up tomatoes and vegetables and stirred everything together. He put in a tablespoon of lemon juice to make it a little sour. He added the last ingredient, fruit juice, to make it sweet. Then he mixed everything together. Finally, he poured everything over the rice. The fruit juice was his secret ingredient. He never forgot it. Sorry, I can't tell you what kind or how much. It's a family secret.

Writer's note

This story has two paragraphs.
A paragraph is two or more sentences about an idea or topic. Indent the first word of each paragraph.

C **Check your understanding. Complete Papi's recipe.**

Cook the ___chicken___ with the ___onions___ , ___garlic___ , and ___a few chilies___ .
             1   2   3   4
Chop up the ___tomatoes___ and vegetables. Put in a tablespoon of ___lemon___ juice and
              5   6
some fruit juice. ___Mix___ everything together. Pour everything over ___the rice___ .
                    7   8

✔ Describe how to prepare a favorite recipe

Unit 6 Lesson 2

Objectives	Grammar	Vocabulary	Correlations
On- and Higher-level: Analyze, write, and edit a story about a favorite recipe **Pre-level:** Read and write about a favorite recipe	Past tense (*He cooked a big meal for everyone.*)	Cooking, ingredients, and food words For vocabulary support, see this **Oxford Picture Dictionary** unit: Food	**CASAS:** 0.1.2, 0.2.1, 2.7.2, 8.2.1 **LCPs:** 39.01, 49.02, 49.03, 49.14, 49.16 **SCANS:** Interprets and communicates, Listening, Writing **EFF:** Convey ideas in writing, Cooperate with others, Listen actively, Read with understanding, Reflect and evaluate, Speak so others can understand

Warm-up and Review

10–15 minutes (books closed)

Review cooking words. Write cooking directions for particular food items on slips of paper, and pass them out to volunteers. Have students use gestures and/or draw on the board to help the class guess what is on their slips. Ask the class member who guesses correctly to write the words on the board. Possible cooking directions: *Peel a carrot, steam broccoli, grate cheese, mix cookie dough, slice an onion, chop a tomato, pour a cup of tea.*

Introduction

5 minutes

1. Say: *In Lesson 1, we talked about cooking. Today we're going to talk about recipes.* Write *recipe* on the board, and elicit a definition or an example from a student. Have students repeat the word. Elicit the number of syllables. (You may need to distinguish *recipe* from *receipt*.)

2. State the objective: *Today we're going to read and write about our favorite recipes.*

1 Read about a family recipe

Presentation

20–25 minutes

A Elicit answers to questions 1 and 2. Write some of the students' favorite foods on the board. If your students are from different countries, ask them to briefly describe their favorite dishes, so other students know what they are.

B 1. Direct students to look at the picture. Ask: *Is this a recent picture or an old picture?*

2. Introduce the reading. Ask: *When you were a child, who was the best cook in the house?* Read the title of the story. Point out that *dish* can mean prepared food as well as a plate, bowl, etc.

3. Direct students to read the story silently. Check comprehension. Ask: *Who was the best cook in the writer's family?* [Papi] *What did the writer and Papi do together?* [cooked a big meal on Sundays]

4. Play the audio. Have students read along silently.

5. Draw students' attention to the *Writer's note.* Ask students to tell you the topic of each paragraph.

Guided Practice I

10 minutes

C Have students work independently to complete the recipe. Ask volunteers to write the answers on the board.

Multilevel Strategies

Seat pre-level students together for 1C.

• **Pre-level** While other students are working on 1C, ask these students Yes/No and Or questions about the reading. *Was the writer's grandfather or grandmother the best cook in the house? Did the writer help him? Was his favorite dish chicken soup? Is the secret ingredient fruit juice?* Allow these students to copy the answers to 1C from the board.

2 Write about a family recipe

Guided Practice II

20–25 minutes

A Read the questions. Elicit students' answers. Write the meals and the special occasions on the board so that students can refer to them as they write.

B 1. Direct students to look back at the model story in 1B. Ask them to read quickly through the story and call out the verbs. Write the words on the board, and elicit the tense. Remind them to use the past tense in their stories.

2. Read the questions for each paragraph aloud. Call on volunteers to answer.

3. Check comprehension of the exercise. Ask: *How many paragraphs are you going to write? Do you need to write the questions? What is the purpose of the questions?*

4. Have students write their paragraphs individually.

> ### Multilevel Strategies
>
> Adapt 2B to the level of your students.
>
> • **Pre-level** Provide these students with a skeleton paragraph to complete. *The best cook in my family was _____. My favorite dish of his/hers was _____. The ingredients were _____.*

C Lead students through the process of using the *Editing checklist*. Read each sentence aloud, and ask students to check their papers before moving onto the next item. Allow students a few minutes to edit their writing as necessary.

Communicative Practice

10 minutes

D 1. Read the instructions aloud. Emphasize to students that they are responding to their partners' work, not correcting it.

2. Use the story in 1B to model the exercise. *I think the part about how the writer helped his/her grandfather is interesting. I'd like to ask the writer if he/she still makes this dish and if it still tastes as good.*

3. Direct students to exchange papers with a partner and follow the instructions. Call on volunteers to share what they found interesting in their partners' stories.

> **TIP**
>
> After students have written and spoken about their favorite recipes, have them look up the recipes on the Internet. Tell students to type the names of the dishes and the word *recipe* into a search engine. Have them print out the recipes they find. Ask them to look for any differences between the online recipe ingredients and instructions and those of their families.
>
> If you don't have Internet access in class, elicit the names of several dishes that your students make at home. Bring in recipes for those dishes, and have students compare them with their family recipes.

Application and Evaluation

15 minutes

TEST YOURSELF

1. Review the instructions aloud. Assign a time limit (ten minutes), and have students work independently.

2. Before collecting students' work, remind them to use the *Editing checklist*. Collect and correct students' writing.

> ### Multilevel Strategies
>
> Adapt the *Test Yourself* to the level of your students.
>
> • **Pre-level** Write questions for these students to answer. *Who was the best cook in your partner's family? When did this person cook special meals? Did your partner help?*

To compress this lesson: Assign the *Test Yourself* for homework.

To extend this lesson: Have students practice giving recipe directions. Review cooking verbs and write them on the board. Pair students. Tell Partner A to give instructions about how to cook something. Tell Partner B to pantomime these instructions. (You can simplify this by providing Partner A with a recipe to read aloud.) Circulate and monitor. Provide feedback as needed.

And/Or have students complete **Workbook 3 page 38** and **Multilevel Activity Book 3 page 70**.

2 Write about a family recipe

A **Talk about the questions with your class.**

1. What were your favorite foods when you were a child?
2. When did your family have special meals?

B **Write about a family recipe. Use the model in 1B
and the questions below to help you.** Answers will vary.

Paragraph 1: Who was the best cook in your family when you were a child?
When did this person cook special meals?
Did you help the person cook? How? If not, what did you do?

Paragraph 2: What was your favorite food that he or she cooked?
How did the person prepare the food? (List three important ingredients.)
Was there a secret ingredient? If so, what was it?

My Favorite Dish
When I was a child the best
cook in my family was...

C **Use the checklist to edit your writing. Check (✔) the true sentences.** Answers will vary.

Editing checklist	
1. I wrote about a favorite family recipe.	
2. I listed three or more ingredients and how to prepare them.	
3. My story has two paragraphs.	
4. I indented the first word of each paragraph.	

D **Exchange stories with a partner. Read and comment
on your partner's work.**

1. Point out one sentence that you think is very interesting.
2. Ask your partner a question about his or her favorite dish.

TEST YOURSELF ✔

Work with a new partner. Listen to the first paragraph of your partner's story.
Then use your own words to write the story you heard.

Adolfo's mother was the best cook in his family. On Friday nights, she cooked...

1 Learn separable phrasal verbs

A **Read the story. What ingredient did Joel and Ming forget?**

Joel and Ming have been classmates since September. They decided to make a cake together at Ming's house for their class party. Joel <u>wrote down</u> a recipe. Ming <u>put in</u> the eggs, flour, and milk. She mixed the ingredients well. Joel <u>turned on</u> the oven and <u>put</u> the cake <u>in</u>. They waited patiently. When they opened the oven and <u>took out</u> the cake, it looked great. They brought the cake to the party and everyone tasted it. Everyone <u>figured out</u> the mistake right away. The cake was missing an important ingredient.

B **Study the chart. Underline the 6 phrasal verbs in the story above.**

Separable phrasal verbs	
She **put in** the eggs.	They **figured out** the mistake.
She **put** the eggs **in**.	They **figured** the mistake **out**.
She **put** them **in**.	They **figured** it **out**.

Notes
• Phrasal verbs are verbs + short words (*put in, figure out, write down*).
• Many phrasal verbs are separable. They can be separated by other words in the sentence.
• Other separable verbs are: *write down, turn on, turn off, take out, leave out, pick up*.

C **Separate the phrasal verbs to write the sentences another way. Use the pronouns *it* or *them* for the underlined words.**

1. Mia wrote down <u>the recipe</u>.   <u>She wrote it down.</u>
2. She picked up <u>the ingredients</u> at the store.   <u>She picked them up.</u>
3. She put in <u>the flour</u>.   <u>She put it in.</u>
4. She always leaves out <u>the salt</u>.   <u>She leaves it out.</u>
5. She turned off <u>the oven</u>.   <u>She turned it off.</u>
6. She took out <u>the cake</u>.   <u>She took it out.</u>

Unit 6 Lesson 3

Objectives	Grammar	Vocabulary	Correlations
On- and Higher-level: Use phrasal verbs to talk about food and cooking and listen for meaning in statements with phrasal verbs **Pre-level:** Recognize and use phrasal verbs to write sentences	Phrasal verbs (*She put the eggs in the bowl.*)	*put in, figure out, write down, turn on, turn off, pick up, leave out, look for, come over, get on, get off, look after* For vocabulary support, see this **Oxford Picture Dictionary** topic: Weights and Measurement, Food Preparation and Safety	**CASAS:** 0.1.2, 1.1.1 **LCPs:** 49.01, 49.02, 49.09, 49.16, 49.17, 50.02 **SCANS:** Acquires and evaluates information, Interprets and communicates information **EFF:** Convey ideas in writing, Cooperate with others, Listen actively, Read with understanding, Reflect and evaluate

Warm-up and Review

10–15 minutes (books closed)

Play a "noun-verb" game with a light ball or a wadded-up piece of paper. Name a food as you toss the ball to someone. That person needs to add a cooking verb. For example: if you say *onion*, the student can say *chop the onion* or *fry the onion*. The student with the ball now names another food and tosses the ball to someone else. The rules of the game are: 1. The words must go together (not *pour the onion*). 2. No food or cooking words should be repeated.

Introduction

5–10 minutes

1. Say: *When I'm cooking, I chop up the vegetables, turn on the stove, and put away the dishes.* Chop up, turn on, *and* put away *are two-word verbs called phrasal verbs.*

2. State the objective: *Today we're going to use phrasal verbs to talk about cooking and other activities.*

1 Learn separable phrasal verbs

Presentation I

20–25 minutes

 1. Direct students to look at the picture. Ask: *What are they eating? Do they like it?*

2. Read the question. Ask students to read the story silently to find the answer. Call on a volunteer for the answer.

B 1. Read the sentences in the grammar chart aloud. Read the *Notes* at the bottom of the chart.

2. Direct students to underline the phrasal verbs in the story in 1A. Go over the answers as a class.

3. Read the chart through sentence by sentence. Then read it again, and have students repeat after you.

4. Assess students' understanding of the chart. Write *sugar* on the board. Say: *Can I say* They left out the sugar? *Can I say* They left the sugar out? Write those sentences on the board. Ask: *What if I want to use the pronoun* it? *Where can I use* it? Write: *They left it out.* Say one of the verbs in the bottom row of the chart and a noun. *Write down—message.* Elicit three sentences. *He wrote down a message. He wrote a message down. He wrote it down.* Repeat with each of the verbs in the bottom row of the chart.

Guided Practice I

15–20 minutes

C Ask students to work individually to rewrite the sentences. Ask volunteers to write the new sentences on the board. Go over the answers with the class.

Multilevel Strategies

For 1C, seat same-level students together.

• **Pre-level** While other students are completing 1C, ask these students to copy the phrasal verbs from 1B into their notebooks. Give them time to copy the answers to 1C after they are written on the board.

2 Learn inseparable phrasal verbs

Presentation II
20–25 minutes

 1. Introduce the new topic: *When I use the phrasal verb* turn on, *I can put the noun between the two words or at the end. For example:* I turn on the oven. I turn the oven on. *But some phrasal verbs are inseparable. I can't put any words between the verb and the preposition.*

2. Read the sentences in the chart aloud. Read the *Notes* section of the chart. Say and have students repeat the verbs listed there.

3. Direct students to look at the pictures. Ask a question about each picture. *What is he/she doing? He/She's getting on the bus.*

4. Have students work individually to complete the sentences. Go over the answers as a class.

TIP

> Write verbs on one side of the board: *pick, turn, put, leave, look, come, write, figure, get.* Write prepositions on the other side of the board: *in, on, off, after, up, over, out, down.* Call on volunteers to say a sentence combining two of the words to make a phrasal verb. As they say each verb, write it on the board. Continue until all of the combinations have been exhausted.

 Say the words in the box, and have students repeat. Have students work individually to complete the conversation. Ask volunteers to read the completed conversation aloud.

Multilevel Strategies

After 2B , provide more practice with phrasal verbs. Adapt the practice to the level of your students. Group same-level students together, and provide each group with a sheet of butcher paper.

- **Pre-level** Tell these students to work together to write sentences with as many of the phrasal verbs from pages 78 and 79 as they can.

- **On-level** Tell these students to use five phrasal verbs from pages 78 and/or 79 in a story. Tell them that they will need to write more than five sentences so that their stories make sense and are not just a list of sentences.

- **Higher-level** Give these students the same instructions as the on-level students, but tell them to incorporate eight phrasal verbs into their stories.

Have all groups post their papers on the wall when they finish. Ask a reporter from each group to read the group's writing aloud.

2 Learn inseparable phrasal verbs

A Study the chart. Look at the pictures. Then complete the sentences with an inseparable phrasal verb.

Inseparable phrasal verbs	
I **looked for** the recipe.	Joel **came over** to my house.
I **looked for** it.	Joel **came over** there.

Notes

- Some phrasal verbs are inseparable. They cannot be separated.
  *I **looked** the recipe **for**. (INCORRECT)
  I looked for the recipe.
- Other inseparable verbs are: *get on, get off, come over, look after*.

get on   get off   look after   get over

1. When you <u> get on   </u> the bus, give the money to the driver.

2. I <u> look after   </u> my baby brother from 4:00–5:00 every day.

3. When the doors open, stand up and <u> get off   </u> the train.

4. When did Ali <u> get over   </u> his cold?

B Complete the conversation. Use the words in the box.

look for   get off   get on   ~~come over~~

A: Do you want to <u> come over </u> to my house for dinner?

B: Sure. How do I get there?

A: You live on 1st Street, so <u> get on   </u> the #5 bus. <u> Get off   </u> at the 12th Street stop. <u> Look for   </u> my house across the street. It's the only blue house on the street.

3 Grammar listening

Listen to the sentences. Which sentence is true? Circle *a* or *b*.

1. (a.) She is sick.
   b. She doesn't like winter.

2. a. He wants a salad with onions.
   (b.) He doesn't want any onions.

3. a. She is looking for the trash.
   (b.) She is going to put the trash outside.

4. (a.) He's looking for a piece of paper.
   b. He's looking in the phone book.

5. a. She is going to her friends' home.
   (b.) Her friends are coming to her home.

6. a. He stayed on the bus.
   (b.) He did not stay on the bus.

4 Practice phrasal verbs

A **Think about a dish you can make. How do you prepare it? Write the steps.**

B **Work with 2 partners. Follow the directions. Then change roles.**

Partner A: Explain to your classmates how to cook a dish.
                    Use as many of the verbs in the list as you can.
Partners B and C: Check (✔) the verbs in the list that you hear.

Phrasal verb list	Partner A's recipe	Partner B's recipe	Partner C's recipe
put in			
chop up			
leave out			
turn on			
turn off			
take out			

C **Work with another group. Tell them about one of the recipes.**

TEST YOURSELF ✔

Write 3 sentences about one or more of the recipes you discussed above.
Use a phrasal verb in each sentence.
For Julio's scrambled eggs, chop up one onion and put it in the eggs.

3 Grammar listening

Guided Practice II

10–15 minutes

1. Say: *Now we're going to listen to people using phrasal verbs in conversation.*

2. Play the audio. Direct students to listen silently without writing.

3. Replay the audio. Ask students to circle the correct answers.

4. Call on volunteers for the answers.

> Have students listen to 3A again. Ask them to take notes about each conversation. Put them in pairs. Assign each pair one of the conversations (1–6). Have students in each pair work together to reconstruct the conversation for their number. Tell them that the rules are 1. Write a conversation that expresses the same idea as the original. 2. Use the phrasal verb. It's not important that their sentences be exactly the same as the ones they heard. Replay the audio, so pairs can focus on their assigned numbers. Have volunteers read their conversations aloud.

4 Practice phrasal verbs

Communicative Practice and Application

20–25 minutes

A 1. Group students and have them discuss dishes they can make. Tell them to write the steps they take to prepare them. Ask for a volunteer, and write the recipe on the board.

B 1. Direct students to look at the chart. Elicit any questions about the verbs. Copy the chart onto the board.

2. Put students in groups of three. Read the instructions aloud. Model the exercise. Call on volunteers to be Partner A and Partner B. Play the role of Partner C, and check off the verbs on the chart.

3. Check comprehension of the exercise. Ask: *Who is Partner A? What are you going to do?*

4. Direct students to switch roles until all three students have played all three roles.

C 1. Provide each student with a letter: *A, B,* or *C* (see p. T-199) that corresponds to their individual roles, and ask them to form a new group with students who have the same letter.

2. Have students tell their new groups about one of the recipes they heard from their original groups.

3. Call on volunteers to share which recipes they thought sounded most delicious.

Evaluation

10–15 minutes

TEST YOURSELF

Ask students to write the sentences independently. Collect and correct their writing.

> ### Multilevel Strategies
>
> Target the *Test Yourself* to the level of your students.
>
> • **Pre-level** Ask these students to write three sentences using their charts from 4B. *Put in the eggs. Chop up the nuts. Turn on the oven.*
>
> • **Higher-level** Have these students write about three of the recipes they discussed.

To compress this lesson: Conduct 1C as a whole-class activity.

To extend this lesson: Provide more practice with the phrasal verbs.
1. Write all of the phrasal verbs from this unit on cards or slips of paper. Make enough slips so that each student in the class can have one.
2. Distribute the phrasal verbs. Direct the students to think of a question using the phrasal verbs. Elicit some sample questions.
3. Have the students stand up and find a partner from another part of the room. Tell them to take turns asking and answering their questions. Then have them switch papers and find a new partner. They can invent a new question or use the one their first partner asked them.
4. Participate in the game, and provide feedback.

And/Or have students complete **Workbook 3 pages 39–40, Multilevel Activity Book 3 pages 71–72,** and the corresponding **Unit 6 Exercises** on the **Multilevel Grammar Exercises CD-ROM 3.**

Unit 6 Lesson 4

Objectives	Grammar	Vocabulary	Correlations
On-, Pre-, and Higher-level: Describe a meal, figure out a tip, and listen for information about a restaurant order	Possessive pronouns (*How was yours?*)	*Spicy, sour, sweet, salty* For vocabulary support, see this **Oxford Picture Dictionary** topic: Food Preparation and Safety, A Restaurant	**CASAS:** 0.1.2, 1.6.4, 2.6.4, 6.0.3, 6.0.4, 6.2.3 **LCPs:** 39.01, 45.03, 49.02, 49.09, 49.16, 49.17, 50.04 **SCANS:** Arithmetic/Mathematics, Interprets and communicates information **EFF:** Cooperate with others, Use math to solve problems and communicate, Reflect and evaluate

Warm-up and Review

10–15 minutes (books closed)

Ask students what they like to order when they go to a restaurant. Tell them about your favorite restaurant and what you like to eat there.

Introduction

5 minutes

1. Say: *Sometimes when we order in a restaurant, we want to ask for more information about the food.*

2. State the objective: *Today we're going to learn how to order a meal, ask for information in a restaurant, and use possessive pronouns to talk about meals.*

1 Learn to order a meal

Presentation I

15–20 minutes

A 1. Direct students to look at the pictures. Ask questions about the food. *What foods are they thinking about?*

2. Play the audio. Direct students to ask and answer the questions with a partner. Call on volunteers for the answers.

Guided Practice

20–25 minutes

B 1. Read the instructions aloud. Play the audio. Ask students to read along silently and listen for the answer to the question. Elicit the answer.

2. Read the idiom note. Point out that people also say: *I'm watching my diet* or *weight*.

3. Ask students to read the conversation with a partner. Circulate and monitor pronunciation. Model and have students repeat difficult words or phrases.

Communicative Practice and Application

15–20 minutes

C 1. Ask students to read the instructions silently. Check their comprehension of the exercise. Ask: *What are the two roles?* Elicit examples of what each person might say.

2. Set a time limit (five minutes). Ask students to act out the role-play in both roles. Ask one to three volunteer pairs to act out their conversations for the class. Tell students who are listening to note something they like about each performance.

Multilevel Strategies

For 1C, adapt the role-play to the level of your students.

• **Pre-level** Provide a simplified conversation for these students to practice. *A: Excuse me, what is a chili dog? B: It's a hot dog with a spicy meat sauce. A: Is the vegetable soup salty? B: No, they're not too salty. A: Good. I'm trying to cut down on my salt.*

• **Higher-level** Ask these students to practice the role-play once as written and another time using a dish of their choice.

1 Learn to order a meal

A **Look at the pictures and listen to the conversations. Then answer the questions below with your classmates.**

1. What does the first customer order? a sloppy joe
2. What does the second customer order? chicken pot pie and a baked apple

B **Listen and read. What is a Denver Omelet?**

Customer: Excuse me. I have a question about the menu. I've never heard of a "Denver Omelet". What is it?

Server: It's an egg dish with cheese, tomatoes, peppers, and ham.

Customer: Sounds good. OK. I'll try it.

Server: Excellent. Ours is the best in town.

Customer: I'd also like some coffee cake. Is yours sweet?

Server: No, it isn't. Our cook doesn't use much sugar.

Customer: Good. I'm trying to cut down on* sugar.

*Idiom note: trying to cut down on = not eating much

C **Role-play a restaurant conversation with a partner. Use the example in 1B to make a new conversation.**

Partner A: You are the customer. You've never heard of a chili dog. Ask the server about it. You also want some vegetable soup. Ask if it is salty. You are trying to cut down on salt.

Partner B: You are the server. Tell the customer that a chili dog is a hot dog with a spicy meat sauce. Also tell the customer that the cook doesn't use much salt.

2 Learn possessive pronouns

A Study the charts. Then work with a partner. Partner A: Say a possessive adjective. Partner B: Say the matching possessive pronoun.

Possessive adjectives	Possessive pronouns	Notes
my	mine	• A possessive pronoun replaces a possessive adjective and a noun:
your	yours	I'd like some coffee cake. Is yours sweet?
his	his	(*yours* = your coffee cake)
her	hers	• Never use a possessive pronoun with another noun:
our	ours	Ours is the best in town.
your	yours	Our Denver Omelet is the best in town.
their	theirs	*Ours Denver Omelet is the best in town. (INCORRECT)

B Circle the correct possessive adjectives or possessive pronouns.

1. (**Their** / Theirs) dinner was good, but (our / **ours**) was terrible.
2. Juanita and I both ate sandwiches today. (My / **Mine**) was delicious, but (her / **hers**) was too spicy.
3. I tried Sonya's recipe for chicken soup today. (Hers / **Her**) recipe is much better than (me / **mine**).
4. I went over to Helen's house today. (**Her** / Hers) kitchen is very organized. (**My** / Mine) kitchen isn't. Is (your / **yours**)?
5. (**Your** / Yours) dessert looks delicious. Can I try some of (your / **yours**)?

3 Practice your pronunciation

A Listen to the linking of the phrasal verbs in these sentences.

1. I can't figure out something on the menu.
2. Please turn on the oven.

B Listen to the conversations. Complete the phrasal verbs you hear.

1. look _for_
2. turn _off_
3. get _off_
4. turn _on_
5. came _over_
6. get _on_

C Listen again and check. Repeat the phrasal verbs in 3B.

2 Learn possessive pronouns

Presentation II and Guided Practice

10–15 minutes

A 1. Introduce the new topic. *Now we're going to talk about possessive pronouns. What is a pronoun?* Write: *Tom went to the restaurant. He ordered fish.* Underline *He.* Say: *Who is he?* [Tom] *He replaces Tom in this sentence. Pronouns replace nouns.*

2. Read aloud the information about possessive pronouns in the right side of the chart. Say: *Adjectives are used with nouns. They describe nouns. Pronouns replace nouns. Pronouns and nouns can't be used together.*

3. Read and have students repeat the adjectives and nouns in the chart.

4. Check comprehension. Say sentences with blanks. Clap to indicate the blanks. Elicit a choral response. *This is your lunch. This lunch is _____. I like salt in _____ soup. Their order is ready. This order is _____. My plate is on the table. This plate is _____.*

> **TIP** For more practice with possessives after 2A, put your students in groups. Tell group members to take personal items out of their bags and put them on the table. They can use anything recognizable—pencil cases, erasers, keys, glasses, candy, cell phone, etc. Have each group member pick up an item that doesn't belong to him/her and ask another student: *Is this yours?* or *Is this your pencil case?* The other student can respond with: *Yes, it's mine.* or *No, it's not mine. I think it's his/hers.*

Communicative Practice

15–20 minutes

B 1. Have students work individually to circle the correct word. Go over the answers as a class.

2. Ask students to write two original (related) sentences. Tell them to use a possessive adjective and a possessive pronoun.

> **TIP** For more practice with menu words, create a "bulletin board" menu.
>
> 1. Put students in pairs or groups of three. Tell them that the class is going to make a menu. Each group needs to choose a dish and write a menu description for it. The description should include a name for the dish, the key ingredients, and at least one adjective to describe it.
>
> 2. Brainstorm an example on the board before students begin. *Spicy Chicken Soup: Lots of chicken and fresh vegetables in a thick, delicious broth!*
>
> 3. Have students read their descriptions aloud. Tack them on the bulletin board. Tell your students it looks like the best menu in town.

3 Practice your pronunciation

Pronunciation Extension

10–15 minutes

A 1. Write *First, chop up the nuts.* on the board. Say the sentence and ask students to repeat it. Draw a line to connect the final *p* in *chop* with the *u* in *up.* Say: *Now we're going to focus on the way sounds link in phrasal verbs.*

2. Play the audio. Direct students to listen for the linking in *figure out* and *turn on.* Ask students to repeat the two sentences.

B Play the audio. Have students listen and complete the phrasal verb. Go over the answers as a class.

C Have students listen again to check their answers. Ask them to repeat the phrasal verbs.

4 Focus on listening

Listening Extension

20–25 minutes

 A 1. Direct students to look at the picture in 4A. Ask: *Have they eaten yet? Who is going to pay the bill? Now we're going to listen to a conversation between the father and the server.*

2. Read the questions aloud, and elicit answers from volunteers.

B 1. Tell students to read the sentences before they listen. Play the audio and have students mark the sentences T (true) or F (false). Go over the answers as a class.

2. Direct students to look at the bill before listening. Tell them they need to listen for the quantities and prices.

3. Replay the audio and have students work individually to fill in the numbers. Go over the answers as a class.

> ## Multilevel Strategies
>
> Replay the conversation to challenge on- and higher-level students while allowing pre-level students to catch up.
>
> • **Pre-level** Have these students listen again to fill in the check.
>
> • **On- and Higher-level** Write questions on the board for these students to answer. *What three things does the father say were great? When does the restaurant include the tip on the bill?*

5 Real-life math

Math Extension

5–10 minutes

1. Read question 1. Call on a volunteer for the answer.

2. Have students work individually to figure out question 2. Ask a volunteer to come to the board and write the problems and the solutions they used in order to answer the question.

> **TIP**
>
> Bring in real restaurant menus. Many restaurants have take-out menus, or you can print them off the Internet. After completing section 5, have students look over the menu for any information about tipping or taxes. Tell them to find one adjective they don't know. Discuss the adjectives.

Evaluation

10–15 minutes

TEST YOURSELF

1. Model the role-play with a volunteer. Then switch roles.

2. Pair students. Check comprehension of the exercise. Ask for some examples of things Partner A and Partner B might say.

3. Set a time limit (five minutes), and have the partners act out the role-play in both roles.

4. Circulate and monitor. Encourage pantomime and improvisation.

5. Provide feedback.

> ## Multilevel Strategies
>
> Target the *Test Yourself* to the level of your students.
>
> • **Pre-level** Ask these students to use this skeleton conversation: *A: My _____ was delicious. How was yours? B: It was _____. A: Would you mind figuring out the tip? B: No problem. A: Lunch is on me. I _____ (reason for paying).*
>
> • **Higher-level** Have these students practice the role-play with several partners.

To compress this lesson: Conduct *Real-life math* as a whole-class activity.

To extend this lesson: Practice telling a restaurant server about a problem.
1. Have students brainstorm problems that sometimes occur with restaurant food—for example, food is cold, food is under/overcooked, part of order didn't arrive, wrong item. Write the problems on the board. Write something polite to say in each situation.
2. Have students role-play a customer telling a server about a problem with the food.

And/Or have students complete **Workbook 3 page 41** and **Multilevel Activity Book 3 page 73**.

4 Focus on listening

A **Talk about the questions with your class.**

1. When you eat at a restaurant, do you usually look at the bill carefully before you pay?
2. Do most restaurants include the tip in the bill?

B **Listen to the conversation. Mark the sentences T (true) or F (false).**

___T___ 1. The customers enjoyed their lunch.

___F___ 2. The service was not good.

___F___ 3. There was a mistake on the bill.

___F___ 4. The tip is included in the total.

C **Listen again and complete the information on the bill.**

BILL

__3__	hamburgers @ $6.00 each =	$18.00
__2__	turkey burgers @ $5.50 each =	$11.00
__3__	lemonades @ _$2.00_ each =	$6.00
__1__	coffee @ _$1.50_ each =	$1.50
	Sub-total =	$36.50
	Tax =	$3.19
	Total =	$39.69

5 Real-life math

Use the bill in 4C to answer the questions.

The Kim family in 4C is very happy with their meal. They want to leave a good tip.

1. How much money should they leave for a 15% tip?
   $36.50 × .15 = _$5.48 ($5.50)_
2. If the Kims leave a 20% tip, how much will they pay for the food, tax, and tip? _$46.99 ($50.00)_

> **Need help?**
>
> **Tipping**
> Most people only tip on the total of the food. It's not necessary to tip on any tax.

TEST YOURSELF ✔

Role-play a restaurant conversation. Partner A: You are the customer. Order something and ask for help with a menu item. Partner B: You are the server. Tell your customer about the menu item. Then change roles.

1 Get ready to read

A Has someone you know ever gotten sick from bad food? What happened?

B Read the definitions.

bacteria: (noun) very small living things that sometimes make people sick
food poisoning: (noun) illness people get by eating food that has dangerous bacteria
leftovers: (noun) extra or uneaten food from a meal that people eat at a later meal
throw out: (phrasal verb, separable) to put in the garbage

bacteria

C Look at the title of each section of the pamphlet in 2A. Name the five ways to protect against food poisoning. clean , cook, separate, refrigerate, check "use by" and expiration dates

2 Read and respond

A Read the pamphlet.

Protect Yourself from Food Poisoning
Follow these steps to stay safe:

Clean

Wash your hands for 20 seconds with soap and warm water before and after you touch food.
Dry your hands with paper towels or a clean dishtowel. Clean counters and dishes with hot, soapy water every time you use them.

Cook

Cook food long enough to kill bacteria. Different foods have different cooking temperatures.
To check food temperatures, put a cooking thermometer deep[1] in the center of the food.

---
[1]deep: far inside
[2]spread: to move

Use the Safe Temperatures chart to cook foods to a safe temperature.

Safe Temperatures
145° F - beef, steaks, and roasts
160° F - ground beef, pork, and eggs
170° F - chicken and turkey breasts
180° F - chicken and turkey (whole)

Separate
Bacteria can spread[2] from food to food. Separate uncooked beef, chicken, and fish from fruits and vegetables in your shopping cart and in your refrigerator.

Unit 6 Lesson 5

Objectives	Grammar	Vocabulary	Correlations
On-, Pre-, and Higher-level: Read about and discuss safe food preparation	*Should (You should only keep fish for two days.)*	*Bacteria, food poisoning, leftovers, throw out, pamphlet, expiration date* For vocabulary support, see this **Oxford Picture Dictionary** topic: Food Preparation and Safety	**CASAS:** 0.1.2, 1.6.1, 3.1.1, 3.4.1, 3.4.2, 3.5.1, 3.5.3, 3.5.5, 8.2.1 **LCPs:** 39.01, 49.02, 49.03, 49.16 **SCANS:** Acquires and evaluates information, Interprets and communicates information **EFF:** Convey ideas in writing, Listen actively, Read with understanding

Warm-up and Review

10–15 minutes (books closed)

Review food names. Write *Meat, Fish, Poultry,* and *Dairy* on the board. Ask volunteers to take turns writing food names in each category until the class runs out of ideas or you have several items in each category.

Introduction

5 minutes

1. Ask students about the food on the board from the warm-up. *How often do you eat chicken? How do you prepare it?*

2. State the objective: *We have been talking about how we prepare foods. Today we're going to talk about food safety.*

1 Get ready to read

Presentation

15–20 minutes

A Read the question aloud. Call on volunteers to share their stories.

B Read the words and definitions. Elicit examples or sample sentences from students.

Pre-Reading

C 1. Read the instructions aloud. Elicit the names of the five sections. Write them on the board.

2. Ask students to cover the pamphlet and predict what each section will say.

2 Read and respond

Guided Practice I

25–30 minutes

A 1. Ask students to read the pamphlet silently.

2. Direct students to underline unfamiliar words they would like to know. Elicit the words and encourage other students to provide definitions or examples.

3. Check students' comprehension. Ask volunteers to share one piece of information from each section.

Multilevel Strategies

Adapt 2A to the level of your students.

• **Pre-level** Provide these students with a summary of the reading. *There are five important steps to safe eating. 1. Wash your hands and clean your dishes well. 2. Cook foods well. Look at a "safe temperatures" chart to see how long you need to cook them. 3. Separate uncooked meat from fruits and vegetables. 4. Keep food cold in the refrigerator. 5. Check the expiration dates on food. If the date has passed, throw the food away.*

Direct these students to read the outline while other students are reading 2A.

Guided Practice II

15–20 minutes

B 1. Play the audio. Have students read along silently.

2. Elicit and discuss any additional questions about the reading.

C Have students work individually to complete the sentences. Ask volunteers to read the completed sentences aloud. Write the answers on the board.

Multilevel Strategies

For 2C, work with pre-level students.

• **Pre-level** Ask these students *Yes/No* and *Either/Or* questions about their summaries while other students are completing 2C. *Is it important to wash your hands and your dishes well?* [yes] *Does the "safe temperatures" chart tell you how long to keep food?* [no] *Should you throw food away or keep it after the expiration date?* [throw it away] As volunteers are reading the sentences in 2C aloud, write the answers on the board, and direct pre-level students to copy them into their books.

3 Talk it over

Communicative Practice

15–20 minutes

A Read the questions aloud. Set a time limit (three minutes). Have students work independently to think about the questions and then note their answers.

B Elicit students' answers to the questions in 3A. For question 2, write the foods they name and their guesses for the safe length of storage time. Ask students to check the answers and report back to the class. They can find the answers by typing *food storage length* into an Internet search engine or by typing the name of the food along with *safe storage*.

TIP If you have Internet access in class, have students look up more food-safety information. By typing *food safety, consumer information, food safety for parents,* or *food safety for your family* into a search engine, students can find many sites with fairly easy-to-read information. Tell them to find one new piece of food-safety information that they didn't learn from the pamphlet. Direct them to write down the source of the information, and ask them to share the information and its source with the class. Discuss the legitimacy of the source.

Application

5–10 minutes

BRING IT TO LIFE

Elicit items that the students might look at. Have students choose the three items they will look at in the market.

To compress this lesson: Conduct 2C as a whole-class activity.

To extend this lesson: Have students make food-safety posters.
1. Group students. Assign each group one of the sections from the pamphlet in 2A: *clean, cook, separate, refrigerate, check expiration dates.*
2. Ask the students to close their books. Tell each group to design a poster to tell the public about the food-safety step. The poster should have an illustration and a couple of sentences to get the point across.
3. Display students' posters around the room.

And/Or have students complete **Workbook 3 page 42** and the **Multilevel Activity Book 3 pages 74–75**.

Refrigerate

Bacteria grows very fast. Refrigerate leftovers within two hours after you cook them. Keep your refrigerator set at 40°F or less to keep food safe from bacteria. Check the temperature with a thermometer every few months.

Check "use by" and expiration dates

Always check the "use by" dates on the things in your refrigerator. "Use by" dates are suggestions. If there is an expiration date on a food product, don't eat or drink it after the date. Expiration dates are there for your safety.

When in Doubt, Throw It Out!

Cooked vegetables:
keep 3 to 4 days

Poultry, fish, or ground meat:
keep 2 days (cooked) or 1 to 2 days (uncooked)

Other cooked meats:
keep 3 to 4 days

Milk: keep 5 to 7 days

Eggs: keep 3 weeks

Source: *State of California Department of Health Services*

B Listen and read the pamphlet again.

C Complete the sentences. Use the information in the pamphlet.

1. Use _____soap_____ and _____water_____ to clean your hands and kitchen counters.
2. Check the food temperature with a _cooking thermometer_.
3. You should cook ground beef until the temperature is _160°F_____.
4. _Bacteria_____ grows very fast and can spread from food to food.
5. Of the foods in the food chart, you can keep _eggs_____ the longest.
6. After two days in the refrigerator, you should _throw out_____ ground meat.
7. _Expiration_____ dates tell you when you must use or throw away a food product.

3 Talk it over

A Think about the questions. Make notes about your answers.

1. Do you think eating in restaurants is as safe as eating in your home? Why or why not?
2. Name 3 foods not listed in the food storage chart. How long do you think it's safe to keep them in the refrigerator? Where can you look to check your answers?

B Talk about the answers with your classmates.

BRING IT TO LIFE

Look at the "use by" dates in the dairy section of a market. Bring a list of 3 items and dates to class. How many days are there between today's date and the "use by" dates on each item? Talk about your answers with the class.

1 Grammar

A Complete the answers with separable phrasal verbs. Change the underlined nouns to pronouns.

1. **A:** Can you pick up <u>Mark</u>?

   B: Yes, I can _____ *pick him up* _____.

2. **A:** Who can figure out <u>these problems</u>?

   B: I can _*figure them out*_____.

3. **A:** Did Danielle leave out <u>the eggs</u> again?

   B: Yes, she _*left them out*_____.

4. **A:** Who took out <u>the trash</u>?

   B: Elsa _*took it out*_____.

5. **A:** Did you write down <u>the recipes</u>?

   B: Yes, I _*wrote them down*_____.

B Complete the sentences. Use the phrasal verbs in the box. Use pronouns for the underlined nouns.

turn off	look after	~~take out~~	put in	look for

1. Why is the <u>trash</u> still here? Can you _____ *take it out* _____?

2. I need a babysitter for the <u>kids</u> on Saturday. Can you _*look after them*_____?

3. Is the <u>stove</u> still on? Can you _*turn it off*_____?

4. I can't find my <u>keys</u>. Can you help me _*look for them*_____?

5. Here are the <u>carrots</u> for the soup. Can you peel them and _*put them in*_____?

C Circle the correct possessive pronouns or adjectives.

A: Did you remember to bring in ((your) / yours) favorite recipe?
₁

B: Yes, I did. This is (my / (mine)). It's actually my grandmother's recipe—tomato salad.
₂

A: You're kidding! (My / (Mine)) is for tomato salad, too. But it's ((my) / mine) father's recipe.
₃ ₄

B: That's interesting. What's in (your / (yours))?
₅

A: ((His) / He) salad uses tomatoes and onions. It also has sugar and vinegar.
₆

B: My grandmother just uses tomatoes, but (his / (hers)) also has vinegar and sugar.
₇

A: ((Their) / Theirs) recipes are almost the same.
₈

Unit 6 Review and expand

Objectives	Grammar	Vocabulary	Correlations
On-, Pre-, and Higher-level: Expand upon and review unit grammar and life skills	Phrasal verbs (*I can pick him up.*) Possessives (*That is my book. That book is mine.*)	Phrasal verbs, food For vocabulary support, see this **Oxford Picture Dictionary** unit: Food	**CASAS:** 0.1.2, 0.1.5, 0.2.1, 1.1.1, 4.8.1, 7.2.6, 7.3.1, 7.3.2 **LCPs:** 39.01, 49.02, 49.03, 49.16, 49.17, 50.01, 50.02 **SCANS:** Acquires and evaluates information, Creative thinking, Seeing things in the mind's eye **EFF:** Convey ideas in writing, Solve problems and make decisions

Warm-up and Review

10–15 minutes (books closed)

1. Review the *Bring It to Life* assignment from Lesson 5.

2. Have students who did the exercise discuss what they learned. Direct students who did not complete the exercise to ask them questions about the items they looked at.

3. Ask students to look for patterns in the information. *Which foods last the longest? The least amount of time? Do some stores have fresher products than others?*

Introduction and Presentation

5 minutes

1. Write *turn off* on the board. Ask a volunteer to give you a sentence with *turn off*. Write it on the board. Ask another volunteer to restate the sentence by moving the noun. Ask another to restate the sentence using an object pronoun.

2. Write *get on* on the board. Ask a volunteer to give you a sentence with *get on*. Write it on the board. Ask if the object can be moved. [no]

3. Write *This is _____ recipe* on the board. Elicit possessive completions—for example, *my, your,* etc. Write: *This recipe is _____.* Elicit possessive completions—for example, *mine, yours,* etc.

4. State the objective: *Today we're going to review phrasal verbs and possessives to talk about cooking and other activities.*

1 Grammar

Guided Practice

40–45 minutes

A Read the example. Point out the position of *him*. Direct students to work individually to complete the answers. Ask volunteers to write the answers on the board. Go over the answers as a class.

B Read the instructions and the phrasal verbs aloud. Ask students to work individually to complete the questions. Ask volunteers to write the questions on the board. Go over the answers as a class.

Multilevel Strategies

For 1A and 1B, seat same-level students together.

- **Pre-level** Work with these students. Read each question and elicit the answers/completions before students write them in their books.

- **On- and Higher-level** After these students complete 1A and 1B, ask them to go through the unit and their notes to find phrasal verbs not included in 1A or 1B. Ask them to write two or three sentences with the verbs. Have volunteers write their sentences on the board.

C 1. Have students work individually to circle the correct possessive pronouns and adjectives.

2. Go over the correct answers as a class. Ask a volunteer pair to read the conversation aloud for the class.

2 Group work

Communicative Practice

20–35 minutes

 1. Direct students, in groups of three to four, to focus on the picture. Ask: *Does this look like a nice restaurant?*

2. Group students and assign roles: leader, recorder, and reporters. Explain that students work with their groups to write the conversation.

3. Check comprehension of the roles. Ask: *Who writes the conversation?* [recorder] *Who will read the conversation to the class?* [reporters] *Who helps everyone and tells the group how much time has passed?* [leader] *Who creates the conversation?* [everyone]

4. Set a time limit (five minutes) to complete the exercise. Circulate and answer any questions.

5. Have reporters from each group read the group's conversation to the class.

Multilevel Strategies

For 2A, use mixed-level groups.

• **Pre-level** Assign these students the role of timekeeper.

• **On-level** Assign these students the role of recorder or reporter.

• **Higher-level** Assign these students the role of leader.

B 1. Have students walk around the room to conduct the interviews. To get students moving, tell them to interview three new people who were not in their groups for 2A.

2. Set a time limit (five minutes) to complete the exercise.

3. Tell students to make notes of their classmates' answers but not to worry about writing complete sentences.

Multilevel Strategies

Adapt the mixer in 2B to the level of your students.

• **Pre-level** Allow these students to ask and answer the questions without writing.

• **Higher-level** Have these students ask two additional questions and write all answers.

 Call on individuals to report what they learned about their classmates. Write the names of highly recommended restaurants and dishes on the board. Encourage students to make generalizations. *Many students like pizza.*

PROBLEM SOLVING

15–25 minutes

 1. Ask: *Do you think it's ever OK not to leave a tip?* Tell students they will read a story about a problem with restaurant service. Direct students to read Dora and Jorge's story silently.

2. Ask: *What were the problems at the restaurant? How was the service?*

3. Play the audio and have students read along silently while listening.

B 1. Elicit answers to question 1. Have volunteers write answers to question 2 on the board until all of the class ideas have been put up.

2. Have the class vote on the best course of action for Dora and Jorge.

Evaluation

10–15 minutes

To test students' understanding of the unit grammar and life skills, have them take the Unit 6 Test on the *Step Forward Test Generator CD-ROM* with *ExamView® Assessment Suite*.

Learning Log

To help students record and discuss their progress, use the *Learning Log* on page T–201.

To extend this review: Have students complete **Workbook 3 page 43, Multilevel Activity Book 3 page 76**, and the **Unit 6 Exercises** on the **Multilevel Grammar Exercises CD-ROM 3**.

2 Group work

A Work with 2–3 classmates. Write a conversation between the people in the picture. Share your conversation with the class.

Server: *Are you ready to order?*
Customer: *Yes, but I have a question about the menu...*

B Complete the sentences. Then interview 3 classmates. Write their answers.

1. My favorite restaurant is _____. What's yours?

2. I like my favorite restaurant because _____. Why do you like yours?

3. My favorite dish is _____. What's yours?

4. I use _____ to prepare my favorite dish. What do you use to prepare yours?

C Talk about the answers with your class.

PROBLEM SOLVING

A Listen and read about Dora and Jorge.

    Today is Dora and Jorge's 25th wedding anniversary. They went out to a nice restaurant for dinner. Unfortunately, the chicken was too salty, the fish was dry, the vegetables were cold, and the dessert was too sweet. Dora and Jorge are upset. The service was good, but the food was terrible, and the meal was expensive. They don't really want to leave a tip for a terrible meal, but the server was very nice. They don't know what to do.

B Work with your classmates. Answer the questions.

1. Why are Dora and Jorge upset? Dora and Jorge don't know what kind of tip to leave because the server was nice but the food was terrible.
2. What should they do? Make a list of 3 or 4 things that they can do.

UNIT **7**

FOCUS ON
- banking
- financial planning
- real conditionals
- billing errors
- identity theft

Money Wise

LESSON **1**   Vocabulary

1 Learn banking vocabulary

A **Talk about the questions with your class.**

1. Do you usually do your banking at the bank, at the ATM, or on your computer?
2. What are some services that banks offer?

B **Work with your classmates. Match the words with the picture.**

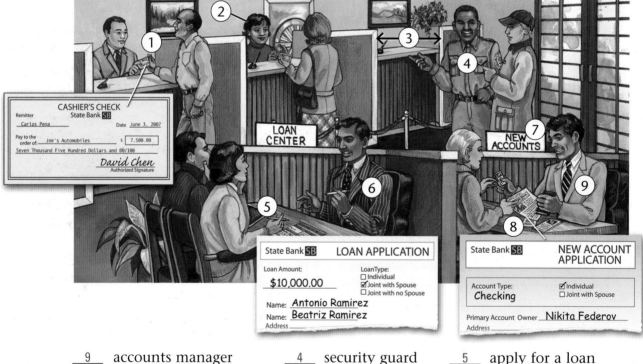

_9_	accounts manager	_4_	security guard	_5_	apply for a loan
_7_	account services desk	_2_	teller	_1_	get a cashier's check
_6_	loan officer	_3_	teller window	_8_	open an account

C **Listen and check. Then read the new words with a partner.**

D **Work with a partner. Write other banking words you know. Check your words in a dictionary.**

Unit 7 Lesson 1

Objectives	Grammar	Vocabulary	Correlations
On-level: Identify bank activities and employees, and describe banking services **Pre-level:** Identify bank activities, employees, and services **Higher-level:** Talk and write about banking using words for activities, employees, and services	Questions with *can* (*How can I avoid bounced checks?*)	Bank employees and services, banking activities For vocabulary support, see this **Oxford Picture Dictionary** topic: The Bank	**CASAS:** 0.1.2, 0.1.5, 1.8.2, 4.8.1, 7.4.5 **LCPs:** 39.01, 42.04, 49.01, 49.02, 49.09, 49.10 **SCANS:** Interprets and communicates information, Seeing things in the mind's eye **EFF:** Cooperate with others, Listen actively, Speak so others can understand, Reflect and evaluate

Warm-up

10–15 minutes (books closed)

Write *Money doesn't grow on trees. Money makes the world go around.* and *Time is money.* on the board. Elicit students' ideas about what the expressions may mean. Ask if they have expressions in their languages with similar meanings. Explain that in this unit, they will be talking about money.

Introduction

5 minutes

1. Ask: *Where do most people keep their money? From where do you borrow money when you want to buy a house?*

2. State the objective: *Today we're going to learn words for bank activities, bank employees, and bank services.*

1 Learn banking vocabulary

Presentation I

20–25 minutes

A Write *banking* on the board, and elicit students' answers to question 1. Tell them your own answer. Elicit their answers to question 2, and write them on the board.

B 1. Direct students to look at the pictures. Ask: *How many people are working at this bank?*

2. Group students and assign roles: leader, fact checker, recorder, and reporter. Explain that students work with their groups to match the words and pictures.

3. Check comprehension of the roles. Ask: *Who looks up the words in a dictionary?* [fact checker] *Who writes the numbers in the book?* [recorder] *Who tells the class your answers?* [reporter] *Who helps everyone and manages the group?* [leader]

4. Set a time limit (three minutes). As students work together, copy the wordlist onto the board.

5. Call "time." Have reporters take turns giving their answers. Write each group's answer on the board next to the word.

C 1. To prepare students for listening, say: *Now we're going to listen to the bank employees and customers.* Ask students to listen and check their answers.

2. Have students check the wordlist on the board and then write the correct numbers in their books.

3. Pair students. Set a time limit (three minutes). Monitor pair practice to identify pronunciation issues.

4. Call "time" and work with the pronunciation of any troublesome words or phrases.

D 1. Ask students to work with a partner from 1C to brainstorm a list of related words.

2. Elicit words from the class. Write them on the board. Ask students to copy them into their vocabulary notes for the unit.

Guided Practice

5–10 minutes

 E 1. Model the conversation with a volunteer. Model it again using other information from 1B.

2. Set a time limit (three minutes). Direct students to practice with a partner.

3. Ask volunteers to act out their conversations for the class.

2 Learn about banking services

Presentation II

15–20 minutes

 A 1. Direct students to look at the bank's website. Introduce the new topic: *Now we're going to talk about the services that the bank offers.*

2. Read the questions aloud, and allow students to look through the website. Go through each vocabulary item, and elicit examples and definitions from students. *What's the difference between a savings account and a checking account? What is a joint account?*

3. Check comprehension of the words. Ask: *What happens if I write a check and I don't have enough money in my account?* [Your check bounces.] *What is it called when my employer sends my paycheck right to my bank account?* [direct deposit]

Guided Practice

10–15 minutes

 B 1. Model the first question and answer with a volunteer.

2. Set a time limit (three minutes). Direct students to ask and answer the questions with a partner.

3. Call on volunteers to repeat each of the questions and answers.

Communicative Practice and Application

10–15 minutes

 C Give students a minute to make notes of their answers to the questions. Call on individuals to share their ideas with the class.

Evaluation

10–15 minutes (books closed)

TEST YOURSELF

1. Make a three-column chart on the board with the headings *Banking, Bank Employees,* and *Bank Services.* Have students close their books and give you an example for each column.

2. Have students copy the chart into their notebooks.

3. Give students five to ten minutes to test themselves by writing the words they recall from the lesson.

4. Call "time" and have students check their spelling in a dictionary. Circulate and monitor students' progress.

5. Direct students to share their work with a partner and add additional words to their charts.

> ### Multilevel Strategies
>
> Target the *Test Yourself* to the level of your students.
>
> • **Higher-level** Have these students complete the chart and then write a sentence defining one word from each column.

To compress this lesson: Conduct 1B as a whole-class activity.

To extend this lesson: Have students look at bank brochures. Bring in copies of two different bank brochures. Put students in groups, and give each group the two brochures. Direct the students to look for differences between the two banks. *Do they advertise different services? Do they have different operating hours? Do the brochures have the information you would want to know when choosing a bank?* Have reporters share each group's conclusions.

And/Or have students complete **Workbook 3 page 44** and **Multilevel Activity Book 3 pages 78–79**.

E Work with a partner. Practice the conversation. Use the picture in 1B.

A: Excuse me, I need to open an account. Where should I go?

B: Go to the account services desk and talk to the accounts manager.

A: Great. Thank you.

2 Learn about banking services

A Look at the bank's website. What kind of accounts, services, and tips do you know about? Which ones are new to you?

B Work with a partner. Partner A: Read the questions. Partner B: Look at the website in 2A. Tell your partner where to click to find the information.

A: How can my spouse and I share a savings account?
B: Click on joint accounts.

1. How can my paycheck go directly into my account? direct deposit
2. How can I use banking services from my home computer? online banking
3. How do I move money from one account to another? transfer money
4. How can I avoid bounced checks? Read the article, "Bye-Bye Bounced Checks."

C Talk about the questions with your class.

1. Name at least three bank jobs. What do these employees do?
2. Name at least two important bank services. Why are they important?

TEST YOURSELF ✔

Close your book. Categorize the new words in 3 lists: *Banking, Bank Employees,* and *Bank Services*. Check your spelling in a dictionary. Compare your lists with a partner.

1 Read about financial planning and goals

A **Look at the picture. Talk about the questions with your class.**

1. What is Kim and her husband's goal?
2. What can they do to reach their goal?

B **Listen and read the story about financial planning.**

Financial Planning for the Future ←
By: Kim Sanchez

    My husband and I are hoping to buy a new car next year. The one we have now is very old, needs many repairs, and uses a lot of gas. We have a plan. My husband and I have a joint account. We're saving money in our account so we can buy the car of our dreams.

    We've learned a lot about saving money. My husband doesn't drive to work alone anymore. He rides with a co-worker, and they share the cost of gas. We never buy our lunch at work anymore. It's cheaper to bring it from home. I plan my grocery shopping carefully. I go to the supermarket once a week. I always make a list, and I use coupons. Saving money isn't easy, but if we work hard, we can reach our goal. With a new car, we'll save money on gas and repair bills. We'll also feel safer on the road.

> **Writer's note**
>
> In a title, use capital letters for all words except articles (*the, a/an*) and prepositions (such as *for, in, on, at*).

C **Check your understanding. Mark the statements T (true), F (false), or NI (no information).**

  _F_ 1. Kim is single.

  _F_ 2. Kim and her husband are happy with the car they own now.

  _T_ 3. They have a joint account.

  _NI_ 4. They saved $100 last month.

  _T_ 5. Kim uses coupons at the supermarket.

Unit 7 Lesson 2

Objectives	Grammar	Vocabulary	Correlations
On- and Higher-level: Analyze, write, and edit a financial plan **Pre-level:** Read a financial plan, and write about financial planning	Verb + infinitive (*I hope to buy a new car.*)	*Goal, anymore, purchase* For vocabulary support, see these **Oxford Picture Dictionary** topics: The Bank, A Mall	**CASAS:** 0.1.2, 0.2.1, 1.8.5, 7.4.7 **LCPs:** 39.01, 49.01, 49.02, 49.03, 49.16, 49.17 **SCANS:** Interprets and communicates information, Reasoning, Seeing things in the mind's eye **EFF:** Convey ideas in writing, Read with understanding, Reflect and evaluate

Warm-up and Review

10–15 minutes (books closed)

Ask: *What do you want to buy in the future?* As students give you ideas, write them on the board in categories. *Furniture, Appliances, Electronics, Transportation, Recreation.* As you put up categories, ask students to brainstorm other items that fit into that category. Leave these words on the board to help students with their 2B writing assignment.

Introduction

5 minutes

1. Ask: *When you want to buy something and you don't have enough money for it, what do you do?*

2. State the objective: *Today we're going to read and write about financial planning and goals.*

1 Read about financial planning and goals

Presentation

20–25 minutes

A Direct students to look at the picture. Elicit answers to questions 1 and 2.

B 1. Say: *This story tells about how Kim and her husband are planning their finances, so they can buy a new car.*

2. Direct students to read the story silently. Check comprehension. Ask: *Why do they want a new car? How are they saving money?*

3. Play the audio. Have students read along silently.

4. Draw student's attention to the *Writer's note.* Elicit examples of prepositions.

Guided Practice I

10 minutes

C Have students work independently to mark the statements T (true), F (false), or NI (no information). Go over the answers as a class.

Multilevel Strategies

For 1C, challenge on- and higher-level students while working with pre-level students.

- **Pre-level** While other students are working on 1C, ask these students *Yes/No* and *Or* questions about the reading. *Does her husband drive to work alone? Do they buy lunch or bring it from home? Will they save money with a new car?* Give students time to copy the answers to 1C from the board.

- **On- and Higher-level** Write this question on the board for these students to answer after they finish 1C: *What are other ways that Kim and her husband could save money?* After allowing students to work individually to answer the question, have volunteers share their ideas. Write the ideas on the board for students to refer to for 2B.

2 Write about a financial plan

Guided Practice II

20–25 minutes

A 1. Read the questions. Elicit students' answers.

2. Write the places where people save money on the board.

B 1. Direct students to look back at the passage in 1B. Focus students' attention on the use of the simple present in the passage. Ask them to look through the passage quickly and underline the simple-present verbs. Elicit the verbs and discuss any questions. Point out that the writer uses the simple present because she's discussing habits.

2. Read the questions for each paragraph aloud. Elicit possible answers.

3. Check comprehension of the exercise. Ask: *How many paragraphs do you need to write?* [two] *Should you write the questions?* [no] *Should you write a list of answers to the questions?* [no] *Does your writing need a title?* [yes] Remind students that they can refer to the words on the board for ideas.

> ### Multilevel Strategies
>
> Adapt 2B to the level of your students.
>
> • **Pre-level** Have these students write one paragraph. Provide a skeleton paragraph to help them get started. *In the future, I plan to buy a _____. There are two ways that I save money. First, _____. Second, _____.*

C 1. Lead students through the process of using the *Editing checklist.* Read each sentence aloud, and ask students to check their papers before moving onto the next item.

2. Allow students a few minutes to edit their writing as necessary.

Communicative Practice

10 minutes

 1. Read the instructions aloud. Emphasize to students that they are responding to their partners' work, not correcting it.

2. Use the passage in 1B to model the exercise. *I think the sentence about riding with a co-worker is interesting. I'd like to ask this writer: What kind of car are you going to buy?*

3. Direct students to exchange stories with a partner and follow the instructions.

4. Call on volunteers to share what they found interesting in their partners' plans.

Application and Evaluation

15 minutes

TEST YOURSELF

1. Read the instructions aloud. Assign a time limit (ten minutes), and have students work independently.

2. Before collecting students' work, remind them to use the *Editing checklist.* Collect and correct students' writing.

> ### Multilevel Strategies
>
> Adapt the *Test Yourself* to the level of your students.
>
> • **Pre-level** Have these students write one paragraph. Provide skeleton sentences to help them get started. *In the future, _____ plans to buy a _____. There are two ways that he/she saves money. First, _____. Second, _____.*

To compress this lesson: Assign the *Test Yourself* for homework.

To extend this lesson: Talk about money mistakes.
1. Say: *Some people have trouble saving money because of bad spending habits. What do they do wrong?*
2. Ask students to brainstorm several answers to your question. Call on volunteers to share their ideas.
3. Have a class discussion about common bad-spending habits—for example, impulse buying, shopping for fun, borrowing on credit cards, always buying brand-name products, etc.

And/Or have students complete **Workbook 3 page 45** and **Multilevel Activity Book 3 page 80.**

2 Write about a financial plan

A **Talk about the questions with your class.**

1. What are some places that people put the money they save?
2. Is saving money easier for you now than it was in the past? Why or why not?

B **Write about your financial plan. Use the model in 1B and the questions below to help you.** Answers will vary.

Paragraph 1: What are you hoping to buy in the future? Why?
What's your plan for saving the money you'll need?

Paragraph 2: What things do you do now to save money?
(Write about three or more things.)
When do you think you will you reach your goal?
How will your new purchase help you?

My Financial Plan
I'm hoping to buy a house in two
years. I live in an apartment now.

C **Use the checklist to edit your writing. Check (✔) the true sentences.** Answers will vary.

Editing checklist	
1. I wrote about something I plan to buy and why I want to buy it.	
2. I wrote about three or more ways I save money.	
3. I used the rules on page 90 for capital letters in the title of my story.	
4. There are two paragraphs in my story.	

D **Exchange stories with a partner. Read and comment on your partner's work.**

1. Point out one way that your partner saves money.
2. Ask your partner a question about his or her financial plan.

TEST YOURSELF ✔

Write a paragraph about your partner's savings plan. Use the information you learned from 2D.
Paulo is hoping to buy a new TV.

1 Learn real conditionals

A Read the conversation. Will the customer buy the coat today?

Customer: I'd like to buy this coat, please.

Salesperson: You know, tomorrow we're having a big sale. <u>If you wait until tomorrow</u>, it'll probably be twenty percent off.

Customer: That's a good deal. But <u>if I wait until tomorrow</u>, someone else might buy it!

Salesperson: You could come in early. You'll save an extra ten percent <u>if you come in before 9 a.m.</u>

Customer: That's perfect! What time do you open?

B Study the chart. Underline the 3 *if* clauses in the conversation above.

Real Conditionals

⸺*If* clause⸺	⸺Main clause⸺	⸺Main clause⸺	⸺*If* clause⸺
If **I buy** the coat tomorrow,	**I'll save** money.	**I'll save** money	if **I buy** the coat tomorrow.
If **she buys** the coat today,	**she won't save** money.	**She won't save** money	if **she buys** the coat today.

Notes

- Real conditionals describe possible events in the future.
- Use the simple present in the *if* clause and *will/won't* in the main clause.
- The *if* clause can come before or after the main clause.

C Complete the sentences. Use the verbs in parentheses.

1. If she ____buys____ the coat tomorrow, she ___will save___ money. (buy, save)

2. If she ___goes___ to the store before 9:00, she ___will pay___ ten percent less. (go, pay)

3. I ___will go___ to the bank if I ___need___ a cashier's check. (go, need)

4. If they ___save___ enough money, they ___will not (won't) need___ a car loan. (save, not need)

5. Ali ___will speak___ to a loan officer if he ___wants___ a car loan. (speak, want)

6. If you ___transfer___ money to your checking account, the check ___will not (won't) bounce___ (transfer, not bounce)

7. If we ___put___ our money in a joint checking account, we ___will save___. money faster. (put, save)

8. The bank ___will give___ free checks if we ___open___ an account today. (give, open)

Unit 7 Lesson 3

Objectives	Grammar	Vocabulary	Correlations
On- and Higher-level: Use future-conditional statements and questions to talk about money, and listen for the future conditional in conversations about money **Pre-level:** Use future-conditional statements to talk about money, and listen for the future conditional in conversations about money	Future conditional (*If I buy the coat today, I'll save money.*)	*If, until, clause* For vocabulary support, see these **Oxford Picture Dictionary** topics: Money, Shopping	**CASAS:** 0.1.2, 0.2.1 **LCPs:** 49.02, 49.03, 49.09, 49.16, 49.17 **SCANS:** Creative thinking, Participates as member of a team, Seeing things in the mind's eye **EFF:** Convey ideas in writing, Cooperate with others, Listen actively, Reflect and evaluate, Speak so others can understand

Warm-up and Review

10–15 minutes (books closed)

Review the future with *will*. Write *In the future, maybe I will _____.* on the board. Ask volunteers to take turns coming to the board to finish the sentence.

Introduction

5–10 minutes

1. Referring to the sentences on the board, say: *All of these are things we may do in the future. We're probably not sure because there is a condition attached.* Use several of the students' ideas to form future-conditional sentences. For example: if the student wrote *Maybe I will buy a house,* say: *If I save enough money, I will buy a house.*

2. State the objective: *Today we'll learn how to use the future conditional to talk about our financial plans.*

1 Learn the real conditional

Presentation I

20–25 minutes

A 1. Direct students to look at the picture. Ask: *What is the customer buying?*

2. Read the instructions aloud. Ask students to read the conversation silently to find the answer to the question. Call on a volunteer for the answer.

3. Play the audio and ask students to read along silently.

B 1. Demonstrate how to read the grammar chart.

2. Direct students to underline the *if* clauses in the conversation in 1A. Go over the answers as a class.

3. Write one of the sentences from the conversation on the board. Elicit the tense of the verb in the *if* clause. [present] Underline the main clause, and elicit its verb tense. [future] Write the sentence with the time clause and main clause order reversed. Point out the change in punctuation.

4. Read the chart through sentence by sentence. Then read it again, and have students repeat after you.

5. Assess students' understanding of the charts. Write *If it rains tomorrow,* on the board, and elicit several main clauses. Write *I will be very excited* on the board, and elicit several *if* clauses. As students provide you with *if* clauses, write some before the main clause and some after. Read the *Notes* aloud.

Guided Practice I

15–20 minutes

C Ask students to work individually to complete the sentences. Ask volunteers to write the answers on the board.

Multilevel Strategies

For 1C, seat same-level students together.

• **Higher-level** Have these students write three to five additional sentences using the future conditional.

Guided Practice II

5–10 minutes

D 1. Read sentences *a* and *b* aloud. Direct students to read numbers 1 and 2 and circle the answers. Go over the answers as a class.

2. Write several future-conditional sentences on the board with no commas, and elicit whether and where a comma is necessary.

Show students that *may/might* and *should* can be used in the main clause. Say: *My sister is thinking about visiting me this weekend. If she visits me, we might go out to dinner. If we go out, we shouldn't spend too much money.* Write two skeleton sentences on the board, and elicit completions from volunteers. *If _____ this weekend, I might _____. If _____ this weekend, I should _____.* Ask students about things they might do this weekend.

2 Learn questions with real conditional

Presentation II

20–25 minutes

A 1. Introduce the new topic. *Now we're going to learn questions with the future conditional.*

2. Read the questions and answers in the chart aloud.

3. Direct students to work individually to match the questions and answers. Have them read the questions and answers with a partner.

Multilevel Strategies

Seat mixed-level students together for 2A and 2B.

• **On and Higher-level** After these students have done the exercises, have them read the questions to their partners.

• **Pre-level** Have these students read the answers to their partners.

Guided Practice I

10–15 minutes

B Read the example question in number 1 aloud. Direct students to work individually to complete the questions. Have them read the questions and answers with a partner.

Multilevel Strategies

After 2B, provide additional practice with the future conditional. Target the practice to the level of your students.

• **Pre-level** Provide these students with main clauses and *if* clauses, and ask them to combine the sentences. *1. If I win the lottery, 2. If it rains tomorrow, 3. If I go to bed early tonight, 4. If I sleep late in the morning, 5. If I exercise every day, a. I'll feel good tomorrow. b. I won't go to the beach. c. I'll buy my mom a house. d. I'll be late to work. d. I'll be healthier.*

• **On- and Higher-level** Put these students in groups and direct them to write a chain story in the third person. Provide this example: *If she wakes up early tomorrow, she'll go downtown. If she goes downtown, she'll buy a jacket. If she buys a jacket, she'll wear it every day. If she wears it every day, it will get old. If it gets old, she'll throw it away. If she throws it away, she'll need a new jacket.* Provide each group with a "starter" clause: *If he moves to this city, if she falls asleep in class, if he stays up late, if she saves her money, if he buys a new car.* Ask a reporter from each group to read the group's story aloud.

D **Get the form. Work with your class. Read the sentences. Then circle *a* or *b*.**

a. If I buy the coat tomorrow, I'll save thirty percent.

b. I'll save thirty percent if I buy the coat tomorrow.

1. Which sentence has a comma?
   a. sentence a
   b. sentence b

2. Complete the rule: Use a comma when ____.
   a. the *if* clause is first.
   b. the main clause is first.

2 Learn questions with real conditionals

A **Study the chart. Then match the questions and answers below.**

Questions and answers with real conditionals	
A: Will you buy a new jacket if it's on sale? **B:** Yes, I will. OR No, I won't.	**A:** How much will they save if they bring their lunch? **B:** They'll save $20 a week.
A: What will you do if you get a loan? **B:** I'll celebrate.	**A:** Where will you go if you need a new computer? **B:** I'll go to Computer World.

___e___ 1. What will Ben do if he needs a loan?

___c___ 2. What will you buy if you save enough money?

___a___ 3. How much will Mateo deposit if he gets paid today?

___b___ 4. Where will you go if you want to open a new account?

___d___ 5. Will he buy the coat if it's on sale?

a. He'll deposit $500.

b. I'll go to the new accounts desk.

c. I'll buy a computer.

d. Yes, he will.

e. He'll talk to a loan officer.

B **Complete the questions.**

1. **A:** What will Safiya do _if she gets the job_ ?

   B: If Safiya gets the job, she will open a new bank account.

2. **A:** What will Jose do _if he finds the right house_ ?

   B: If he finds the right house, Jose will apply for a loan.

3. **A:** How much _will they save if they take the bus_ ?

   B: If they take the bus, they will save $10.00 a week.

4. **A:** Where _will they go if they need a new TV_ ?

   B: If they need a new TV, they'll go to Atlas Electronics.

3 Grammar listening

🎧 **Listen to the questions. Circle *a* or *b*.**

1. a. I'll look for a car this weekend.
   b. I'll get a loan. *(circled)*
2. a. I'll buy a new jacket.
   b. I'll withdraw $200. *(circled)*
3. a. No, I won't.
   b. I'll use the ATM. *(circled)*
4. a. I'll deposit money.
   b. I'll go to the mall. *(circled)*
5. a. Yes, he will. *(circled)*
   b. Yes, I will.
6. a. I'll reach it by the end of the year. *(circled)*
   b. Yes, I will.

4 Practice talking about future plans

A **Work with 3 classmates. Talk about what you see in the picture.**

B **What do you think will happen? Write 5 sentences with your group. Use an *if* clause and a main clause in each sentence.**

If the manager sees the security guard, he'll be angry.

C **Read your sentences with another group.**

┌─ **TEST YOURSELF** ✔ ─────────────────────────────
│ Close your book. Write 5 sentences about what you will do if you have free
│ time this weekend. Use an *if* clause and a main clause in each sentence.

3 Grammar listening

Guided Practice II

10–15 minutes

1. Say: *Now we're going to listen to short conversations about money. Listen for the future conditional.*

2. Play the audio. Direct students to read along silently without writing.

3. Replay the audio. Ask students to circle the correct answers. Go over the answers as a class.

> ### Multilevel Strategies
>
> Replay the *Grammar listening* to challenge higher-level students while you allow pre-level students to catch up.
>
> • **Pre-level** Have these students listen again for the answers to the *Grammar listening*.
>
> • **On- and Higher-level** Direct these students to take notes or write the questions they hear. After you have gone over the answers to the *Grammar listening*, call on volunteers to share what they remember. As a class, reconstruct the questions on the board. Play the audio again to see if they understood the main idea behind each question.

4 Practice talking about future plans

Communicative Practice and Application

20–25 minutes

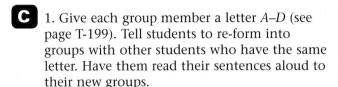 Group students and direct them to talk about what they see in the picture. *Where are these people? What are they doing?*

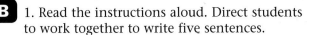 1. Read the instructions aloud. Direct students to work together to write five sentences.

2. Check comprehension of the exercise. Ask: *Who is going to write the sentences?* [everyone] *Is everyone going to write the same sentences or different sentences?* [the same] *What tense should the sentences be in?* [future conditional] Assign a time limit (five minutes).

C 1. Give each group member a letter *A–D* (see page T-199). Tell students to re-form into groups with other students who have the same letter. Have them read their sentences aloud to their new groups.

2. Call on a student from each group to read one of the group's sentences.

Evaluation

10–15 minutes (books closed)

TEST YOURSELF

Ask students to write the sentences independently. Collect and correct their writing.

> ### Multilevel Strategies
>
> Target the *Test Yourself* to the level of your students.
>
> • **Pre-level** Ask these students to follow this skeleton sentence: *If I _____, I will _____.*
>
> • **Higher-level** Have these students write seven or eight sentences.

To compress this lesson: Conduct 2A as a whole-class activity.

To extend this lesson: Write possible results using future conditional sentences. Write a series of situations on the board. Have students work with a partner to write different possible outcomes for the situations. Do the first one as a class. *Tom left his ATM card in the machine.* Discuss possible results. *If he remembers the card, he'll come back for it. If he leaves the card there too long, the machine will swallow it. If someone finds it, they might steal his money.* Consider other situations. *Mary only has $10 in her checking account. Mark wants to apply for a loan. Sara charged $2,000 on her credit card. Joe has $1,000 under his mattress at home.* Call on volunteers to share their sentences with the class.

And/Or have students complete **Workbook 3 pages 46–47** and **Multilevel Activity Book 3 pages 81–82,** and the **Unit 7 Exercises** on the **Multilevel Grammar Exercises CD-ROM 3**.

Unit 7 Lesson 4

Objectives	Grammar	Vocabulary	Correlations
On-, Pre-, and Higher-level: Report a billing or banking error, and listen for account information	Future time clauses (*After we review your application, we'll call you.*)	*Balance, customer, endorse, representative, service, statement* For vocabulary support, see these **Oxford Picture Dictionary** topics: The Bank, Money	**CASAS:** 0.1.2, 1.5.3, 6.0.3, 6.0.4, 6.2.3 **LCPs:** 49.02, 49.03, 49.09, 49.16, 49.17 **SCANS:** Arithmetic/Mathematics, Creative thinking, Seeing things in the mind's eye **EFF:** Listen actively, Reflect and evaluate, Use math to solve problems and communicate

Warm-up and Review

10–15 minutes (books closed)

Write *billing problem* on the board. Ask if any students have had problems with a credit card, bank statement, or bill. Allow volunteers to share their stories with the class.

Introduction

5 minutes

1. Tell students about a time you experienced a billing or banking problem and how you handled it.

2. State the objective: *Today we're going to learn how to report problems on our bank statements and how to listen for account information over the phone.*

1 Learn to report a billing or banking error

Presentation I

15–20 minutes

 1. Direct students to look at the picture. Ask: *What's the problem?*

2. Play the audio. Give students time to mark the sentences T (true), F (false), or NI (no information). Go over the answers as a class.

Guided Practice

20–25 minutes

 1. Read the instructions aloud. Play the audio. Ask students to read along silently and listen

for the answer to the question. Elicit the answer.

2. Ask students to read the conversation with a partner. Model and have students repeat difficult words or phrases.

3. Say and have students repeat the expressions in the *In other words* box. Elicit the placement of the *In other words* expressions in the conversation. Ask volunteers to model the conversation using expressions from the box.

Communicative Practice and Application

15–20 minutes

 1. Ask students to read the instructions silently. Check their comprehension of the exercise. *What are the two roles?* Elicit examples of what the customer and the customer service agent might say.

2. Pair students. Set a time limit (five minutes), and have the partners act out the role-play in both roles. Have a volunteer pair act out its conversation for the class. Tell students who are watching the role-play to write the answer to this question: *Is the customer happy with the customer service?*

Multilevel Strategies

For 1C, adapt the role-play to the level of your students.

• **Pre-level** Provide a simplified conversation for these students. *A: I'm calling to report a problem with my cell phone bill. B: What's the problem? A: It says I called India, but I don't know anybody in India. B: OK. We'll review the bill. A: Thank you.*

1 Learn to report a billing or banking error

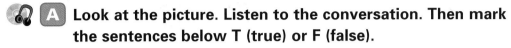

A Look at the picture. Listen to the conversation. Then mark the sentences below T (true) or F (false).

  _T_ 1. Min is upset about her credit card bill.

  _F_ 2. She lives in Pacific City.

  _T_ 3. She doesn't have to pay her bill this month.

B Listen and read. What is the problem with the bill?

Customer:	I'm calling to report a problem on my credit card bill.
Customer Service:	What seems to be the problem?
Customer:	It says I spent $100 at Tom's Market last week, but that's impossible. I've never been to Tom's Market.
Customer Service:	OK. I'll talk to my supervisor and ask him to review it before we send your next bill.
Customer:	So, do I have to pay the $100 charge this month?
Customer Service:	Let's wait and see what my supervisor says. When you receive your next bill, you'll see your new balance.

In other words...

Asking about problems

What seems to be the problem?
What's the problem?
How can I help you?

C Role-play a telephone conversation with a partner. Use the example in 1B to make a new conversation.

Partner A: You are a customer. Call customer service at your cell phone company and report a problem on your cell phone bill. You received a bill that says that you owe $300 for phone calls to India. You don't know anybody in India.

Partner B: You are a customer service representative for the cell phone company. Ask the customer to tell you the problem. Say that your supervisor will review the charge before you send the next bill.

2 Learn future events with time clauses

A Study the chart. Then match the clauses below to make complete sentences.

Describing future events with time clauses	
── Main clause ── ── Time clause ──	
We'll review the statement **before** we send the next bill.	
You'll see your new balance **when** you receive your next bill.	
I'll pay the bill **after** I get my next statement.	

Notes

- Time clauses give information about when things happen.
- A time clause can come before or after the main clause.
- Use *will* in the main clause and the simple present in the time clause.

<u> b </u> 1. The bank will review the statement   a. we'll apply for a home loan.

<u> c </u> 2. I will sign the check   b. before they send the next one.

<u> d </u> 3. We will know how much to pay   c. before I deposit it.

<u> a </u> 4. After we find a house,   d. when we receive our bill.

B Complete the sentences with your own ideas.
Practice your sentences with a partner. Answers will vary.

1. If I have time this weekend...
2. Before I leave class today...

3. After I finish this class...
4. When I go home today...

3 Practice your pronunciation

A Look at the chart. Listen to the pronunciation of the linked words in these sentences.

Sentence	Linked words	Note
I'll ask her.	ask ~~h~~er	When two words are linked, speakers often don't pronounce the beginning "h" sound in the second word.
What's his name?	What's ~~h~~is	
Come here now!	Come ~~h~~ere	

B Listen. Circle the linked words.

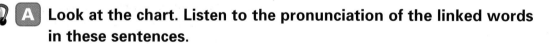

1. Your sister (brought her) friend. (What's her) friend's name?
2. Tim will (brush his) teeth (before he) goes to bed.
3. He'll go to the bank (before he) comes home.
4. (When he) (gets his) paycheck, Jack will buy a new TV.

C Listen again and check. Repeat the sentences.

2 Learn future events with time clauses

Presentation II and Guided Practice

30–35 minutes

A 1. Introduce the new topic. *Now we're going to look at time clauses using* before, when, *and* after. *They work just like future* if *clauses.*

2. Copy the sentences from the chart on the board. Read them aloud. Elicit the sequence of the action in each sentence. Ask: *Which will happen first,* review the statement *or send the next bill?* Write *1* and *2* above the correct clause to indicate the sequence of the action. Point out that *when* uses the same sequence as *after* and actually means immediately after.

3. Read the *Notes.* Reverse the clause order of one of the sentences on the board, and elicit the comma placement.

4. Ask students to work individually to match the sentence parts. Go over the answers as a class.

Communicative Practice

10–15 minutes

B 1. Have students work individually to complete the sentences with their own ideas.

2. Ask students to read their sentences to several partners. Call on individuals to share something interesting that one of their partners said.

> For more practice with time clauses, call out a verb phrase: *eat dinner.* Have one volunteer say a sentence with *before. Before I eat dinner, I'll wash my hands.* Have another say a sentence with *after. After I eat dinner, I'll watch TV.* Have a third say a sentence with *when. When I eat dinner, I'll relax.* Switch to a new verb phrase, and call on more volunteers. Possible phrases: *go home, go shopping, do my homework,* etc.

3 Practice your pronunciation

Pronunciation Extension

10–15 minutes

A 1. Write *He has a problem with his bill.* on the board. Say the sentence with relaxed pronunciation. Underline the *h* in *has* and *his.* Repeat the sentence, and ask students to listen for how the "h" sounds are dropped. Say: *Now we're going to focus on linked words. We often don't pronounce the beginning* h *on the second word of two linked words.*

2. Ask students to read the sentences in the chart. Play the audio. Encourage students to notice how the "h" sound is dropped.

B Play the audio again. Have students circle the linked words. Ask volunteers to read the sentences aloud to demonstrate the silent *h.*

C 1. Ask students to listen and repeat the sentences.

2. Have students read the sentences in 3A and 3B to a partner. Monitor and provide feedback on pronunciation.

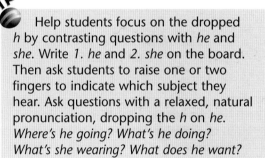

> Help students focus on the dropped *h* by contrasting questions with *he* and *she.* Write *1. he* and *2. she* on the board. Then ask students to raise one or two fingers to indicate which subject they hear. Ask questions with a relaxed, natural pronunciation, dropping the *h* on *he. Where's he going? What's he doing? What's she wearing? What does he want?*

4 Focus on Listening

Listening Extension

20–25 minutes

A Read the questions aloud, and elicit answers from volunteers. Encourage students to respond to each other's ideas. After one student speaks, ask other students for their opinions. *Do you agree or disagree with what he/she said? Why?*

B Direct students to read the three sentences before listening. Play the audio and ask them to mark the sentences T (true) or F (false). Go over the answers as a class.

C 1. Direct students to look over the account information. Ask: *What kind of information are you going to be writing?*

2. Replay the audio and have students work individually to write the dates, check numbers, and amounts. Go over the answers as a class.

Multilevel Strategies

Replay the audio to challenge higher-level students while allowing pre-level students to catch up.

Pre-level Have these students listen again to write the missing numbers.

On-level Direct these students to listen again and check their answers.

Higher-level Direct these students to listen with their books closed and write all of the information (date, check number, and amount).

5 Real-life math

Math Extension

5–10 minutes

1. Direct students to focus on the savings account information. Ask: *How much is the interest on a Gold Savings account? How much money do you need to open a Premiere Savings account?*

2. Ask students to work individually to answer the questions. Go over the answers as a class.

Evaluation

10–15 minutes

TEST YOURSELF

1. Model the role-play with a volunteer. Then switch roles.

2. Pair students. Check comprehension of the exercise by asking what the two roles are.

3. Set a time limit (five minutes), and have the partners act out the role-play in both roles.

4. Circulate and monitor. Encourage pantomime and improvisation.

5. Provide feedback.

Multilevel Strategies

Target the *Test Yourself* to the level of your students.

• **Pre-level** Ask these students to use this skeleton conversation: A: There's a problem on my bank statement. B: What's the problem? A: It says _____, but I never _____. B: OK. We'll review the statement and send you a new statement. A: Thank you.

• **Higher-level** Ask these students to practice the role-play with several partners.

To compress this lesson: Have students read the sentences in 2B with only one partner.

To extend this lesson: Write a follow-up letter.
1. Tell students to imagine that the situation from the *Test Yourself* was not resolved and that it is now necessary to put the complaint in a follow-up letter. Elicit the information you'll need to include in the letter: account number, description of problem, date and time of first complaint, request for action, and the name of the teller.
2. Compose the letter as a class, and write it on the board. Ask students to copy it into their notebooks.

And/Or have students complete **Workbook 3 page 48** and **Multilevel Activity Book 3 page 83**.

4 Focus on listening

A **Talk about the questions with your class.**

1. What kind of information can you get about your bank accounts over the phone?
2. Is it easy or difficult to get account information over the phone?

B **Listen to the account information. Mark the sentences T (true) or F (false).**

_T_ 1. The recording has information for two kinds of accounts.

_F_ 2. The customer is listening to information about a savings account.

_F_ 3. The customer wrote these checks after March 15th.

C **Listen again. Complete the account information.**

Checking Account			
1.	3/07	#266	$44.73
2.	3/07	#_268_	$106.50
3.	3/09	#267	_$56.00_
4.	_3/09_	#270	_$27.61_
5.	_3/09_	_#271_	_$175.90_

5 Real-life math

Read about Town Bank's Savings Accounts. Answer the questions below. Then compare your answers with the class.

1. Sara wants to open a savings account with $500. Which account can she get?

   Basic savings

2. Adam has $10,000 in a Premiere Savings Account. How much interest will he earn this year?

   $10,000 \times .05 =$ _$500.00_

Internet Search _ □ x

Address http://www.townbanksavings.mypage.com ▾ Go

Town Bank Savings Accounts
Compare our accounts.

	Interest rate	Minimum balance
Basic Savings Click to Apply	2%	None
Gold Savings Click to Apply	4.03%	$2,500
Premiere Savings Click to Apply	5%	$8,000

TEST YOURSELF ✔

Role-play a conversation in a bank. Partner A: There's a mistake on your bank statement. Talk to the teller. Partner B: You're the teller. Help the customer. Then change roles.

1 Get ready to read

A **Has anyone ever used your name or credit card number to buy something without your permission?**

B **Read the definitions.**

crime: (noun) an action that breaks the law

criminal: (noun) a person who breaks the law

identity theft: (noun) the crime of using another person's name, social security number, credit card number, or other personal information without permission

C **Look at the title and pictures in the article. What is the article is about?** identity theft

2 Read and respond

A **Read the article.**

Identity Theft: Are You Safe?

Identity theft is a growing problem in the U.S. This crime affects 10 million people a year. A criminal can use your personal information to apply for credit cards, take money from your bank account, or even buy a new home!

Unfortunately, it can be easy for the wrong person to get your information. The U.S. Department of Justice lists the most common[1] ways people steal information and how you can protect yourself.

If you are a victim of identity theft, you should contact the Federal Trade Commission at *www.ftc.gov* or look in the government pages of your phone book.

[1]common: usual, popular

Shoulder surfing

Be careful with your information in public places. A person behind you can listen to you or watch over your shoulder and get your information

Dumpster diving

Some criminals look in trash cans outside of homes to get information. Always cut up papers with your personal information before you throw them away.

Phishing

Criminals can pretend to be your bank or credit card company. They send an email that looks real and asks you for personal information such as your social security or credit card numbers. If you get an email with your bank's name on it and it asks you to send personal information, don't do it.

Source: *U.S. Federal Trade Commission*

Unit 7 Lesson 5

Objectives	Grammar	Vocabulary	Correlations
On-, Pre-, and Higher-level: Read about and discuss identity theft	Future time clauses (*I'll cut up my bank statement before I throw it away.*)	*Crime, criminal, identify theft, common, dumpster* For vocabulary support, see these **Oxford Picture Dictionary** topics: Personal Information, Money	**CASAS:** 0.1.2, 5.3.7, 7.3.1, 7.4.7 **LCPs:** 49.01, 49.03, 49.04, 49.16, 49.17 **SCANS:** Problem Solving, Reading, Speaking **EFF:** Read with understanding, Solve problems and make decisions, Speak so others can understand

Warm-up and Review

10–15 minutes (books closed)

Write the words *thief* and *theft* on the board, and elicit definitions. Ask students how they protect themselves from theft at home and away from home. Ask them what kinds of things thieves usually steal. Write their ideas on the board.

Introduction

5 minutes

1. Go over the items on the board. Say: *We protect our houses by locking doors and buying dogs. We protect our cars with alarms and electronic keys. But many people don't protect their personal information.*

2. State the objective: *Today we're going to read and discuss identity theft.*

1 Get ready to read

Presentation

15–20 minutes

 Read the question aloud. Call on volunteers to share their stories, and tell students about any experiences you have had with credit-card theft.

B Read the words and definitions. Elicit sample sentences from students using *crime* and *criminal*. Discuss identity theft: *Is it worse if someone steals your money or if they steal your credit-card number? Why?*

Pre-Reading

C 1. Read the instructions. Elicit an answer to the question.

2. Have students scan the article and identify the sections: *Shoulder surfing, Dumpster diving, and Phishing.* Ask if they can guess what these are based on the pictures.

2 Read and respond

Guided Practice I

25–30 minutes

 1. Ask students to read the article silently.

2. Direct students to underline unfamiliar words they would like to know. Elicit the words and encourage other students to provide definitions or examples.

3. Check students' comprehension. Ask: *What is shoulder surfing?* [looking over someone's shoulder to steal their information]

Multilevel Strategies

Adapt 2A to the level of your students.

• **Pre-level** Provide these students with a summary of the reading. *Identity theft is a big problem in the U.S. There are three common ways that people steal personal information. 1. Shoulder surfing—a thief looks over your shoulder and copies your information. 2. Dumpster diving—a thief looks for personal information in the trash. 3. Phishing—a thief pretends to work for your bank or credit-card company and sends email asking for your personal information.*

Direct these students to read the summary while other students are reading 2A.

Guided Practice II

15–20 minutes

B 1. Play the audio. Have students read along silently.

2. Elicit and discuss any additional questions about the reading.

C Have students work individually to mark the sentences T (true), F (false), or NI (no information). Go over the answers as a class.

Multilevel Strategies

For 2C, work with pre-level students.

• **Pre-level** Ask these students *Yes/No* and *Or* questions about their summaries while other students are completing 2C. *Is personal identity theft a big problem in the U.S.? Do you need to be careful when you give out personal information? Should you put your credit-card statements in the trash whole or should you tear them up?* Give students time to copy the answers to 2C from the board.

D 1. Read the words and the information in the chart aloud. Elicit and discuss any questions the students have about the meanings of the words or the suffix *–al*. Have students repeat the words.

2. Direct students to work individually to circle the correct word to complete the sentences. Ask volunteers to read the completed sentences aloud.

Multilevel Strategies

For 2D, seat same-level students together.

• **Pre-level** Allow these students extra time to complete 2D. Provide individual assistance as necessary.

• **On- and Higher-level** While pre-level students are finishing 2D, ask these students to brainstorm nouns they could combine with the adjectives in the chart—for example, *personal problem, personal information, national anthem, national government, musical talent, musical voice, professional clothing, professional advice.* Or provide the nouns, and ask students to match them with as many of the adjectives as possible.

3 Talk it over

Communicative Practice

15–20 minutes

A Read the questions aloud. Set a time limit (three minutes). Have students work independently to think about the questions and write their answers in note form.

B Discuss students' ideas as a class. Ask them if they have additional questions about identity theft.

Application

5–10 minutes

BRING IT TO LIFE

Read the instructions aloud. As a class, brainstorm items that they might find.

To compress this lesson: Conduct the word study in 2D as a whole-class activity.

To extend this lesson: Review theft-prevention advice.
1. Put students in mixed-level groups of three or four. Tell them to close their books and make a poster giving advice on how to protect against identity theft. Ask them to include four or five pieces of advice.
2. Have a reporter from each group read the group's poster to the class. Display the posters around the room.

And/Or have students complete **Workbook 3 page 49** and **Multilevel Activity Book 3 pages 84–85**.

B Listen and read the article again.

C Mark the sentences T (true), F (false), or NI (no information).

_F_ 1. Ten billion people a year are victims of identity theft.

_F_ 2. Fortunately, it's very difficult for a criminal to get your personal information.

_F_ 3. Criminals won't look for information in a trash can.

_T_ 4. A criminal can listen to you in public and steal your information.

_T_ 5. If an email asks for your bank password, you shouldn't give it.

_NI_ 6. The author of the article was a victim of identity theft.

D Study the chart. Circle the correct words in the sentences below.

> **Word Study: The suffix -al**
>
> Add –al to some nouns to form adjectives.
> person + -al = personal   You should protect your **personal** information.
>
> | accident | accidental | music | musical |
> | nation | national | profession | professional |

1. Identity theft is a (nation /(national)) problem.
2. It can be easy for a ((person)/ personal) to steal your identity.
3. Sandra is very (music /(musical)). She can sing, play the piano, and play the guitar.
4. There was a car ((accident)/ accidental) on the corner yesterday.
5. When Eli has a job interview, he always wears (profession /(professional)) clothing.

3 Talk it over

A Think about the questions. Make notes about your answers.

1. How can you say "no" if someone asks for your personal information on the telephone?
2. Why do you think there is more and more identity theft in the U.S. every year?

B Talk about the answers with your classmates.

> **BRING IT TO LIFE**
>
> Look around your home for two letters, papers, or other things that you should cut up before you throw away. Tell the class what you found.

1 Grammar

A Match the clauses to make complete sentences.

_c_ 1. When I save enough money,

_d_ 2. I'll pay the bills

_a_ 3. I'll do my homework in the morning

_b_ 4. If the bus comes on time,

a. if I don't have time tonight.

b. I'll go to the gym before work.

c. I'll buy a house.

d. when I get my paycheck.

B Circle the correct words to complete the sentences.

1. If Inez and Rubin (won't spend /(don't spend)) all their money, they'll put it in the bank.

2. If Jorge needs help with his homework, ((he'll call)/ he calls) a classmate.

3. If Alma's husband ((forgets)/ will forget) her birthday, she'll be upset.

4. I (go /(will go)) to the bank if I need a cashier's check.

5. Yukio will be a little nervous if he ((applies)/ will apply) for a home loan.

C Write answers to the questions. Answers will vary.

1. What will you do when you complete this class?

_____

2. How will you feel when you speak fluent English?

_____

3. Where will you go if you take a vacation?

_____

4. What will you do if it rains tomorrow morning?

_____

D Complete the sentences with *before, when,* or *after*.

1. Ella will fill out the application __before__ she gives it to the loan officer.

2. I'll ask a supervisor __when__ I need help.

3. Jamal will mail the letters __after__ he buys stamps.

4. __Before__ you deposit a check, you will need to endorse it.

5. We'll open an account __after__ we talk to the accounts manager.

6. __When__ I have enough money, I'll buy a car.

Unit 7 Review and expand

Objectives	Grammar	Vocabulary	Correlations
On-, Pre-, and Higher-level: Expand upon and review unit grammar and life skills	Time clauses (*I'll eat dinner after I get home.*)	*interest, annual fee, transfer balance* For vocabulary support, see this **Oxford Picture Dictionary** topic: The Bank, Money	**CASAS:** 0.1.2, 0.1.5, 0.2.1, 1.8.5, 4.8.1, 7.2.6, 7.3.1, 7.3.2, 7.3.4, 8.3.2 **LCPs:** 39.01, 49.01, 49.02, 49.03, 49.16, 49.17, 50.08 **SCANS:** Creative thinking, Interprets and communicates information **EFF:** Convey ideas in writing, Listen actively, Solve problems and make decisions

Warm-up and Review

10–15 minutes (books closed)

1. Review the *Bring It to Life* assignment from Lesson 5.

2. Have students who did the exercise share what they found. Write the items on the board. Ask students who didn't do the exercise to brainstorm other things they should cut up before throwing away.

Introduction and Presentation

5 minutes

1. Review future time clauses and *if* clauses. Ask questions and call on volunteers to answer. *What will you do before you eat dinner tonight? What will you do if I give a surprise test today? What will you do if your husband/wife brings you flowers tonight? What will you do when you first come to class tomorrow?* Write students' answers on the board in complete sentences.

2. State the objective: *Today we're going to review future time clauses and* if *clauses to talk about money.*

1 Grammar

Guided Practice

40–45 minutes

A Have students work individually to match the sentence parts. Call on volunteers to read the completed sentences aloud. Write the answers on the board.

B Read the example sentence (number 1) aloud. Ask students to work individually to circle the correct word(s) to complete the sentences. Call on volunteers to read the completed sentences aloud.

C Direct students to work individually to answer the questions with complete sentences. Have them take turns asking and answering the questions with a partner.

D Have students work with their partners to choose the correct word. Tell them to take turns reading the sentences aloud.

Multilevel Strategies

For 1C and 1D, seat same-level students together.

• **Pre-level** Work with this group. Read each item aloud. Elicit the answer from the group. Have all group members copy the answers into their books.

• **On- and Higher-level** While you are working with pre-level students, ask these students to work with their partners to complete 1C and 1D, and then to write three additional questions and answers with *before, when,* and *after.*

2 Group work

Communicative Practice

20–35 minutes

 1. Direct students, in groups of three or four, to focus on the picture. Ask: *Which one is the customer? Which one is the teller?*

2. Group students and assign roles: leader, recorder, timekeeper, and reporters. Explain that students work with their groups to write the conversation between the customer and the teller.

3. Check comprehension of the roles. Ask: *Who writes the conversation?* [recorder] *Who will read the conversations to the class?* [reporters] *Who helps everyone and manages the group?* [leader] *Who tells the group how much time has passed?* [timekeeper] *Who creates the sentences?* [everyone]

4. Set a time limit (five minutes) to complete the exercise. Circulate and answer any questions.

5. Have reporters from each group read the group's conversation to the class.

Multilevel Strategies

For 2A, use mixed-level groups.

- **Pre-level** Assign these students the role of timekeeper
- **On-level** Assign these students the role of recorder or reporter.
- **Higher-level** Assign these students the role of leader.

B 1. Have students walk around the room to conduct the interviews. To get students moving, tell them to interview three new people not in their groups from 2A.

2. Set a time limit (five minutes) to complete the exercise.

3. Tell students to make a note of their classmates' answers but not to worry about writing complete sentences.

C Call on individuals to report what they learned about their classmates. Encourage students to make generalizations. *Three out of four students have a financial goal.*

PROBLEM SOLVING

15–25 minutes

A 1. Ask: *Do you get credit-card offers in the mail? Do you read them?* Tell students they will read a story about a man who is trying to compare his credit-card offers. Direct students to read Li's story silently.

2. Ask: *How many credit-card offers does he get? How are they different?*

3. Play the audio and have the students read along silently.

B 1. Elicit answers to question 1. Ask volunteers to write their answers on the board. Continue until all of the class ideas have been put up.

2. As a class, decide which things are most important.

Evaluation

30–35 minutes

To test students' understanding of the unit grammar and life skills, have them take the Unit 7 Test in the *Step Forward Test Generator CD-ROM* with *ExamView® Assessment Suite.*

Learning Log

To help students record and discuss their progress, use the *Learning Log* on page T–202.

To extend this review: Have students complete **Workbook 3 page 50, Multilevel Activity Book 3 page 86,** and the **Unit 7 Exercises** on the **Multilevel Grammar Exercises CD-ROM 3.**

2 Group work

A Work with 2-3 classmates. Write a conversation between the customer and the teller in the picture. Share your conversation with the class.

Customer: Excuse me, there's a mistake on my bank statement. Could you check my account?

Teller: Sure. What seems to be the problem?

B Interview 3 classmates. Write their answers.

1. Do you enjoy financial planning? Why or why not?
2. Do you have a financial goal right now? What is it?
3. When you reach your goal, what will you do next?

C Talk about the answers with your class.

PROBLEM SOLVING

A Listen and read about Li.

Li is thinking about getting a credit card. Every week he receives 3 or 4 credit card offers in the mail. All the offers are a little different. For example, one card offers 0% interest for 6 months and 12% interest after that. Another card offers 7% interest all the time. Another card offers no annual fee and only 5% interest on balance transfers. All the cards promise to be the best. Li isn't sure what to think. They can't all be the best.

B Work with your classmates. Answer the questions.

1. What is Li's problem? Li doesn't know which credit card company is best.
2. What should Li do? Think of 2–3 things that Li should do before he decides which credit card to get.

UNIT 8

Living Well

FOCUS ON
- the body and health care
- wellness
- past actions with *used to*
- following doctor's advice
- drug safety

LESSON 1 Vocabulary

1 Learn parts of the body

A Talk about the questions with your class.

1. Do you think scientists and doctors know a little or a lot about the human body?
2. Do you think the study of the human body is interesting? Why or why not?

B Work with your classmates. Match the words with the pictures.

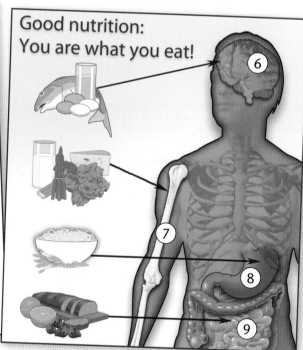

_5_	blood	_3_	heart	_4_	muscles
_7_	bones	_9_	intestines	_1_	skin
_6_	brain	_2_	lungs	_8_	stomach

C Listen and check. Then read the new words with a partner.

D Work with a partner. Write other parts of the body you know. Check your words in a dictionary.

Unit 8 Lesson 1

Objectives	Grammar	Vocabulary	Correlations
On-level: Identify parts of the body, and describe medical departments **Pre-level:** Identify parts of the body and medical departments **Higher-level:** Talk and write about health using parts-of-the-body vocabulary and medical-department vocabulary	Present perfect and simple past (*I have been in the hospital. I had a broken arm.*)	Parts of the body and medical departments For vocabulary support, see these **Oxford Picture Dictionary** topics: The Body, Hospital	**CASAS:** 0.1.2, 0.1.5, 0.2.1, 2.5.1, 3.1.1, 3.1.3, 3.5.9, 4.8.1, 7.4.5 **LCPs:** 39.01, 49.02, 49.09, 49.10 **SCANS:** Listening, Participates as a member of a team, Seeing things in the mind's eye **EFF:** Cooperate with others, Reflect and evaluate, Speak so others can understand

Warm-up and Review

10–15 minutes (books closed)

Review body parts. Have a volunteer come to the front of the room and call out body parts. Ask the rest of the class to stand and point to or touch the correct body part. Have another student write the words on the board as the first volunteer says them.

Introduction

5 minutes

1. Ask: *Are any of these body parts on the inside of our bodies? Which ones?* Circle students' answers.

2. State the objective: *Today we're going to learn the names of more body parts and talk about areas of the hospital where we go when we have trouble with them.*

1 Learn parts of the body

Presentation I

20–25 minutes

A Write *Health* on the board, and elicit students' answers to the questions.

B 1. Direct students to look at the pictures. Ask: *What is aerobic exercise? What does you are what you eat mean?*

2. Group students and assign roles: leader, fact checker, recorder, and reporter. Explain that students work with their groups to match the words and pictures.

3. Check comprehension of the roles. Ask: *Who looks up the words in a dictionary?* [fact checker] *Who writes the numbers in the book?* [recorder] *Who tells the class your answers?* [reporter] *Who helps everyone and manages the group?* [leader]

4. Set a time limit (three minutes). As students work together, copy the wordlist onto the board.

5. Call "time." Have reporters take turns giving their answers. Write each group's answer on the board next to the word.

C 1. To prepare students for listening, say: *Now we're going to listen to some advice about staying healthy.* Ask students to listen and check their answers.

2. Have students check the wordlist on the board and then write the correct numbers in their books.

3. Pair students. Set a time limit (three minutes). Monitor pair practice to identify pronunciation issues.

4. Call "time" and work with the pronunciation of any troublesome words or phrases.

5. Replay the audio and challenge students to listen for more information about each item. Call on volunteers to share what they remember about each item.

D 1. Ask students to work with their partners from 1C to brainstorm a list of related words.

2. Elicit words from the class. Write them on the board. Ask students to copy them into their vocabulary notes for the unit.

Guided Practice

5–10 minutes

 1. Model the conversations with a volunteer. Model them again using other information from 1B.

2. Set a time limit (three minutes). Direct students to practice with a partner.

3. Ask volunteers to repeat one of their conversations for the class.

2 Learn about medical departments

Presentation II

15–20 minutes

 1. Direct students to look at the hospital directory. Introduce the new topic: *Now we're going to talk about places in the hospital.*

2. Read the department names aloud, and ask students to point to the correct department on the map. Elicit the purpose of each department.

3. Ask students to work individually to write the department names next to the sentences.

4. Call on volunteers for the answers.

5. Check comprehension. Ask: *Where does a nine-year-old go when he/she's sick?* [Pediatrics] *Where does a woman go when she's pregnant?* [Maternity] *Where do you go if you break a bone?* [Emergency]

Guided Practice

10–15 minutes

 1. Model the conversation with a volunteer. Model it again using a different word from 2A.

2. Set a time limit (three minutes). Direct students to practice with a partner. Call on volunteers to say one of their conversations for the class.

Communicative Practice and Application

10–15 minutes

 1. Give students time to make notes of their answers to the questions. Call on individuals to share their ideas with the class.

2. Write students' ideas for question 2 on the board. Have the class vote for the part of the body they think doctors most need to learn about.

Evaluation

10–15 minutes (books closed)

TEST YOURSELF

1. Direct students to work individually to write a list of words from the lesson. Assign a time limit (three minutes). Call "time" and direct students to work with a partner to combine their lists and put the words in alphabetical order.

2. Circulate and monitor students' progress.

3. Ask a volunteer pair to write its list on the board. Ask other students to add words to the list.

> ### Multilevel Strategies
>
> Target the *Test Yourself* to the level of your students.
>
> • **Pre-level** Have students work in pairs to write their lists.
>
> • **Higher-level** After these students have worked with a partner to alphabetize their lists, ask them to write three to five sentences that demonstrate the meanings of words from the list.

To compress this lesson: Conduct 1B as a whole-class activity.

To extend this lesson: Talk about health problems. Elicit the names of body parts discussed in this unit. Write the words on the board. As a class, discuss the most common ailments that are associated with particular organs/body parts—for example, lungs and pneumonia, blood and leukemia, muscles and sprains or pulls. Give students time to copy the ailment words, and allow volunteers to share stories or ask questions about these illnesses.

And/Or have students complete **Workbook 3 page 51** and **Multilevel Activity Book 3 pages 88–89**.

E Work with a partner. Practice the conversation. Use the pictures in 1B.

A: What are milk and cheese good for?

B: They're good for your bones.

A: What is aerobic exercise good for?

B: It's good for your heart and lungs.

2 Learn about medical departments

A Look at the hospital directory. Write the department names next to the sentences below.

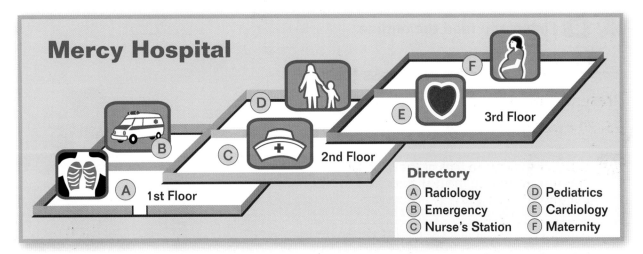

Radiology	1. Zack might have a broken bone. He needs an X-ray.
Nurse's Station	2. Alan's mom is in the hospital. He needs to talk to a nurse.
Maternity	3. Rita is going to have a baby.
Emergency	4. Ted had a car accident. He came to the hospital in an ambulance.
Pediatrics	5. Ok Sook has a stomach problem. She's ten years old.
Cardiology	6. Habib needs to have some tests done on his heart.

B Work with a partner. Practice the conversation. Use the words in 2A.

A: Excuse me. Where is Maternity?

B: It's on the third floor, near Cardiology.

A: Thank you.

C Talk about the questions with a partner.

1. Which medical departments have you been to?
2. Which parts of the body do doctors need to learn more about? Why?

TEST YOURSELF ✔

Close your book. Work with a partner. Make a list of as many new words from the lesson as you can. Alphabetize your list.

1 Read an outline about staying healthy

A **Look at the pictures. Talk about the questions with your class.**

1. What things do you do to take care of your health?
2. What do you think is the most important thing people can do to stay healthy?

B **Listen and read the outline.**

Maria's Wellness Plan

I. Improve Eating Habits
   A. Eat less fast food
   B. Eat low-fat ice cream
   C. Eat more fresh vegetables at lunch and dinner

II. Get in Shape
   A. Do aerobics three times a week
   B. Lift weights for strong bones and muscles

III. Stay Well
   A. Make medical and dental appointments
      1. See the doctor for a physical exam
      2. See the dentist for a cleaning
      3. Get an eye exam
   B. Manage Stress
      1. Relax with my family
      2. Don't worry about little things

C **Check your understanding. Circle *a* or *b*.**

1. Maria plans to eat less ____.
   a. fast food
   b. fresh vegetables

2. Maria will ____ three times a week.
   a. do aerobics
   b. get an eye exam

3. The three main parts of Maria's plan are about ____.
   a. nutrition, doctors, and stress
   b. nutrition, exercise, and staying well

4. Maria has only two details about ____.
   a. eating habits
   b. managing stress

Unit 8 Lesson 2

Objectives	Grammar	Vocabulary	Correlations
On and Higher-level: Analyze, write, and edit a wellness plan **Pre-level:** Read a wellness plan, and write about health care and wellness	Present tense (*I exercise every day.*)	*Aerobics, weights, immunizations, nutrition, wellness, prescription, stress* For vocabulary support, see these **Oxford Picture Dictionary** topics: Taking Care of Your Health, Illnesses and Medical Conditions	**CASAS:** 0.1.2, 0.2.1, 0.2.4, 3.5.2, 3.5.8, 7.1.2, 7.1.3, 7.2.7, 7.4.2 **LCPs:** 39.01, 41.06, 49.02, 49.02, 49.16, 49.17 **SCANS:** Decision making, Listening, Organizes and maintains information **EFF:** Convey ideas in writing, Read with understanding, Speak so others can understand

Warm-up and Review

10–15 minutes (books closed)

Talk about health problems. Write *Health Problems* on the board, and elicit the most common health problems—for example, common cold, flu, cancer, heart disease, asthma, diabetes, depression, allergies, etc.

Introduction

5 minutes

1. Ask students which of the problems on the board can be avoided or made less likely by a person's behavior.

2. State the objective: *Today we're going to read and write about health care and staying well.*

1 Read an outline about staying healthy

Presentation

20–25 minutes

A 1. Direct students to look at the pictures. Ask: *Does she look healthy?*

2. Elicit answers to questions 1 and 2.

B 1. Direct students to look at the title. Ask: *What do you think a wellness plan is?*

2. Ask students to read the wellness plan silently. Check students' comprehension. Ask: *Why is Maria going to do aerobics and lift weights? How is she going to manage stress?* Elicit what Maria is doing in each of the pictures.

3. Play the audio. Have students read along silently.

> **TIP**
> Teach students the expression *stop and smell the roses*, as it relates to Maria's stress-management plan (and the accompanying picture).

Guided Practice I

10 minutes

C Read each sentence aloud, and direct students to choose *a* or *b*. Go over the answers as a class.

Multilevel Strategies

For 1C, challenge on- and higher-level students while working with pre-level students.

- **Pre-level** While other students are working on 1C, ask these students *Yes/No* and *Or* questions about the wellness plan. *Is Maria going to eat more or less fast food? Is she going to eat ice cream? Is she going to see her doctor?*

- **On- and Higher-level** Have these students come up with one additional idea for each section of the wellness plan. Ask volunteers to share their ideas with the class.

2 Write an outline about staying healthy

Guided Practice II
20–25 minutes

A 1. Read the questions aloud.

2. Write categories on the board: *Eat, Don't Eat, Exercise, Health problems*. As you elicit students' answer to the questions, write their ideas in the correct category.

B 1. Direct students to look back at the model in 1B. Focus their attention on how Maria's plan is organized. Point out the roman numerals, letters, and numbers.

2. Draw a model outline on the board with *Improve Eating Habits, Get in Shape, and Stay Well* as the main headings. Elicit possible completions for subcategories.

3. Direct students to work individually to write their plan, using ideas from the board and Maria's plan as a model.

Multilevel Strategies

Adapt 2B to the level of your students.

• **Pre-level** Work with these students to create a short plan—two sections, two subcategories in each section. Elicit ways to improve nutrition, to get in shape, etc. Give them time to write down each idea before you move on to the next category.

• **Higher-level** Ask these students to expand on Part III (*Stay Well*). Tell them to include a number 3 in parts A and B, or to add a part C. Write the possible outlines on the board to clarify your instructions.

C 1. Lead students through the process of using the *Editing checklist*. Read each sentence aloud, and ask students to check their papers before moving on to the next item.

2. Allow students a few minutes to edit their writing as necessary.

Communicative Practice
10 minutes

D 1. Read the instructions aloud. Emphasize to students that they are responding to their partners' work, not correcting it.

2. Use the outline in 1B to model the exercise. *I like the idea* Don't worry about little things. *I'd like to ask this writer for an example of a little thing she's not going to worry about.*

3. Direct students to exchange plans with a partner and follow the instructions in numbers 1 and 2.

4. Call on volunteers to share something interesting they read in their partners' plan.

Application and Evaluation
15 minutes

TEST YOURSELF

1. Review the instructions aloud. Assign a time limit (ten minutes), and have students work independently.

2. Before collecting students' work, remind them to use the *Editing checklist*. Collect and correct students' writing.

To compress this lesson: Assign the *Test Yourself* for homework.

To extend this lesson: Practice talking about health.
1. Provide students with role-play instructions. *Partner A: Tell your partner you don't feel well lately. Answer your partner's questions. You have been working long hours, and you have been stopping for fast food on the way home. You're having trouble sleeping at night, and you don't have time to exercise. Partner B: Ask your partner questions about his/her health habits. Give some advice.*
2. Elicit some questions that Partner B can ask. *Do you have a lot of stress? Do you exercise? How long do you sleep at night? What do you eat?*
3. Have students practice the role-play with a partner and then switch roles.
4. Ask volunteers to share any good advice they got from their partners.

And/Or have students complete **Workbook 3 page 52** and **Multilevel Activity Book 3 page 90**.

2 Write an outline about staying healthy

A **Talk about the questions with your class.**

1. What food is healthy?
2. What kind(s) of exercise do you do?
3. Why do people see the doctor and dentist?
4. What are some ways to manage stress?

B **Write an outline of your plan for good health. Use the model in 1B and your answers to the questions in 2A.** Answers will vary.

My Wellness Plan

I. _____
   A. _____
   B. _____
   C. _____
II. _____
   A. _____
   B. _____
III. _____
   A. _____
     1. _____
     2. _____
   B. _____
     1. _____
     2. _____

C **Use the checklist to edit your writing. Check (✔) the true sentences.** Answers will vary.

Editing checklist	
1. I wrote at least three points about good eating habits.	
2. I wrote two different ways to stay well, and I wrote details for each one.	
3. I used a dictionary to check the spelling of words I wasn't sure about.	
4. All lines in my outline begin with a capital letter.	

D **Exchange outlines with a partner. Read and comment on your partner's work.**

1. Point out one part of the plan that you think is very interesting.
2. Ask your partner a question about his or her wellness plan.

TEST YOURSELF ✔

What wellness advice do you think a doctor or other healthcare worker would give? Write a new outline.

1 Learn *used to*

A **Look at the pictures and read the paragraph. What changes do you see in Sam?**

Sam wants to take better care of his health, so he has made some changes in his life. He <u>used to</u> eat a lot of junk food. He doesn't eat it anymore. He <u>didn't use to</u> eat fruit and vegetables. Now, he eats more healthy food. Sam <u>used to</u> watch a lot of TV. He <u>didn't use to</u> exercise. Now, he walks every day. Sam <u>didn't use to</u> have many friends. Now, he feels great and has made many new friends.

Before

After

B **Study the charts. Underline the 5 examples of *used to* in the paragraph above.**

USED TO

Affirmative statements					
I You He She	**used to**	eat junk food.	We You They	**used to**	eat junk food.

Negative statements					
I You He She	**didn't use to**	exercise last year.	We You They	**didn't use to**	exercise last year.

Note
Use *used to* + verb to talk about a habit or situation that was true in the past but is not true now.

C **Read the sentences about the things that Sam used to do, but doesn't do now. Rewrite the sentences with the correct forms of *used to*.**

1. Sam watched a lot of TV last year.   <u>Sam used to watch a lot of TV.</u>

2. Sam didn't go outside very often.   <u>Sam didn't use to go outside very often.</u>

3. Sam drank too much soda.   <u>Sam used to drink too much soda.</u>

4. Sam didn't lift weights.   <u>Sam didn't use to lift weights.</u>

5. Sam stayed inside a lot.   <u>Sam used to stay inside a lot.</u>

✔ Use *used to* to discuss health habits and choices

Unit 8 Lesson 3

Objectives	Grammar	Vocabulary	Correlations
On- and Higher-level: Use *used to* to talk about health habits, and listen for information about health habits **Pre-level:** Recognize *used to* in conversations about health habits	*Used to (I used to exercise.)*	*Junk food, jogging, take care of yourself, steamer* For vocabulary support, see these **Oxford Picture Dictionary** topics: Taking Care of Your Health, Recreation	**CASAS:** 0.1.2, 0.1.5, 0.2.1, 7.4.7 **LCPs:** 39.01, 41.06, 49.02, 49.09, 49.13, 49.16, 49.17 **SCANS:** Interprets and communicates information, Listening, Reading, Writing **EFF:** Convey ideas in writing, Listen actively, Read with understanding, Reflect and evaluate

Warm-up and Review

10–15 minutes (books closed)

Write *Exercise* and *Eating Habits* on the board. Ask students to share what they did for exercise when they were younger and what they do now. Write the ideas on the board. Ask what things they ate when they were younger that they don't eat now and vice versa. Write the foods on the board.

Introduction

5–10 minutes

1. Say: *Many people's eating and exercise habits change during their lives.* Restate the information on the board with *used to.* *Now I eat a lot of salad. I used to eat a lot of French fries.*

2. State the objective: *Today we're going to learn to use* used to *to talk about our past habits.*

1 Learn *used to*

Presentation I

20–25 minutes

 1. Direct students to look at the pictures. Ask: *Did Sam have healthy habits before? Does he have healthy habits now?*

2. Read the question. Ask students to look at the pictures and decide what has changed. Call on individuals to share their ideas.

 1. Demonstrate how to read the grammar charts.

2. Direct students to underline the examples of *used to* in the paragraph in 1A. Go over the answers as a class.

3. Read the *Note* aloud. Ask: *Does Sam eat a lot of junk food now?*

4. Read the chart through sentence by sentence. Then read it again, and have students repeat after you.

5. Assess students' understanding of the charts. Ask students to tell you which items from the warm-up represent things they used to do or used to eat. Remind them that they can't use *used to* to describe things they still do.

Guided Practice I

15–20 minutes

 Ask students to work individually to rewrite the sentences with *used to.* Ask volunteers to write the answers on the board.

Multilevel Strategies

For 1C, seat same-level students together.

• **Pre-level** While other students are completing 1C, ask these students to use the charts in 1B to write two affirmative and two negative sentences. Give them time to copy the answers to 1C after they are written on the board.

• **On- and Higher-level** When these students finish 1C, have them write four original sentences using *used to.* Tell them to write two affirmative sentences and two negative sentences.

TIP For more practice with statements with *used to* before you begin 2A, talk about the "old days." Write: *What was different?* on the board along with several years: *1960, 1800, 1400.* Have a class discussion about each era. *How was nutrition different then from now? How was medicine different? How were people's exercise habits and health awareness different?* Write students' ideas on the board. Ask students to work with a partner to write sentences about the different eras with *used to* and *didn't use to.* Have volunteers write their sentences on the board. Correct them together.

2 Learn questions with *used to*

Presentation II

20–25 minutes

A 1. Introduce the new topic. *Now we're going to ask questions with* used to.

2. Read the questions and answers in the chart aloud. Ask students to underline both parts of the verb in one of the questions. Point out that *use to* is used in questions. Write a negative sentence on the board. *I didn't use to like spinach.* Then remind students that *use* is also used in negative sentences.

3. Have students work individually to match the questions and answers. Call on volunteers to read the matching questions and answers aloud.

TIP Before 2B, write some question words and verbs on the board to help students practice creating questions with *use to.* Write *where, when,* and *what* on one side of the board. Write *go to school, live, work, do for fun* on the other side. Call on volunteers to ask questions. *Where did you use to go to school?* Answer the questions.

Guided Practice I

10–15 minutes

B Give students time to read each sentence. Write the choices on the board, and ask for a show of hands about each one. If necessary, refer students back to the chart in 2A. Have students circle the correct words in their books.

Multilevel Strategies

Seat same-level students together for 2C.

• **Pre-level** Provide these students with the questions for the exercise, and direct them to write the answers.

• **Higher-level** Ask these students to write two or three additional questions that they could ask a classmate. After you have gone over the 2B questions and answers on the board, call on individuals to ask their questions. Call on other students to answer.

C Have students work individually to complete the questions. Ask volunteers to write the completed questions on the board. Go over the questions as a class.

TIP To provide more practice writing sentences with *used to,* have students "illustrate" their past habits with pictures from magazines. Demonstrate the activity. Choose pictures of things, places, or people and tape them on the board. Then write sentences about your life. For example: with a picture of a park, a person running, and a carton of milk, write: *I used to live near a park. I used to run every day. I didn't use to drink much milk.* Pass out magazines and ask students to cut out three pictures and write sentences about them. Have students sit with a group and share their pictures and their sentences. Encourage group members to ask follow-up questions. *How much did you run? Did you use to be on a team?* Monitor and provide feedback. To have more control over the content of this activity, specify the kind of pictures you want students to use—for example, pictures of food, pictures of activities, health-related pictures, etc.

2 Learn questions with *used to*

Study the chart. Then match the questions below with the answers.

Questions and answers with *used to*	
A: Did Jim **use to smoke**? **B:** Yes, he did. OR No, he didn't.	**A:** Did they **use to see** Dr. Jones? **B:** No, they **didn't use to see** Dr. Jones.
A: When did you **use to exercise**? **B:** We **used to exercise** after work.	**A:** What doctor did they **use to see**? **B:** They **used to see** Dr. Green.

___b___ 1. What did Mia use to eat all the time?   a. No, she didn't.

___c___ 2. Where did Mia use to eat?   b. She used to eat fast food.

___d___ 3. What problem did Mia use to have?   c. She used to eat in her car.

___a___ 4. Did Mia use to take care of herself?   d. She used to have stomach problems.

___f___ 5. Why did Mia use to eat fast food?   e. Yes, she does.

___e___ 6. Does Mia take care of herself now?   f. She used to be too busy to cook.

B **Get the form. Work with your class. Circle the correct words in the sentences.**

1. Write ((used to) / use to) + *verb* for affirmative sentences.
2. Write *didn't* (used to / (use to)) + *verb* for negative sentences.
3. Write (used to / (use to)) in questions with *did*.

C **Complete the questions and answers. Use the correct form of *used to* and the words in parentheses.**

1. **A:** How often _did Tom use to get a physical exam_____? (Tom, get a physical exam)

   B: He used to get a physical exam once a year when he was younger.

2. **A:** Did _Mr. and Mrs. Diaz use to live_____ in Mexico? (Mr. and Mrs. Diaz, live)

   B: Yes, they did. They _use to live_____ in Mexico City 5 years ago. (live)

3. **A:** Did _Sara use to study_____? (Sara, study)

   B: Yes, she used to study a lot when she was a student.

4. **A:** When _did Bill use to lift weights_____? (Bill, lift weights)

   B: He used to lift weights when he was in college.

5. **A:** When she was a child, how often _did Fatima use to eat breakfast_____? (Fatima, eat breakfast)

   B: She used to eat breakfast every day when she was a child.

3 Grammar listening

A Listen to the health habits of the Martinez family. Mark the sentences T (true) or F (false).

<u> F </u> 1. Livia eats white bread now.

<u> T </u> 2. Carlos didn't use to go to the park.

<u> F </u> 3. Tomas used to save a lot of money.

<u> F </u> 4. Paulo didn't use to exercise on the weekend.

<u> T </u> 5. Elena can't play basketball because she hurt her knee.

B Listen and check (✔) *used to, didn't use to,* or Question with *use to.*

	used to	*didn't use to*	Question with *use to*
1.			✔
2.		✔	
3.	✔		
4.			✔
5.		✔	

4 Practice *used to*

A Think about your answers to these questions.

1. What exercise did you use to do that you don't do now?
2. What food did you use to eat that you don't eat anymore?
3. What places did you use to go that you don't go now?
4. What habit did you use to have that you don't have anymore?

B Work with 3 classmates. Compare your answers from 4A.

A: *I used to play at the playground when I was in elementary school.*
B: *I used to play volleyball, but now I don't have time.*

C Talk about your answers with the class.

Nadia and I used to eat beef, but we don't eat it anymore.

> **TEST YOURSELF** ✔
>
> Close your book. Write 4 sentences about yourself and 4 sentences about your classmates. Use *used to* and the information you learned in 4B and 4C.
> *Ali used to play soccer, but he doesn't anymore.*

3 Grammar listening

Guided Practice II

10–15 minutes

 1. Say: *Now we're going to listen to some sentences about the health habits of the Martinez family.*

2. Play the audio. Direct students to read along silently without writing.

3. Replay the audio. Ask students to mark the sentences T (true) or F (false).

4. Go over the sentences as a class.

Multilevel Strategies

Replay the *Grammar listening* to challenge on- and higher-level students while allowing pre-level students to catch up.

- **Pre-level** Have these students listen again to mark the sentences T (true) or F (false).

- **On- and Higher-level** Have these students write one or more sentences with *used to* about the Martinez family.

B **1.** Read the instructions aloud. Play the audio and ask students to check the appropriate column in the chart.

2. Replay the audio. Stop after each item to elicit which column students checked. Call on volunteers to repeat what they heard.

4 Practice *used to*

Communicative Practice and Application

20–25 minutes

 1. Direct students to look at the photo. Ask: *Can you do that?*

2. Read the questions aloud. Elicit one or two possible answers for each question. Ask students to work individually to write their answers.

B **1.** Put students in groups of four.

2. Direct students to take turns asking and answering the questions from 4A in their groups. Tell them to make notes of each other's answers. Model the exercise by asking a volunteer the first question. Have the class tell you how to write the answer in note form.

3. Check comprehension of the exercise. Ask: *How many people are you going to talk to?* [three] *Whose answers are you going write?* [everyone's] *Are you going to write complete sentences?* [no]

C Call on volunteers to share what they learned about their classmates. Ask them what similarities and differences they found.

TIP

Before students write the sentences for the *Test Yourself,* practice connecting clauses with *but.* Write several pairs of sentences, and ask students to connect them with *but. Tom used to eat donuts for breakfast. Now he doesn't eat donuts. I didn't use to lift weights. Now I lift weights.*

Evaluation

10–15 minutes

TEST YOURSELF

Ask students to write the sentences independently. Collect and correct their writing.

Multilevel Strategies

Target the *Test Yourself* to the level of your students.

- **Pre-level** Provide skeleton sentences for these students to complete. *I didn't use to _____, but now I do. I used to _____, but now I don't. _____ (partner's name) used to _____, but he/she doesn't anymore. _____ (partner's name) didn't use to _____, but now he/she _____.*

- **Higher-level** Have these students write a paragraph in response to this question and prompt: *How have your health habits changed? Write about what you used to do and what you do differently now.*

To compress this lesson: Conduct 2A as a whole-class activity.

To extend this lesson: As a follow-up to 4C, have students write generalizations about the class on the board: *Most of us used to exercise more often. Some of us used to smoke.* Read the sentences and ask for a show of hands to find out if the generalization is true.

And/Or have students complete **Workbook 3 pages 53–54, Multilevel Activity Book 3 pages 91–92,** and the corresponding **Unit 8 Exercises** on the **Multilevel Grammar Exercises CD-ROM 3**.

Unit 8 Lesson 4

Objectives	Grammar	Vocabulary	Correlations
On-, Pre-, and Higher-level: Give and accept advice, and listen for health information	Present perfect continuous (*I haven't been feeling well lately.*)	Health and exercise vocabulary For vocabulary support, see these **Oxford Picture Dictionary** topics: Taking Care of Your Health, Symptoms and Injuries, Illnesses and Medical Conditions	**CASAS:** 0.1.2, 0.1.5, 3.5.8, 6.0.3, 6.0.4, 6.2.3 **LCPs:** 41.03, 41.06, 49.02, 49.09, 49.16, 50.02, 51.03 **SCANS:** Arithmetic/Mathematics, Listening, Reading **EFF:** Listen actively, Observe critically, Read with understanding, Reflect and evaluate, Use math to solve problems and communicate

Warm-up and Review

10–15 minutes (books closed)

Write some problems on the board. *I'm overweight. I'm under a lot of stress. I feel tired all the time. I can't sleep at night.* Elicit a piece of advice for each problem, and write it on the board.

Introduction

5 minutes

1. Point out that all of the problems on the board can be helped to some degree by exercise. Say, *That's why health-care workers often advise us to exercise.*

2. State the objective: *Today we're going to learn how to give and respond to health advice.*

1 Learn to follow a doctor's advice

Presentation I

15–20 minutes

A 1. Direct students to look at the pictures. Read the questions aloud.

2. Play the audio. Give students time to answer the questions. Go over the answers as a class.

Guided Practice

20–25 minutes

B 1. Read the instructions aloud. Ask students to read silently for an answer to the question. Elicit the answer.

2. Ask students to read the conversation with a partner. Circulate and monitor pronunciation. Model and have students repeat difficult words or phrases.

3. Say and have students repeat the expressions in the *In other words* box. Elicit the placement of the expressions in the conversation. Ask volunteers to read the conversation using expressions from the box.

Communicative Practice and Application

15–20 minutes

C 1. Ask students to read the instructions silently. Check their comprehension of the exercise. Ask: *What are the two roles? What is the situation?* Elicit examples of what the doctor and the patient might say.

2. Set a time limit (five minutes). Ask students to act out the role-play in both roles. Ask one to three volunteer pairs to act out their conversations for the class. Tell students who are listening to note the expressions used for giving and accepting advice.

Multilevel Strategies

For 1C, adapt the role-play to the level of your students.

• **Pre-level** Provide a simplified conversation for these students. *A: I'm concerned about your heart. B: I'm always tired. A: Do you exercise? B: I used to ride my bike, but I don't have time now. A: You could ride your bike to work. B: OK, I'll start tomorrow.*

---

1 Learn to follow a doctor's advice

A Look at the pictures. Listen to the conversation.
Then check the correct patient.

Patient 1

Patient 2

1. Which patient used to go to the gym? ☐ Patient 1 ☑ Patient 2
2. Which patient used to jog? ☑ Patient 1 ☐ Patient 2

B Listen and read. What does the doctor suggest for this patient?

Doctor: I'm a little concerned about your blood pressure.

Patient: I've been under a lot of stress recently.

Doctor: Have you been getting enough exercise?

Patient: Well, I used to go to the gym, but it was too expensive.

Doctor: Heart disease runs in your family,* so you need to exercise. Why don't you walk in the park?

Patient: OK. I can do that. I'll start today.

*****Idiom note:** run in the family = to be common in a family

> **In other words...**
>
> **Making suggestions**
> Why don't you...
> You might...
> You could...
>
> **Accepting suggestions**
> I can do that.
> Good idea. I'll try it.
> I'll give it a try.

C Role-play a doctor/patient conversation with a partner. Use the example in 1B to make a new conversation.

Partner A: You are a doctor. You are concerned about your patient's heart. Ask about the patient's exercise habits. Suggest that your patient ride a bike to work.

Partner B: You're the patient. You've been tired a lot recently. You used to ride your bike after work, but now you don't have time. Accept your doctor's suggestion.

2 Learn present perfect continuous

A Look at the time line and study the chart. Then read the sentences with a partner.

Tomas has been working at a restaurant for two years.

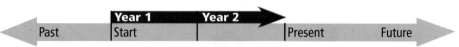

The present perfect continuous		
⌐Subject⌐	⌐have/has + been + verb + *ing*⌐	
I	**have been walking**	to work since April.
They	**haven't been getting**	enough exercise recently.
He	**has been working**	at a restaurant for two years.
She	**hasn't been feeling**	well this week.

Note

Use the present perfect continuous to talk about actions or situations that began in the past and are continuing now.

B Complete the sentences. Use the words in parentheses.

1. Stan _____has been waiting_____ to see the doctor for an hour. (wait)

2. We __have been walking_____ for 30 minutes. (walk)

3. I __have been cooking_____ since 4:30. (cook)

4. They __have not been feeling_____ well recently. (not feel)

5. Roya __has not been exercising_____ three times a week. (not exercise)

3 Practice your pronunciation

A Listen to the pronunciation of *use* in each sentence. Which *use* has the *z* sound? Which has the *s* sound?

1. I **use** the microwave to cook vegetables.
   "z" sound

2. I didn't **use** to eat a lot of vegetables.
   "s" sound

B Listen and complete the sentences. Use *use, didn't use,* or *didn't use to.* Then read the sentences with a partner.

1. What do most people __use_____ to cook vegetables?

2. These days, they __use_____ steamers and microwaves.

3. There was a time when people __didn't use to_____ eat a lot of vegetables.

4. They __didn't use_____ microwaves, because there weren't any!

C Listen again and check. Repeat the sentences.

2 Learn present-perfect continuous

Presentation II

15–20 minutes

 A 1. Introduce the new topic. *Now we're going to learn a new tense, the present perfect continuous.* Direct students to look at the timeline and read the sentence about Tomas.

2. Ask questions about the timeline. *Is Tomas working at the restaurant now? Did he work there in the past?* Say: *When we talk about an action beginning in the past and continuing to the present, we use present perfect continuous.*

3. Write the sentence about Tomas on the board, and elicit the three parts of the verb. [*have + be + -ing*]

4. Read the sentences in the chart. Point out the time expressions: *since April, recently, for two years, this week.* Read the *Note.*

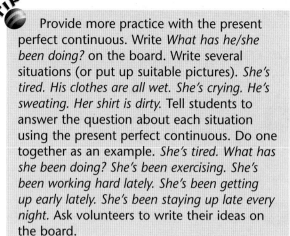

TIP
Point out that with some verbs, like *work* and *live*, we can use the present perfect to express the same idea, but with most actions, we use the present perfect continuous.

Guided Practice and Communicative Practice

15–20 minutes

B Have students work individually to complete the sentences. Ask volunteers to write the answers on the board.

TIP
Provide more practice with the present perfect continuous. Write *What has he/she been doing?* on the board. Write several situations (or put up suitable pictures). *She's tired. His clothes are all wet. She's crying. He's sweating. Her shirt is dirty.* Tell students to answer the question about each situation using the present perfect continuous. Do one together as an example. *She's tired. What has she been doing? She's been exercising. She's been working hard lately. She's been getting up early lately. She's been staying up late every night.* Ask volunteers to write their ideas on the board.

3 Practice your pronunciation

Pronunciation Extension

10–15 minutes

A 1. Write *She used to use too much salt.* on the board. Say the sentence and ask students to repeat it. Underline the *s* in *used to* and *use*, and repeat each word. Say: *Now we're going to focus on the pronunciation of* used to *and the verb* use.

2. Play the audio. Direct students to read the sentences.

3. Elicit the answers to the questions. Replay the audio or say the sentences and have students repeat.

B Play the audio. Direct students to fill in the blanks.

C 1. Replay the audio. Ask students to check their answers.

2. Call on volunteers to read the sentences aloud. Then have students take turns reading the sentences with a partner. Monitor and provide feedback on pronunciation.

4 Focus on Listening

Listening Extension

20–25 minutes

A Read the questions aloud, and elicit answers from volunteers. Encourage students to respond to each other's ideas. After one student speaks, ask other students for their opinions. *Do you agree or disagree with what he/she said? Why?*

B 1. Direct students to read the sentences before they listen.

2. Play the audio. Ask students to listen and circle the correct word(s). Ask volunteers to read the completed sentences aloud.

C 1. Ask students to look at the list of activities. Ask: *Which one burns the fewest calories?* Play the audio and ask students to write the number of calories next to each activity.

2. Go over the answers as a class.

Multilevel Strategies

Replay the audio to challenge on- and higher-level students while allowing pre-level students to catch up.

• **Pre-level** Have these students listen again to write the number of calories.

• **On- and Higher-level** Tell these students to listen for the answer to these questions: *What do experts say is the best way to lose weight? What is one of the benefits of swimming?* Go over the answers as a class.

---

5 Real-life math

Math Extension

5–10 minutes

1. Direct students to look at the chart. Ask: *Which exercise burns the most calories?*

---

2. Ask students to read the paragraph about Mario and work individually to answer the questions.

3. Call on volunteers to answer each question. Ask them to write the problem and answer on the board.

TIP

If students are interested in learning more about calories per activity, have them type *calories* and *activity* into an Internet search engine. They can find the average number of calories burned for many activities. They can also find calculators to tell them how many calories they should consume every day based on their age, weight, and activity level.

Evaluation

10–15 minutes

TEST YOURSELF

1. Model the role-play with a volunteer. Then switch roles.

2. Pair students. Check comprehension of the exercise by eliciting things the doctor and patient might say.

3. Set a time limit (five minutes), and have the partners act out the role-play in both roles.

4. Circulate and monitor. Encourage pantomime and improvisation.

5. Provide feedback.

Multilevel Strategies

Target the *Test Yourself* to the level of your students.

• **Pre-level** Ask these students to use this skeleton conversation: *A: I'm concerned about your health. B: I've been tired a lot lately. A: How much do you exercise? B: _____ A: You could _____. B: OK, I'll start tomorrow.*

• **Higher-level** Ask these students to practice their role-play with several partners.

To compress this lesson: Conduct 2B as a whole-class activity.

To extend this lesson: Have students evaluate their activity levels.
1. Ask students to make a list of all of the activities they did over the last weekend.
2. Have students sit with a partner and together decide which activities and which partner probably burned the most calories over the weekend.
3. Ask if anyone's partner was exceptionally active. Ask those people to share what their partners did over the weekend.

And/Or have students complete **Workbook 3 page 55** and **Multilevel Activity Book 3 page 93**.

4 Focus on listening

A **Talk about the questions with your class.**

1. What are some reasons people don't get enough exercise?
2. What do you think is the best kind of exercise?

B **Listen to the radio program. Circle the correct words.**

1. Katie wants to ((lose weight)/ eat better food).
2. Katie's health is ((good)/ not good).
3. Donna tells Katie about ways to (clean the house / (use more calories)).

C **Listen again. How many calories do these activities burn? Write how many calories each activity burns per hour.**

_60_	watching TV	_300_	walking	_550_	running
_225_	cleaning house	_425_	swimming		

5 Real-life math

Read about Mario. Use the chart to answer the questions.

Mario had a busy weekend. On Saturday, he played soccer for three hours. After that, he came home and vacuumed his apartment for thirty minutes. Then he played the guitar for an hour.

On Sunday, he went for a 1-hour bike ride. Then he played soccer again for 90 minutes.

Activity	Calories/hour
bike riding	350
playing guitar	175
playing soccer	400
vacuuming	200

1. How many calories did Mario burn on Saturday? _1475_
2. How many calories did he burn on Sunday? _950_
3. On which day did Mario burn the most calories? _Saturday_

TEST YOURSELF ✔

Role-play a conversation between a doctor and a patient. Partner A: Ask about your patient's exercise habits. Make a suggestion to increase your patient's exercise. Partner B: Accept your doctor's suggestion. Then change roles.

1 Get ready to read

A **What kinds of medication do people take most often?**

B **Read the definitions.**

generic drug: (noun) a drug with no brand name that has the same ingredients as a more expensive drug with a brand name. For example: *Aspirin is a generic drug.*

side effect: (noun) something uncomfortable that happens when a patient takes medication. For example: *Headaches are a side effect of this heart medication.*

C **Look at the title of the brochure in 2A. Talk about the questions with your classmates.**

1. What are some questions you should ask before taking a new medication?
2. What kind of information is usually on a prescription label?

2 Read and respond

A **Read the brochure.**

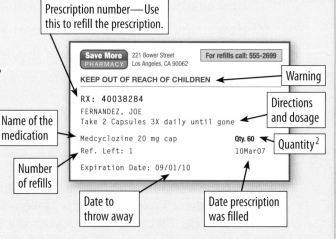

Using Medication Safely

In a study, 63 percent of Americans say they have taken vitamins in the last six months. 59 percent say they have taken over-the-counter (OTC) medication. 54 percent say they have taken a prescription medicine. Here are some ways to be sure you are using medication correctly and safely.

Ask the doctor or pharmacist these questions about the medication:

- Does this medicine have any side effects?
- What should I do if I have side effects?
- Is it safe to take this medicine with other medications or vitamins I take?
- Can I use a less expensive, generic drug?
- When should I start to feel better?

[1]dosage: the amount of medicine to take
[2]quantity: how many or how much of something

Read and understand the label:

Follow the directions:

- Each time you take the medicine, read the label again.
- Take the exact dosage.[1]
- Take the medicine until the directions tell you to stop.

Prescription number—Use this to refill the prescription.

Save More PHARMACY 221 Bower Street Los Angeles, CA 90062 For refills call: 555-2699

KEEP OUT OF REACH OF CHILDREN — Warning

RX: 40038284
FERNANDEZ, JOE
Take 2 Capsules 3X daily until gone — Directions and dosage

Medcyclozine 20 mg cap **Qty. 60** — Quantity[2]
Ref. Left: 1 10Mar07

Expiration Date: 09/01/10

Name of the medication

Number of refills

Date to throw away

Date prescription was filled

Source: *National Council on Patient Information and Education © 2002–2006*

Unit 8 Lesson 5

Objectives	Grammar	Vocabulary	Correlations
Pre-, On-, and Higher-level: Read about and discuss medication safety	Questions (*Does this medication have any side effects?*)	*Generic drug, side effect, quantity* For vocabulary support, see this **Oxford Picture Dictionary** topic: Taking Care of Your Health	**CASAS:** 0.1.2, 0.1.5, 3.1.3, 3.3.1, 3.3.2, 3.3.3, 3.4.1, 3.4.2, 7.2.3, 7.4.7 **LCPs:** 41.04, 49.04, 49.09, 49.16, 49.17 **SCANS:** Reading, Reasoning, Speaking **EFF:** Observe critically, Read with understanding, Speak so others can understand, Take responsibility for learning

Warm-up and Review

10–15 minutes (books closed)

Bring in empty bottles of some familiar over-the-counter medications and prescriptions (with the patient's name blacked out). Pass the bottles around to different areas of the room. Ask the students with the bottles to say the name of the medication and what it's for. Ask them to find the adult dosage on the label. After students have spoken, have them pass the bottle, so others can check the information.

Introduction

5 minutes

1. Say: *All of these medicines can be helpful when used correctly and dangerous when not used correctly.*

2. State the objective: *Today we're going to read and discuss medical safety.*

1 Get ready to read

Presentation

15–20 minutes

A Read the question aloud. When students answer, ask if you can buy those medications without a prescription. Write *over the counter* on the board, and tell students that it means medicines you can buy without a prescription.

B Read the words and definitions. Tell students that *acetaminophen* and *ibuprofen* are generic names. Ask them if they know the popular brand names. Elicit other common side effects besides headaches.

Pre-Reading

C Ask students to look at the title of the brochure. Read the questions aloud, and elicit their answers. Write the questions they come up with for number 1 on the board.

2 Read and respond

Guided Practice I

25–30 minutes

A 1. Ask students to read the brochure silently.

2. Direct students to underline unfamiliar words they would like to know. Elicit the words and encourage other students to provide definitions or examples.

3. Check students' comprehension. Ask: *What are the three ways of being sure you are using medicine safely?*

Multilevel Strategies

Adapt 2A to the level of your students.

• **Pre-level** While other students are reading 2A, direct these students to read the medicine label. Write these words on the board: *prescription, refill, quantity, expiration.* Ask students to copy the words and look them up in their dictionaries.

Guided Practice II

15–20 minutes

B 1. Play the audio. Have students read along silently.

2. Elicit and discuss any additional questions about the reading.

C Have students work individually to mark the sentences T (true), F (false), and NI (no information). Go over the answers as a class.

Multilevel Strategies

For 2C, work with pre-level students.

• **Pre-level** Ask these students *Yes/No* and *Either/Or* questions about the medicine label while other students are completing 2C. *Should Joe take three capsules a day? Should he throw the medicine away in September or January? Can he refill the prescription once more or twice more?* Give students time to copy the answers to 2C from the board.

TIP If you have access to the Internet in class, have students compare generic prices to brand-name prices at an online pharmacy.

D 1. Read the information in the chart aloud. Elicit and discuss any questions the students have about the meanings of the words or the prefix *re-*. Say the words and have students repeat them.

2. Direct students to work individually to complete each sentence. Ask volunteers to read the completed sentences aloud.

Multilevel Strategies

For 2D, seat same-level students together.

• **Pre-level** While other students are completing 2D, ask these students to write sentences with *print, read, use,* and *write*.

• **Higher-level** After these students finish 2D, have them write sentences demonstrating the contrast between the two forms of each word. Ask volunteers to write their sentences on the board.

3 Talk it over

Communicative Practice

15–20 minutes

A Read the statistics and the questions aloud. Set a time limit (three minutes). Have students work independently to think about the questions and write their answers in note form.

B Call on volunteers to share their ideas. Encourage students to respond to one another's ideas. After one student speaks, ask other students for their opinions. *Do you agree or disagree with what he/she said? Why?*

Application

5–10 minutes

BRING IT TO LIFE

Ask students what common over-the-counter medicines they have in their houses. Have them choose one and write down the information to share with the class.

To compress this lesson: Conduct the word study in 2D as a whole-class activity.

To extend this lesson: Have students practice asking questions about medicine labels.
1. Use the label on page 112, or pass out empty medicine bottles. As a class, brainstorm the questions students can ask about the label. *How often do I need to take this? What's the dosage? How long should I take it? What's it for? What's the expiration date? Can my child take this medicine?*
2. Have students practice asking and answering the questions with a partner.

And/Or have students complete **Workbook 3 page 56** and the **Multilevel Activity Book 3 pages 94–95**.

B Listen and read the brochure again.

C Mark the sentences T (true), F (false), or NI (no information).

   _T_ 1. It's important to ask your doctor about possible side effects.

   _F_ 2. You should throw away all medicine after six months.

  _NI_ 3. Vitamin C is the most popular vitamin that people take.

   _T_ 4. It's important to take the correct amount of medicine.

D Study the chart. Complete the sentences below.

> **Word Study: The prefix _re-_**
>
> Add _re-_ to the beginning of some verbs to mean _do the action again_.
> fill - refill
> The pharmacist filled my prescription last month. I took all the pills, so the pharmacist will **refill** the prescription this month.
>
> print reprint | read reread | use reuse | write rewrite

1. I can't read the number you wrote. Please ___rewrite___ it.
2. You should _reread_____ a medicine label each time you take the medicine.
3. There was a mistake on the label. The pharmacist has to _reprint_____ the label.
4. Don't throw that away! I think we can _reuse_____ it.

3 Talk it over

A Read the statistics. Think about the questions. Make notes about your answers.

1. Do these statistics surprise you? Why or why not?
2. Why do you think some people take too much medication?

Medication Statistics

- Of all the over-the-counter medications people buy, 78 percent are pain relievers.
- About 33 percent of people in the U.S. say they take more medication than the directions recommend.

Source: _National Council on Patient Information and Education_ © 2002–2006

B Talk about the answers with your classmates.

BRING IT TO LIFE

Look for an over-the-counter medicine at the pharmacy or in your home.
Write down the name, use, dosage, any side effects, and the expiration date.
Bring the information to class.

1 Grammar

A **Complete the sentences with *used to* and the correct form of the verbs in parentheses.**

1. Now Greg eats healthy food. He _____used to eat_____ junk food. (eat)
2. We _used to stay_____ home every evening, but now we take a walk. (stay)
3. Rita _didn't use to see_____ the doctor often. Now she goes every year. (not see)
4. I _didn't use to think_____ about my health, but now I think about it. (not think)

B **Complete the questions and answers with the correct form of *used to*.**

1. **A:** _Did_____ you _____use to_____ live in Florida?
   B: No, I didn't. I _____used to live_____ in New Jersey.
2. **A:** Where _did_____ you _use to_____ live?
   B: I _used to live_____ in Cleveland, Ohio. (live)
3. **A:** What _did_____ they _use to_____ study?
   B: They _used to study_____ Spanish. (study)
4. **A:** Where _did_____ your sister _use to_____ work?
   B: She _used to work_____ at the bank. (work)

C **Complete the sentences. Use the present perfect continuous and the verbs in parentheses.**

1. My brother _____has been driving_____ since he was 17. (drive)
2. He _has not been driving_____ this week. (not drive)
3. He _has been walking_____ to work instead. (walk)
4 The mechanic _has been fixing_____ his car all week. (fix)

D **Complete the questions and answers.**

1. **A:** _Where have_____ you been working?
   B: _I've been working_____ in a drugstore.
2. **A:** _How long has_____ John been studying English?
   B: _He's been studying_____ English for two years.
3. **A:** _How long have_____ Marcia and Lucy been swimming?
   B: _They've been swimming_____ since they were in elementary school.
4. **A:** _Where has_____ Alma been buying these delicious vegetables?
   B: _She's been buying_____ them at the farmers market downtown.

Unit 8 Review and expand

Objectives	Grammar	Vocabulary	Correlations
On-, Pre-, and Higher-level: Expand upon and review unit grammar and life skills	*Used to (I used to swim every day.)* Present perfect continuous (*I've been swimming since I was five.*)	Health habits vocabulary For vocabulary support, see these **Oxford Picture Dictionary** topics: Health Care, Daily Routines, Food Preparation, Recreation	**CASAS:** 0.1.2, 0.1.5, 0.2.1, 3.5.8, 7.2.6, 7.3.1, 7.3.2 **LCPs:** 41.06, 49.02, 49.16, 50.02 **SCANS:** Acquires and evaluates information, Interprets and communicates information, Listening, Participates as member of a team **EFF:** Cooperate with others, Read with understanding, Solve problems and make decisions

Warm-up and Review

10–15 minutes (books closed)

1. Review the *Bring It to Life* assignment from Lesson 5.

2. Have students who did the exercise discuss what they learned. For students who didn't do the exercise, provide medicine bottles.

3. As students share the information they found, ask them to group the medicines according to the ailment each medicine treats. *Which are painkillers?*

Introduction and Presentation

5 minutes

1. Tell students something you used to do. *I used to live in Arizona.* Ask: *What did you use to do?* Write your question and some of their answers on the board.

2. Tell students about something you have been doing lately. *I've been waking up early lately.* Ask what they have been doing, and write a few of their sentences on the board.

3. State the objective: *Today we're going to review* used to *and the present perfect continuous to talk about living well.*

1 Grammar

Guided Practice

40–45 minutes

A Read number 1 aloud. Ask students to work individually to complete the sentences. Call on volunteers to read the completed sentences aloud.

B Read number 1 aloud. Ask students to work individually to complete the questions and answers. Tell them to read the completed questions and answers with a partner.

C Ask students to work with their partners to complete the sentences. Have them take turns reading the sentences aloud. Ask volunteers to write the answers on the board.

D Ask students to work with their partners to complete the questions and answers. Have them take turns reading the questions and answers with a partner. Ask volunteers to write the completed questions and answers on the board.

Multilevel Strategies

For 1B, 1C, and 1D, seat same-level students together.

• **Pre-level** Work with these students on 1B and 1C. Allow them to copy the answers to 1D from the board.

• **On- and Higher-level** Ask these students to complete 1B, 1C, and 1D with their partners. Have them write two new questions and answers with the present perfect continuous. Go over the answers to 1B and 1C on the board. Then elicit their new questions and answers.

2 Group work

Communicative Practice

20–35 minutes

A 1. Direct students, in groups of three to four, to focus on the picture. Ask: *Has this woman changed her habits?*

2. Group students and assign roles: leader, recorder, timekeeper, and reporter. Explain that students work with their groups to write sentences about the woman's life.

3. Check comprehension of the roles. Ask: *Who writes the sentences?* [recorder] *Who will read the sentences to the class?* [reporter] *Who helps everyone and manages the group?* [leader] *Who tells the group how much time has passed?* [timekeeper] *Who creates the sentences?* [everyone]

4. Set a time limit (five minutes) to complete the exercise. Circulate and answer any questions.

5. Have a reporter from each group read the group's sentences to the class.

Multilevel Strategies

For 2A, use mixed-level groups.

• **Pre-level** Assign these students the role of timekeeper.

• **On-level** Assign these students the role of recorder or reporter.

• **Higher-level** Assign these students the role of leader.

B 1. Have students walk around the room to conduct these interviews. To get students moving, tell them to interview three new people not in their group for 2A.

2. Set a time limit (five minutes) to complete the exercise.

3. Tell students to make a note of their classmates' answers but not to worry about writing complete sentences.

Multilevel Strategies

Adapt the mixer in 2B to the level of your students.

• **Pre-level** Allow these students to ask and answer the questions without writing.

• **Higher-level** Have these students ask two additional questions and write all answers.

C Call on individuals to report what they learned about their classmates. Encourage students to make generalizations. *Three out of five people don't see the doctor enough.*

PROBLEM SOLVING

15–25 minutes

A 1. Ask: *Have you ever broken a bone?* Tell students they will read a story about a woman who hurts her ankle. Direct students to read Juan and Anita's story silently.

2. Ask: *How did she hurt her ankle? Why do they think her ankle is broken? Why don't they go home?*

3. Play the audio and have students read along silently.

B 1. Elicit answers to question 1. Have the class brainstorm a list of things Juan and Anita can do. Write the list on the board.

2. Come to a class consensus on Juan and Anita's best course of action.

Evaluation

30–35 minutes

To test students' understanding of the unit grammar and life skills, have them take the Unit 8 Test in the *Step Forward Test Generator CD-ROM* with *ExamView® Assessment Suite*.

Learning Log

To help students record and discuss their progress, use the *Learning Log* on page T-202.

To extend this review: Have students complete **Workbook 3 page 57, Multilevel Activity Book 3 page 96,** and the **Unit 8 Exercises** on the **Multilevel Grammar Exercises CD 3.**

2 Group work

A Work with 2–3 classmates. Write 5 sentences about the woman's life *before* and *after* she made some changes. Share your sentences with the class.

Before

After

She used to be tired. Now she feels great.

B Interview 3 classmates. Write their answers.

1. What's a quick, healthy meal you like to eat or prepare?
2. Do you think that most people eat well every day? Why or why not?
3. Is it easy or difficult for most people to exercise every day? Why?

C Talk about the answers with your class.

PROBLEM SOLVING

A Listen and read about Juan and Anita.

   Juan and his wife, Anita, were riding their bicycles in a large state park. Anita fell off her bike and hurt her ankle. She can't move it, and it really hurts. Juan and Anita think it might be broken. It doesn't look like Anita can walk. Juan has a cell phone, but they don't know where they are in the park. Juan used to have a map of the park, but he doesn't have it now.

B Work with your classmates. Answer the questions.

1. What is Juan and Anita's problem? Juan and Anita need to call for help, but they don't know how to describe where they are.
2. What should they do? Outline a plan or make a list of what they should do.

Hit the Road

FOCUS ON
- parts of a car
- describing travel
- time clauses
- buying a car
- lemon laws

LESSON **1** Vocabulary

1 Learn automobile vocabulary

A Talk about the questions with your class.

1. Have you ever changed the oil in a car before?
2. What is Quick Change's recommendation for oil changes? Do you agree?

B Work with your classmates. Match the words with the picture.

_9_ bumper	_4_ hood	_7_ trunk
_6_ gas tank	_8_ license plate	_5_ turn signal
_2_ headlight	_3_ tire	_1_ windshield

C Listen and check. Then read the new words with a partner.

D Work with a partner. Write other automobile words you know. Check your words in a dictionary.

Unit 9 Lesson 1

Objectives	Grammar	Vocabulary	Correlations
On-level: Identify interior and exterior automobile parts and describe their functions **Pre-level:** Identify interior and exterior automobile parts **Higher-level:** Talk and write about automobiles	Simple-present tense (*You use the rearview mirror to see behind you.*)	Interior and exterior automobile parts For vocabulary support, see this **Oxford Picture Dictionary** topic: Parts of a Car, Buying and Maintaining a Car	**CASAS:** 0.1.2, 0.1.5, 1.9.6, 4.8.1 **LCPs:** 39.01, 49.02, 49.10 **SCANS:** Listening, Organizes and maintains information, Participates as a member of a team, Seeing things in the mind's eye **EFF:** Cooperate with others, Listen actively, Observe critically, Reflect and evaluate

Warm-up

10–15 minutes (books closed)

Find out how many car words the students already know. Draw a simple car on the board, and ask students to brainstorm words they associate with it. Write their ideas on the board.

Introduction

5 minutes

1. Ask how many of your students have a car. Ask if any of them can fix a car.

2. State the objective: *Today we're going to learn words for talking about cars.*

1 Learn automobile vocabulary

Presentation I

20–25 minutes

A Write *Parts of a Car* on the board, and elicit students' answers to the questions. If some students have changed their oil, ask them how they learned to do it and how often they do it.

B 1. Direct students to look at the picture. Ask students if they go to an oil-changing place like the one in the picture.

2. Group students and assign roles: leader, fact checker, recorder, and reporter. Explain that students work with their groups to match the words and pictures.

3. Check comprehension of the roles. Ask: *Who looks up the words in a dictionary?* [fact checker] *Who writes the numbers in the book?* [recorder] *Who tells the class your answers?* [reporter] *Who helps everyone and manages the group?* [leader]

4. Set a time limit (three minutes), and have students work together to complete the exercise. As students work together, copy the wordlist onto the board.

5. Call "time." Have reporters take turns giving their answers. Write each group's answer on the board next to the word.

C 1. To prepare students for listening, tell them that they're going to hear an employee from the Quick Change station talk about cars. Ask students to listen and check their answers.

2. Have students check the wordlist on the board and then write the correct numbers in their books.

3. Pair students. Set a time limit (three minutes). Monitor pair practice to identify pronunciation issues.

4. Call "time" and work with the pronunciation of any troublesome words or phrases.

5. Replay the audio and challenge students to listen for the advice Ramiro gives. Ask volunteers to share what they heard.

D 1. Ask students to work with their partners from 1C to brainstorm a list of related words.

2. Elicit words from the class. Write them on the board. Ask students to copy them into their vocabulary notes for the unit.

Guided Practice

5–10 minutes

 1. Model the conversation with a volunteer. Model it again using other information from 1B.

2. Set a time limit (three minutes). Direct students to practice with a partner. Ask volunteers to act out one of their conversations for the class.

2 Learn about the interior of a car

Presentation II

15–20 minutes

 1. Direct students to look at the automobile owner's manual. Introduce the new topic: *Now we're going to look at the inside of a car.*

2. Read the words aloud, and ask about each one. *What do you do with the steering wheel? What's the ignition for?* Have students repeat each word.

3. Ask students to work individually to complete the paragraph. Call on volunteers to read the completed sentences aloud. Write the answers on the board.

4. Check comprehension. Ask: *What tells you how fast the car is going? What do you use to see out the back window?*

Multilevel Strategies

Adapt 2A to the level of your students.

• **Pre-level** Direct these students to copy the words from the owner's manual and add a quick illustration or explanation.

• **Higher-level** After they complete 2A, ask these students to look at the picture of the inside of a car in *The Oxford Picture Dictionary* or another picture dictionary. Have them write two or three additional sentences about parts inside of a car.

Guided Practice

10–15 minutes

 1. Model the conversation with a volunteer. Model it again using a different word from 2A.

2. Set a time limit (three minutes). Direct students to practice with a partner. Call on volunteers to say one of their conversations for the class.

Communicative Practice and Application

10–15 minutes

 1. Give students time to make notes of their answers to the questions. Call on individuals to share their ideas with the class.

2. Find out whether students feel that their cars are safe or unsafe and why.

Evaluation

10–15 minutes (books closed)

TEST YOURSELF

1. Direct students to work individually to write a list of words from the lesson. Assign a time limit (three minutes). Call "time" and direct students to work with a partner to combine their lists and put the words in alphabetical order.

2. Circulate and monitor students' progress. Ask a volunteer pair to write their list on the board. Ask other students to add words to the list.

Multilevel Strategies

Target the *Test Yourself* to the level of your students.

• **Higher-level** After these students have worked with a partner to alphabetize their lists, ask them to write three to five sentences using words from the list.

To compress this lesson: Conduct 1B as a whole-class activity.

To extend this lesson: Discuss how cars have changed. Tell students that although cars have always had engines, steering wheels, and tires, they have changed in many ways in recent years. As a class, brainstorm a list of modern car features—for example, remote door locks, on-board navigation, side air bags, and hybrid engines. Write the list on the board. Ask students to rank these features from the one they would most like to have in their car to the ones they want the least.

And/Or have students complete **Workbook 3 page 58** and **Multilevel Activity Book 3 pages 98–99**.

E **Work with a partner. Practice the conversation. Use the words in 1B.**

A: *Where's the windshield?*
B: *The windshield is on the front of the car, near the hood.*

A: *Where are the tires?*
B: *The tires are under the car. There are two in the front and two in the back.*

2 Learn about the interior of a car

A **Look at the picture from an owner's manual. Match the definitions and the words below.**

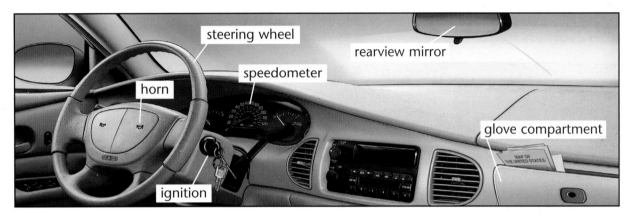

  _d_   1. Use this to check the road behind you.

  _e_   2. Use this to check your speed as you drive.

  _c_   3. Use this to steer the car.

  _a_   4. Use this to start the car.

  _f_   5. Use this to keep the owner's manual safe.

  _b_   6. Use this to warn other drivers.

a. ignition

b. horn

c. steering wheel

d. rearview mirror

e. speedometer

f. glove compartment

B **Work with a partner. Practice the conversation. Use the owner's manual in 2A.**

A: What's the steering wheel for?
B: You use it to steer the car.

A: What's the rearview mirror for?
B: You use it to see behind you.

C **Talk about the questions with your class.**

1. Have you ever owned a car? Do you own one now?
2. Which parts of the car are most important for safety or protection? Why?
3. Can you name three or more parts of a car that hold or store things?

TEST YOURSELF ✔

Close your book. Work with a partner. Make a list of as many new words from the lesson as you can. Alphabetize your list.

1 Read about a road trip

A Look at the pictures. Talk about the questions with your class.

1. Does this kind of vacation look fun to you?
2. Have you ever taken a driving vacation before?

B Listen and read the story about a road trip.

Arizona: A Beautiful Place to Visit

My family likes to take driving trips. We love to put our bags in the trunk and hit the road!* My wife reads the maps while I drive. We haven't gotten lost yet! We all like road trips because we can stop any time we want to.

Last summer my family took a road trip through Arizona. First, we went to Phoenix. We stayed there for two days. After we visited Phoenix, we drove through the Sonora Desert. It was beautiful, but it was very hot during the day. We didn't see any gas stations for miles. We stayed one night in the desert at a comfortable motel. The next day, we went to the Grand Canyon. The Grand Canyon is incredible! You should see it sometime. It was definitely my favorite part of the trip.

Arizona is a beautiful place, but take my advice. If you drive through the desert, be sure you have enough gas and water in the car before you go. It's hot and there aren't many places to stop.

*Idiom note: hit the road = to leave, or go away in a car

C Check your understanding. Mark the statements T (true), F (false), or NI (no information).

<u>F</u> 1. The writer's family drove to Arizona last spring.

<u>T</u> 2. They drove through the Sonora Desert.

<u>F</u> 3 The desert is usually cool during the day.

<u>T</u> 4. They stayed at a motel.

<u>T</u> 5. The writer's favorite part of the trip was the Grand Canyon.

<u>NI</u> 6. Their car didn't have enough gas and water.

Unit 9 Lesson 2

Objectives	Grammar	Vocabulary	Correlations
On- and Higher-level: Analyze, write, and edit a story about a vacation **Pre-level:** Read a travel story and write about a vacation	Past tense (*Last year I went to San Francisco.*)	*Navigator, road trip, motel, luxury* For vocabulary support, see these **Oxford Picture Dictionary** topics: Places to Go, Taking a Trip	**CASAS:** 0.1.2, 0.1.5, 0.2.1 **LCPs:** 39.01, 49.02, 49.03, 49.13, 49.16, 49.17 **SCANS:** Creative thinking, Interprets and communicates information, Listening, Reading **EFF:** Convey ideas in writing, Listen actively, Observe critically, Read with understanding, Reflect and evaluate

Warm-up and Review

10–15 minutes (books closed)

Write *Vacations* on the board. Underneath it, write *Where, How, Where do you sleep? What do you do?* Have volunteers come to the board and write the kinds of places people go on vacation (mountains, beaches, cities, landmarks, etc), methods of travel, kinds of accommodations, and vacationing activities. Leave this on the board.

Introduction

5 minutes

1. Tell students about a trip you have been on. Include the kinds of information on the board.

2. State the objective: *Today we're going to read and write about traveling.*

1 Read about a road trip

Presentation

20–25 minutes

 1. Direct students to look at the pictures. Ask: *Where did this family go?*

2. Elicit answers to question 1. Ask students why they like or don't like this kind of vacation. Elicit their experiences with vacations that involve driving.

 1. Draw students' attention to the asterisk in the second sentence and the footnote below. Tell them they are going to read a description of the vacation in the pictures.

2. Direct students to read the story silently. Check comprehension. Ask: *Who is writing this story?* [the father] *Where did they stay in the desert?* [a comfortable motel] *What was his favorite part of the trip?* [the Grand Canyon]

3. Play the audio. Have students read along silently.

Guided Practice I

10 minutes

C Have students work independently to mark the statements T (true), F (false), or NI (no information). Go over the answers as a class.

Multilevel Strategies

For 1C, challenge on- and higher-level students while working with pre-level students.

• **Pre-level** While other students are working on 1C, ask these students *Yes/No* and *Or* questions about the reading. *Does the writer like to drive? Did he enjoy the Grand Canyon? Is Arizona hot or cold?*

• **On- and Higher-level** Ask these students to write two additional *True/False* sentences about the story. Ask volunteers to write one of their sentences on the board. Have the class say whether the statement is true or false.

2 Write about a trip

Guided Practice II
20–25 minutes

A Read the questions. Elicit students' answers. List some information about the students' trips on the board.

B 1. Direct students to look back at the model in 1B. Focus their attention on the past and present tense verbs. Ask them to look through the story quickly and mark past and present verbs. Discuss the reasons for the tense choices.

2. Read the questions aloud. Elicit answers from volunteers. Write some of their ideas for vacation advice on the board.

3. Check students' comprehension of the exercise. Ask: *How many paragraphs is your story going to be?* [three] *Are you going to write the questions?* [no]

4. Have students work individually to write their stories.

> ### Multilevel Strategies
> Adapt 2B to the level of your students.
>
> • **Pre-level** Have these students write one paragraph. Tell them to answer the questions for paragraph 2 only. Read the questions and call on individuals to answer aloud before they write.
>
> • **Higher-level** Tell these students to include some details about their favorite parts of the trip. *How was the weather? What did you see there? What did you do there?*

C 1. Lead students through the process of using the *Editing checklist*. Read each sentence aloud, and ask students to check their papers before moving on to the next item.

2. Allow students a few minutes to edit their writing as necessary.

> **TIP** If you have access to the Internet in class, have students look up pictures of their vacation spots. Encourage them to share the pictures with their partners when they exchange stories. Post their completed stories with the pictures on your bulletin board.

Communicative Practice
10 minutes

D 1. Read the instructions aloud. Emphasize to students that they are responding to their partners' work, not correcting it.

2. Use the story in 1B to model the exercise. *I think the sentence about driving without any buildings or cars around is interesting. I'd like to ask this writer why he thinks the Grand Canyon is incredible.*

3. Direct students to exchange their stories with a partner and follow the instructions in numbers 1 and 2.

Application and Evaluation
15 minutes

TEST YOURSELF

1. Review the instructions aloud. Assign a time limit (ten minutes), and have students work independently.

2. Before collecting students' work, remind them to use the *Editing checklist*. Collect and correct students' writing.

To compress this lesson: Assign the *Test Yourself* for homework.

To extend this lesson: Talk about a vacation.
1. Pass out pictures of beautiful vacation spots, or tell students to imagine a place they would love to go, and have them quickly draw a "postcard" of it.
2. Tell students to imagine a "dream vacation." Write these questions on the board: *Where did you go? Who did you go with? How did you get there? How long did you stay? What did you do?* Elicit possible answers to these questions. Encourage them to use their imaginations.
3. Have students meet with several partners to show their "postcards" and ask and answer the questions.

And/Or have students complete **Workbook 3 page 59** and **Multilevel Activity Book 3 page 100**.

2 Write about a trip

A Talk about the questions with your class.

1. Think about your last trip. Was it for a vacation, work, or family business?
2. Are vacations and travel important for good health, why or why not?

B Write about a trip you have taken. Use the model in 1B and the questions below to help you. Answers will vary.

Paragraph 1: How do you and your family or friends like to travel?
How do you like about traveling?

Paragraph 2: Where did you go on your last trip?
When did you go?
How long did you stay?
What was your favorite part?

Paragraph 3: What advice do you have for somebody who wants to take the same trip?

Our Trip across Canada
My friends and I like to travel by train.
We all like trains because we can relax...

C Use the checklist to edit your writing. Check (✔) the true sentences. Answers will vary.

Editing checklist	
1. I gave my story a title.	
2. I gave some advice to help someone who wants to take this trip.	
3. I used capital letters for the names of places in my story.	
4. My story has three paragraphs.	

D Exchange stories with a partner. Read and comment on your partner's work.

1. Point out one sentence that you think is very interesting.
2. Ask your partner a question about his or her trip.

TEST YOURSELF ✔

Write a paragraph about your partner's trip. Describe where your partner went and what he or she did.

1 Learn to describe events with time clauses

A **Read the story. What is the mechanic going to do?**

Peter had a car problem this morning. <u>When he started the car</u>, the engine made a strange noise. <u>Before he got to work</u>, a red light came on near the speedometer.

He took the car to the garage and talked to his mechanic. Peter said, "<u>When I start the car</u>, the engine makes a strange noise."

The mechanic asked, "Have you changed the oil recently?" Peter said, "Yes. I changed the oil <u>before I drove to Denver last week</u>." The mechanic replied, "OK. I'll take a look at it tomorrow." Peter said, "<u>OK. After I finish work</u>, I'll call you."

B **Study the chart. Underline the 5 examples of time clauses in the story above.**

Describing present, past, and future events with time clauses	
Present	**When I start the car**, the engine makes a strange noise. The engine makes a strange noise **when I start the car.**
Past	**Before I drove to Denver last week,** I changed the oil. I changed the oil **before I drove to Denver last week.**
Future	**After I finish work**, I'll call you. I'll call you **after I finish work.**

Note
Time clauses give information about when things happen or happened. A time clause can come before or after the main clause.

C **Match the clauses to make sentences.**

   _e_ 1. Peter talked to the mechanic,   a. before we go on vacation.

   _a_ 2. We always buy maps   b. when she drives.

   _b_ 3. Tina always listens to the radio   c. we take the car to the mechanic.

   _d_ 4. We'll go shopping   d. after we go to the bank.

   _c_ 5. When we hear a strange noise,   e. after he finished work.

Unit 9 Lesson 3

Objectives	Grammar	Vocabulary	Correlations
On- and Higher-level: Use past and present time clauses to talk about driving, and listen for the order of events **Pre-level:** Recognize past and present time clauses in conversations about driving	Past and present time clauses (*He put on his seat belt before he drove away. She listens to the radio when she drives.*)	Automobiles For vocabulary support, see these **Oxford Picture Dictionary** topics: Parts of a Car, Buying and Maintaining a Car, Prepositions of Motion, Directions and Maps, Traffic Signs	**CASAS:** 0.1.2, 0.2.1, 7.4.2 **LCPs:** 49.02, 49.09, 49.13, 49.16, 49.17 **SCANS:** Creative thinking, Interprets and communicates information, Listening, Reading, Writing **EFF:** Convey ideas in writing, Listen actively, Read with understanding, Reflect and understand

Warm-up and Review

10–15 minutes (books closed)

Ask for a show of hands of students who drove to school today. Choose a volunteer and use pantomime to coach him or her through a detailed description of driving away from home. *I put the keys in the ignition. I turned on the engine. I checked the rearview mirror. I backed out of the driveway.* Leave these sentences on the board.

Introduction

5–10 minutes

1. Say: *If we want to combine some of these sentences to show the sequence of events, we can use time words. After Jorge got in the car, he put the keys in the ignition.*

2. State the objective: *Today we're going to use past and present time clauses to talk about driving.*

1 Learn to describe events with time clauses

Presentation I

20–25 minutes

A 1. Direct students to look at the picture. Ask: *Who are these men?*

2. Read the question. Ask students to read the story silently to find the answer. Call on a volunteer for the answer.

B 1. Copy the first sentence from the grammar chart on the board. Underline and label the main clause and the time clause. Elicit the verb tenses. [present] Read the *Notes* and the other sentences in the chart. Ask students to identify the time clause in each sentence.

2. Direct students to underline the examples of time clauses in the story in 1A. Go over the answers as a class.

3. For each underlined sentence in the story, elicit which action came first. *Did he get to work first or did the red light next to the speedometer go on first?*

4. Assess students' understanding of the charts. *Can you use past-tense verbs in time clauses? Can you use present-tense verbs?*

5. Ask volunteers to combine some of the sentences from the warm-up using *when, before,* and *after.*

Guided Practice I

15–20 minutes

C Ask students to work individually to match the clauses. Ask volunteers to write the answers on the board.

Multilevel Strategies

For 1C, seat same-level students together.

• **Pre-level** While other students are completing 1C, provide these students with skeleton sentences to complete.
1. You should put on your seat belt _____ you drive away. 2. You need to stop _____ you see a red light. 3. You should change the oil _____ you drive for 3,000 miles. Give them time to copy the answers to 1C after they are written on the board.

Guided Practice II

5–10 minutes

D Ask volunteers to copy the sentences on the board. Go over each sentence and ask which action happened first. Have students circle the correct words in their books.

2 Compare time clauses

Presentation II

20–25 minutes

1. Write this skeleton sentence on the board: *I usually _____ my car before I _____.* Elicit a present-tense completion. Write *Yesterday, I _____ my car before I _____.* Elicit a past-tense completion. Write *Tomorrow, I _____ my car before I _____.* Elicit a future-tense completion. Say: *Now we're going to compare time clauses with* when, before, *and* after *in the past, present, and future.*

2. Underline each of the verbs. Draw students' attention to the use of the present-tense verb in the future time clause. Reverse the order of the clauses to illustrate that the verb tenses don't change when the clauses are reversed.

A Have students work individually to circle the correct words. Go over the answers as a class.

> **TIP** For more practice with time clauses, play a variation of the game from the *Tip* on page T-96. Write *past, present,* and *future* on the board. Under each tense, write one of the time words: *before, after,* or *when*. Call out a verb phrase—for example, *eat dinner*. Call on a volunteer to say a sentence using the first time word with the first tense. For example, if *before* is under *past*, the student might say, *I washed my hands before I ate dinner*. Call on different volunteers to use the same verb phrase using the other time words and tenses. Erase the time words, and write them under different tenses. Switch to a new verb phrase, and call on more volunteers.

Guided Practice I

10–15 minutes

> **TIP** Before 2B, point out that *should* and *might* can be used in present and future time clauses but not in past time clauses. *When it rains, you should drive carefully. When you go to the mountains this summer, you might see some snow.*

B Have students work individually to write answers to the questions. Ask volunteers to write the answers on the board.

> ### Multilevel Strategies
>
> Seat same-level students together for 2B.
>
> • **Pre-level** Help these students write the answers by prompting them with the beginning of the sentence. *When you get in a car, you should _____.* Give them time to write each sentence before you move on to the next one.
>
> • **On- and Higher-level** Ask these students to write additional questions like the ones in the exercise. Have them write one question in each tense. After you go over the answers to 2B, call on volunteers to ask their questions. Call on other students to answer.

> **TIP** For more practice with time clauses, show a short video clip with a variety of actions in it. Seat students in multilevel groups, and direct them to write sentences with time clauses about what happened in the clip. *He put his suitcase on the bed before he started packing. When the clothes wouldn't fit, he sat on the suitcase.* When groups have run out of ideas for past-tense sentences, ask them to write two or three future sentences with time clauses predicting what will happen next.

D **Get the form. Work with your class. Read the sentences. Then circle the correct word.**

When I have car problems, I take my car to a mechanic.
After the mechanic looked at the car, he told me what was wrong.
Before I go on vacation, I'll ask him to fix the car.

1. If both things happen in the present, both clauses are in the (present / past) tense.
2. If both things happen in the past, both clauses are in the simple (present / past) tense.
3. If both things happen in the future, the time clause is in the simple present tense. The main clause is in the (present / future).

E **Get the meaning. Work with your class. Write *1st* or *2nd* to put the events in each sentence in order. If the events happen at the same time, write *same*.**

1. <u>Mel learned to drive a car</u> after <u>he came to Los Angeles</u>.
   _____2nd_____   _____1st_____

2. <u>Min puts on her seat belt</u> before <u>she starts the car</u>.
   __1st_____   __2nd_____

3. After <u>we take a long trip</u>, <u>we're always happy to come home</u>.
   __1st_____   __2nd_____

4. When <u>I listened carefully</u>, <u>I heard a strange noise under the hood</u>.
   __same_____   __same_____

2 Compare time clauses

A **Circle the correct words.**

1. Marta and I studied together before we (take / took) the driving test.
2. We were both nervous before we (took / will take) the test.
3. I was tired after I (leave / left) the DMV.
4. Marta (bought / will buy) a new car after she passes the test.

B **Write answers to the questions.**

1. When you get in a car, what should you do first? Answers will vary.
   You should put on your seat belt when you get in a car.

2. What things do people usually check before they take a road trip?

   _____

3. When should you use your turn signals?

   _____

4. After you leave class today, where will you go?

   _____

3 Grammar listening

🎧 **Listen to the sentences. Which event happens first? Circle *a* or *b*.**

1. (a.) We called the mechanic.
   b. We took the car to the garage.

2. (a.) Ana stopped at the gas station.
   b. Ana picked me up.

3. (a.) I stopped the car.
   b. I saw my friend on the corner.

4. a. Mr. Chen took his driving test.
   (b.) Mr. Chen was nervous.

5. a. Susan will buy a new car.
   (b.) Susan will sell her old car.

6. (a.) Anthony will move to Los Angeles.
   b. Anthony will learn to drive.

7. (a.) I got an oil change.
   b. I went on a trip.

8. (a.) Karla starts the car.
   b. Karla adjusts the rearview mirror.

4 Practice time clauses

A **Work with a partner. Choose 1 of the topics below and take notes on your ideas.**

Topic 1: Vacation time: List 5 things you do before and after you take a trip.

OR

Topic 2: Moving day: List 5 things you do before and after you move to a new place.

B **Talk about your ideas with your class.**

A: *We lock all the doors of our houses before we take a trip.*
B: *We fill out change of address cards before we move.*

C **Work with your classmates. Make a "Top 5" list for each topic in 4A.**

vacation time

moving day

TEST YOURSELF ✔

Close your book. Think about the last trip you took or the last time you moved. Write 5 sentences about the experience. Include a time clause in each sentence.

3 Grammar listening

Guided Practice II

10–15 minutes

1. Tell students that they are going to hear a series of sentences with time clauses and that they'll need to decide which action happens first in the sentence. Give them time to read the sentences before they listen.

2. Play the audio. Direct students to read along silently without writing.

3. Replay the audio. Ask students to circle the event that happens first.

4. Call on volunteers to read their answers. If necessary, replay the audio and write sentences on the board to demonstrate their meaning.

4 Practice time clauses

Communicative Practice and Application

20–25 minutes

 1. Direct students to look at the picture. Ask: *Is he moving or going on vacation?*

2. Put students in pairs. Read the two assignment options.

3. Check comprehension of the exercise. Ask: *Should you write about vacations and moving?* [no—choose one] *If one partner does something but another partner doesn't, can that be one of your sentences?* [no—something both people do] *How many things do you need to list?* [five] *Who needs to write?* [both partners]

B 1. Give each group member a letter A–D (see page T-199). Tell students to re-form in groups with other students who have the same letter.

2. Read the sample sentences aloud. Direct students to share their answers with their new groups.

C 1. Write *Vacation Time* and *Moving Day* on the board.

2. Elicit students' ideas for both categories, and then write them on the board. Have the class vote for the top five in each category.

Evaluation

10–15 minutes

TEST YOURSELF

Ask students to write the sentences independently. Collect and correct their writing.

Multilevel Strategies

Target the *Test Yourself* to the level of your students.

• **Pre-level** Allow these students to write first-person sentences. *I always _____ before I go on a trip. I always _____ after I go on a trip. I always _____ before I move to a new place. I always _____ after I move to a new place.*

• **Higher-level** Have these students write a paragraph in response to these questions: *How do you prepare for a trip (or for moving)? What do you do afterwards? How is what you do the same or different from what your classmates do?*

To compress this lesson: Conduct 1C as a whole-class activity.

To extend this lesson: Have students give travel advice.
1. Give students several time clauses to get started with and then elicit completions.
   Before you go overseas, you should _____.
   When you travel in a foreign country, you should _____.
   After you drive for several hours, you should _____.
2. Ask students to work with a partner to come up with more travel advice using *when, before,* and *after.* Call on volunteers to share their ideas with the class.

And/Or have students complete **Workbook 3 pages 60–61, Multilevel Activity Book 3 pages 101–102**, and the **corresponding Unit 9 Exercises** on the **Multilevel Grammar Exercises CD-ROM 3.**

Unit 9 Lesson 4

Objectives	Grammar	Vocabulary	Correlations
On-, Pre-, and Higher-level: Negotiate prices and listen for information about car buying	Conjunctions (*I like that car, and he does too. I don't like it, and neither does he.*)	*Negotiate, dealer, interior, make a deal* For vocabulary support, see these **Oxford Picture Dictionary** topics: Parts of a Car, Buying and Maintaining a Car, Cars and Trucks	**CASAS:** 0.1.2, 1.2.2, 1.7.1, 1.9.5, 1.9.6, 1.9.8, 6.03., 6.0.4, 6.2.3 **LCPs:** 45.01, 49.02, 49.09, 49.16, 51.01 **SCANS:** Acquires and evaluates Information, Arithmetic/Mathematics, Listening, Reading **EFF:** Read with understanding, Use math to solve problems and communicate

Warm-up and Review

10–15 minutes (books closed)

Ask: *Where could you find a new or used car for sale?* Write *Dealership, Newspaper, Internet,* and *Friend* on the board. Ask students to name an advantage and disadvantage of each one.

Introduction

5 minutes

1. Tell students that usually when we buy things in a store in the U.S., we don't negotiate prices. One major exception to that rule is the car dealership.

2. State the objective: *Today we're going to learn how to negotiate prices and listen for information about buying a car.*

1 Learn to negotiate price

Presentation I

15–20 minutes

 1. Direct students to look at the picture. Ask questions. *Where are they? How does the woman feel? Why?*

2. Play the audio. Give students time to answer the questions. Go over the answers as a class. Ask additional questions. *How long is the warranty? What are the problems with the car?*

Guided Practice

20–25 minutes

 1. Read the instructions aloud. Play the audio. Ask students to read along silently for the answer to the question. Elicit the answer.

2. Ask students to read the conversation with a partner. Circulate and monitor pronunciation. Model and have students repeat difficult words or phrases.

3. Say and have students repeat the expressions in the *In other words* box. Elicit the placement of the expressions in the conversation. Ask volunteers to model the conversation using expressions from the box.

Communicative Practice and Application

15–20 minutes

C 1. Ask students to read the instructions silently. Check their comprehension of the exercise. Ask: *What are the two roles?* Elicit examples of what the salesperson and the customer might say.

2. Set a time limit (five minutes). Ask students to act out both roles. Have volunteers act out their conversation for the class. Ask students who are listening to note the customer's final decision.

Multilevel Strategies

For 1C, adapt the role-play to the level of your students.

- **Pre-level** Provide a simplified conversation for these students. *A: This is a very stylish car. It has 17,000 miles on it and a two-year warranty. B: How much is it? A: It's $8,000. B: That's too expensive. The turn signals don't work. A: I'll talk to my manager.*

1 Learn to negotiate price

 A **Look at the picture. Listen to the conversation. Then answer the questions below with your classmates.**

1. How many miles does the car have on it? 30,000 miles
2. Name two things on the car that are new. stereo and paint
3. How much is the car? $12,500

 B **Listen and read. What's wrong with the car?**

Car dealer: This is a great car. It only has 15,000 miles on it, and it has a one-year warranty.

Customer: It sure is beautiful. How much is it?

Car dealer: It has new tires and a beautiful interior, too.

Customer: Uh-huh. And how much is it?

Car dealer: It's going for $10,000. It's a fantastic price.

Customer: $10,000! But the radio doesn't work, and the CD player doesn't either!

Car dealer: Uhhh…Let me talk to my manager. I'm sure we can work something out.

> **In other words...**
>
> **Making a deal**
> I'm sure we can work something out.
> We're flexible.

C **Role-play a conversation between a car dealer and a customer with a partner. Use the example in 1B to make a new conversation.**

Partner A: You are a car dealer. Your customer is looking at a stylish car. It has 17,000 miles and a two-year warranty. Tell the customer it has a new stereo and CD player. You want to sell it for $8,000.

Partner B: You're the customer. You like the car you're looking at, but it's too expensive. The rearview mirror is broken, and the turn signals don't work.

✔ Identify features and defects in a product; negotiate for a lower car price **123**

2 Learn *and...too, and...not either, but*

A Study the chart. Complete the sentences below with *and, too, either,* or *but.*

Conjunctions: *and...too, and...not either, but*	
and...too	I like the red car. Tom likes the red car. I like the red car, **and** Tom does, **too**.
and... not either	The radio doesn't work. The CD player doesn't work. The radio doesn't work, **and** the CD player doesn't **either**.
but	I don't like the blue car. My wife likes the blue car. I don't like the blue car, **but** my wife does.

1. This door doesn't lock, and the trunk doesn't ____either____.

2. That's a nice car, __and__ it's a great price, too!

3. We don't need gas, __but__ we need some oil.

4. I don't like to fly, and my friends don't __either__.

B Use *and, too, not either,* or *but* to make a new sentence for the two sentences.

1. Jun doesn't drive. Mary doesn't drive.

   __Jun doesn't drive, and Mary doesn't either.__

2. I enjoy road trips. Josh doesn't enjoy road trips.

   __I enjoy road trips, but Josh doesn't.__

3. Lee drives carefully. Karen drives carefully.

   __Lee drives carefully, and Karen does, too.__

4. Miguel doesn't like to travel. Naomi doesn't like to travel.

   __Miguel doesn't like to travel and Naomi doesn't either.__

3 Practice your pronunciation

A Study the chart. Listen to the pronunciation of the schwa sound in these words.

The schwa sound
We pronounce some vowels (a,e,i,o,u) in certain words as "uh". This is the *schwa sound*. It is the most common sound in English. Dictionaries show the schwa sound as the symbol (ə). manager   CD player   warranty

B Listen and circle the letters with the schwa sounds.

1. sign(a)l   3. mirr(o)r   5. th(e)   7. Ar(i)zona

2. eith(e)r   4. trav(e)l   6. c(o)mput(e)r   8. Grand Cany(o)n

C Listen again and check. Repeat the words.

2 Learn *and... too, and... not either, but*

Presentation II and Guided Practice

30–35 minutes

 1. Introduce the new topic. *Now we're going to learn how to combine sentences with the conjunctions* and *and* but.

2. Direct students to look at the first sentence in the chart. Read it aloud. Ask: *Do Tom and I agree or disagree?* [Agree] *Do we use* and *or* but *to show agreement?* [and] *Do we use* too *or* either? [too] Read the second sentence. *Are we saying the same thing about the radio and the CD or something different?* [same] *Do we use* and *or* but *when the two parts of the sentence agree or say the same thing?* [and] *Both parts of the sentence are negative. Do we use* too *or* either *with negatives?* [either] Read the third sentence. *When do we use* but? [to show difference] *Do we use* too *or* either *with* but? [no]

3. Have students work individually to complete the sentences. Go over the answers as a class.

 If you have access to the Internet in class, have your students look up information about cars. Tell them to choose a car year, make, and model. They can find safety test results, gas mileage, and reliability ratings. They can also find out where the car is being sold nearby and for how much. Have students share their information with each other or with the class.

Communicative Practice

15–20 minutes

B 1. Conduct this as a whole-class exercise. As you go through each example, elicit which conjunction is required, whether *too* or *either* is required, and how to deal with the second verb. For example: Ask if you should replace it with *does* or *doesn't*.

2. Have volunteers write the completed sentences on the board.

3 Practice your pronunciation

Pronunciation Extension

10–15 minutes

 1. Write *He doesn't have a warranty on the engine.* on the board. Say the sentence with relaxed pronunciation, and ask students to repeat it. Underline the *oe* in *doesn't*, the word *a*, the second *a* in *warranty,* and the *i* in *engine.* Say: *Now we're going to focus on the most common sound in English, the "uh" sound. This sound can be spelled with any vowel and is very common in unstressed syllables.*

2. Read the chart. Draw the schwa symbol (ə) on the board.

3. Play the audio. Direct students to listen for the schwa sound. Ask which vowels produce the sound. Point out that any vowel can have the schwa sound and that it is particularly common in unstressed vowels.

 Direct students to circle the schwa sounds.

C 1. Play the audio. Have students check their answers and repeat the words.

2. Ask them to take turns reading the words aloud with a partner. Monitor and provide feedback on pronunciation.

4 Focus on listening

Listening Extension

20–25 minutes

A 1. Direct students to look at the picture. Ask: *What is he worried about?*

2. Read the quotation and the questions aloud, and elicit answers from volunteers.

B Tell students that they are going to listen to a radio show where people call in and ask advice about their cars. Direct them to check the items they hear people talk about.

C 1. Direct students to read the sentences before listening.

2. Replay the audio and have students work individually to complete the sentences. Go over the answers as a class.

5 Real-life math

Math Extension

5–10 minutes

1. Read the first problem aloud. Ask students to work individually to figure out the answer. Ask a volunteer to write the problem and answer on the board.

2. Read the second problem aloud. Read the information in the *Need help?* box. Ask students to work individually to figure out the answer. Ask a volunteer to write the problem and answer on the board.

Evaluation

10–15 minutes

TEST YOURSELF

1. Model the role-play with a volunteer. Then switch roles.

2. Pair students. Check comprehension of the exercise by eliciting what the customer and the salesperson might say.

3. Set a time limit (five minutes), and have the partners act out the role-play in both roles.

4. Circulate and monitor. Encourage pantomime and improvisation.

5. Provide feedback.

Multilevel Strategies

Target the *Test Yourself* to the level of your students.

• **Pre-level** Ask these students to use this skeleton conversation: *A: This is a very good car. It has _____ miles on it and a two-year warranty. B: How much is it? A: It's _____. B: That's too expensive. A: I'll talk to my manager.*

• **Higher-level** Have these students practice the role-play with several partners.

To compress this lesson: Conduct 2A and/or *Real-life math* as a whole-class activity.

To extend this lesson: Do a car-for-sale corners jigsaw.
1. In large letters, write four car descriptions on four separate poster boards as follows: *Dealership A: 4-door sedan, 30,000 miles, interior like new, gets 25 mpg, cracked rearview mirror, $8,000. Dealership B: small 2-door sedan, 15,000 miles, gets 40 mpg, broken turn signal, $10,000. Dealership C: van, 10,000 miles; car seat torn, gets 20 mpg, exterior like new, $9,000. Dealership D: station wagon, 20,000 miles, exterior and interior like new, gets 25 mpg, $9,000.* Hang each in a different corner of the room.
2. Put students in groups of four. Tell them that they are going to choose a car to buy and that each group member is going to a different dealership to look at cars. Assign each group member a letter A–D (see p. T-199), and explain which letters go to which corners.
3. Tell each student to memorize the information about the car at his/her dealership. Encourage students to talk to each other about the car. Say: *Ask the other customers at the dealership if they think the car is a good deal.*
4. Have students return to their original groups and describe their car. Tell the groups to discuss the pros and cons of each car and decide which one to buy. Call on a reporter from each group to share which car they chose and why.
5. As a follow-up, have the groups write sentences about the cars using *and* or *but*. *The van costs $9,000, and the station wagon does, too.*

And/Or have students complete **Workbook 3 page 62** and **Multilevel Activity Book 3 page 103**.

4 Focus on listening

A Read the statement. Talk about the questions
with your class.

"I can afford to buy a car, but I can't afford to own one."

1. What does this statement mean? There are many other things
   you need to have and buy when you own a car.
2. After you buy a car, what new expenses should you

   expect to have? Some expenses are a license, registration, insurance,
   repairs, and gas.

B Listen to the conversation. Check (✔) the items you hear
the people talk about.

1. ✔ car maintenance   3. ✔ car insurance   5. ____ car accidents

2. ____ car owner's manual   4. ✔ gas mileage   6. ✔ car taxes

C Listen again and complete the sentences.

1. Most people pay car insurance every _____month_____ .

2. The average person drives _15,000_____ miles per year.

3. Good mileage means anything above _30_____ miles per gallon.

4. In many states, people pay car taxes every _year_____ .

5. An example of car maintenance is an oil change every _5,000_____ miles.

5 Real-life math

Read the problems about car expenses. Write the answers.

1. Josh gets the oil changed in his car every three months. The price of an oil change is
   $36.99, but every 4th one is free. How much does he pay for oil changes every year?

   _$110.97_____

2. Eva drives 16,000 miles per year. Her car gets 32 miles
   per gallon. The average price of gas last year was $2.50
   per gallon. How much did she spend for gas last year?

   _$1,250.00_____

   > **Need help?**
   >
   > Total cost = Total miles ÷
   > miles per gallon x price

TEST YOURSELF ✔

Role-play a conversation at a used car lot. Partner A: You're the car dealer. Tell
the customer about the mileage, warranty, and price of one car. Partner B:
You're the customer. You think the price is too high. Talk about the car's
problems. Then change roles.

1 Get ready to read

A **What do you do when you buy something that doesn't work?**

B **Read the definitions.**

consumers: (noun) customers, people who buy things

defect: (noun) something that is wrong with, or missing from, a product

lemon: (noun) 1. a sour, yellow fruit

(noun) 2. a product that has a defect that is difficult or impossible to fix

C **Look at the picture in 2A. Which definition of _lemon_ is this article about?**

Definition 2: a product that has a defect that is difficult or impossible to fix

2 Read and respond

A **Read the article.**

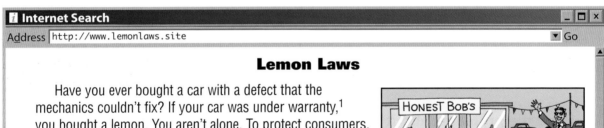

| Internet Search | _ □ x |

Address `http://www.lemonlaws.site` ▼ Go

Lemon Laws

Have you ever bought a car with a defect that the mechanics couldn't fix? If your car was under warranty,[1] you bought a lemon. You aren't alone. To protect consumers, most states have lemon laws. Lemon laws say that a car company has to fix a car that is under warranty. If the car cannot be fixed, then the company must give the customer another car or a refund.

In general, if the car can't be fixed after three or four repairs for the same defect, it is a lemon.

Frequently asked questions (FAQs) about lemon laws:

Do lemon laws protect used-car buyers?
Sometimes. Some states have lemon laws for used cars. For example, in New York, when you buy a used car with fewer than 100,000 miles, you are probably protected.

Am I protected when I buy a car from a friend or neighbor?
No. When you buy a car from a neighbor, friend, or other private individual, there are no lemon laws. You must buy the car from a car dealer for the laws to protect you.

When I buy a car, is there anything I need to do to be sure I'm protected?
Yes. Be sure you receive a warranty with the car. After you buy the car, write down all repairs and maintenance. Here is a sample of a Repair and Maintenance Log.

[1]under warranty: protected by a written promise that a product is reliable and in good condition

Unit 9 Lesson 5

Objectives	Grammar	Vocabulary	Correlations
Pre-, On-, and Higher-level: Read about and discuss lemon laws	Time clauses (*When you buy a car from a friend, lemon laws don't protect you.*)	*consumer, defect, lemon, maintenance, condition, log, warranty* For vocabulary support, see this **Oxford Picture Dictionary** topic: Parts of a Car, Buying and Maintaining a Car	**CASAS:** 0.1.2, 1.6.3, 7.4.4 **LCPs:** 38.01, 49.09, 49.16, 49.17 **SCANS:** Interprets and communicates information, Reading, Reasoning, Uses computers to process information **EFF:** Observe critically, Learn through research, Take responsibility for learning, Read with understanding,

Warm-up and Review

10–15 minutes (books closed)

Write *Car Problems* on the board. Ask students to brainstorm common problems that people have with their cars (brakes don't work, battery dies, hoses break, electrical system fails, air conditioner doesn't work, etc.) Help them with vocabulary, and write their ideas on the board.

Introduction

5 minutes

1. Tell students that everyone expects these things to happen eventually, but sometimes they happen when we first buy a car.

2. State the objective: *Today we're going read about and discuss laws that protect car buyers.*

1 Get ready to read

Presentation

15–20 minutes

 Read the question aloud. Elicit student responses. Encourage them to share their experiences with buying defective cars, appliances, or machines.

B Read the words and definitions. Elicit sample sentences from students using the words.

Pre-Reading

C 1. Direct students to look at the picture in 2A. Call on a volunteer for the answer. Ask students to guess what a "lemon law" is.

2. Have students look for the bolded questions in the article in 2A. Tell them the article is going to answer those questions.

2 Read and respond

Guided Practice I

25–30 minutes

 1. Ask students to read the article silently.

2. Direct students to underline unfamiliar words they would like to know. Elicit the words and encourage other students to provide definitions or examples.

3. Check students' comprehension. Ask: *What is a lemon law?* [a law that says if a defective car is under warranty, it must be repaired or replaced] *What can you do to be sure you're protected?* [keep a maintenance log]

Multilevel Strategies

Adapt 2A to the level of your students.

• **Pre-level** Ask these students to read the last portion of the article beginning with the question *Do lemon laws protect used-car buyers?* During the comprehension check, elicit questions about vocabulary. Write words and definitions on the board.

Guided Practice II

15–20 minutes

B 1. Play the audio. Have students read along silently.

2. Elicit and discuss any additional questions about the reading.

C Have students work individually to circle the correct answer. Go over the answers as a class.

Multilevel Strategies

For 2C, work with pre-level students.

• **Pre-level** Ask these students *Yes/No* questions about the section they read while other students are completing 2C. *In New York, if I buy a car with 150,000 miles on it, am I protected by lemon laws? Am I protected if I buy a car from my friend? Should I write down the day and the mileage when I get an oil change?* Give students time to copy the answers to 2C from the board.

3 Talk it over

Communicative Practice

15–20 minutes

A Read the questions aloud. Set a time limit (three minutes). Have students work independently to think about the questions and write their answers in note form.

B Elicit students' answers to the questions. Encourage students to respond to each other's stories and opinions.

TIP After 3B, encourage students to discuss other purchases they've made for which a lemon law would have come in handy. Put students in groups, and tell them to list anything they've bought that broke, fell apart, or stopped working right away. Find out if there are any commonalities, and tell students to propose new lemon laws. *I think we need a lemon law for shoes. If the soles come loose in the first month, you should get your money back!*

Application

5–10 minutes

BRING IT TO LIFE

Read the instructions aloud. Ask students what kind of car they will be looking for. Have them brainstorm kinds of cars (sedan, sports car, convertible, SUV, etc.) and adjectives to describe cars (luxurious, sporty, sleek, fast, vintage, etc.).

To compress this lesson: Conduct 2C as a whole-class activity.

To extend this lesson: Role-play a conversation with a mechanic.
1. Brainstorm car problems and write them on the board: *Brakes are squealing; engine is making a funny noise; car isn't starting; engine dies when I stop.*
2. Put up a skeleton conversation.
   Mechanic: What seems to be the problem?
   Customer: _____.
   Mechanic: OK. I'll check it out.
   Customer: Can you give me an estimate?
   Mechanic: I'll let you know after I look at it.
3. Have students practice the conversation with a partner. Tell them to practice in both roles.

And/Or have students complete **Workbook 3 page 63** and **Multilevel Activity Book 3 pages 104–105.**

Repair and Maintenance Log

License plate #: 2NNU 636   Date of Purchase: 01-08-05

Date In	Date out	Mileage	Mechanic or Garage	Description of problem	Work Performed	Price
12-11-06	12-13-06	51, 274	Mid-City Auto	regular maintenance	tune-up	$149.99
03-22-07	03-22-07	54,890	Quick Change		oil Change	$39.95
06-07-07	06-08-07	56,122	Mid-City Auto	left headlight not working	repaired headlight	no charge

Source: *The Center for Auto Safety*

B Listen and read the article again.

C Complete the sentences. Circle *a* or *b*.

1. A car is a lemon if ____.
   a. it has problems that can't be fixed
   b. it can be fixed after two repairs

2. Ms. Jones is my co-worker. If I buy a car from her, lemon laws ____.
   a. protect me
   b. do not protect me

3. To be protected by lemon laws, ____.
   a. keep a record of all maintenance and repairs
   b. only buy a used car

4. Based on the information in the Repair and Maintenance Log in 2A, the car ____.
   a. is a lemon
   b. isn't a lemon

5. The main idea of the article is: lemon laws can help you ____.
   a. if you buy a car with defects from a dealer
   b. if you buy a car with defects from a neighbor

3 Talk it over

A Think about the questions. Make notes about your answers.

1. Has someone you know ever bought a lemon? If so, what happened?
2. Is it better to buy a car from a dealer or a private individual? Why?

B Talk about the answers with your classmates.

BRING IT TO LIFE

Look in magazines, in newspapers, or online. Find a picture of your dream car.
Bring the picture to class. Tell your classmates why it's the perfect car for you.

1 Grammar

A Circle the correct words.

1. The mail arrived before Fernando (comes /(came)) home.
2. When Raisa calls, we always ((talk)/ talked) for a long time.
3. Paul stopped for gas after he (goes /(went)) to the market.
4. Before I decided on my new car, I ((asked)/ ask) a lot of questions.
5. Alex leaves the house after the kids ((go)/ went) to school.

B Match the clauses to make sentences.

_e_ 1. Before I got my driver's license,   a. after she finishes school.

_d_ 2. I fill the gas tank   b. when they were in Florida.

_f_ 3. Before we go on a trip,   c. he will drive to school.

_a_ 4. Raquel will visit us   d. when it's empty.

_c_ 5. After he fixes the car,   e. I usually took the bus.

_b_ 6. They went to Orlando   f. we often check the oil and tires.

C Circle the correct words.

1. Marco wears his seat belt and Esteban does, ((too)/ either).
2. Kwan likes to read maps, (either /(but)) Angelo doesn't.
3. I always wash my windshield, (and /(but)) Alan never does.
4. My car gets good gas mileage, ((and)/ but) Taka's car does, too.
5. I don't have my license yet, and Juanita doesn't, (too /(either)).

D Complete the paragraph. Use the words in the box.

and	before	tires	too	after	but	~~trip~~	when

Vicky took a ___trip___ to San Diego last summer. ___Before___ she went, she took
                      1   2

her car to the mechanic. The mechanic told Vicky that the car was in good condition,

___but___ it needed new ___tires___. He also wanted $75 to fix the radio. Vicky
        3   4

wasn't sure if she had enough money, but ___after___ she checked her account, she
                                                 5

decided to buy the tires ___and___ fix the radio, ___too___. Vicky was happy she
                                6   7

did. She didn't have any problems with the car ___when___ she went on her trip and
                                                          8

she had a great time.

Unit 9 Review and expand

Objectives	Grammar	Vocabulary	Correlations
On-, Pre-, and Higher-level: Expand upon and review unit grammar and life skills	Time clauses (*She'll call when she gets home.*) Conjunctions (*Tom doesn't like to drive and Shirley doesn't either.*)	Car parts For vocabulary support, see these **Oxford Picture Dictionary** topics: Parts of a Car, Buying and Maintaining a Car, Cars and Trucks	**CASAS:** 0.1.2, 0.1.5, 2.2.3, 4.8.1, 7.2.6, 7.3.1, 7.3.2, 7.3.4 **LCPs:** 49.16, 49.17 **SCANS:** Interprets and communicates information, Participates as member of a team, Seeing things in mind's eye **EFF:** Read with understanding, Solve problems and make decisions, Speak so others can understand

Warm-up and Review

10–15 minutes (books closed)

1. Review the *Bring It to Life* assignment from Lesson 5.

2. Have students who did the exercise show the picture of their dream car and describe it. Ask other students to describe the car of their dreams and explain their choices.

Introduction and Presentation

5 minutes

1. Ask a volunteer to describe his or her typical morning. Write the information on the board as a series of simple sentences. *Hugo gets up at 6:00. He walks his dog. He takes a shower. He eats eggs for breakfast.* After you have four or five sentences, call on another student to provide information about the same time of day. Write his/her sentences on the board as well.

2. Call on volunteers to combine some of the sentences on the board with *when, before,* and *after. Hugo walks his dog before he takes a shower. Hugo eats breakfast after he takes a shower.*

3. Call on other volunteers to compare the two students' stories using *and* and *but. Hugo gets up at 6:00, but Kate doesn't. She gets up at 7:00. Hugo takes a shower in the morning, and Kate does, too.*

4. State the objective: *Today we're going to review time clauses and conjunctions to talk about driving and transportation.*

1 Grammar

Guided Practice

40–45 minutes

A Have students work individually to circle the correct words. Ask volunteers to read the completed sentences aloud.

B Have students work individually to match the clauses. Ask volunteers to read the completed sentences aloud.

C Have students work individually to circle the correct word. Ask them to take turns reading the sentences with a partner. Go over the answers as a class.

D Have students work with their partners to complete the paragraph. Ask them to take turns reading it aloud when they have finished. Go over the answers as a class.

Multilevel Strategies

For 1C and 1D, seat same-level students together.

- **Pre-level** Work with this group on 1C and 1D. Elicit each answer, and allow students time to write it before you move on.

- **On- and Higher-level** After these students finish reading the exercises with a partner, tell them to work with their partners to write a short story about a vacation using *but, either, too, after,* and *before.*

2 Group work

Communicative Practice

20–35 minutes

A 1. Direct students in groups to focus on the picture. Ask: *Does this look like a good place to buy a car? Why or why not?*

2. Group students and assign roles: leader, recorder, timekeeper, and reporters. Explain that students work with their groups to write a conversation between the customers and the salesperson.

3. Check comprehension of the roles. Ask: *Who writes the conversation?* [recorder] *Who will read the conversation to the class?* [reporters] *Who helps everyone and manages the group?* [leader] *Who tells the group how much time has passed?* [timekeeper] *Who creates the conversation?* [everyone]

4. Set a time limit (five minutes) to complete the exercise. Circulate and answer any questions.

5. Have reporters from each group read the group's conversation to the class.

> ### Multilevel Strategies
>
> For 2A, use mixed-level groups.
>
> • **Pre-level** Assign these students the role of timekeeper.
>
> • **On-level** Assign these students the role of recorder or reporter.
>
> • **Higher-level** Assign these students the role of leader.

B 1. Have students walk around the room to conduct these interviews. To get students moving, tell them to interview three new people not in their groups for 2A.

2. Set a time limit (five minutes) to complete the exercise.

3. Tell students to make a note of their classmates' answers but not to worry about writing complete sentences.

> ### Multilevel Strategies
>
> Adapt the mixer in 2B to the level of your students.
>
> • **Pre-level** Allow these students to ask and answer the questions without writing.
>
> • **Higher-level** Have these students ask two additional questions and write all answers.

C Call on individuals to report what they learned about their classmates. Encourage students to make generalizations. *Two out of four students think _____ is the worst problem people have after they buy a car.*

Problem Solving

15–25 minutes

A 1. Ask: *Did your car ever break down while you were driving?* Tell students they will read a story about a man with car problems. Direct students to read Frank's story silently.

2. Ask: *Where was Frank when his car broke down?*

3. Play the audio. Have students read along silently.

B 1. Elicit answers to question 1. Have the class brainstorm a list of things Frank can do. Write the list on the board.

2. Ask students what Frank should do first. Come to a class consensus about the order of the list.

Evaluation

30–35 minutes

To test students' understanding of the unit grammar and life skills, have them take the Unit 9 Test in the *Step Forward Test Generator CD-ROM* with *ExamView® Assessment Suite.*

> ### Learning Log
>
> To help students record and discuss their progress, use the *Learning Log* on page T-202.

To extend this review: Have students complete **Workbook 3 page 64, Multilevel Activity Book 3 page 106**, and the **Unit 9 Exercises** on the **Multilevel Grammar Exercises CD-ROM 3.**

2 Group work

A Work with 2–3 classmates. Write a conversation between the people in the picture. Share your conversation with the class.

Customer: *How many miles does this car have on it?*
Car dealer: *It only has 20,000 miles on it.*

B Interview 3 classmates. Write their answers.

1. In your city, do you think it's easy to go places by car? Why or why not?
2. What's the worst problem people have when they shop for a car?
3. What's the worst problem people have after they buy a car?

C Talk about the answers with your class.

PROBLEM SOLVING

A Listen and read about Frank.

Everyday, Frank takes his kids to school before he drives to work. This morning, after he took the kids to school, his car made a strange noise and stopped in the middle of a busy intersection. Now, cars are honking, and people are getting angry. Frank's car won't start. He doesn't know what to do.

B Work with your classmates. Answer the questions.

1. What is Frank's problem? Frank's car has stopped in the middle of traffic.
2. Make a list of things Frank can do. Put the list in order.
   Start with what Frank should do first.

UNIT **10**

FOCUS ON
- crime and safety
- home security
- gerunds as subjects
- reporting a crime
- careers in public safety

Crime Doesn't Pay

1 Learn safety vocabulary

A   Talk about the questions with your class.

1. How do you stay safe in your home?
2. How do you stay safe when you are out at night?

B   Work with your classmates. Match the words with the pictures.

_8_	arrest a suspect	_2_	protect your wallet or purse
_5_	commit a crime	_7_	report a crime
_3_	don't walk alone at night	_4_	walk in well-lit areas
_1_	lock the doors	_6_	witness a crime

C   Listen and check. Then read the new words with a partner.

D   Work with a partner. Write other safety words you know.
Check your words in a dictionary.

Unit 10 Lesson 1

Objectives	Grammar	Vocabulary	Correlations
On-level: Identify safety vocabulary, and describe the criminal justice system **Pre-level:** Identify safety and criminal justice system vocabulary **Higher-level:** Talk and write about safety and the criminal justice system	Present-tense questions and answers (*What does the judge do? He listens to cases.*)	Safety and criminal justice system vocabulary For vocabulary support, see these **Oxford Picture Dictionary** topics: Public Safety, The Legal System	**CASAS:** 0.1.2, 0.1.5, 0.2.1, 3.5.9, 5.5.3 **LCPs:** 39.01, 44.02, 49.02, 49.10 **SCANS:** Creative thinking, Interprets and communicates information, Listening, Participates as member of a team, Speaking **EFF:** Cooperate with others, Reflect and evaluate, Speak so others can understand

Warm-up and Review

10–15 minutes (books closed)

Write *Crime* on the board. Elicit words students know for different kinds of crime: *car theft, mugging, bank robbery, murder, kidnapping, identity theft*.

Introduction

5 minutes

1. Ask students how many of them worry about crime in their neighborhoods.

2. State the objective: *Today we're going to learn words for talking about safety and the criminal justice system.*

1 Learn safety vocabulary

Presentation I

20–25 minutes

A Write *Staying Safe* on the board, and elicit students' answers to questions 1 and 2. If they have ideas about staying safe that are not included in 1B, write those words on the board.

B 1. Direct students to look at the pictures. Ask: *Which place looks dangerous?*

2. Group students and assign roles: leader, fact checker, recorder, and reporter. Explain that students work with their groups to match the words and pictures.

3. Check comprehension of the roles. Ask: *Who looks up the words in a dictionary?* [fact checker] *Who writes the numbers in the book?* [recorder] *Who tells the class your answers?* [reporter] *Who helps everyone and manages the group?* [leader]

4. Set a time limit (three minutes). As students work together, copy the wordlist onto the board.

5. Call "time." Have reporters take turns giving their answers. Write each group's answer on the board next to the word.

C 1. To prepare students for listening, say: *You're going to hear some advice about how to stay safe from crime.* Ask students to listen and check their answers.

2. Have students check the wordlist on the board and then write the correct numbers in their books.

3. Pair students. Set a time limit (three minutes). Monitor pair practice to identify pronunciation issues.

4. Call "time" and work with the pronunciation of any troublesome words or phrases.

5. Replay the audio and challenge students to listen for additional information.

D 1. Ask students to work with their partners from 1C to brainstorm a list of related words.

2. Elicit words from the class. Write them on the board. Ask students to copy them into their vocabulary notes for the unit.

Guided Practice

5–10 minutes

 1. Model the conversation with a volunteer. Model it again using other information from 1B.

2. Set a time limit (three minutes). Direct students to practice with a partner.

3. Ask volunteers to act out one of their conversations for the class.

2 Learn about the criminal justice system

Presentation II

15–20 minutes

 1. Direct students to look at the picture. Introduce the new topic: *Now we're going to talk about the criminal justice system.*

2. Read the words aloud. Discuss what each person is doing in the courtroom.

3. Ask students to work individually to complete the paragraph.

4. Call on volunteers to read the completed sentences aloud. Write the answers on the board. Read and have students repeat the words.

5. Check comprehension. Ask: *Who listens to the case?* [judge and jury] *Who is the person on trial?* [defendant]

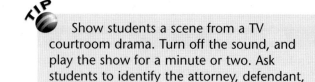 Show students a scene from a TV courtroom drama. Turn off the sound, and play the show for a minute or two. Ask students to identify the attorney, defendant, judge, witness, and jury.

Guided Practice

10–15 minutes

 Read the questions aloud. Give students time to think and take notes. Then call on volunteers to share their ideas.

Evaluation

10–15 minutes (books closed)

TEST YOURSELF

1. Pair students. Direct Partner B to close the book and listen to Partner A dictate five words from page 130. Ask students to switch roles when they finish, and have Partner B dictate five words from page 131.

2. Direct both partners to open their books and check their spelling when they finish.

3. Circulate and monitor student work.

Multilevel Strategies

Target the *Test Yourself* to the level of your students.

- **Higher-level** Direct these students to write a sentence defining each of the words their partner dictates.

To compress this lesson: Conduct 1B as a whole-class activity.

To extend this lesson: Have students listen for safety mistakes.

1. Read students this short story about someone who commits a number of safety "no-nos": *Tom overslept this morning, so he rushed out of the house without locking the doors and windows. He had to stop by the post office before work, so he left his car running to save time while he ran inside to mail the cash for his rent. After work, he walked down a dark alley to his favorite restaurant. He left his credit card on the table for the waitress while he went to the bathroom.*
2. Reread the story. Tell students to make a list of everything Tom did wrong. Call on volunteers to share the list.

And/Or have students complete **Workbook 3 page 65** and **Multilevel Activity Book 3 pages 108–109**.

E Work with a partner. Practice the conversation. Use the pictures in 1B.

A: *What are they doing in the first picture?*

B: *They're leaving their apartment. She's locking the door.*
He's protecting his wallet. He's putting it in his jacket.

2 Learn about the criminal justice system

A Look at the picture. Complete the article about the picture.

Maple Lane Trial Begins

courtroom   judge   attorney

witness

jury

defendant

Everyone inside the ____courtroom____ was quiet. The __judge__
                        1   2
listened to the case. Mary Gold (standing), an __attorney__, questioned
                                                                3
the __witness__. All twelve people on the __jury__ listened
         4   5
carefully, too. The __defendant__ sat quietly next to his attorney.
                         6

B Talk about the questions with your class.

1. What does an attorney do?
2. How many people are on a jury?
3. Who do you think has the most difficult job in the courtroom? Why?
4. How would you feel about being a witness to a crime?

TEST YOURSELF ✔

Work with a partner. Partner A: Read the vocabulary words in 1B to your
partner. Partner B: Close your book. Write the words. Ask your partner for help
with spelling as necessary. Then change roles. Partner B: Use the words in 2A.

1 Read about home security

A Look at the pictures. Talk about the questions with your class.

1. What home security features do you see in the pictures?
2. How many home or auto security features can you name?

B Listen and read the story about home security.

> **Home Security: Safe at Home**
> by Sandi Lopez
>
> I live in an apartment downtown. My neighborhood is a great place to live. It's clean, convenient, and it's usually pretty safe. Even so, sometimes I think of ways to make my home safer. The other day, I decided to look around and check the security of my home.
>
> I'm happy with the deadbolt locks on the doors in my apartment. I also have a chain lock. I'd like to get a peephole for the front door so I can see who's at the door before I open it. I'm going to ask the landlord to install one. The lights in my building's hallways are fine, but my neighbors and I would like to have better lighting on the sides of the building.
>
> Last week, one of my neighbors said, "We should have a neighborhood email group to make the neighborhood safer." Now we write emails if we see something strange or unusual in the neighborhood. Keeping a neighborhood safe takes a little work, but I think people sleep better at night when they feel safe at home.

> **Writer's note**
> Use quotation marks (" ") to show a person's exact words. Use a comma before you begin the quotation.

C Check your understanding. Complete the sentences.

1. The writer's neighborhood is usually pretty _____safe_____.
2. The writer wants to make her home __safer_____.
3. The writer wants the landlord to put a __peephole_____ in the front door.
4. Her neighbors want more lights on the __sides_____ of the building.
5. Neighbors can use email to report anything __strange_____ or
   __unusual_____.

Unit 10 Lesson 2

Objectives	Grammar	Vocabulary	Correlations
On- and Higher-level: Analyze, write, and edit an essay about home security and neighborhood safety **Pre-level:** Read and write about home security	Present tense (*I have a security alarm.*)	*buzzer, intercom, deadbolt, peephole* For vocabulary support, see these **Oxford Picture Dictionary** topics: Apartments, Different Places to Live	**CASAS**: 0.1.2, 0.2.1, 8.1.4 **LCPs**: 39.01, 44.02, 49.01, 49.02, 49.13, 49.16 **SCANS**: Creative thinking, Interprets and communicates information, Listening, Observe critically, Reading, Writing **EFF**: Convey ideas in writing, Read with understanding

Warm-up and Review

10–15 minutes (books closed)

Write *Safe Neighborhood* and *Unsafe Neighborhood* on the board. Ask students what makes a neighborhood safe or unsafe. Write their ideas in the correct column.

Introduction

5 minutes

1. Looking at the "unsafe" column, ask students which of these things the neighbors themselves could take care of and which require the help of city government.

2. State the objective: *Today we're going to read and write about home security.*

1 Read about home security

Presentation

20–25 minutes

A 1. Direct students to look at the pictures. Ask: *Do these homes look safe?*

2. Elicit answers to questions 1 and 2. Write the names of the security features on the board.

B 1. Tell students they are going to read a woman's description of the security at her apartment.

2. Direct students to read the article silently. Check comprehension. Ask: *What safety features does she have at her apartment?* [deadbolt locks, chain lock, lights in hallways, neighborhood email group]

3. Play the audio. Have students read along silently.

4. Draw students' attention to the *Writer's note.* Elicit the quote in the reading.

Guided Practice I

10 minutes

C Have students work independently to complete the sentences. Write the answers on the board.

Multilevel Strategies

Seat pre-level students together for 1C.

• **Pre-level** While other students are working on 1C, ask these students *Yes/No* and *Or* questions about the reading. *Does the writer have good locks on her doors? Does she have a peephole? Do they want new lights in the hallways or on the sides of the building?* Give students time to write the answers to 1C.

2 Write about home security

Guided Practice II
20–25 minutes

 1. Read the questions. Elicit students' answers.

2. Add any additional security features students name to the list on the board from the warm-up.

 1. Direct students to look back at the article in 1B. Ask students to look through the article quickly and tell you what tense most of the verbs are in. [simple present]

2. Read the questions for each paragraph. Elicit possible answers from several students to help others get ideas.

3. Check comprehension of the exercise. *How many paragraphs do you write?* [three] *Do you need to write the questions?* [no] *What is the purpose of the questions?* [to guide writing]

4. Have students work individually to write their essays.

Multilevel Strategies

Adapt 2B to the level of your students.

• **Pre-level** Have these students write one paragraph in response to the questions for paragraph 2.

• **Higher-level** Ask these students to include a fourth paragraph comparing the security of their current home to the security of a place where they used to live.

---

 1. Lead students through the process of using the *Editing checklist*. Read each sentence aloud, and ask students to check their papers before moving on to the next item.

2. Allow students a few minutes to edit their writing as necessary.

Communicative Practice
10 minutes

 1. Read the instructions aloud. Emphasize to students that they are responding to their partners' work, not correcting it.

2. Use the article in 1B to model the exercise. *I think the sentence about the neighborhood email group is interesting. I'd like to ask this writer how many emails she has received and what they said.*

3. Direct students to exchange papers with a partner and follow the instructions.

4. Call on volunteers to share something interesting they read in their partners' papers.

Application and Evaluation
15 minutes

TEST YOURSELF

1. Review the instructions aloud. Assign a time limit (ten minutes), and have students work independently.

2. Before collecting students' work, remind them to use the *Editing checklist*. Collect and correct students' writing.

To compress this lesson: Assign the *Test Yourself* for homework.

To extend this lesson: Have students role-play calling a neighbor.
1. With the class, brainstorm possible "suspicious" events in the neighborhood and appropriate responses to those events. Write them on the board.
2. Provide students with role-play instructions: *Partner A: Tell your partner you saw something suspicious—for example, a strange car parked with someone sitting in it. Partner B: Thank your neighbor for calling and tell him/her what you'll do. For example: Ask the police to drive down the street.*
3. Ask volunteer pairs to perform one of their role-plays for the class.

And/Or have students complete **Workbook 3 page 66** and **Multilevel Activity Book 3 page 110**.

2 Write about home security

A Talk about the questions with your class.

1. Do you ever think about how safe your home is?
2. Have you added any security features to your home since you've lived there?

B Write a story about security in your home and your neighborhood.
Use the model in 1B and the questions below to help you. Answers will vary.

Paragraph 1: Where do you live? Why do you like living there?
Do you ever think about home security?

Paragraph 2: What security feature(s) in your home are you happy with?
What other security features would you like to have? Why?

Paragraph 3: What have your neighbors or family members suggested to make the
neighborhood safer? If possible, include a quotation about safety from a
family member or neighbor. Why is it important to work together?
Does it take a little work or a lot of work to keep a neighborhood safe?
Why do you think people want to feel safe?

My Home Security
I live in …

C Use the checklist to edit your writing. Check (✔) the true sentences. Answers will vary.

Editing checklist	
1. I wrote about one or more good security features in my home.	
2. I wrote about one or more security features I would like to have.	
3. I followed the rules on page 132 for quotations.	
4. There are three paragraphs in my essay.	

D Exchange stories with a partner. Read and comment on your partner's work.

1. Point out one security feature that you think is very important.
2. Ask your partner a question about his or her neighborhood.

TEST YOURSELF ✔

Think about safety and security at your school. Write a new story about the
security features at your school and any security features you would like to
have at school.

1 Learn gerunds as subjects

A **Read the article. What crime happened at Millie's house?** Two men came into the house and tried to take her TV.

"Locking the doors is more important than it used to be," says Millie Olsen, age 82. Millie knows because she was at home last night when two men broke into her house and tried to take her TV. Millie was not sleeping, so she quietly called 911 from another room. Calling was the right thing to do. It saved Millie's TV, and maybe even her life. What's Millie going to do next? "Thanking the police will be the first thing on my list. Buying newer, stronger locks is the

second. I guess my old locks weren't as strong as I thought they were."

B **Study the chart. Underline the 4 examples of gerunds as subjects in the article above.**

Gerunds as subjects
┌Gerund┐
Calling   was the right thing to do.
Locking   the doors is important.
Thanking the police will be the first thing I do.

Notes
• Form a gerund by adding *-ing* to the base form of a verb.
• A gerund acts as a singular noun in a sentence.

C **Complete the sentences. Use the verbs in the box to make gerunds. Then read your sentences to a partner.**

call   walk   ~~lock~~   protect   report   park

1. _Locking_____ your car doors is a good idea.
2. _Reporting_____ a crime quickly can save lives.
3. _Walking_____ alone at night is not a good idea.
4. _Parking_____ near a streetlight is safer than parking on a dark street.
5. _Calling_____ the police to report crimes can make everyone safer.
6. _Protecting_____ our neighborhood is important to everyone.

Unit 10 Lesson 3

Objectives	Grammar	Vocabulary	Correlations
On- and Higher-level: Use gerunds to talk about safety, distinguish gerunds from present-continuous verbs, and listen for gerunds in sentences about crime **Pre-level:** Identify gerunds in conversations about safety and crime	Gerunds as subjects (*Locking your doors is a good idea.*)	*break in, install, give out* For vocabulary support, see this **Oxford Picture Dictionary** topic: Public Safety	**CASAS:** 0.1.2, 0.2.1, 8.1.4 **LCPs:** 44.01, 49.16 **SCANS:** Acquires and evaluates information, Decision making, Participates as member of a team, Reading, Writing **EFF:** Convey ideas in writing, Observe critically, Read with understanding, Solve problems and make decisions

Warm-up and Review

10–15 minutes (books closed)

Write *Safety Habits* on the board, and elicit as many as students recall from the previous lesson. Write expressions on the board beginning with a simple verb: *Lock doors, call or email neighbors, report crimes, install window bars, have strong locks, close windows, leave lights on, install an alarm.*

Introduction

5–10 minutes

1. Use the sentences on the board to form sentences with gerunds as subjects. *Locking doors is a good idea. Installing an alarm can be expensive.*

2. State the objective: *Today we're going to learn how to use gerunds as subjects to talk about safety.*

1 Learn gerunds as subjects

Presentation I

20–25 minutes

A 1. Direct students to look at the photo. Ask: *How old do you think she is?*

2. Read the question. Ask students to read the article silently to find the answer to the question. Call on a volunteer for the answer.

B 1. Read the sentences in the chart aloud.

2. Direct students to underline the examples of gerunds in the article in 1A. Go over the answers as a class.

3. Copy one of the sentences from the article on the board. Ask students to identify the verb. [*is* or *was*] Ask students to identify the subject. [the gerund]

4. Assess students' understanding of the charts. Ask: *Is* locking *the verb in the first sentence?* [no] *Can I use* lock *as the subject?* [no]

5. Ask students to use the expressions on the board from the warm-up to create sentences with gerunds.

Guided Practice I

15–20 minutes

C Ask students to work individually to complete the sentences. Ask volunteers to write the answers on the board.

TIP Provide extra practice with gerunds. Write active verbs on the board in simple form. *Run, walk, write, speak, give, learn, go, live, dream, build, sit, stand.* Tell students to work with partners. Partners should take turns saying sentences that use the verbs on the board as subject gerunds. Have them continue taking turns until they have used all of the words on the board. When students finish, elicit a sample sentence for each verb.

Guided Practice II

5–10 minutes

D Read the sentence aloud. Read each of the choices, and ask for a show of hands for each answer.

2 Compare gerunds and the present continuous

Presentation II

20–25 minutes

A 1. Introduce the new topic. Say: *The –ing form can be used as a noun (a gerund), or it can be part of a verb (the present continuous). Now we're going to look at the difference between the gerund and the present continuous.*

2. Direct students to read the chart. While they are reading, copy a gerund sentence and a present-continuous sentence from the chart onto the board. Ask students to identify the subject and the verb in each sentence. Ask: *Is the present-continuous verb complete with only the –ing form?* [No—it requires a form of be.]

3. Ask students to work individually to label the sentences *G* or *P*. Go over the answers as a class. Elicit the subject of each sentence.

TIP For more practice with present continuous versus gerund, try the following activities:
   1. Give each student an index card with *gerund* written on one side and *present continuous* on the other. Say sentences. Have students show the sides of their cards that indicate which forms they heard. *I'm reporting the accident.* [present continuous] *Reporting crimes to the police is important.* [gerund] *I think she's calling the police.* [present continuous] *Calling the police isn't necessary.* [gerund]
   2. Have students line up in two teams at the board. Explain the rules: *The first team member writes a present-continuous sentence. For example,* I'm looking for a new car. *The second team member writes a sentence using the same verb as a gerund subject. For example,* Looking for a new car isn't easy.

The third team member writes a sentence using the present continuous with a different verb. The fourth team member uses that verb as a gerund subject. Team members can call for assistance. Writers can finish and/or correct previous sentences, but only one person can write at a time.
   3. Call out *Switch!* every 20 seconds as a signal for the next team member to come to the board. The game ends after the last team member has written. The team with the most correct sentences at the end of the game wins.

Guided Practice I

10–15 minutes

B 1. Direct students to look at the art. Ask: *Where are these women? What do you think they are talking about?*

2. Read the beginning of the conversation aloud. Elicit the subject and verb of numbers 1 and 2. Tell students to work individually to complete the sentences with the present continuous or a gerund. Ask them to read the conversation with a partner when they finish. Ask two volunteers to read and act out the conversation for the class.

Multilevel Strategies

While on- and higher-level students are completing 2B, go over the basics with pre-level students.

• **Pre-level** Provide these students with simple sentences, and ask them to identify the subject and verb. *Running is good exercise. The suspect is running away. Walking in the dark isn't safe. She is walking on a well-lit street. Speaking English is fun. She is speaking in front of the class.*

• **On- and Higher-level** After these students finish 2B, ask them to work with their partners to write two additional sentences with gerund subjects and two with present-continuous verbs. Have volunteers write their sentences on the board. Ask other students to identify the gerunds and present-continuous verbs.

D Get the form. Work with your class. Read the sentence.
Then circle the correct words.

Adding streetlights makes a neighborhood safer.

1. In this sentence, the gerund is (*neighborhood* /(*Adding*)).
2. The gerund is the ((subject) / verb) in the sentence.
3. When a gerund is the subject of a sentence in the simple present tense,
   the verb is singular and ends with ((-s) / -er).

2 Compare gerunds and the present continuous

A Study the charts. Then read the sentences below. Write *G* for gerund
or *P* for present continuous.

Gerunds
Reporting crime is the right thing to do.
Walking alone isn't safe.

Present continuous
Irina **is reporting** the crime to the police.
Jack **isn't walking** alone now.

  _P_ 1. Michelle is installing new locks on her windows.

  _P_ 2. The attorneys are speaking with the judge.

  _G_ 3. Protecting your wallet is easy to do.

  _P_ 4. Dana is walking in a well-lit area.

  _G_ 5. Listening carefully is the jury's job.

B Complete the sentences. Use a gerund or present continuous form.

A: My neighborhood is very safe. Why should I **lock** the door?

B: ___Locking___ the door protects you and your home.
         1

A: OK, I _'m locking___ the door right now.
            2

B: And you should **put** your wallet in your purse.

A: I know, I know. _Putting_____ my wallet in my
                       3
purse will keep it safe.

B: Right! Look, I _'m putting____ my wallet in my purse.
                     4

A: And now, you're going to tell me how to **walk**.

B: Well, _walking_____ in the dark isn't smart.
            5

A: Hah! I _'m_____ not _walking_____. I plan
            6   7
to **drive**!

B: I guess _driving_____ in the dark is OK, but don't forget to turn your lights on.
              8

3 Grammar listening

Listen to the sentences and check (✔) *Gerund* or *Present continuous*.

	Gerund	Present continuous
1.		✔
2.	✔	
3.	✔	
4.		✔
5.		✔
6.	✔	

4 Practice gerunds

A Read the chart. Check (✔) *Safe* or *Dangerous* for each situation. Answers will vary.

Is the situation dangerous or safe?	Safe	Dangerous
1. sleeping with the windows open		
2. talking to people you don't know		
3. going out alone		
4. driving alone at night		
5. opening the front door to a stranger		
6. giving out your phone number to a stranger		

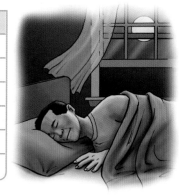

B Work with 3 classmates. Compare your answers to the survey.

A: *I think sleeping with the windows open is safe.*

B: *I agree. Sleeping with the windows open is safe if you keep the doors locked.*

C: *I disagree. Sleeping with the windows open is dangerous. Someone could come in through the windows.*

C Take a class poll. How many students think each situation in 4A is safe? How many think each situation is dangerous?

TEST YOURSELF ✔

Close your book. Write 4 sentences about situations that are safe and 4 sentences about situations that are dangerous. Use a gerund in each sentence.

---

3 Grammar listening

Guided Practice II

10–15 minutes

1. Elicit some of the courtroom words students learned in the first lesson: *judge, jury, defendant.* Say: *Now we're going to listen to sentences that describe what's going on in a courtroom. Decide if each sentence uses a gerund subject or a present-continuous verb.*

2. Play the audio. Direct students to read along silently without writing.

3. Replay the audio. Ask students to check the correct column in the chart.

4. Copy the chart on the board while students are listening. Elicit the correct answers and check them off.

> ### Multilevel Strategies
>
> Replay *Grammar listening* to allow pre-level students to catch up while you challenge on- and higher-level students.
>
> • **Pre-level** Have these students listen again to complete the chart.
>
> • **On- and Higher-level** Have these students take notes on the sentences as they listen again. As you go over the chart on the board elicit what they remember about each sentence.

4 Practice gerunds

Communicative Practice and Application

20–25 minutes

A 1. Direct students to look at the picture. Ask: *Is the man safe?*

2. Tell students to work individually to complete the survey.

B 1. Put students in groups of four. Read the sample conversation aloud. Point out that they may feel the situation is safe in some circumstances but not in others. *Driving alone at night may be safe sometimes and not safe other times.*

2. Check comprehension of the exercise. Ask: *Are you talking to one partner or to the whole group?* [the group] *Who is giving their opinions?* [everyone]

3. Direct students to compare their survey answers with others in their groups.

C Ask for a show of hands about each item on the survey. Encourage students to share their ideas about circumstances in which the activity would be safer or less safe.

Evaluation

10–15 minutes

TEST YOURSELF

1. Ask students to write the sentences independently.

2. Collect and correct students' writing.

> ### Multilevel Strategies
>
> Target the *Test Yourself* to the level of your students.
>
> • **Pre-level** Ask these students to write four sentences. Provide this structure: _____ *is dangerous;* _____ *is safe.*
>
> • **Higher-level** Have these students write a total of ten sentences.

To compress this lesson: Conduct 2A as a whole-class activity and/or assign 2B as homework.

To extend this lesson: Discuss safety for children. Ask students what kind of advice they give their children to teach them about safety. Write their ideas on the board. Elicit categories for the advice: *Sports Safety, Safety from Crime, Safety for Pedestrians.*

And/Or have students complete **Workbook 3 pages 67–68** and **Multilevel Activity Book 3 pages 111–112,** and the corresponding **Unit 10 Exercises** on the **Multilevel Grammar Exercises CD-ROM 3.**

Unit 10 Lesson 4

Objectives	Grammar	Vocabulary	Correlations
On-, Pre-, and Higher-level: Report a crime and listen for a crime description	Gerunds and infinitives (*Locking the door is a good idea. It's a good idea to lock the door.*)	*sudden, suddenly, hold on, purse-snatching, mugging* For vocabulary support, see these **Oxford Picture Dictionary** topics: Crime, The Legal System	**CASAS:** 0.1.2, 5.3.8, 6.7.2 **LCPs:** 39.01, 44.01, 49.02, 49.09, 49.16, 51.05 **SCANS:** Arithmetic/Mathematics, Creative thinking, Listening, Reading **EFF:** Listen actively, Observe critically, Use math to solve problems and communicate, Read with understanding, Reflect and evaluate

Warm-up and Review

10–15 minutes (books closed)

Write these words on the board: *a ran away hair man a student's the man had and thin long blond was laptop tall he he stole grabbed the laptop and.* Tell students someone saw a crime. The words make sentences that describe what he/she saw. Ask them to create sentences with the scrambled words. Call on volunteers to write their sentences on the board. Praise all correct sentences. *A man stole a student's laptop. The man had long blond hair. He was tall and thin. He grabbed the laptop and ran away.*

Introduction

5 minutes

1. Write up the unscrambled version of the story. Say: *This is a statement from a witness who is reporting a crime.*

2. State the objective: *Today we're going to learn how to report a crime and listen to a description of a crime.*

1 Learn to report a crime

Presentation I

15–20 minutes

A 1. Direct students to look at the pictures. Read the questions below the pictures.

2. Play the audio. Give students time to answer the questions. Go over the answers as a class.

Guided Practice

20–25 minutes

B 1. Read the instructions aloud. Play the audio. Ask students to read along silently and listen for the answer to the question.

2. Ask students to read the conversation with a partner. Circulate and monitor pronunciation. Model and have students repeat difficult words or phrases.

3. Say and have students repeat the expressions in the *In other words* box. Elicit the placement of the expressions in the conversation. Ask volunteers to read the conversation using expressions from the box.

Communicative Practice and Application

15–20 minutes

C 1. Ask students to read the instructions silently. Check their comprehension of the exercise. Ask: *What are the two roles? What is the situation?* Elicit examples of what the witness and the police officer might say.

2. Set a time limit (five minutes). Ask students to act out the role-play in both roles. Ask volunteers to act out their conversations for the class. Tell students who are listening to note some of the questions that the desk officer asks.

Multilevel Strategies

For 1C, adapt the role-play to the level of your students.

• **Pre-level** Provide a simplified conversation for these students to practice as their role-play. *A: I'd like to report a crime. B: What happened? A: I saw some teenagers painting on a building. B: What happened after that? A: They broke a few windows and ran away. B: Thank you for reporting the crime.*

1 Learn to report a crime

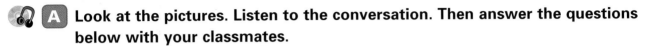

A Look at the pictures. Listen to the conversation. Then answer the questions below with your classmates.

1. What did the witness see? a man breaking into an apartment and taking a TV
2. What did the man do when he saw the witness? He ran away.

B Listen and read. What did the person witness?

Desk Officer: Police department. How can I direct your call?
Witness: I'd like to report a crime I witnessed.
Desk Officer: OK. Please tell me what happened.
Witness: Well, while I was waiting for the bus, I saw a man across the street. First, he broke a car window. Then he opened the car door.
Desk Officer: What happened after that?
Witness: I think he saw me because, all of a sudden, he ran away.
Desk Officer: OK. Hold on. An officer will fill out a complete report. Reporting this was the right thing to do.
Witness: Thank you.

> **In other words...**
>
> **Sequencing events**
> first
> then
> after that
> next
> all of a sudden
> suddenly

C Role-play a conversation between a witness and a police officer with a partner. Use the example in 1B to make a new conversation.

Partner A: You're the witness. Call and report a crime. While you were walking to work, you saw some teenagers behind a building. First, they painted some words on the building. Then, they broke a few windows. After that, they ran away.
Partner B: You're a desk officer at the police station. Ask the witness about the crime.

2 Learn to use infinitives and gerunds

A Study the chart. Circle the correct words below.

Gerunds and infinitives	
Gerund	Infinitive
Reporting crime is important.	It's important **to report** crime.
Walking alone isn't safe.	It isn't safe **to walk** alone.
Locking your car is a good idea.	It's a good idea **to lock** your car.

Note
The infinitive form of a verb is *to* + the base form of the verb.

1. It's important (**to listen** / listening) to the judge in a courtroom.
2. (Go / **Going**) out alone at night isn't always a good idea.
3. (Talk / **Talking**) to neighbors is good for the neighborhood.
4. It's a good idea (**to walk** / walking) in well-lit areas.

B Underline the gerunds or infinitives in the sentences. Then write a new sentence with the same idea. Use a gerund or an infinitive.

1. <u>Walking</u> down a dark street is dangerous.

   It's dangerous to walk down a dark street.

2. It isn't safe <u>to leave</u> the garage door open at night.

   Leaving the garage door open at night isn't safe.

3. <u>Understanding</u> the criminal justice system is important.

   It's important to understand the criminal justice system.

4. It's important <u>to make</u> sure your home is safe.

   Making sure your home is safe is important.

3 Practice your pronunciation

A Study the chart. Listen to the words that are stressed in these sentences.

Stressed words in sentences	
He broke the car window.	**He** broke the window. She didn't do it.
He broke the **car** window.	He broke a **car** window, not a house window.
He broke the car **window**.	He broke the **window**, not the horn or door.

B Listen and circle the sentences you hear.

1. **(a.)** **I** called the police.
   b. I called the **police**.

2. a. **They** ran that way.
   (b.) They ran **that** way.

3. **(a.)** We walk every **evening**.
   b. We **walk** every evening.

C Listen again and check. Repeat the sentences.

2 Learn to use infinitives and gerunds

Presentation II and Guided Practice

10–15 minutes

1. Introduce the new topic. Write *infinitive* and *gerund* on the board. Elicit the infinitive and gerund forms of the verb *call*.

2. Read the sentences in the chart. Ask students to identify the subject of each sentence.

3. Check comprehension of the chart. Ask: *Do we use the infinitive as a subject?*

4. Direct students to circle the correct words in the sentences below the chart. Ask volunteers to read the completed sentences aloud.

Communicative Practice

10–15 minutes

1. Read number 1 aloud. Tell students to work individually to write new sentences with the same idea. Ask volunteers to write their sentences on the board.

2. Ask students to take turns reading their sentences with a partner.

> ### Multilevel Strategies
>
> Seat same-level students together for 2B.
>
> • **Pre-level** Lead these students through the process of re-stating each idea with an infinitive or gerund.
>
> • **On- and Higher-level** Have these students write two more pairs of infinitive/gerund sentences that express the same idea. Ask volunteers to write one of their sentence pairs on the board.

3 Practice your pronunciation

Pronunciation Extension

15–20 minutes

1. Write *I locked the doors.* on the board. Say: *I locked the doors. You didn't lock them!* Ask students which word you stressed. Then say: *I locked the doors. I didn't just close them.* Ask students which word you stressed. Say: *I locked the doors. I didn't lock the windows.* Ask students which word you stressed. Say: *Now we're going to focus on using stress to show contrast.*

2. Play the audio. Direct students to listen for the stressed words as they read the sentences in the chart.

3. Elicit the stressed words. Ask students why those words were stressed. [to emphasize contrast]

B Have students look at number 1. Point out the bold-faced type that indicates a stressed word. Ask them to listen to the audio and circle the sentence they hear.

C Replay the audio. Have students listen and check their answers. Go over the answers as a class. Have students repeat the sentences.

> **TIP**
> For more practice with describing a crime, have students write a witness's statement.
>
> 1. Tell students they are going to witness a crime and they need to report it in writing. They should include what happened and what the suspect looked like. Allow them to work with a partner.
>
> 2. Show a short clip of a crime in progress from a TV show or movie. (Don't choose anything very violent or disturbing.) Have students work with their partners to describe what they saw. If you don't have access to a television in class, show pictures of the "criminals" for about 30 seconds. Have students invent the crime, but give descriptions of the people they saw.
>
> 3. Have volunteers share their statements with the class. Replay the video or show the pictures to check the accuracy of their descriptions.

◄ Focus on Listening

Listening Extension

20–25 minutes

A Read the questions aloud, and elicit answers from volunteers. Encourage students to respond to each other's ideas. After one student speaks, ask other students for their opinions. *Do you agree or disagree with what he/she said? Why?*

B 1. Tell students they are going to listen to someone reporting a crime to the police. Direct them to read the questions before they listen.

2. Play the audio. Tell students to answer the questions. Go over the answers as a class.

C 1. Direct students to read the sentences before listening. Check comprehension of the exercise. Ask: *Why is there a number 1 next to* Ms. Aziz was sitting in the park? [because that happened first]

2. Replay the audio and have students work individually to put the sentences in order. Go over the answers as a class.

> ### Multilevel Strategies
>
> Replay the conversation to challenge on- and higher-level students while allowing pre-level students to catch up.
>
> • **Pre-level** Have these students listen again to put the sentences in order.
>
> • **On- and Higher-level** Write questions on the board. *What did the man look like? What was the victim yelling? What are Ms. Aziz and the victim supposed to do now?* After you have gone over the answers to 4C, have volunteers share their answers to the questions.

5 Real-life math

Math Extension

5–10 minutes

1. Direct students to look at the graph. Review the meaning of *mugging* and *identity theft*.

2. Ask students to work individually to answer the questions. Call on volunteers for the answers.

3. Take a class poll to find out which of these safety issues students are most concerned about. Write the numbers on the board. Write the total number of students, and elicit how to figure out the percentages. Compare the class percentages to the percentages in the chart.

Evaluation

10–15 minutes

TEST YOURSELF

1. Model the role-play with a volunteer. Then switch roles.

2. Pair students. Check comprehension of the exercise by eliciting what the witness and the police officer might say.

3. Set a time limit (five minutes), and have the partners act out the role-play in both roles.

4. Circulate and monitor. Encourage pantomime and improvisation.

5. Provide feedback.

> ### Multilevel Strategies
>
> Target the *Test Yourself* to the level of your students.
>
> • **Pre-level** Ask these students to use this skeleton conversation: *A: I'd like to report a crime. B: What happened? A: I saw _____. B: What happened after that? A: _____. B: Thank you for reporting the crime.*
>
> • **Higher-level** Ask these students to practice the role-play with several partners.

To compress this lesson: Do not ask students to act out their conversation for the class in 1C. Conduct 2B as a whole-class activity.

To extend this lesson: Bring in articles about crimes from the local newspaper. (Some small-town and local newspapers have a "police blotter" or "crime beat" section.) Have students look through the section and circle words that they have learned in this unit. Answer questions about other crime and safety-related vocabulary.

And/Or have students complete **Workbook 3 page 69** and **Multilevel Activity Book 3 page 113**.

4 Focus on listening

A **Talk about the questions with your class.**

1. Have you ever reported a crime?
2. What are some reasons people might not want to report a crime?

 B **Read the questions. Then listen to the telephone conversation. Answer the questions.**

1. Where was Ms. Aziz? <u>sitting on a park bench</u>
2. Was the victim a man or a woman? <u>a woman</u>
3. What happened to the victim? <u>her purse was stolen</u>
4. What should the women do now? <u>wait for the police</u>

 C **Listen to the conversation. Put the events in the correct order. Number the items from 1–6.**

 <u>3</u> A woman ran by and said the purse was hers.

 <u>5</u> The woman asked Ms. Aziz to call the police.

 <u>6</u> The police officer sent a police car.

 <u>4</u> The man fell down and dropped the purse.

 <u>1</u> Ms. Aziz was sitting in the park.

 <u>2</u> A man ran by carrying a lady's purse.

5 Real-life math

Study the survey. Answer the questions.

A survey asked 200 people what crimes they were worried about. Here's what they said.

1. Which crime were people most worried about?

 <u>identity theft</u>

 Which crime were people least worried about?

 <u>mugging</u>

3. How many people in the survey were worried about school safety? <u>200</u> x <u>36</u> % = <u>72</u>

Source: Loveland, Colorado Police Department

TEST YOURSELF ✔

Role-play reporting a crime. Partner A: You're the witness. Tell the police officer about a crime you witnessed. Partner B: You're the police officer. Ask for more information. Then change roles.

1 Get ready to read

A **Name some jobs that help keep the public safe.** It's about where people can find jobs in public safety.

B **Read the definitions.**

options: (noun) things to choose from

law enforcement: (noun) police officers, and others who make sure that people obey the laws

rewarding: (adj.) giving a feeling of happiness

C **Look at the first sentence in the article. What is the article about?**

2 Read and respond

A **Read the article.**

Where the Jobs Are

Thinking about a career in public safety or law enforcement? Statistics show that these careers are growing, have great benefits, and can be very rewarding. Police officer, paramedic, and firefighter are some of the most popular jobs in this field; but there are hundreds of public safety jobs to think about—everything from police officers who protect people to driver's license examiners who test driving skills.

For example, Angela Bloom is an animal control worker for the city. She and her co-workers pick up animals that are lost, sick, or dangerous. They also

Angela Bloom has been an animal control worker for 16 years. Animal control is one of many careers in public safety.

investigate reports of animal abuse.[1] Being in good physical condition is important for this job. People with a high school diploma or GED can usually apply for this job.

Martin Lee is a health inspector. He looks for health problems in places where people prepare and serve food. There are many kinds of jobs for inspectors. Public safety inspectors look for safety violations

Occupation	Average Annual Salary (2004)	Growth Rate (2014)
animal control worker	$17,420	18–26%
building inspector	$43,670	18–26%
fire inspector	$46,340	18–26%
police officer	$45,210	9–17%

[1]abuse: the act of hurting or injuring someone or something

Unit 10 Lesson 5

Objectives	Grammar	Vocabulary	Correlations
Pre-, On-, and Higher-level: Read about and discuss careers in public safety	Simple present (*Health inspectors look for problems in restaurants.*)	*law enforcement, rewarding, options, abuse* For vocabulary support, see these **Oxford Picture Dictionary** topics: Public Safety, Civic Rights and Responsibilities, Jobs and Occupations	**CASAS:** 0.1.2, 5.5.6, 7.4.4 **LCPs:** 38.01, 49.09, 49.16, 49.17 **SCANS:** Acquires and evaluates information, Applies technology to task, Creative thinking, Interprets and communicates information, Reading **EFF:** Learn through research, Read with understanding, Take responsibility for learning

Warm-up and Review

10–15 minutes (books closed)

Review job titles. Write *Good Jobs* on the board, and ask students to brainstorm a list of jobs they would consider to be good jobs. Then elicit the reasons. *What makes a job good?* Write those ideas on the board. Ask how many of the jobs involve helping people.

Introduction

5 minutes

1. Ask students if any of the jobs on the board involve keeping people safe. Tell them that although most people might think of firefighters and police officers, there are many other jobs involved with public safety.

2. State the objective: *Today we're going read about and discuss careers in public safety.*

1 Get ready to read

Presentation

15–20 minutes

A Elicit students' ideas and write them on the board.

B Read the words and definitions. Elicit sample sentences from students for *options* and *rewarding*. Ask: *Who is responsible for law enforcement?*

Pre-Reading

C 1. Read the question. Call on a volunteer for the answer.

2. Ask students to look at the picture and read the caption about Angela Bloom. Ask: *Do you think working in animal control would be a good career?*

2 Read and respond

Guided Practice I

25–30 minutes

A 1. Ask students to read the article silently.

2. Direct students to underline unfamiliar words they would like to know. Elicit the words and encourage other students to provide definitions or examples.

3. Check students' comprehension. Ask: *What are some advantages of a job in public safety?* [They're growing, have great benefits, and can be rewarding.]

Multilevel Strategies

Adapt 2A to the level of your students.

• **Pre-level** Provide these students with definitions for the occupations in the chart, and ask them to look at the chart. *Animal control workers pick up animals that are lost, sick, or dangerous. Building inspectors make sure that buildings are safe for people to live and work in. Crossing guards help people cross the street. Fire inspectors look for problems that could cause fires.*

Direct students to read this summary while other students are reading 2A.

Guided Practice II

15–20 minutes

B 1. Play the audio. Have students read along silently.

2. Elicit and discuss any additional questions about the reading.

C Have students work individually to circle *a* or *b*. Ask volunteers to read the answers aloud. Write the letters on the board.

Multilevel Strategies

For 2C, work with pre-level students.

• **Pre-level** Ask these students to identify public safety occupations while other students are completing 2C. *Who picks up lost animals?* [animal control workers] Give students time to copy the answers to 2C from the board.

• **Higher-level** Ask these students to choose two of the jobs from the article and write three advantages and disadvantages of each job. After you go over the answers to 2C, call on volunteers to share their ideas with the class.

3 Talk it over

Communicative Practice

15–20 minutes

A Read the questions aloud. Set a time limit (three minutes). Ask students to work independently to think about the questions and write their answers in note form.

B Ask for a show of hands about each job to find out which ones most students think are the best. Write them on the board. Include those jobs as choices for the *Bring It to Life* investigation.

TIP For information about job training and education requirements, as well as average salaries and growth potential, direct students to look online for the Department of Labor's *Occupational Outlook Handbook*. The same kind of information can be found on many career information sites. If you have access to computers in class, have each student choose an occupation and write a list of questions for them to answer on the board: *What is the starting salary for this job? What education/training is required? What are the working conditions?* Direct students to scan through the information on the website looking for the answers to the questions.

Application

5–10 minutes

BRING IT TO LIFE

Find out if any of your students know people with public safety jobs. Have students decide in class which job they are going to research and how they are going to conduct their research.

To compress this lesson: Conduct 2C as a whole-class activity.

To extend this lesson: Do a "career counselor" role-play.
1. Write this role-play situation on the board. *Partner A: You are looking for a job. Tell the counselor what you are good at and what you like to do. Partner B: You are the counselor. Recommend a job for your partner. Say why it's a good match.*
2. Brainstorm things each person might say, and write them on the board.
3. Have students practice the role-play in both roles. Call on volunteers to share whether or not their partners had good career matches.

And/Or have students complete **Workbook 3 page 70** and **Multilevel Activity Book 3 pages 114–115**.

or dangerous workplaces. Fire inspectors look for problems in buildings that could cause fires. Problem solving skills are important for these jobs. A college degree is often necessary.

These are only a few of the job options available. So remember, if you like working with the public, and are looking for a good job, a career in public safety might be perfect for you.

Source: *U.S. Department of Labor*

B Listen and read the article again.

C Read the sentences. Circle *a* or *b*.

1. A driver's license examiner tests people's driving skills.

   (a.) They make sure that unsafe drivers don't get licenses.

   b. They make sure that people can cross the street.

2. Health inspectors look for problems in places where people serve food.

   (a.) They might inspect hospitals and schools.

   b. They might inspect banks and pharmacies.

3. Public safety employees often feel good because they protect and help people.

   a. They feel good because they make a lot of money.

   (b.) They feel good because their jobs are rewarding.

4. Fire inspectors look for problems in buildings that could cause fires.

   a. They can check the plumbing in the building.

   (b.) They can check the electrical system in a building.

3 Talk it over

A Think about the questions. Make notes about your answers.

1. What do you think are the three best things about a job in public safety?
2. Which job in the chart do you think is the best? Why?

B Talk about the answers with your classmates.

BRING IT TO LIFE

Choose one of the public safety jobs from the article in 2A. Talk to someone who has this job or search online to learn what education and training is required for the job. Bring the information to class.

1 Grammar

A **Unscramble the sentences.**

1. in the neighborhood / everyone / helps / talking / to neighbors

   Talking to neighbors helps everyone in the neighborhood.

2. locked / keeping / is / doors and windows / important

   Keeping doors and windows locked is important.

3. at night / is not / alone / walking / safe

   Walking alone at night is not safe.

4. a light on / a good idea / leaving / is / at night

   Leaving a light on at night is a good idea.

B **Complete the sentences with a gerund or the present continuous. Use the verbs in parentheses.**

1. To me, _____working_____ with my neighbors is fun and rewarding. (work)

2. _Managing_____ the building is a big job. (manage)

3. The landlord _is installing_____ some new lights in the hallways. (install)

4. _Taking_____ time for safety is important. (take)

5. Our neighborhood group _is starting_____ a new project. (start)

6. _Raising_____ money for a safer playground is our goal. (raise)

C **Circle the correct words.**

1. It's important (working /(to work)) together.

2. ((Helping)/ To help) others makes you feel good.

3. It is possible (making /(to make)) our neighborhood safer.

4. It's difficult (stopping /(to stop) all crime.

5. ((Living)/ To live) in that old building is dangerous.

6. It's not smart (walking /(to walk)) down that dark street at night.

D **Rosa is reporting a crime to the police. Put the events in the correct order.**

   _4_ After that, a man ran out of a building.

   _2_ I saw two teenagers break a car window.

   _1_ It was about 8:00, and I was walking home from the bus stop.

   _6_ The two kids drove away and I called the police.

   _3_ Next, they got into the car and tried to start it.

   _5_ The man yelled, "They're stealing my car."

Unit 10 Review and expand

Objectives	Grammar	Vocabulary	Correlations
On-, Pre-, and Higher-level: Expand upon and review unit grammar and life skills	Gerunds and infinitives (*Calling the police was a good idea. It was a good idea to call the police.*)	*raise, yell, suspicious* For vocabulary support, see these **Oxford Picture Dictionary** topics: Public Safety, Crime	**CASAS:** 0.1.2, 0.1.5, 4.8.1, 5.3.8, 5.6.1, 7.2.6, 7.3.1, 7.3.2, 7.3.4 **LCPs:** 39.01, 44.01, 49.02, 49.17, 50.02 **SCANS:** Acquires and communicates information, Listening **EFF:** Convey ideas in writing, Read with understanding, Solve problems and make decisions

Warm-up and Review

10–15 minutes (books closed)

1. Review the *Bring It to Life* assignment from Lesson 5.

2. Have students who did the exercise discuss what they learned. Have students who didn't do the exercise ask their classmates questions.

3. Find out if any students have changed their minds about a job based on their research. *Is the job better than you thought it was? Or not as good?*

Introduction and Presentation

5 minutes

1. Write several familiar verbs on the board: *study, practice, speak.* Then write: *Present Continuous, Gerund, Infinitive.* Elicit example sentences with the verbs for each category. *I am studying English. Studying English is fun. It's a good idea to study every day.*

2. State the objective: *Today we're going to review the present continuous, gerunds as subjects, and it + infinitive to talk about safety.*

1 Grammar

Guided Practice

40–45 minutes

A Read the example in number 1. Ask students to work individually to unscramble the sentences. Have volunteers write the unscrambled sentences on the board.

B Ask students to work individually to complete the sentences with a gerund or a present-continuous verb. Have students take turns reading the sentences aloud with a partner.

C Have students work with their partners to choose the correct form. Tell them to take turns reading the sentences aloud.

Multilevel Strategies

For 1B and 1C, seat same-level students together.

• **Pre-level** Read each sentence aloud for these students and help them choose the correct form. Allow everyone to circle the correct answer before you move on to the next item.

• **On- and Higher-level** After these students finish reading the sentences with their partners, ask them to write six additional sentences, two with present continuous, two with a gerund subject, and two with *it* + infinitive. Have volunteers write their sentences on the board. Ask other students to identify the subjects and verbs.

D Have students work individually to put the events in order. Call on volunteers to read the sentences aloud in the correct order.

2 Group work

Communicative Practice

20–35 minutes

A 1. Direct students, in groups of three to four, to focus on the picture. Ask: *What do you think they're talking about?*

2. Group students and assign roles: leader, recorder, and reporters. Explain that students work with their group to write the conversation.

3. Check comprehension of the roles. Ask: *Who writes the conversation?* [recorder] *Who will read the conversation to the class?* [reporters] *Who helps everyone and tells the group how much time has passed?* [leader] *Who creates the conversation?* [everyone]

4. Set a time limit (five minutes) to complete the exercise. Circulate and answer any questions.

5. Have reporters from each group read the group's conversation to the class.

> ### Multilevel Strategies
> For 2A, use mixed-level groups.
> - **Pre-level** Assign these students the role of timekeeper.
> - **On-level** Assign these students the role of recorder or reporter.
> - **Higher-level** Assign these students the role of leader.

B 1. Have students walk around the room to conduct the interviews. To get students moving, tell them to interview three new people not in their group for 2A.

2. Set a time limit (five minutes) to complete the exercise.

3. Tell students to make a note of their classmates' answers but not to worry about writing complete sentences.

> ### Multilevel Strategies
> Adapt the mixer in 2B to the level of your students.
> - **Pre-level** Allow these students to ask and answer the questions without writing.
> - **Higher-level** Have these students ask two additional questions and write all answers.

C Call on individuals to report what they learned about their classmates. Encourage students to make generalizations. *One out of four students has seen a safety problem in the neighborhood.*

PROBLEM SOLVING

15–25 minutes

A 1. Ask: *Do you know anyone whose house has been broken into?* Tell students they will read a story about a woman who lives in a neighborhood where houses have been broken into. Direct students to read Delia's story silently.

2. Check students' comprehension. Ask: *Why is the truck suspicious?* [no license plates, driving slowly up and down the street, people sitting inside truck for 20 minutes]

3. Play the audio. Have students read along silently.

B 1. Elicit answers to question 1. Have the class brainstorm a list of things Delia can do. Write the list on the board.

2. Ask students what the best thing is for Delia to do. Come to a class consensus on the best idea.

Evaluation

30–35 minutes

To test students' understanding of the unit grammar and life skills, have them take the Unit 10 Test on the *Step Forward Test Generator CD-ROM* with *ExamView®* Assessment Suite.

> ### Learning Log
> To help students record and discuss their progress, use the *Learning Log* on page T-203.

To extend this review: Have students complete **Workbook 3 page 71, Multilevel Activity Book 3 page 116,** and the **Unit 10 Exercises** in the **Multilevel Grammar Exercises CD-ROM 3.**

2 Group work

A Work with 2–3 classmates. Write a conversation between the people in the picture. Share your conversation with the class.

Witness: *I'd like to report what I witnessed.*
Police officer: *OK. Please tell me what happened.*

B Interview 3 classmates. Write their answers.

1. What safety problems have you seen in your neighborhood?
2. Which public safety workers do you see most often in your neighborhood?
3. If you were a safety worker, what kind would you be?

C Talk about the answers with your class.

PROBLEM SOLVING

A Listen and read about Delia.

Some people broke into two houses in Delia's neighborhood last week. Delia is feeling a little nervous. This evening, she saw something strange on her street. A truck drove slowly up and down the street. It didn't have a license plate. Delia doesn't think the people in the truck are neighbors. Now the truck has been parked on the street for 20 minutes, but the people are still inside. Delia is worried. Forgetting about it doesn't feel right, but she doesn't want to call the police.

B Work with your classmates. Answer the questions.

1. What is the problem? Deila doesn't know what to do about a suspicious truck in her neighborhood.
2. What can Delia do? Make a list and discuss your ideas. What is the best thing for Delia to do?

UNIT **11**

That's Life

FOCUS ON
- life events
- attending social events
- the present passive voice
- responding to news
- buying or renting a home

LESSON 1 | **Vocabulary**

1 Learn life-event vocabulary

A **Talk about the questions with your class.**

1. Look at the picture. How many of these life events have you experienced?
2. Life events are exciting but sometimes stressful. Which are the most stressful?

B **Work with your classmates. Match the words with the pictures.**

___1___	be born	___4___	get engaged	___6___	have a baby
___9___	become a grandparent	___5___	get married	___8___	retire
___3___	get a promotion	___2___	graduate	___7___	start a business

C **Listen and check. Then read the new words with a partner.**

D **Work with a partner. Write other life-event words you know. Check your words in a dictionary.**

Unit 11 Lesson 1

Objectives	Grammar	Vocabulary	Correlations
On-level: Identify life events and describe special occasions **Pre-level:** Identify life-event and special-occasion vocabulary **Higher-level:** Talk and write about life events and special occasions	Past tense (*When was the wedding?*)	Life events and special occasions For vocabulary support, see this **Oxford Picture Dictionary** topic: Life Events and Documents	**CASAS:** 0.1.2, 0.1.5, 0.2.1, 1.2.5, 4.8.1 **LCPs:** 49.02, 49.10 **SCANS:** Interprets and communicates information, Listening, Participates as member of a team, Seeing things in the mind's eye, Speaking **EFF:** Cooperate with others, Reflect and evaluate, Speak so others can understand

Warm-up and Review

10–15 minutes (books closed)

Write a series of years on the board that represent events in your life—for example, the year you were born, graduated from high school/college, got married, had your first child, started working at this school. Ask students to guess what happened to you that year. When someone gets it right, write the word next to the year—*born, married,* etc.

Introduction

5 minutes

1. Have students tell you which of the items on the board would be considered major life events.

2. State the objective: *Today we're going to talk about life events and special occasions.*

1 Learn life-event vocabulary

Presentation I

20–25 minutes

A Write *Life Events* on the board. Direct students to look at the pictures in 1B, and elicit their answers to questions 1 and 2. Ask: *Which life event is the least stressful?*

B 1. Group students and assign roles: leader, fact checker, recorder, and reporter. Explain that students work with their groups to match the words and pictures.

2. Check comprehension of the roles. Ask: *Who looks up the words in a dictionary?* [fact checker] *Who writes the numbers in the book?* [recorder] *Who tells the class your answers?* [reporter] *Who helps everyone and manages the group?* [leader]

3. Set a time limit (three minutes), and have students work together to complete the exercise. As students work together, copy the wordlist onto the board.

4. Call "time." Have reporters take turns giving their answers. Write each group's answer on the board next to the word.

C 1. To prepare students for listening, tell them they are going to hear the life story of a man named Carlos Ortega. Ask students to listen and check their answers.

2. Have students correct the wordlist on the board and then write the correct numbers in their books.

3. Pair students. Set a time limit (two minutes). Monitor pair practice to identify pronunciation issues.

4. Call "time" and work with the pronunciation of any troublesome words or phrases.

5. Replay the audio and challenge students to listen for more information. *When was he born? What job was he promoted to? Where did he get engaged?* Call on volunteers for the answers.

D 1. Ask students to work with a partner to brainstorm a list of related words.

2. Elicit words from the class. Write them on the board. Ask students to copy them into their vocabulary notes for the unit.

Guided Practice

5–10 minutes

 E 1. Model the conversation with a volunteer. Model it again using other information from 1B.

2. Set a time limit (three minutes). Direct students to practice with a partner.

3. Ask volunteers to act out one of their conversations for the class.

2 Learn about life events and special occasions

Presentation II

15–20 minutes

A 1. Direct students to look at the newspaper announcements and read the section titles. Ask: *Do you ever read this section of the newspaper?*

2. Have students ask and answer the questions with a partner. Set a time limit (three minutes).

3. Ask volunteers to share their answers with the class.

 Point out the image of the stork bringing the baby. The legend that storks bring babies began in Germany, where storks were a sign of good luck. Ask students if they know of other superstitions or customs associated with birth.

Guided Practice

10–15 minutes

 B 1. Model the conversations with a volunteer. Model them again using a different word from 2A.

2. Set a time limit (three minutes). Direct students to practice with a partner.

3. Call on volunteers to say one of their conversations for the class.

Communicative Practice and Application

10–15 minutes

 C 1. Give students a minute to make notes of their answers to the questions. Call on individuals to share their ideas with the class.

2. Ask students if they can think of other important family events, perhaps ones that are particularly important in their cultures. Ask them to share information about how those events are celebrated.

Evaluation

10–15 minutes (books closed)

TEST YOURSELF

1. Pair students. Direct Partner B to close the book and listen to Partner A dictate five words from 1B. Ask students to switch roles when they finish.

2. Direct both partners to open their books and check their spelling when they finish.

3. Circulate and monitor student work.

> ### Multilevel Strategies
>
> Target the *Test Yourself* to the level of your students.
>
> • **Pre-level** Have these students dictate three words each.
>
> • **Higher-level** Direct these students to write a sentence defining each of the words their partner dictates.

To compress this lesson: Conduct 1B as a whole-class activity.

To extend this lesson: Have students discuss their important life events.
1. Have students write a series of years or dates representing important life events. Tell them not to write the events.
2. Direct them to sit with a partner and say one sentence about each date. *This is the year I was born. This is the year I got married.* Instruct the partner to ask one question about that event. *Where were you born? Did you have a big wedding? What's your son's name?*

And/Or have students complete **Workbook 3 page 72** and **Multilevel Activity Book 3 pages 118–119**.

E Work with a partner. Practice the conversation. Use the words in 1B.

A: I just heard from my friend. His first child was born last week!

B: Hey! That's great news!

2 Learn about life events and special occasions

A Look at the newspaper announcements. Ask and answer the questions below with a partner.

Sun Valley News   **About Town**   *Section C*

 Wedding Announcements

Lilly and Sam Rodriquez were married April 30th in Valley Park. The happy couple are in Hawaii for a ten-day honeymoon.

Birth Announcements

George Allen Lee was born May 9th to Joe and Linda Lee. Simon Lee and Ann Lee are the grandparents.

Death Notices

Jerry Jones, age 101, died at his home on May 6th. The funeral will be on May 10th at Valley Funeral Home.

1. Which section has information about babies? Birth Announcements
2. Which section has funeral information? Death Notices
3. Which section has information about marriages? Wedding Announcements

B Work with a partner. Practice the conversations.
Use the newspaper announcements in 2A.

A: *When was the wedding?*   A: *Where will the funeral be?*

B: *It was April 30th.*   B: *It'll be at Valley Funeral Home.*

C Talk about the questions with your class.

1. When did the man in 1B look the happiest? When did he look nervous?
2. Which life events are family events? Which are work events?

TEST YOURSELF ✔

Work with a partner. Partner A: Read the vocabulary words in 1B to your partner. Partner B: Close your book. Write the words. Ask your partner for help with spelling as necessary. Then change roles. Partner B: Use the words in 2A.

1 Read responses to an invitation

A Look at the pictures. Talk about the questions with your class.

1. What are some ways people respond to invitations?
2. What kinds of invitations have you received recently? How did you respond?

B Listen and read the invitation and the responses.

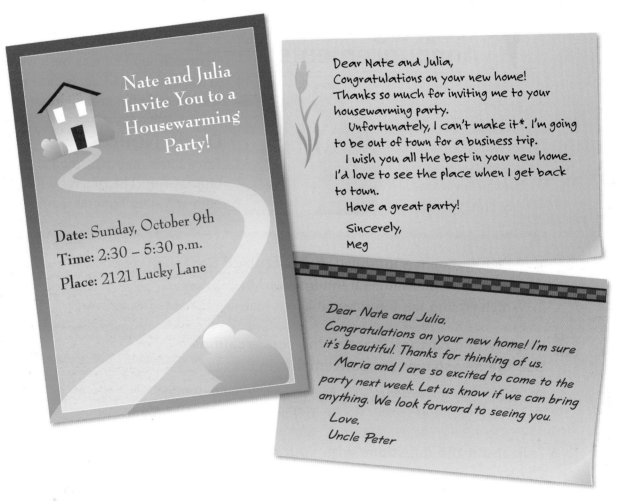

Nate and Julia
Invite You to a
Housewarming
Party!

Date: Sunday, October 9th
Time: 2:30 – 5:30 p.m.
Place: 2121 Lucky Lane

Dear Nate and Julia,
Congratulations on your new home!
Thanks so much for inviting me to your
housewarming party.
  Unfortunately, I can't make it*. I'm going
to be out of town for a business trip.
  I wish you all the best in your new home.
I'd love to see the place when I get back
to town.
  Have a great party!

  Sincerely,
  Meg

Dear Nate and Julia,
Congratulations on your new home! I'm sure
it's beautiful. Thanks for thinking of us.
  Maria and I are so excited to come to the
party next week. Let us know if we can bring
anything. We look forward to seeing you.
  Love,
  Uncle Peter

*Idiom note: make it = to attend

C Check your understanding. Circle the correct words.

1. ((Nate and Julia)/ Uncle Peter and Meg) are having a housewarming party.
2. (Nate /(Peter)) is invited to the party.
3. Peter is ((happy)/ sorry) to come to the party.
4. Meg (can /(cannot)) come to the party.
5. Meg is going (to another party /(out of town)).

Unit 11 Lesson 2

Objectives	Grammar	Vocabulary	Correlations
On- and Higher-level: Analyze, write, and edit an invitation and a response to an invitation **Pre-level:** Read an invitation and write a response	Gerunds (*Thanks for thinking of us. We look forward to coming.*)	*Respond, look forward to, housewarming, unfortunately, make it* For vocabulary support, see these **Oxford Picture Dictionary** topics: Life Events and Documents, A Birthday Party	**CASAS:** 0.1.2, 0.2.1, 0.2.3 **LCPs:** 39.01, 39.04, 49.02, 49.03, 49.13 **SCANS:** Creative thinking, Interprets and communicates information, Listening, Reading **EFF:** Convey ideas in writing, Read with understanding, Reflect and evaluate

Warm-up and Review

10–15 minutes (books closed)

Write *Housewarming Party* on the board. Elicit the meaning and find out if students have any experience with housewarming parties. *Have you ever been to or had a housewarming party? Are they traditional in your native country? What are some good gifts to bring to a housewarming party?* Write students' "good gift" ideas on the board. Ask: *Are there any bad gifts?*

Introduction

5 minutes

1. Tell students: *In order to have a party, you have to invite people. Normally if it's going to be a big party, we send out written invitations. When you receive an invitation, it's polite to respond, whether you are going to the party or not.*

2. State the objective: *Today we're going to read and write a response to a party invitation.*

1 Read responses to an invitation

Presentation

20–25 minutes

A Direct students to look at the pictures in 1B. Elicit answers to questions 1 and 2.

B 1. Write *invitation* on the board. Ask students if they have ever given out a written invitation for anything. Elicit the events.

2. Ask students to read the invitation silently. Check comprehension. Ask: *Which one is the invitation? Which is a yes response? Which is a no?*

3. Play the audio. Have students read along silently.

Guided Practice I

10 minutes

C Have students work independently to circle the correct words to complete the sentences. Go over the answers as a class.

Multilevel Strategies

For 1C, challenge on- and higher-level students while working with pre-level students.

• **Pre-level** While other students are working on 1C, ask these students *Yes/No* and *Or* questions about the reading. *Is this invitation for a birthday party? Is Uncle Peter coming to the party? Is Meg coming to the party or going out of town?*

• **On- and Higher-level** Ask these students to brainstorm possible excuses for not attending. After you go over the answers to 1C, have volunteers write their excuses on the board. Have the class decide if the excuses sound legitimate. Leave them on the board to help students with their 2B writing assignment.

2 Write responses to invitations

Guided Practice II
20–25 minutes

 1. Read the questions. Elicit students' answers.

2. Write the list of events and any new reasons for not attending on the board.

 1. Direct students to look back at the responses in 1B. Elicit expressions used in the acceptance and in the rejection. Write them on the board.

2. Ask students to look at the two invitations. Ask what occasions they are for. Elicit the day and time. Ask: *Can you go to both of them?* [no] Tell students to choose which one they will attend and write a response to each invitation.

3. Read through the questions. Remind students to use the model in 1B to help them. Have them work individually to write their responses.

> ### Multilevel Strategies
>
> Adapt 2B to the level of your students.
> • **Pre-level** Have these students write one response.

 1. Lead students through the process of using the *Editing checklist*. Read each sentence aloud, and ask students to check their papers before moving onto the next item.

2. Allow students a few minutes to edit their writing as necessary.

Communicative Practice
10 minutes

 1. Read the instructions aloud. Emphasize to students that they are responding to their partners' work, not correcting it.

2. Use Meg's response in 1B to model the exercise. *I like the sentence:* We wish you all the best in your new home. *I'd like to ask this writer where she is going on her business trip.*

3. Call on volunteers to share something interesting they read in their partners' responses.

> **TIP**
>
> Bring in examples of pre-made invitations. You can find them on the Internet or in stores. Have students decide which category each invitation belongs in—for example, adult birthday party, child's birthday party, baby shower, wedding shower, graduation party, housewarming party, or retirement party. Many invitations have idioms and expressions on them. Ask your more advanced students to guess what they mean.

Application and Evaluation
15–20 minutes

TEST YOURSELF

1. Review the instructions aloud. Assign a time limit (five minutes), and have students work independently. Ask them to exchange invitations with a partner.

2. Direct students to write responses to their partners' invitations. Assign a time limit (five minutes). Have them read their responses aloud to their partners.

3. Before collecting students' work, remind them to use the *Editing checklist*. Collect and correct students' writing.

To compress this lesson: Assign the *Test Yourself* for homework.

To extend this lesson: Practice accepting and rejecting invitations orally.
1. Write a skeleton conversation on the board for students to follow.
  A: Hi. I'm having a party this Saturday for _____. Can you come?
  B: What time?
  A: _____.
  B: [accept or reject]
  A: [respond]
2. Elicit things that each person could say to accept or reject the invitation, and write them on the board. Have students practice with a partner.

And/Or have students complete **Workbook 3 page 73** and **Multilevel Activity Book 3 page 120**.

2 Write responses to invitations

A **Talk about the questions with your class.**

1. What are some of the special events you have celebrated in your life?
2. What was the last event you were invited to? Did you go? Why or why not?

B **Read the two invitations. Choose one party that you will attend and one that you won't attend. Write responses to both invitations. Use the model in 1B and the suggestions below to help you.** Answers will vary.

1. Congratulate the person.
2. Tell the person if you will or will not attend.
3. Ask the person if you can bring something.
4. Suggest meeting at a later date if you can't attend.

> Dear Anna,
>   Congratulations on your
> retirement...

C **Use the checklist to edit your writing. Check (✔) the true sentences.** Answers will vary.

Editing checklist	
1. I congratulated Anna and Paolo.	
2. I thanked them for the invitations.	
3. I used a comma after the greetings and the closings.	
4. My handwriting is neat and easy to read.	

D **Exchange responses with a partner. Read and comment on your partner's work.**

1. Point out one sentence that you think is interesting.
2. Ask your partner a question about his or her response.

TEST YOURSELF ✔

Write an invitation for a party this weekend. Include the date, time, and location. Exchange invitations with a classmate. Write a response to your classmate's invitation.

1 Learn the present passive

A Read the flyer. How is this retirement community different
from an apartment building? In the retirement community, they serve meals for the people living there and there are events planned for the people.

Welcome to Oak View Apartments Retirement Community!

Please pay attention to the following information. If you have any questions or need assistance, please call the office.

- We serve delicious meals daily. Dinner <u>is served</u> in the dining room from 5 p.m. to 7 p.m. every day.

- Swimming <u>is not permitted</u> after 10 p.m.

- Trash <u>is picked up</u> every Thursday.

- Mail <u>is picked up</u> and delivered before 12 p.m.

- A monthly calendar of events <u>is kept</u> next to the reception desk.

B Study the chart. Underline the 5 examples of the present passive
in the flyer above.

THE PRESENT PASSIVE

The present passive		
be + past participle		
Dinner	**is served**	between 5 p.m. and 7 p.m.
Mail	**is delivered**	before 12 p.m.

Notes
• We usually use the active voice in English. We say what people or things do.
We serve delicious meals daily.
• We use the passive voice when we do not know who performed the action, when it is not important who performed the action, or when it is clear who performed it.
Dinner is served between 5 p.m. and 7 p.m.

C Complete the sentences. Use the present passive and the words
in parentheses.

1. My family _____is invited_____ to Ernesto's graduation party. (invite)

2. Usually, food __is served_____ at graduation parties. (serve)

3. Party invitations __are mailed_____ to guests a month in advance. (mail)

4. Transportation to graduation parties __is not provided_____. (not provide)

5. A party __is planned_____ for Julio's graduation, too. (plan)

Unit 11 Lesson 3

Objectives	Grammar	Vocabulary	Correlations
• **On- and Higher-level:** Use the present passive to talk about parties and community events, and listen for meaning in present passive in sentences about parties and community events • **Pre-level:** Recognize the present passive in sentences about parties and community events	Present passive (*Dinner is served at 6:00.*)	*retirement, deliver, serve, permit, announcement* For vocabulary support, see this **Oxford Picture Dictionary** topic: Life Events and Documents	**CASAS:** 0.1.2, 0.1.5, 0.2.1, 1.4.2, 4.8.1 **LCPs:** 39.01, 49.02, 49.09, 49.13, 49.17 **SCANS:** Creative thinking, Listening, Participates as member of a team, Reading, Speaking, Writing **EFF:** Convey ideas in writing, Cooperate with others, Listen actively, Read with understanding

Warm-up and Review

10–15 minutes (books closed)

Say: *We've been talking in this unit about life events—growing up, getting married, getting a promotion, but let's think for a moment about when we were young. Life was easy then because we didn't have to do so many things for ourselves. For example, when you're a child, someone feeds you, someone buys you clothes, someone brushes your hair. What else?* Write a series of simple-present sentences on the board. *Someone cleans your room. Someone washes your clothes. Someone takes you to school.*

Introduction

5–10 minutes

1. Point out that in all the sentences on the board, it's not important who did the actions. The main idea is that the child didn't have to do them. The point is not that *someone* cleaned the room but that *the room was cleaned.*

2. State the objective: *Today we're going to learn how to use the present passive to talk about daily life and community events.*

1 Learn the present passive

Presentation I

20–25 minutes

A 1. Direct students to look at the flyer. Ask: *What kind of community is this?*

2. Read the question. Ask students to read the flyer silently to find the answer. Call on individuals to share their ideas.

B 1. Demonstrate how to read the grammar charts.

2. Direct students to underline the examples of the present passive in the flyer in 1A. Go over the answers as a class.

3. Check comprehension of sentences in the flyer. Ask: *Who picks up the trash? Who permits swimming?* Point out that these sentences are passive because the emphasis is on what is done, not on who does it.

4. Read the *Notes.* Ask students to identify the forms of *be* and the past participles in the sentences in the chart.

5. Assess students' understanding of the charts. Elicit passive versions of the sentences on the board from the warm-up. *Your room is cleaned. Your clothes are washed.*

Guided Practice I

15–20 minutes

C Ask students to work individually to complete the sentences. Ask volunteers to write the answers on the board.

Multilevel Strategies

For 1C, seat same-level students together.

• **Pre-level** While other students are completing 1C, ask these students to copy the sentences from 1B into their notebooks. Give them time to copy the answers to 1C after they are written on the board.

Guided Practice II

10–15 minutes

 D Ask a volunteer to read the instructions and the paragraph aloud. Direct students to read numbers 1 and 2 and circle the answers. Go over the answers as a class.

2 Learn the passive with *by*

Presentation II

20–25 minutes

 A 1. Introduce the new topic. *Sometimes we want to say who performed the action in a passive sentence. Then we use a* by *phrase.*

2. Read the active and passive voice sentences in the chart and the *Note* aloud. Have students match the parts of the sentences.

> **TIP** Most passive sentences have a *by* phrase. We often use the *by* phrase when we want to put known information at the beginning of the sentence: For example: In the sentence *Dinner is served by experienced servers,* the listener may already know that there is a dinner. The new information is who serves it.

Guided Practice I

10–15 minutes

 B 1. Have students work individually to answer the questions.

2. Direct students to take turns reading the questions and answers with a partner.

> **Multilevel Strategies**
>
> For 2B, adapt the exercise to the level of your students.
>
> • **Pre-level** Provide these students with more complete versions of the answers. Ask them to complete the sentences with time words. *1. In my neighborhood, mail is delivered _____. 2. Trash is picked up _____. 3. Newspapers are delivered _____. 4. The streets are cleaned _____.*

> **TIP** Write *Baby Shower* on the board, and elicit what students know about baby showers. Read aloud this information: *In the U.S., when a woman is going to have a baby, her friends or family usually host a baby shower for her. It is traditional to invite only women to baby showers, but nowadays they sometimes include men. Everyone brings a gift for the baby or the mother. Women usually play games at baby showers. You can find books of baby shower games at any bookstore.*
>
> After you read the information, write sentences on the board for students to complete: *The baby shower is usually hosted by _____. Traditionally, only women _____ to a baby shower. _____ are brought for the baby and the mother. Usually games _____ at the shower. Books about baby shower games can be bought at any _____.*
>
> Read the information again, and ask students to work individually to complete the sentences on the board. Have volunteers come to the board to complete the sentences. Ask students if baby showers are traditional in their countries.

D Get the meaning. Work with your class. Read the sentences.
Then circle the correct words.

The mail carrier works very quickly. The mail is always delivered before 12 p.m.
Oak View Apartments were built in 1975. They've been in this neighborhood
a long time.

1. We ((know) / don't know) who delivers the mail.
2. We (know / (don't know)) who built Oak view apartments.

2 Learn the passive with *by*

A Study the chart. Match the parts of the sentences below.

The present passive with *by*	
Active Voice	The bride's parents send the wedding invitations. (The focus is on the bride's parents.)
Passive Voice	The wedding invitations are sent by the bride's parents. (The focus is on the wedding invitations.)

Note
Use *by* + person/thing when you want to say who performs the action in a passive sentence.

_b_ 1. Wedding invitations are sent
_e_ 2. Dinner is served
_d_ 3. Music is performed
_c_ 4. Photos are taken
_a_ 5 Presents are given

a. by friends and family.
b. by the bride and groom.
c. by a professional photographer.
d. by an excellent band.
e. by experienced servers.

B Write the answers. Then ask and answer the questions with a partner. Answers will vary.

1. When is the mail delivered in your neighborhood?

   In my neighborhood, mail _____.

2. When is the trash picked up?

   Trash _____.

3. When are newspapers delivered?

   Newspapers _____.

4. When are the streets cleaned?

   The streets _____.

3 Grammar listening

Listen to the sentences. Circle the letter of the sentence with the same idea.

1. (a.) You can't smoke in the restaurant.
   b. You can smoke in some sections.

2. a. They haven't planned a reception.
   (b.) The reception is after the wedding.

3. (a.) The hospital has good nurses.
   b. The hospital doesn't have good nurses.

4. (a.) Tina and Lim are having a party.
   b. Tina and Lim are going to a party.

5. a. The guests welcome the bride.
   (b.) The bride welcomes the guests.

6. a. Announcements aren't in the paper.
   (b.) The paper has announcements.

4 Practice the present passive

A Work with 3 classmates. What types of parties do you like to attend? What happens at these parties? Use the present passive. Complete the chart with your group.

Types of parties	What happens at parties?
Birthday party	Food is served

B Talk about the chart with your classmates.

A: *What types of parties do you like to attend?*
B: *I like to attend New Year's parties.*
A: *What happens at New Year's parties?*
B: *Music is played.*

TEST YOURSELF ✔

Close your book. Write 5 sentences about what happens at parties. Use the information in 4B.

Food is served at parties.

3 Grammar listening

Guided Practice II

10–15 minutes

1. Tell students that they are going to listen to six sentences. For each one, they need to choose the active-voice sentence with the same meaning.

2. Play the audio. Direct students to read along silently without writing.

3. Replay the audio. Ask students to circle *a* or *b*.

4. Ask volunteers to read the correct sentences aloud. Write the number-letter match on the board.

Multilevel Strategies

Replay the *Grammar listening* to challenge on- and higher-level students while allowing pre-level students to catch up.

- **Pre-level** Have these students listen again to circle the sentence with the same meaning.

- **On- and Higher-level** Have these students listen again and write down the verbs they hear. As you go over the answers to the *Grammar listening*, see if students can reconstruct the passive sentence they heard on the audio.

---

4 Practice the present passive

Communicative Practice and Application

20–25 minutes

 1. Direct students to look at the picture. Ask: *What's happening in this picture?*

2. Read the instructions aloud. Put students in groups of four. Direct them to complete the chart with their groups.

B Call on individuals to share their ideas. List the different types of parties on the board. Ask volunteers to write their passive sentences on the board.

Evaluation

10–15 minutes

TEST YOURSELF

1. Ask students to write the sentences independently.

2. Collect and correct students' writing.

Multilevel Strategies

Target the *Test Yourself* to the level of your students.

- **Pre-level** Provide skeleton sentences for these students to complete about a type of party. *Presents are given at _____. Invitations are written for _____. A big meal is served at _____.*

- **Higher-level** Have these students write a paragraph in response to this question and prompt: *What was the best party you ever went to? Describe what was done at the party.*

To compress this lesson: Conduct 1C as a whole-class activity.

To extend this lesson: Compare cultures and discuss the use of the passive.
1. Brainstorm a list of life events, and write them on the board—for example, birth, important birthdays, graduation, wedding, retirement, moving.
2. Put students in groups. Give each group a large sheet of paper. Tell them to list some differences between how these events are celebrated or recognized in their native countries and how they are celebrated here. Have each group write five sentences. Tell them it isn't necessary to write about all of the events.
3. Post students' sentences at the front of the room, and use them as a springboard for discussing the passive voice. For most sentences, there is no reason to use the passive. *In Korea, pregnant women eat a special seaweed soup.* Other sentences may lend themselves to the passive. *In Mexico, a huge party is thrown on a girl's fifteenth birthday.*

And/Or have students complete **Workbook 3 pages 74–75, Multilevel Activity Book 3 pages 121–122,** and the corresponding **Unit 11 Exercises** on the **Multilevel Grammar Exercises CD-ROM3.**

Unit 11 Lesson 4

Objectives	Grammar	Vocabulary	Correlations
On-, Pre-, and Higher-level: Respond to good and bad news, and listen for information about weddings	Present passive (*Dishes are broken for good luck.*)	*Terrific, tradition, gown, honeymoon,* For vocabulary support, see this **Oxford Picture Dictionary** topic: Life Events and Documents	**CASAS:** 0.1.2, 0.2.1, 2.7.2, 2.7.3, 6.0.3, 6.0.4, 6.1.1, 6.1.3, 6.1.4 **LCPs:** 39.01, 49.02, 49.03, 49.09, 49.16 **SCANS:** Acquires and evaluates information, Arithmetic/Mathematics, Listening, Problem solving **EFF:** Read with understanding, Use math to solve problems and communicate

Warm-up and Review

10–15 minutes (books closed)

Write *That's great!* and *That's too bad.* on the board. Say: *Which one do you say if I tell you I broke my leg? Which one do you say if I tell you my son just graduated from college?* Ask students for more examples of things people might say to elicit these responses. Write their ideas in the correct column.

Introduction

5 minutes

1. Say: *These are all examples of good news and bad news.*

2. State the objective: *Today we're going to practice responding to good and bad news, and we're going to listen for information about wedding traditions.*

1 Learn to talk about life events

Presentation I

10–15 minutes

A Direct students to look at pictures. Ask: *Which person has the good news?* Play the audio. Give students time to answer the questions. Go over the answers as a class.

Guided Practice

20–25 minutes

B 1. Read the instructions aloud. Play the audio. Ask students to read along silently and listen for the answer to the question. Elicit the answer.

2. Ask students to read the conversation with a partner. Circulate and monitor pronunciation. Model and have students repeat difficult words or phrases.

3. Say and have students repeat the expressions in the *In other words* box. Elicit the placement of the expressions in the conversation. Ask volunteers to read the conversation using the expressions.

TIP Make sure that students understand that *Terrific!* means good. They may be confused by its similarity to *terrible, terror,* and *terrify.*

Communicative Practice and Application

15–20 minutes

C 1. Ask students to read the instructions. Check their comprehension of the roles. Ask: *What are the two roles?* Elicit examples of what each person might say.

2. Set a time limit (five minutes). Ask students to act out the role-play in both roles. Ask volunteers to act out their conversations for the class. Tell students who are listening to note how Partner B responds to the good news.

Multilevel Strategies

For 1C, adapt the role-play to the level of your students.

• **Pre-level** For these students, provide a simplified conversation. A: *I have some good news and bad news.* B: *What's the bad news?* A: *I got a huge credit-card bill this month.* B: *Oh, that's too bad. What's the good news?* A: *I got a promotion and a raise! I'll be able to pay off my bill next month.* B: *Congratulations! Let's celebrate tonight.*

1 Learn to talk about life events

A Look at the pictures. Listen to the conversation. Then answer the questions below with your classmates.

1. What is Min's bad news? Min had car trouble and was almost late for her final exam.
2. What is her good news? Min got an A on the test.
3. What does her friend want to do? Her friend wants to celebrate this weekend.

B Listen and read. What's the good news?

A: Hello, Dan? It's Maria. I've got some good news and some bad news.

B: Oh, no. What's the bad news?

A: Well, I took my driving test today. It was really difficult.

B: Oh, no. That's too bad.

A: Yes, but the good news is that I passed. I'll be able to get my license right away.

B: Congratulations! That's fantastic! Let's celebrate tonight.

A: That sounds great. I'm on my way home now.

> **In other words...**
>
> **Responding to good news**
> Congratulations!
> That's fantastic!
> That's great news!
> That's terrific!

C Role-play a good news/bad news conversation with a partner. Use the example in 1B to make a new conversation.

Partner A: Call a friend and tell him or her your good news and bad news. The boss asked to talk to you this morning. You got very nervous. You got a promotion and a raise! You'll be able to pay all your bills.

Partner B: Respond to the bad news. Congratulate your friend on the good news. Invite him or her to celebrate.

2 Learn *be able to* + verb for ability

A Study the chart. Then complete the sentences below. Use the words in parentheses.

BE ABLE TO+VERB FOR ABILITY

Future
I will **be able to** drive next year.
Ben won't **be able to** retire.
We'll **be able to** take a vacation next month.
They won't **be able to** start college in June.

Note

In the present, it is more common to use *can* for ability, not *be able to*.
 	
  I can drive. (more common) = I am able to drive. (less common)
 	
In the past, it is more common to use *could* for ability.
 	
  I couldn't drive last year. (more common) =
  I wasn't able to drive last year. (less common)

1. We ___will be able to attend___ Frank's graduation next week. (attend)

2. Jack is sorry, but he __won't_____ be able to attend the graduation. (not go)

3. They're happy because they __will/'ll be able to get married____ this June. (get married)

4. Sue's sorry, but she ___won't be able to sing_____ at their wedding. (not sing)

B Complete the sentences with *be able to* + verb. Use your own ideas. Answers will vary.

1. Last year, _I wasn't able to use a computer_____.

2. Last week, _____.

3. Next year, _____.

4. In twenty years, _____.

5. In 100 years, doctors _____.

3 Practice your pronunciation

A Study the chart. Listen to intonation in these sentences.

Showing excitement
Congratulations! Let's celebrate tonight. That's great! I'm so happy for you. Terrific! I knew you could do it.

Note
Use an exclamation point (!) to show excitement when you write. Use rising intonation to show excitement when you speak.

B Listen to the sentences. Is the speaker excited? Check (✔) *yes* or *no*.

1. ☑ yes ☐ no   3. ☐ yes ☑ no   5. ☑ yes ☐ no

2. ☐ yes ☑ no   4. ☑ yes ☐ no   6. ☐ yes ☑ no

C Listen again and check.

2 Learn *be able to* + verb for ability

Presentation II and Guided Practice

30–35 minutes

A 1. Introduce the new topic. *In the conversation in 1B, Maria said:* I'll be able to get my license right away. *What does that mean? Can she get her license soon?* [yes]

2. Read the sentences in the chart and the *Note*.

3. Go through the sentences below the chart as a class. Elicit the correct forms of *be able to,* and have students circle them in their books.

4. Check comprehension. Write *I'm sorry I _____ to come to your party yesterday.* and *I'm sorry. I _____ to come to your party tomorrow.* on the board. Elicit the completions.

B Direct students to work individually to complete the sentences. Call on volunteers to share their sentences with the class.

> **TIP**
>
> After 2B, try some oral practice with *will be able to* and *was able to.* Ask one student a question. *Will you be able to come to school tomorrow?* After that student answers, ask another student to say a sentence about the first student. *He/She won't be able to come to class tomorrow.* Elicit other possible questions. *Were you able to find a good parking spot this morning? Were you able to get to school on time today? Will you be able to pass the test for this unit? Will you be able to attend school next summer?*

3 Practice your pronunciation

Pronunciation Extension

10–15 minutes

A 1. Write *That's wonderful.* on the board. Read the sentence aloud in a bored tone of voice with falling intonation. Add an exclamation point, and read the sentence again in an excited voice with rising intonation. Ask students how your voice changed the second time. Say: *Now we're going to focus on using rising intonation to show excitement.*

2. Play the audio. Direct students to listen for rising intonation and falling intonation.

B Play the audio. Direct students to check *Yes* or *No* to indicate whether the speaker is excited or not.

C Have students listen and check their answers. Ask for a show of hands about each number.

4 Focus on listening

Listening Extension

20–25 minutes

A Read the questions aloud, and elicit answers from volunteers. Encourage students to respond to each other's ideas. After one student speaks, ask other students: *Have you had a similar experience at weddings? Have you experienced something different?*

B 1. Tell students they are going to listen to a story about wedding traditions. Direct them to read the sentences before listening.

2. Have students listen and mark the statements T (true) or F (false).

3. Go over the answers as a class.

C 1. Direct students to read the traditions and the country names before listening.

2. Replay the audio and have students work individually to match the tradition to the place. Go over the answers as a class.

Multilevel Strategies

Replay the story to challenge on- and higher-level students while allowing pre-level students to catch up.

• **Pre-level** Have these students listen again to match the traditions with the places.

• **On- and Higher-level** Write these questions on the board for these students to answer: *What do the bride and groom do in Venezuela?* [sneak away without saying goodbye] *Why?* [good luck] Have volunteers write their answers on the board.

5 Real-life math

Math Extension

5–10 minutes

1. Read number 1 aloud. Elicit the steps in the problem, and write them on the board. *What's the total? What do I need to subtract? How much does that leave? Now what do I need to do? How many people will they be able to invite?*

2. Direct students to work individually to solve number 2. Ask a volunteer to write the problem and solution on the board and explain the steps.

Evaluation

10–15 minutes

TEST YOURSELF

1. Model the role-play with a volunteer. Then switch roles.

2. Pair students. Check comprehension of the exercise by eliciting things that each partner might say.

3. Set a time limit (five minutes), and have the partners act out the role-play in both roles.

4. Circulate and monitor. Encourage pantomime and improvisation.

5. Provide feedback.

Multilevel Strategies

Target the *Test Yourself* to the level of your students.

• **Pre-level** Ask these students to use a skeleton conversation: A: *I have some good news and bad news.* B: *What's the bad news?* A: _____. B: *Oh, that's too bad. What's the good news?* A: _____. B: *Congratulations!*

• **Higher-level** Have these students practice the role-play with several partners.

To compress this lesson: Conduct *Real-life math* as a whole-class activity.

To extend this lesson: Write about wedding traditions.
1. Put students in groups. If possible, group them by country of origin. Give each group a large sheet of paper, and ask the groups to write about wedding traditions in their native countries. Provide questions to help them get started: *Who pays for the reception? What are the before-wedding traditions? Where is the wedding held? Who participates in the wedding? What food is served? What are traditional gifts?*
2. Have a reporter from each group read the group's writing to the class.

And/Or have students complete **Workbook 3 page 76** and **Multilevel Activity Book 3 page 123**.

4 Focus on listening

A Talk about the questions with your classmates.

1. What happens at the weddings you go to?
2. Have you ever been to a wedding with traditions that were new to you? Describe what you saw or did.

B Listen to the story. Then mark the statements T (true) or F (false).

__T__ 1. The story talks about wedding traditions in different countries.

__T__ 2. The story talks about weddings in the U.S.

__T__ 3. The story talks about things that brides and grooms do.

__F__ 4. The story talks about the age that people marry in different countries.

__T__ 5. The story talks about weddings in China.

C Listen again. Match the traditions with the places.

__d__ 1. The groom gives the bride 13 gold coins.

__c__ 2. Dishes are broken for good luck.

__b__ 3. People throw rice.

__a__ 4. A red gown is worn by the bride.

    a. China and India

    b. The U.S.

    c. Greece

    d. Mexico and Panama

5 Real-life math

Read about Jorge and Gina. Answer the questions.

1. Jorge and Gina are planning their wedding reception. The band will cost $400. The reception hall will cost $300 to rent. Dinner will cost $25 per person including the tip. Jorge and Gina plan to spend $3,200 for their reception. How many people will they be able to invite? __100 people__

2. After the wedding, Jorge and Gina want to go to San Francisco for three nights and four days for their honeymoon. The plane tickets are $300 each and the hotel is $175 per night. They plan to spend $150 a day on food and entertainment. How much will the trip cost? __$1,725__

> **TEST YOURSELF** ✔
>
> Role-play a conversation. Partner A: Tell your partner some bad news and good news that happened to you recently. Partner B: Respond and suggest a time to celebrate. Then change roles.

1 Get ready to read

A How many times have you moved in your life?

B Read the definitions.

disability: (noun) a mental or physical condition that makes it difficult for a person to do some things

discrimination: (noun) unequal treatment based on race, religion, or something else

fair: (adj.) equal

rights: (noun) things you are allowed to do

C Look at the title and the picture's caption in the article.
What do you think the article is about? People moving to new homes and reasons why they move.

2 Read and respond

A Read the article.

MOVE Moving On

In an average year, 14 to 20 percent of the U.S. population moves to a new home. Some people move to new cities to start a career or to enjoy retirement. Others move across town to be closer to family. There's a good chance that you will move in the future. Whatever your reason for moving, it's important to know your rights and to be careful when you buy or rent a home.

The U.S. government has laws to protect people from discrimination. When you buy or rent a home, the Fair Housing Act says that discrimination is not permitted based on race, religion, familial status,[1] or disability. When you buy a home, the Equal Opportunity Credit Act protects you and your credit application from discrimination. If you have experienced housing discrimination, contact the U.S. Department of Housing and Urban Development (HUD).

First, read the lease. Then unpack.

[1]familial status: married, divorced, or with children

☑ Interpret information about renting or buying a home

Unit 11 Lesson 5

Objectives	Grammar	Vocabulary	Correlations
Pre-, On-, and Higher-level: Read about and discuss housing laws and leases	*It* + infinitive (*It's important to know your housing rights.*)	*Disability, discrimination, fair, familial status, lease* For vocabulary support, see these **Oxford Picture Dictionary** topics: Finding a Home, Different Places to Live, Apartments	**CASAS:** 0.1.2, 0.2.1, 1.4.3 **LCPs:** 45.07, 49.01, 49.02 **SCANS:** Acquires and evaluates information, Decision making, Interprets and communicates information, Listening, Reading **EFF:** Convey ideas in writing, Read with understanding, Take responsibility for learning

Warm-up and Review

10–15 minutes (books closed)

Tell your students how many different homes you have lived in during your life. Give them a moment to think back on their lives and count how many places they have lived in. Have all students stand. Ask: *Has anybody lived in only two homes?* If any student has lived in only two places, ask him/her to sit down. Ask: *Has anybody lived in only three homes?* Then have those students sit down. Continue until you find the person who has moved the most times.

Introduction

5 minutes

1. Say: *Most people move several times in their lives. Moving is expensive and it can be difficult, so it's important that we know our housing rights.*

2. State the objective: *Today we're going to read about and discuss housing rights and leases.*

1 Get ready to read

Presentation

15–20 minutes

A Read the question aloud. Call on various students to answer the question.

B Read the words and definitions. Elicit sample sentences from students using the words.

Pre-Reading

C 1. Read the instructions aloud. Ask volunteers to share their ideas with the class. Ask: *What*

does cost of living *mean? What costs are included?*

2. Write *discrimination* and *lease* on the board. Ask students to predict what they will read. *What do you think the law says about housing discrimination? This article gives advice about signing lease agreements. What do you think it will say?*

2 Read and respond

Guided Practice I

25–30 minutes

A 1. Ask students to read the article silently.

2. Direct students to underline unfamiliar words they would like to know. Elicit the words and encourage other students to provide definitions or examples.

3. Check students' comprehension. Ask: *What does the Fair Housing Act say?*

Multilevel Strategies

For 2A, adapt your comprehension questions to the level of your students.

- **Pre-level** Ask these students *Yes/No* questions. *Is it important to get a copy of the lease?* [yes]

- **On-level** Ask these students information questions. *Who should you contact if you experience discrimination?* [HUD]

- **Higher-level** Ask these students inference questions. Explain: *The article says that you might be in for a surprise if you sign an incomplete lease.* Ask: *What does that mean? What could the surprise be?*

Guided Practice II

15–20 minutes

B 1. Play the audio. Have students read along silently.

2. Elicit and discuss any additional questions about the reading.

C Have students work individually to choose the best heading. Call on volunteers for the answers. Ask students to explain their answers.

> ### Multilevel Strategies
>
> • **Pre-level** Ask these students *True/False* questions. *1. It's important to know your rights.* [T] *2. Housing discrimination is legal in the U.S.* [F] *3. You should read and understand your lease.* [T] Tell them to circle the answers to 1C when you go over it with the class.

3 Talk it over

Communicative Practice

15–20 minutes

A Read the questions aloud. Show students how to multiply by .25 to come up with the recommended rent or mortgage allowance. Discuss typical rents in your area for a two-bedroom or three-bedroom apartment and for a house. Set a time limit (three minutes). Allow students to work individually to think about the questions and write their answers in note form.

> **TIP**
>
> Make a transparency of part of the rental section of the classified ads. Talk about the average rents, and discuss what factors affect the rents—for example, size, age, convenience, neighborhood, and schools. Have students choose the ad that looks most appealing to them and explain why they like it. Discuss any abbreviations they don't understand.

B Call on individuals to share their ideas with the class.

Application

5–10 minutes

BRING IT TO LIFE

Read the instructions aloud. Ask students whether they have leases or mortgage agreements at home. Check comprehension of the exercise. *Should you bring your lease to class?* [no] *How many rules are you going to copy?* [three]

To compress this lesson: Conduct 2C as a whole-class activity.

To extend this lesson: Practice questions for the landlord.

1. As a class, brainstorm a list of questions that a prospective tenant might want to ask about the lease agreement. *Are utilities included? Which ones? When can the landlord raise the rent? By how much? What are the rules about pets? What are the rules about visitors? Does the lease cover repairs?* Write the questions on the board.

2. Have the students practice the questions with a partner. Tell the "tenant" to ask the questions and the "landlord" to invent the answers.

And/Or have students complete **Workbook 3 page 77** and **Multilevel Activity Book 3 pages 124–125**.

When you rent an apartment or a house, it's your job to read and understand the lease[2] before you sign it. Are utilities included? When can the landlord raise the rent? How much is the security deposit? Don't be afraid to ask questions if something isn't clear. Never sign a lease if information is missing. You might be in for a surprise. Finally, you should get a copy of the lease immediately after you sign it. Moving can be stressful. However, if you know your rights and understand your lease, moving may be easier!

[2]lease: a rental agreement

Source: *U.S. Department of Justice, HUD*

B **Listen and read the article again.**

C **Choose the best heading for each paragraph of the article.**

1. Paragraph 1
   a. Buying a Home
   (b.) Reasons People Move
   c. Enjoying Retirement

2. Paragraph 2
   (a.) Understanding Housing Laws
   b. Preparing to Move
   c. Renting or Buying

3. Paragraph 3
   a. Preparing to Move
   b. Signing and Security
   (c.) Understanding the Lease

3 Talk it over

A **Read the information. Think about the questions. Make notes about your answers.**

1. What are some reasons a person might want to spend only 25 to 30 percent of his or her salary on rent?
2. Is this easy, difficult, or impossible, to do in your city?

How much should you spend on your home?

Financial professionals recommend that you spend between 25 and 30 percent of your total income on your rent or mortgage.

B **Talk about the answers with your classmates.**

BRING IT TO LIFE

Read the small print from your lease or mortgage agreement (homeowner's contract). Write 3 rules that you think are important. Bring the information to class.

1 Grammar

A **Complete the sentences. Use the present passive and the verbs in parentheses.**

1. You _____ are invited _____ to a party next month. (invite)
2. A large meal _is planned_____ for the guests. (plan)
3. Coffee and tea _are included_____ with dinner. (include)
4. This party _is held_____ every year. (hold)
5. The invitations _are mailed_____ on the first of the month. (mail)

B **Match the parts of the sentences.**

_d_ 1. A birth announcement is usually written   a. by the employer.

_c_ 2. Cards are often sent to the graduate   b. by a moving company.

_a_ 3. A retirement present is given   c. by friends and family.

_b_ 4. Furniture is taken to a new house   d. by the parents.

C **Complete the sentences with the past of *be able to*. Use the verbs in parentheses.**

1. Jack _____ was able to clean _____ the garage but not the pool. (clean)
2. We _were not able to cut_____ the grass because it rained. (not cut)
3. I tried, but I _was not able to fix_____ the lights. (not fix)
4. We _were able to paint_____ the kitchen. (paint)
5. Our neighbor _was able to help_____ us with the garden. (help)

D **Complete the sentences with the future of *be able to*. Use the verbs in parentheses.**

1. Next year, we _____ will be able to swim _____ in the new pool. (swim)
2. When the new parking lot is finished, we _will be able to park_____
   closer to the building. (park)
3. The kids _won't be able to play_____ in the field after the parking lot
   is built over it. (not play)
4. In a few years, everyone _will be able to shop_____ in the mall next
   to the apartments. (shop)
5. In a few months, seniors _will be able to use_____ the new senior
   center. (use).

Unit 11 Review and expand

Objectives	Grammar	Vocabulary	Correlations
On-, Pre-, and Higher-level: Expand upon and review unit grammar and life skills	Present passive (*Dinner is served at 6:00.*) Be able to (*We weren't able to go.*)	Events and celebrations For vocabulary support, see these **Oxford Picture Dictionary** topics: Life Events and Documents, Finding a Home	**CASAS:** 0.1.2, 0.1.5, 0.2.1, 2.7.1, 2.7.2, 2.7.3, 4.8.1, 7.2.6, 7.3.1, 7.3.2, 7.3.4, 7.4.7 **LCPs:** 39.01, 49.02, 49.16 **SCANS:** Acquires and communicates information, Reading **EFF:** Convey ideas in writing, Read with understanding, Solve problems and make decisions

Warm-up and Review

10–15 minutes (books closed)

1. Review the *Bring It to Life* assignment from Lesson 5.

2. Have students who did the exercise share the rules from their leases/mortgages. For students who did not do the exercise, bring in a copy of a lease. You can find sample lease agreements on the Internet. Ask these students to look over the agreement and share one rule they find.

Introduction and Presentation

5 minutes

1. Restate the rules from the lease and mortgage agreements using the present passive and *be able to*. Write examples on the board. *Pets are not permitted. Visitors are allowed for three days. Repairs are paid for by the landlord. If the rent is five days late, the landlord will be able to charge a fine. If the apartment is damaged, the landlord will be able to keep the security deposit.*

2. State the objective: *Today we're going to review the present passive and* be able to *to talk about life events.*

1 Grammar

Guided Practice

40–45 minutes

A 1. Write sentence 1 on the board, and review the form of the present passive (*be* + past participle).

2. Ask students to work individually to complete the exercise. Have volunteers write the answers on the board.

B Have students work individually to match the first part of the sentence with the *by* phrase.

> ### Multilevel Strategies
>
> For 1B, challenge on- and higher-level students while allowing pre-level students to catch up.
>
> • **Pre-level** Give these students additional time to match the sentence parts.
>
> • **On- and Higher-level** Ask these students to rewrite the sentences in 1B as active-voice sentences. *The parents write the birth announcement.*

C 1. Write sentence number 1 on the board. Check comprehension. Ask: *Did Jack clean the garage?* [yes] *Did he clean the pool?* [no] *If I change* Jack *to* they, *what changes in the sentence?* [*was* becomes *were*]

2. Ask students to work individually to complete the sentences. Have volunteers write the answers on the board.

D 1. Tell students that these sentences use the future form of *be able to*. Elicit the positive and negative forms, and write them on the board. [*will be able to* + verb; *won't be able to* + verb]

2. Ask students to work individually to complete the sentences. Ask volunteers to write the answers on the board.

2 Group work

Communicative Practice

20–35 minutes

A 1. Direct students, in groups of three to four, to focus on the picture. Ask: *Where are these people? What are they celebrating?*

2. Group students and assign roles: leader, recorder, and reporters. Explain that students work with their groups to write the conversation.

3. Check comprehension of the roles. Ask: *Who writes the conversation?* [recorder] *Who will read the conversation to the class?* [reporters] *Who helps everyone and lets the group know how much time has passed?* [leader] *Who creates the conversation?* [everyone]

4. Set a time limit (five minutes) to complete the exercise. Circulate and answer any questions.

5. Have reporters from each group read the group's conversation to the class.

Multilevel Strategies

For 2A, use mixed-level groups.

- **Pre-level** Assign these students the role of timekeeper.
- **On-level** Assign these students the role of recorder or reporter.
- **Higher-level** Assign these students the role of leader.

B 1. Have students walk around the room to conduct the interviews. To get students moving, tell them to interview three new people not in their groups for 2A.

2. Set a time limit (five minutes) to complete the exercise.

3. Tell students to make a note of their classmates' answers but not to worry about writing complete sentences.

Multilevel Strategies

Adapt the mixer in 2B to the level of your students.

- **Pre-level** Allow these students to ask and answer the questions without writing.
- **Higher-level** Have these students ask two additional questions and write all answers.

C Call on individuals to report what they learned about their classmates. Encourage students to make generalizations. *Two out of four students have gone to a birthday party recently.*

PROBLEM SOLVING

15–25 minutes

A 1. Ask: *Would you take a day off work to go to a wedding?* Tell students they will read a story about a woman who received a wedding invitation that conflicted with work. Direct students to read Soo's story silently.

2. Check comprehension. Ask: *Did Soo ask for a vacation day?* [yes] *What did her boss say?* [no— the day was too busy] *Why didn't Soo respond to her cousin right away?* [She wanted to think about her response.] *When is the wedding?* [next week]

3. Play the audio. Have students read along silently.

B Elicit answers to question 1. Have the class brainstorm a list of things Soo can do. Write the list on the board. Discuss the pros and cons of each item on the list.

Evaluation

30–35 minutes

To test students' understanding of the unit grammar and life skills, have them take the Unit 11 Test on the *Step Forward Test Generator CD-ROM* with *ExamView® Assessment Suite*.

Learning Log

To help students record and discuss their progress, use the *Learning Log* on page T–203.

To extend this review: Have students complete **Workbook 3 page 78, Multilevel Activity Book 3 page 126**, and the **Unit 11 Exercises** on the **Multilevel Grammar Exercises CD-ROM 3**.

2 Group work

A Work with 2–3 classmates. Write a conversation between the people in the picture. Share your conversation with the class.

A: *Congratulations on your retirement, Jack.*
B: *Thank you.*

B Interview 3 classmates. Write their answers.

1. Have you received any invitations or gone to any parties recently?
2. What events do you celebrate with your friends or family every year?
3. How do you celebrate these events?

C Talk about the answers with your class.

PROBLEM SOLVING

A Listen and read about Soo.

Soo received a wedding invitation from her cousin many weeks ago. She wanted to go to the wedding, but she needed to ask her boss for a vacation day. Her boss said that he wasn't able to give Soo a day off. Soo didn't want to say no to her cousin, so she didn't respond to the invitation right away. She wanted to think about her response. She just looked at the invitation again. The wedding is next week! Soo is embarrassed, and she doesn't know what to do now.

B Work with your classmates. Answer the questions.

1. What is Soo's problem? Soo doesn't know what to do about a wedding invitation that she forgot to acknowledge in a timely fashion.
2. What can Soo do? Make a list of things that Soo can do.

Doing the Right Thing

FOCUS ON
- civic rights and responsibilities
- community involvement
- infinitives and gerunds after verbs
- protecting your rights
- the Civil Rights Movement

LESSON 1 **Vocabulary**

1 Learn civics vocabulary

A **Talk about the questions with your class.**

1. Look at the pictures. Which things apply to all U.S. residents?
2. Which things apply to U.S. citizens only?

B **Work with your classmates. Match the words with the pictures.**

Rights and Freedoms In The United States

__5__ freedom of peaceful assembly
__2__ freedom of speech
__3__ freedom of the press

__6__ the right to carry a U.S. passport
__4__ the right to a fair trial
__1__ the right to vote

C **Listen and check. Then read the new words with a partner.**

D **Work with a partner. Write other civics words you know. Check your words in a dictionary.**

Unit 12 Lesson 1

Objectives	Grammar	Vocabulary	Correlations
On-level: Discriminate between civil rights and responsibilities, and use civics vocabulary **Pre-level:** Identify civil rights and responsibilities **Higher-level:** Talk and write about civil rights and responsibilities using civics vocabulary	*Can* and *have to* (*Can you vote? Do you have to vote?*)	Civil rights and responsibilities For vocabulary support, see this **Oxford Picture Dictionary** topic: Civic Rights and Responsibilities	**CASAS:** 0.1.2, 0.1.5, 0.2.1, 4.8.1, 5.1.1, 5.1.6 **LCPs:** 39.01, 49.02, 49.10 **SCANS:** Acquires and evaluates information, Participates as member of a team, Seeing things in the mind's eye **EFF:** Cooperate with others, Listen actively, Reflect and evaluate, Speak so others can understand

Warm-up

10–15 minutes (books closed)

Write *Freedom* on the board. Ask students to brainstorm about freedom. *Do you have freedom in the U.S.? What are you free to do? Can you say negative things about the government? Can you write negative things about the government? Can you travel where you want to?*

Introduction

5 minutes

1. Say: *We have been talking about the things that we are allowed to do in this country. These are our rights. There are also things we have to do. These are our responsibilities.*

2. State the objective: *Today we're going to talk about civic rights and responsibilities.*

1 Learn civics vocabulary

Presentation I

20–25 minutes

A Write *Rights* and *Freedoms* on the board. Discuss what the people are doing in each picture in 1B. *This man is speaking in the park.* Elicit students' answers to questions 1 and 2.

B 1. Group students and assign roles: leader, fact checker, recorder, and reporter. Explain that students work with their groups to match the words and pictures.

2. Check comprehension of the roles. Ask: *Who looks up the words in a dictionary?* [fact checker] *Who writes the numbers in the book?* [recorder] *Who tells the class your answers?* [reporter] *Who helps everyone and manages the group?* [leader]

3. Set a time limit (three minutes). As students work together, copy the wordlist onto the board.

4. Call "time" and have the reporters take turns giving their answers. Write each group's answer on the board next to the word.

C 1. To prepare students for listening, say: *Now we are going to hear a description of each of these rights.* Ask students to listen and check their answers.

2. Have students check the wordlist on the board and then write the correct numbers in their books.

3. Pair students. Set a time limit (two minutes). Monitor pair practice to identify pronunciation issues.

4. Call "time" and work with the pronunciation of any troublesome words or phrases.

5. Replay the audio. Challenge students to listen for which rights and freedoms apply to all U.S. residents. Have volunteers share their answers with the class.

D 1. Ask students to work with their partners from 1C to brainstorm a list of related words.

2. Elicit words from the class. Write them on the board. Ask students to copy them into their vocabulary notes for the unit.

Guided Practice

5–10 minutes

 1. Direct a volunteer to ask you the questions. Model the answers.

2. Set a time limit (three minutes). Direct students to practice with a partner. Ask volunteers to share their ideas with the class.

2 Learn about civic responsibilities

Presentation II

15–20 minutes

 1. Direct students to look at the pamphlet. Introduce the new topic: *Now we're going to talk about civic responsibilities.*

2. Say and have students repeat the phrases. Read the definitions. Discuss the examples in the artwork. Elicit students' knowledge about each of the items. *What is a "No littering" law? When do you pay federal taxes? What does respect the rights of others mean? How do you know when it's time for you to serve on a jury? How can you get informed?*

3. Ask students to work individually to complete the paragraph. Call on a volunteer to read the paragraph.

4. Check comprehension. Say sentences with missing words, and have the class complete them. *If you are called to jury duty, you need to _____. You have to pay federal, state, and local _____.*

> ### Multilevel Strategies
> While other students are completing 2A, provide pre-level students with an alternate activity.
>
> • **Pre-level** Have these students match the verb to the rest of the phrase. *1. obey 2. pay 3. respect 4. serve 5. be a) the rights of others b) taxes c) the laws d) informed e) on a jury.* Ask volunteers to write the phrases on the board.

Guided Practice

10–15 minutes

 Model the conversations. Model them again using a different word from 2A. Set a time limit (three minutes). Direct students to practice with a partner. Call on volunteers to say one of their conversations for the class.

Communicative Practice and Application

10–15 minutes

 1. Give students time to make notes of their answers to the questions. Call on individuals to share their ideas with the class.

2. Write ideas for staying informed on the board. Ask for a show of hands about the voting age. Call on volunteers to explain their reasons.

Evaluation

10–15 minutes (books closed)

TEST YOURSELF

1. Direct students to work individually to write a list of words from the lesson. Assign a time limit (three minutes). Call "time" and direct students to work with a partner to combine their lists and put the words in alphabetical order.

2. Circulate and monitor students' progress. Ask a volunteer pair to write its list on the board. Ask other students to add words to the list.

> ### Multilevel Strategies
> Target the *Test Yourself* to the level of your students.
>
> • **Higher-level** After these students have worked with a partner to alphabetize their lists, ask them to write three to five sentences defining words from the list.

To compress this lesson: Conduct 1B as a whole-class activity.

To extend this lesson: Have students use modals to write about rights and responsibilities. Write *can, can't, should,* and *have to* on the board. Ask students to work with a partner and use the words to write about the rights and responsibilities of U.S. residents. Have volunteers put their sentences on the board.

And/Or have students complete **Workbook 3 page 79** and **Multilevel Activity Book 3 pages 128–129**.

Work with a partner. Talk about the questions. Use the pictures in 1B.

1. In your opinion, which freedom is the most important? Why?
2. In your opinion, which right is the most important? Why?

2 Learn about civic responsibilities

A **Look at the pamphlet. Complete the paragraph.**

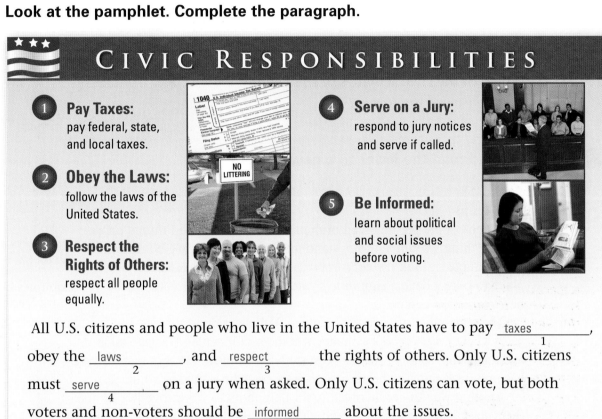

★ ★ ★

CIVIC RESPONSIBILITIES

1 **Pay Taxes:** pay federal, state, and local taxes.

2 **Obey the Laws:** follow the laws of the United States.

3 **Respect the Rights of Others:** respect all people equally.

NO LITTERING

4 **Serve on a Jury:** respond to jury notices and serve if called.

5 **Be Informed:** learn about political and social issues before voting.

All U.S. citizens and people who live in the United States have to pay _taxes_ ,
                                                                          1
obey the _laws_ , and _respect_ the rights of others. Only U.S. citizens
            2   3
must _serve_ on a jury when asked. Only U.S. citizens can vote, but both
        4
voters and non-voters should be _informed_ about the issues.
                                    5

B **Work with a partner. Practice the conversations. Use the words in 2A.**

A: *Can U.S. residents vote?*
B: *No, they can't. Only U.S. citizens can vote.*

A: *Do U.S. citizens have to pay taxes?*
B: *Yes, they do.*

C **Talk about the questions with your class.**

1. How can people stay informed about the issues?
2. The voting age in the U.S. is eighteen. Do you agree or disagree with this age limit? Why?

TEST YOURSELF ✓

Close your book. Work with a partner. Make a list of as many new words from the lesson as you can. Alphabetize your list.

1 Read about civic involvement

A **Look at the picture. Talk about the questions with your class.**

1. Have you ever written a letter to a newspaper?
2. Which of the civic activities in the picture is more interesting to you?

B **Listen and read the letter to a newspaper.**

Dear Editor,

When people get involved in their communities, good things happen.

One thing we can all do is stand up for* the things we believe in. For example, I think it's very important to give children a safe place to play. I have a sign in my yard telling people to vote for the new recreation center.

There are other ways to get involved. Volunteer opportunities are everywhere. My neighbor volunteers at the senior center. He eats lunch and visits with seniors. He has been studying English. He says that his English has improved, and he's heard great stories since he started to volunteer.

Another way to get involved is for neighbors to work together to make their neighborhoods great. I read about a group that planted trees together to improve their neighborhood. I'm planning to try it this spring. If we work together, we can all make positive changes for the future.

Ernie Rodriguez
Freehold, New Jersey

> **Writer's note**
>
> Examples help make your ideas clear.

*__Idiom note:__ stand up for = to show you agree with something

C **Check your understanding. Mark the statements T (true), F (false), or NI (no information).**

__T__ 1. Ernie thinks people should be involved in their communities.

__T__ 2. He wants people to vote "yes" for a new recreation center.

__F__ 3. He isn't interested in political issues.

__NI__ 4. His neighbor volunteers five hours each month.

__F__ 5. If you don't speak English well, you shouldn't volunteer.

__T__ 6. Planting trees is one way to improve your neighborhood.

Unit 12 Lesson 2

Objectives	Grammar	Vocabulary	Correlations
On- and Higher-level: Analyze, write, and edit a letter to a newspaper about civic involvement **Pre-level:** Read a letter to the newspaper, and write about civic involvement	Present tense (*He goes to the senior center once a month.*)	*Get involved, stand up for, issues* For vocabulary support, see this **Oxford Picture Dictionary** topic: Community Cleanup	**CASAS:** 0.1.2, 0.2.1, 0.2.3, 5.6.2, 5.6.3 **LCPs:** 39.01, 49.02, 49.13, 49.16, 49.17 **SCANS:** Creative thinking, Interprets and communicates information, Listening, Reading, Writing **EFF:** Advocate and influence, Convey ideas in writing, Read with understanding, Reflect and evaluate

Warm-up and Review

10–15 minutes (books closed)

Write *My neighborhood* on the board. Draw a smiley face and a frowning face. Ask students to think about what they like and don't like about their neighborhoods. *Are your neighbors friendly? How often do you talk to them? What do you talk about? Is there a nice park in your neighborhood? Good schools? Are the streets safe?* Ask volunteers to come to the board and write things they like and don't like about their neighborhoods.

Introduction

5 minutes

1. Point to the list of things that students don't like about their neighborhoods. Ask: *Can you do anything about these things? What can you do?*

2. State the objective: *Today we're going to read and write about civic involvement.*

1 Read about civic involvement

Presentation

20–25 minutes

A 1. Direct students to look at the pictures. Ask about what is happening in the picture. *What are these people doing?*

2. Elicit answers to questions 1 and 2. Ask students if they ever read the "letters" section of the newspaper.

B 1. Tell students they are going to read a letter to the editor about different ways that people can get involved with their communities.

2. Direct students to read the letter silently. Check comprehension. Ask: *What are the three ways he recommends getting involved?* [learn about political issues and stand up for what you believe, volunteer, work with your neighbors to improve the community] Write these ideas on the board.

3. Play the audio. Have students read along silently.

4. Draw students' attention to the *Writer's note.* Elicit the example the writer uses to illustrate each of the three main ideas.

Guided Practice I

10 minutes

C Have students work independently to mark the statements T (true), F (false), or NI (no information). Go over the answers as a class.

Multilevel Strategies

Adapt 1C to the level of your students.

- **Pre-level** While other students are working on 1C, provide these students with an outline of the letter. *How to Get Involved: 1. Learn about political issues and stand up for what you believe. I'm asking people to vote for the new recreation center. 2. Volunteer. My friend volunteers at the senior center. 3. Work with your neighbors. One group planted trees together to improve the neighborhood.*

Direct students to complete 1C using this outline.

2 Write a letter to a newspaper

Guided Practice II
20–25 minutes

 A 1. Read the questions. Elicit students' answers.

2. Write students' ideas for community involvement on the board.

B 1. Read the questions aloud. Direct students to look back at the paragraphs in 1B. Call on volunteers to identify how each paragraph answers the questions. Elicit and write on the board additional ideas for community involvement.

2. Check comprehension of the exercise. Ask: *How many paragraphs are you going to write?* [three] *Do you need to write the questions?* [no] *What is the purpose of the questions?* [to guide writing]

3. Have students work individually to write their letters, using the questions, the model in 1B, and the information on the board from the warm-up.

> ### Multilevel Strategies
>
> Adapt 2B to the level of your students.
>
> • **Pre-level** Ask these students to write a list of ideas for community involvement. Tell them they can use the ideas on the board, but they should put their lists in order from the most interesting to the least interesting.

C 1. Lead students through the process of using the *Editing checklist*. Read each sentence aloud, and ask students to check their papers before moving onto the next item.

2. Allow students a few minutes to edit their writing as necessary.

Communicative Practice
10 minutes

 D 1. Read the instructions aloud. Emphasize to students that they are responding to their partners' work, not correcting it.

2. Use the letter in 1B to model the exercise. *I think the example about his friend who volunteers in the senior center is interesting. I'd like to ask this writer about his plan for planting trees with his neighbors.*

3. Direct students to exchange letters with a partner and follow the instructions.

4. Call on volunteers to share something interesting they read in their partners' letters.

Application and Evaluation
15 minutes

TEST YOURSELF

1. Review the instructions aloud. Have the class brainstorm other possible writing topics. *Why is it important for people to _____?* Write their ideas on the board. Assign a time limit (ten minutes), and have students work independently.

2. Before collecting students' work, remind them to use the *Editing checklist*. Collect and correct students' writing.

To compress this lesson: Assign the *Test Yourself* for homework.

To extend this lesson: Have students ask and answer questions about community involvement.
1. Using the ideas from this lesson about community involvement, brainstorm a list of questions. *Have you ever or would you like to in the future work with your neighbors on a project? Gone to a city council meeting? Voted? Volunteered? Do you pay attention to politics? Do you talk to your neighbors?*
2. Direct students to ask and answer the questions in groups of three. Encourage them to supply additional information after they have given their *Yes/No* answer.

And/Or have students complete **Workbook 3 page 80** and **Multilevel Activity Book 3 page 130**.

2 Write a letter to a newspaper

A **Talk about the questions with your class.**

1. Do you think civic involvement is important? Why or why not?
2. Which community projects have people you know participated in?

B **Write a letter to a newspaper. Use the model in 1B and the questions below to help you.** Answers will vary.

Opening: Begin your letter with "Dear Editor,".

Paragraph 1: What's one thing people can do to be involved in their community? Give an example of something you've done in your community.

Paragraph 2: What's another way that people can be involved? Give an example of something another person has done.

Paragraph 3: How can people work together to make the community better? Give an example.

Closing: Sign your name and write your city and state.

> Dear Editor,
>   It's important for people to be
> involved in their community. One
> thing people can do is...

C **Use the checklist to edit your writing. Check (✔) the true sentences.** Answers will vary.

Editing checklist	
1. I wrote "Dear Editor," to begin my letter.	
2. I used an example from my experience.	
3. I used an example from another person's experience.	
4. I signed my name and wrote my city and state.	

D **Exchange letters with a partner. Read and comment on your partner's work.**

1. Point out one sentence that you think is very interesting.
2 Ask your partner a question about his or her letter.

TEST YOURSELF ✔

Write a new opinion letter to a newspaper. Use your own idea or write an answer to this question: Why is it important for citizens to vote?

1 Learn verbs + infinitives

A Read the form. Which job would you like to volunteer for?

FIVE-MILE WALK/RUN IN THE PARK

Dear neighbors,
    Please join us this Saturday for our community walk/run event. All money collected will go to the River City Children's Hospital. We need your help! Please let us know how you can help.

Name: _____
Address: _____
Phone Number: _____

☐ I plan to walk.   ☐ I volunteer to serve food.
☐ I plan to run.   ☐ I volunteer to clean up.
☐ I agree to pledge $ _____ for _____ .
                                              Name of runner/walker

B Study the chart. Underline the 5 examples of infinitives in the form above.

Verb + infinitive	
I plan **to walk**.	I don't plan **to run**.
Judy agreed **to serve** food.	She didn't agree **to clean up**.
I will volunteer **to clean up**.	I won't volunteer **to serve** food.

Notes
• An infinitive is *to* + the base form of the verb. • These verbs are often followed by an infinitive: want   agree   volunteer   plan   decide   hope   need   forget

C Complete the sentences with infinitives. Use the verbs in the box.

volunteer   go   mail   ~~serve~~   pledge   run

1. I agreed ____to serve____ food at the event on Saturday.
2. Paul and Ellen decided _to volunteer_____ at the event. They will help clean up.
3. Ellen wants _to pledge_____ some money. Do you know any runners?
4. Henri hoped _to run_____, but he hurt his knee and can't do it now.
5. David doesn't plan _to go_____ to the event on Saturday because he has to work.
6. Maggie forgot _to mail_____ her pledge form, but she will bring it on Saturday.

Unit 12 Lesson 3

Objectives	Grammar	Vocabulary	Correlations
On- and Higher-level: Use verb + infinitive or gerund to talk about community involvement, and listen for information about community involvement **Pre-level:** Recognize verb + infinitive or gerund in conversations about community involvement, and use the infinitive	Verb + infinitive or gerund (*I plan to walk. He began working.*)	*Pledge* For vocabulary support, see this **Oxford Picture Dictionary** topic: Community Cleanup	**CASAS**: 0.1.2, 0.1.5, 0.2.1, 0.2.4, 4.8.1, 5.6.2 **LCPs**: 39.01, 49.02, 49.03, 49.09, 49.17 **SCANS**: Creative thinking, Interprets and communicates information, Listening, Speaking, Writing **EFF:** Convey ideas in writing, Cooperate with others, Listen actively, Reflect and evaluate

Warm-up and Review

10–15 minutes (books closed)

Write these words (include punctuation) *homework. I to volunteer enjoy children, school. I working with don't but I elementary at the like to correct want* on the board. Ask students to unscramble the words to make sentences. Have volunteers share their ideas. Accept any logical, correct sentence. Write the original order on the board: *I want to volunteer at the elementary school. I enjoy working with children, but I don't like to correct homework.*

Introduction

5–10 minutes

1. Underline *want to volunteer, enjoy working,* and *don't like to correct* in the example on the board. Say: *With* want, *we use a* to *form, or an infinitive. With* enjoy, *we use an –ing form or a gerund.*

2. State the objective: *Today we're going to learn some verbs that are followed by infinitives and some that are followed by gerunds, and we'll talk about participating in our community.*

1 Learn verbs + infinitives

Presentation I

20–25 minutes

A 1. Direct students to look at the flyer. Elicit their answers to the question.

2. Ask: *What are they raising money for?* Ask students to read the flyer silently to find the answer. Call on a volunteer for the answer.

B 1. Read the sentences in the grammar chart.

2. Direct students to underline the examples of infinitives in the flyer in 1A. Go over the answers as a class.

3. Read the *Note.* Use the verbs listed to demonstrate that the infinitive is not affected by tense. *Yesterday I agreed to help my son's teacher. I need to call my neighbor tonight. I will volunteer to bake cookies for the sale.*

4. Assess students' understanding of the charts. Call on volunteers to make new sentences using the verbs in the chart.

Guided Practice I

15–20 minutes

C Ask students to work individually to complete the sentences. Ask volunteers to write the answers on the board.

Multilevel Strategies

For 1C, seat same-level students together.

- **Pre-level** While other students are completing 1C, ask these students to write three sentences with infinitives. Provide these skeletons: *I want to _____. I hope to _____. I need to _____.*

- **Higher-level** Have these students write four additional sentences using infinitives. Provide them with these verbs: *expect, promise, offer, seem.*

Guided Practice II

5–10 minutes

 1. Read each question aloud. Demonstrate answering with a complete sentence by telling students your own answers.

2. Ask students to work individually to write answers to the questions.

3. Have students ask and answer the questions with a partner.

2 Learn verbs + gerund or infinitive

Presentation II

20–25 minutes

 1. Introduce the new topic: *Now we're going to look at some verbs that are followed by gerunds and infinitives.*

2. Read and have students repeat the sentences in the chart.

3. Ask students to work individually to choose the correct form(s) to complete the sentences. Call on volunteers to read the completed sentences aloud.

> **TIP** After 2B, provide more practice with infinitives and gerunds. Put up the following incomplete story on the board, and ask students to work with a partner to complete it: *My uncle Hal didn't like to get involved with the community. He never volunteered _____. His neighbors said, "Don't you like _____," and he said, "No, I have always disliked _____." His neighbor Mary continued _____, and finally, Hal began _____. Now, I think he even enjoys _____!* Tell students they need to use infinitives and gerunds, but they can add other things as well to make their stories clearer. Elicit possibilities for the first blank: *to do anything, to work on community clean-up days, to help with the neighborhood yard sale.* Have volunteers share their versions of the story with the class.

Guided Practice I

10–15 minutes

 1. Read the first sentence aloud. Ask students to find *continue* on the grammar chart. Ask: *Can* continue *be followed by an infinitive?* [yes] Ask a volunteer to write a new sentence using the infinitive on the board.

2. Read each sentence and direct students to find the verb on the chart before they answer. Have a different volunteer write each sentence on the board.

> 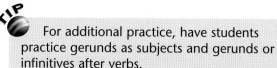 **TIP** For additional practice, have students practice gerunds as subjects and gerunds or infinitives after verbs.
> 1. Provide this model conversation:
>   A: *I want/plan/have decided to volunteer at my son's school.*
>   B: *Why?*
>   A: *Volunteering at the school is a good way to practice my English.*
> 2. Elicit other possible completions for the conversation and write them on the board.
> 3. Set a time limit (five minutes). Have students walk around the room practicing the conversation with as many different people as possible.

D **Write answers to the questions.** Answers will vary.

1. What did you volunteer to do last year?

   _____

2. What do you try to do every day?

   _____

3. What do you hope to do this weekend?

   _____

4 What will you volunteer to do this year?

   _____

5. What class(es) have you decided to take when this class ends?

   _____

2 Learn verbs + gerund or infinitive

A **Study the charts. Then circle a gerund or infinitive to complete the sentences below. Circle two answers when possible.**

Verb + gerund
We enjoy **studying**.
Tom disliked **running**.
I will practice **speaking** English.

Verb + gerund or infinitive	
We like **playing**.	We like **to play**.
He began **working**.	He began **to work**.
I will continue **studying**.	I will continue **to study**.

Note
These verbs are often followed by gerunds: enjoy   dislike   practice

Note
These verbs can be followed by gerunds or infinitives: like   begin   continue

1. Regina likes ((meeting)/(to meet)) new neighbors.
2. When do you practice ((playing)/ to play) the piano?
3. Do you enjoy ((listening)/ to listen) to the radio?
4. Do you think we should continue ((learning)/(to learn)) English?

B **Get the form. Work with your class. Which sentences can be rewritten as verb + infinitive? Rewrite the sentences when possible. Write "no change possible" when not possible.**

1. They continued working last night.   _They continued to work last night._
2. I like volunteering.   _I like to volunteer._
3. Sue enjoys helping people.   _No change possible._
4. He began studying at 8:00.   _He began to study at 8:00._

3 Grammar listening

Listen and circle *a* or *b* to complete the sentences.

1. **a.** to volunteer this summer.
   b. volunteering this summer.

2. **a.** to clean up after the dance.
   b. cleaning up after the dance.

3. a. to speak Spanish every day.
   b. speaking Spanish every day.

4. a. to serve food.
   b. serving food.

5. a. to be on a jury.
   b. being on a jury.

6. **a.** to get involved.
   b. getting involved.

4 Practice gerunds and infinitives

A **Complete the chart with your own ideas. Use gerunds or infinitives.**

My Community Involvement		
I like...	I dislike...	I plan...
talking to my neighbors.	going to neighborhood meetings.	to volunteer at a school.

B **Work with a group of 3 students. Ask and answer questions about the chart. Take notes about answers that are the most interesting to you.**

A: *What do you like doing in your community?*
B: *I like volunteering at the senior center.*

C **Tell your classmates about the interesting things you learned.**

Irma likes talking to her neighbors, but she dislikes going to neighborhood meetings.

TEST YOURSELF ✔

Write 6 complete sentences about your classmates' likes, dislikes, and plans.
Use the chart in 4A.

3 Grammar listening

Guided Practice II

10–15 minutes

 1. Say: *Now we're going to listen to sentences about people getting involved with their communities. You will only hear the beginning of the sentence. You need to choose the correct ending.*

2. Play the audio. Direct students to read along silently without writing.

3. Replay the audio. Ask students to choose the correct endings.

4. Call on volunteers for the answers.

Multilevel Strategies

Replay the *Grammar listening* to challenge on- and higher-level students while allowing pre-level students to catch up.

• **Pre-level** Have these students listen again to choose the correct answers.

• **On- and Higher-level** Ask these students to listen again and write the main verb they hear. Elicit the verbs and write them on the board.

4 Practice gerunds and infinitives

Communicative Practice and Application

20–25 minutes

A Read the instructions. Direct students to work individually to complete the chart.

B 1. Put students in groups of three. Model the conversation with a volunteer. Then model it again using real information.

2. Direct students to take turns asking and answering the questions in their groups. Tell them to make notes of at least one of each person's answers.

3. Check comprehension of the exercise. Ask: *How many people are you going to talk to?* [two] *Do you need to write everything down?* [no]

C Ask volunteers to share something interesting they learned about their partners.

Evaluation

10–15 minutes

TEST YOURSELF

Ask students to write the sentences independently. Collect and correct their writing.

Multilevel Strategies

Target the *Test Yourself* to the level of your students.

• **Pre-level** Provide skeleton sentences for these students to complete. _____ (classmate's name) *likes* _____. _____ (classmate's name) *dislikes* _____. _____ (classmate's name) *plans* _____.

• **Higher-level** Have these students write a paragraph in response to this prompt and questions: *Compare yourself to one of your classmates. How are your likes, dislikes, and plans the same? How are they different?*

To compress this lesson: Conduct 2A or 1C as a whole-class activity.

To extend this lesson: Provide more practice with gerunds and infinitives.
1. Show students pictures of famous people, or pass out magazines, and ask students to find pictures of people involved in different activities.
2. Tell students to write sentences about the people using infinitives and gerunds. *He enjoys playing basketball. She likes working in the garden.*

And/Or have students complete **Workbook 3 pages 81–82, Multilevel Activity Book 3 pages 131–132,** and the corresponding **Unit 12 Exercises** on the **Multilevel Grammar Exercises CD-ROM 3.**

Unit 12 Lesson 4

Objectives	Grammar	Vocabulary	Correlations
On-, Pre-, and Higher-level: Use a community agency, and listen for information in a town hall meeting	Reported requests (*He told her to sit down.*)	*Tenant, town meeting, express opinions* For vocabulary support, see this **Oxford Picture Dictionary** topic: Civic Rights and Responsibilities	**CASAS:** 0.1.2, 0.2.1, 5.6.1 **LCPs:** 39.01, 49.02, 49.16, 49.17 **SCANS:** Arithmetic/Mathematics, Creative thinking, Interprets and communicates information, Problem solving, Reading **EFF:** Cooperate with others, Observe critically, Use math to solve problems and communicate

Warm-up

10–15 minutes (books closed)

Write *Neighbors, Work,* and *City* on the board. Tell students you want to brainstorm ideas about legal problems and put them in these categories. Ask: *What kinds of problems do people have with their neighbors?* Write them on the board. Do the same with *Work* and *City*.

Introduction

5 minutes

1. Ask if any of the problems on the board might cause you to ask for legal help.

2. State the objective: *Today we're going to learn how to ask for help at a legal clinic and listen for information at a town hall meeting.*

1 Learn to protect your rights

Presentation I

15–20 minutes

A 1. Direct students to look at the flyer. Ask questions. *What kinds of legal services do they offer at this clinic?*

2. Say: *We're going to listen to two people talk about their legal problems.* Read questions 1 and 2 aloud.

3. Play the audio. Give students time to answer the questions. Go over the answers as a class.

Guided Practice

20–25 minutes

B 1. Read the instructions aloud. Play the audio. Ask students to listen for the answer to the question. Elicit the answer.

2. Ask students to read the conversation with a partner. Circulate and monitor pronunciation. Model and have students repeat difficult words or phrases.

3. Say and have students repeat the expressions in the *In other words* box. Elicit the placement of the expressions in the conversation. Ask volunteers to read the conversation using expressions from the box.

Communicative Practice and Application

15–20 minutes

C 1. Ask students to read the instructions silently. Check their comprehension of the exercise. Elicit examples of what Partner A and Partner B might say.

2. Set a time limit (five minutes). Ask students to act out the role-play in both roles. Ask volunteers to act out their conversations for the class. Tell students who are listening to note any expressions from the *In other words* box.

Multilevel Strategies

For 1C, adapt the role-play to the level of your students.

• **Pre-level** Provide a simplified conversation for these students to use as their role-play. *A: How can I help you? B: My neighbor's kids broke my car windshield. A: Did you ask your neighbor to pay for it? B: Yes, I did. But he didn't pay, and I never see him now. B: OK. I think I can help you.*

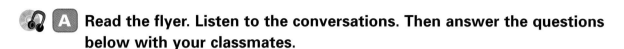

1 Learn to protect your rights

A **Read the flyer. Listen to the conversations. Then answer the questions below with your classmates.**

1. What is Mrs. Delgado's problem?
 Mrs. Delgado's landlord told her she has to move.
2. What is Mr. Tran's problem?
 Mr. Tran's car has been broken three times since he bought it and the dealer is telling him there is no lemon law.

COMMUNITY LEGAL CLINIC
Providing community-based legal services for all

SERVICES INCLUDE:

- Tenant Rights
- Employment Rights
- Immigration
- Traffic Accidents
- Credit Problems

CALL 555-8495

B **Listen and read. Why does the man think he was fired?**

Client:	Hello. I called yesterday. The man on the phone told me to come in.
Law Clerk:	How can I help you today?
Client:	Well, I don't know what to do. I've worked at the same company for 20 years. Two weeks ago my boss told me to go home. He fired me, and now I don't have a job.
Law Clerk:	Do you have any idea why?
Client:	No. I work hard and I'm never late. It might be because I'm over 55. Can they do that?
Law Clerk:	No, they can't. I think I can help you.

In other words...

Describing possible reasons
It might be because...
I think it's because...
I suspect it's because...

C **Role-play a conversation at a legal clinic with a partner. Use the example in 1B to make a new conversation.**

Partner A: You're a client. You've lived in the same apartment for eight months. Last week, the landlord told you that you have to move next month. You have a one-year lease and you're a good tenant. You think the owner wants to give the apartment to his sister.

Partner B: You are a law clerk at the legal clinic. Ask about the problem. Offer to help.

2 Learn to report requests

A Study the pictures. Then circle the correct words in the sentences below.

Pick up the kids.

Don't forget to write.

Notes

- To report an affirmative request, use *told* + person + infinitive.
- To report a negative request, use *told* + person + *not* + infinitive.

She told him to *pick up the kids.*   They *told her not to forget* to write.

1. Frank told me (to call)/ call) him later.
2. She told him (write /(to write)) what happened.
3. They told us ((not to)/ to don't) worry about it.

4. I told (she /(her)) to come to the office tomorrow.
5. We told them ((to ask)/ ask) for help.

B Read about Sasha. Then write reported requests.

Yesterday Sasha had jury duty. Here are some things the court clerk told her to do.

1. "Sit down over there."   _The clerk told Sasha to sit down_ .
2. "Fill out this form."   _Then he told her to fill out the form._ .
3. "Don't leave the building." _Next, he told her not to leave the building.,_ .
4. "Listen to the judge's instructions." _Finally, he told her to listen to the judge's instructions._ .

3 Practice your pronunciation

A Study the chart. Listen to the pronunciation of the homophones in these sentences.

Homophones	
I don't know what **to** do. I was fired **two** weeks ago.	**They're** at school. **There** are five pens. **Their** books are on the table.
We can protect our **rights**. Jim **writes** opinion letters.	

Note

Homophones are words that are spelled differently but that are pronounced the same.

B Listen to the sentences. Underline the homophones.

1. a. I get the <u>mail</u> every day.
   b. Pat is a 10-year old <u>male</u>.
2. a. I need to <u>buy</u> some food.
   b. The market is <u>by</u> the bank.

3. a. Tim is a <u>new</u> citizen.
   b. He <u>knew</u> he could pass the exam.
4. a. <u>I'll</u> go to the market.
   b. Apples are in <u>aisle</u> six.

C Listen again and check. Repeat the sentences.

2 Learn to report requests

Presentation II and Guided Practice
30–35 minutes

 A 1. Introduce the new topic. *Now we're going to learn how to report requests with the verb* tell.

2. Direct students to look at the pictures. *Who is the woman calling? Where do you think the daughter is going?*

3. Have students work individually to circle the correct answers. Ask volunteers to read the completed sentences aloud.

 TIP For more practice with reported requests after 2A, have students think of or write down a request. Tell half the class (side A) that their requests should be affirmative and the other half (side B) that their requests should be negative. Call on a student from side A to make a request of a B-side student. Have the B-side student report the request (*He told me to _____.*) and then make his/her own request to a different A-side student. Call on your more advanced students to report in the third person. *What did Suki tell Karim to do?*

Communicative practice
10–15 minutes

B 1. Illustrate the transformation of quotation to reported request by having your students make requests. Pass out slips of paper to several students with requests on them. *Erase the board. Turn off the light. Don't close the door.* Have each student read the request. Respond with the reported version. *Marcos told me to erase the board.* Ask students to make new requests. Respond with the reported versions.

2. Have students work individually to write the reported version of each sentence.

3. Ask volunteers to write their sentences on the board.

Multilevel Strategies
Adapt 2B to the level of your students.

• **Pre-level** Provide these students with the beginnings of sentences 3–4. *3. He told her not to _____. 4. He told her to listen for her _____.*

3 Practice your pronunciation

Pronunciation Extension
10–15 minutes

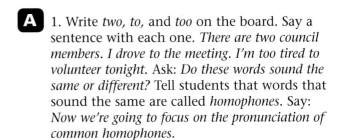 **A** 1. Write *two, to,* and *too* on the board. Say a sentence with each one. *There are two council members. I drove to the meeting. I'm too tired to volunteer tonight.* Ask: *Do these words sound the same or different?* Tell students that words that sound the same are called *homophones.* Say: *Now we're going to focus on the pronunciation of common homophones.*

2. Play the audio. Direct students to listen for the words that sound the same.

3. Elicit the words. Read the *Note* about homophones aloud. Write *deer* on the board, and elicit the homophone. [dear]

B Play the audio. Direct students to underline the homophones.

C Replay the audio. Have students check their sentences. Elicit the homophone for each pair of sentences. Have students take turns reading the sentences with a partner.

TIP Play the "flyswatter" game with homophones. Write on the board six pairs of homophones (for a total of twelve words) in a grid pattern. Don't put the pairs next to each other. Divide the class into two teams. Line up the teams at the board, and give the first person in each line a flyswatter. Say a sentence using one of the homophones. *I have a new car.* The first person to swat the correct homophone wins a point for that team. [knew] Have that person pass the flyswatter to the next and say a new sentence.

4 Focus on Listening

Listening Extension

20–25 minutes

A Read the questions aloud, and elicit answers from volunteers. Write their ideas about community concerns on the board.

B 1. Have students read the sentences before they listen to the audio.

2. Play the audio and give students time to circle the correct answers. Go over their answers as a class.

C 1. Direct students to read the sentences before listening.

2. Replay the audio and have students work individually to mark the sentences T (true) or F (false). Go over the answers as a class.

Multilevel Strategies

Replay the audio to challenge on- and higher-level students while allowing pre-level students to catch up.

• **Pre-level** Have these students listen again to mark the sentences T (true) or F (false).

• **On- and Higher-level** Write questions on the board for these students to answer. *Why doesn't Mrs. Bailey want the school on Green Street? Why does Ms. Martinez want the school on Green Street? What is Ms. Neal's solution?* Call on individuals to share their answers with the class.

5 Real-life math

Math Extension

5–10 minutes

1. Direct students to look at the poll. Ask: *What is this poll about? Does the high school look nice?*

2. Have students work individually to answer the questions. Go over the answers as a class.

Evaluation

10–15 minutes

TEST YOURSELF

1. Model the role-play with a volunteer. Then switch roles.

2. Pair students. Check comprehension of the exercise by eliciting things Partner A and Partner B might say. Write them on the board.

3. Set a time limit (five minutes), and have the partners act out the role-play in both roles.

4. Circulate and monitor. Encourage pantomime and improvisation.

5. Provide feedback.

Multilevel Strategies

Target the *Test Yourself* to the level of your students.

• **Pre-level** Ask these students to use this skeleton conversation: *A: How can I help you? B: I'm a landlord. My tenant _____. A: Did you ask your tenant to _____? B: Yes, I did. But he didn't _____. B: Okay. I think I can help you.*

• **Higher-level** Have these students practice the role-play using two different problems.

To compress this lesson: Conduct 2A as whole-class activity.

To extend this lesson: Have students write a letter requesting legal help.
1. Put students in groups of three or four. Ask the groups to write a short letter explaining their legal trouble and asking for help.
2. Have a reporter from each group read the letter to the class. Ask the class to decide whether the problem could be dealt with by a legal clinic. In some cases, the person might be able to deal with it him/herself, or police help might be needed.

And/Or have students complete **Workbook 3 page 83** and **Multilevel Activity Book 3 page 133**.

4 Focus on listening

A Talk about the questions with your class.

1. Have you ever attended a town meeting?
2. What issues in your community are people concerned about right now?

B Listen to the town meeting. Circle the correct words.

1. The people at the meeting are talking about the location of a new (street /(high school)).
2. Some people don't want a school on ((Green)/ Central) Street.
3. The people at the meeting (agree /(disagree)) about the proposal.

C Listen again. Mark the sentences T (true) or F (false).

__T__ 1. Many people want to express their opinions.

__T__ 2. A lot of people have strong feelings about the high school.

__T__ 3. Some people don't want a new school.

__F__ 4. The city wants to buy property on Green Street.

__T__ 5. One woman told everyone to calm down.

5 Real-life math

Study the voter poll. Answer the questions.

1. How do most people feel about the high school?

   They want it.

2. If half of the undecided people vote "no" for the high school, which side will win?

   the "yes" side

3. How many undecided people must vote "yes" for the high school to pass?

   one

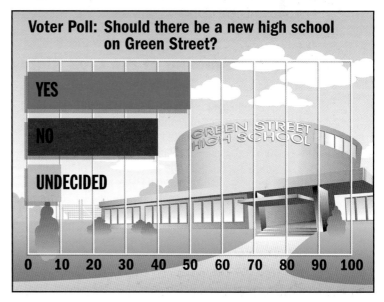

Voter Poll: Should there be a new high school on Green Street?

YES

NO

UNDECIDED

0 10 20 30 40 50 60 70 80 90 100

TEST YOURSELF ✓

Role-play a conversation at a legal clinic. Partner A: You're a landlord. You're having a problem with a tenant. Partner B: You work at the clinic. Ask for more information and offer to help. Then change roles.

1 Get ready to read

A **What are some ways people in the U.S. can protect their rights?** demonstrations, petitions, parades, writing letters, voting

B **Read the definitions.**

movement: (noun) a large group of people who work for the same goal

boycott: (verb) to refuse to buy or use something to show protest or disagreement

Civil Rights Act: (noun) a set of laws passed in 1964 that promises equal treatment in public places to all people in the U.S.

C **Look at the title of the article and the photograph. Complete the sentences.**

1. From the title, I know this article is about ___the Civil Rights Movement___.

2. From the photograph I know that ___Rosa Parks___ was an important person in the Civil Rights Movement.

2 Read and respond

A **Read the article.**

ℹ Internet Search   _ □ ×

Address | http://www.civilrights.movement   ▼ Go

The Beginning of the Civil Rights Movement

In 1955, bus seats for African Americans and whites were segregated[1] in parts of the U.S. On December 1, 1955, in the city of Montgomery, Alabama, a conflict, or disagreement, started when an African American woman named Rosa Parks refused to give her bus seat to a white man and go to the back of the bus. The police took 42-year-old Parks to jail.

The African American community was extremely angry. They had a meeting and decided to work together to protest discrimination. They agreed to boycott the buses on the day that Parks went to court. The day was a success. Empty buses drove through the streets. The city lost money. The community decided to continue the boycott. They elected a man named Martin Luther King, Jr. to be the leader.

The boycott continued for more than one year. It was difficult for African Americans to get to work

without buses, but they didn't stop the boycott. The city continued to lose money. Finally, the U.S. Supreme Court decided that Montgomery's bus laws were unfair and gave the African American community equal rights. On December 21, 1956, after 376 days, the bus boycott ended.

Rosa Parks

The Montgomery Bus Boycott was the beginning of the Civil Rights Movement. The movement eventually led to the Civil Rights Act in 1964, a set of laws that made discrimination a crime. During the Montgomery Bus Boycott, people worked together to change the government. Today, people in the U.S. continue to work together for change. Now hundreds of organizations and community groups work to protect the rights of U.S. citizens and residents.

[1]segregated: separated

Unit 12 Lesson 5

Objectives	Grammar	Vocabulary	Correlations
On-, Pre-, and Higher-level: Read about and discuss the Civil Rights Movement	Nouns and verbs (*They don't permit smoking here. He has a driving permit.*)	*boycott, civil rights, discrimination, segregated* For vocabulary support, see this **Oxford Picture Dictionary** topic: Civic Rights and Responsibilities	**CASAS:** 0.1.2, 0.2.1, 5.2.1, 5.6.3 **LCPs:** 39.01, 49.02, 49.03, 49.13, 49.16 **SCANS:** Acquires and evaluates information, Decision making, Interprets and communicate information, Reading **EFF:** Convey ideas in writing, Listen actively, Take responsibility for learning

Warm-up

10–15 minutes (books closed)

Write *Segregation* on the board. Ask if anyone knows what it means. Find out what students know about the history of African Americans in this country. List ways in which African Americans and other minorities were segregated and discriminated against. *Separate schools and neighborhoods, separate areas of restaurants, job discrimination, and laws against mixed marriage.*

Introduction

5 minutes

1. Ask students if they know when the segregation and discrimination they have discussed became illegal.

2. State the objective: *Today we're going to read about the first important protest against segregation. After this protest, thousands of people fought against racial discrimination for years. We call it the Civil Rights Movement.*

1 Get ready to read

Presentation

15–20 minutes

A Read the question aloud. Elicit students' ideas.

B Read the words and definitions. Ask students if they can think of any examples of boycotts.

Pre-Reading

C Ask students to read the title and look at the photograph in 2A. Give them time to answer the questions. Call on volunteers for the answers. Ask students to scan the article for dates. Elicit the dates and write them on the board.

2 Read and respond

Guided Practice I

25–30 minutes

A Ask students to read the article silently. Direct them to underline unfamiliar words they would like to know. Elicit the words and encourage other students to provide definitions or examples. Check comprehension. Elicit what happened on each of the dates on the board.

Multilevel Strategies

For 2A, adapt the reading assignment to the level of your students.

• **Pre-level** Provide these students with a summary of the reading. *1. In 1955, buses were segregated. An African-American woman named Rosa Parks refused to give her seat to a white man. She went to jail. 2. African Americans decided to boycott the buses. They didn't ride the buses for one year, so the city lost money. Martin Luther King, Jr. was their leader. On December 21, 1956, the Supreme Court told the city to change its bus laws. The boycott ended. 3. This was the beginning of the Civil Rights Movement. In 1964, the Civil Rights Act was passed. The Civil Rights Act made discrimination a crime.*

Direct students to read this summary while other students are reading 2A.

Guided Practice II

15–20 minutes

B 1. Play the audio. Have students read along silently.

2. Elicit and discuss any additional questions about the reading.

C 1. Read the instructions. Elicit the meaning of *summary*.

2. Work with the class to write an answer to the first question. Have students work independently to answer the rest of the questions. Ask volunteers to put their sentences on the board.

> ### Multilevel Strategies
>
> Adapt 2C to the level of your students.
>
> **Pre-level** Have these students write short answers to the questions.

D 1. Read the words in the chart aloud. As you say each word, write a sentence on the board using it in its noun and verb form. *They had a <u>conflict</u> about civil rights. Their ideas <u>conflict</u> with ours. I need to <u>research</u> the problem. I do a lot of <u>research</u>. He has a <u>permit</u> to drive. They won't <u>permit</u> you to park here. We should <u>protest</u> against injustice. The <u>protest</u> was very large. They <u>object</u> to discrimination. There's a strange <u>object</u> on the table.* Say each sentence and elicit the stressed syllable. Underline the stressed syllable. Then elicit whether the word is a noun or a verb.

2. Direct students to work individually to underline the stressed syllable. Ask volunteers to read the completed sentences aloud.

> ### Multilevel Strategies
>
> For 2D, seat pre-level students together.
>
> • **Pre-level** Direct these students to copy the words from the chart into their notebooks. Allow them to look in their dictionaries for definitions if necessary.

E Play the audio and have students check their answers.

3 Talk it over

Communicative Practice

15–20 minutes

A Read the questions aloud. Set a time limit (three minutes). Have students work independently to think about the questions, and write their answers in note form.

B Call on volunteers to share their answers with the class. Encourage students to respond to each other's ideas. After one student speaks, call on others to give their opinions. *Do you agree with what he/she said? Why or why not?*

Application

5–10 minutes

BRING IT TO LIFE

Ask students whom they are going to tell Rosa Park's story to. Elicit any additional questions that they have about Rosa Parks. Write the questions on the board, and ask them to look on the Internet or in the library for answers.

To compress this lesson: Conduct the word study in 2D as a whole-class activity.

To extend this lesson: Talk about people who led change in the students' native countries.
1. Say: *Rosa Parks is famous because her action started a movement that changed the whole country. Martin Luther King, Jr. is famous because he was the leader and the most important voice of that movement. Think of someone who is important in the history of your native country. How did that person change the country?* Call on volunteers for ideas, and write the names on the board.
2. Have students sit in same-country groups. Tell them to choose one of the names and write about what he/she did. If you have too many different countries represented in your class to make same-country groups possible, have students sit in groups and tell each other about the leader from their country.
3. Have a reporter from each group read the group's story to the class. Or have volunteers share what they learned from their classmates.

And/Or have students complete **Workbook 3 page 84** and **Multilevel Activity Book 3 pages 134–135**.

B Listen and read the article again.

C Write a summary of the article by answering the questions in your own words. Answers will vary.

1. Why did the African-American community boycott the buses in Montgomery?

   _____.

2. Why did the boycott end?

   _____.

3. When was the Civil Rights Act passed?

   _____.

D Study the chart. Underline the word stress in the sentences below.

> **Word Study: Word stress in nouns and verbs**
>
> Change the stress within the word to change a noun to a verb.
> **con**flict (noun) — con**flict** (verb)
>
> **per**mit (noun) — per**mit** (verb) | **ob**ject (noun) — ob**ject** (verb)
> **pro**test (noun) — pro**test** (verb) |

1. Did you hear? A construction company got a **permit** to make City Park into a parking lot!
2. Oh, no! The city can't **permit** that! Let's start a **protest**.
3. We want to avoid **conflict** with the company. Let's talk to them first.
4. First, we **object** strongly. Then we listen to what they have to say.
5. We can meet at 9:00. Any other time will **conflict** with my classes.

E Listen and check your answers.

3 Talk it over

A Think about the questions. Make notes about your answers.

1. Think about a protest you've seen or read about. Describe what you saw or read.
2. Would you ever participate in a boycott? Why or why not?

B Talk about the answers with your classmates.

> **BRING IT TO LIFE**
>
> Tell a friend or family member the story of Rosa Parks and the Civil Rights Movement. Write what they say about the story. Bring their comments to class.

1 Grammar

A Read the first sentence. Complete the second sentence with an infinitive. Use the underlined verbs.

1. Andy will <u>speak</u> about the new taxes.

   Andy wants _to speak about the new taxes_ .

2. Emily will <u>volunteer</u> at the senior center.

   She hopes _to volunteer at the senior center._ .

3. We will <u>report</u> the traffic accident to the police.

   We agreed _to report the traffic accident to the police._ .

4. The police immediately <u>checked</u> the driver's license.

   The police didn't wait _to check the driver's license._ .

5. Please <u>sign up</u> for the community event.

   Don't forget _to sign up for the community event._ .

B Complete the sentences with gerunds. Answers will vary.

1. In class we practice _reading English_ .

2. My best friend enjoys _____.

3. I dislike _____.

4. Next month I will begin _____.

5. We will continue _____.

C Answer the questions with an infinitive or gerund. Answers will vary.

1. What do you dislike doing? _____

2. What did you practice last week? _____

3. What do you enjoy doing? _____

4. What class did your friends decide to take? _____

5. What do you plan to do next weekend? _____

D Read the first sentence. Complete the second sentence to make reported requests.

1. "Take a break." My boss told me _to take a break_ .

2. "Get some milk at the store." My sister told me _to get some milk at the store_ .

3. "Sign up for another class." My teacher told me _to sign up for another class_ .

4. "Come to the town meeting." My neighbor told me _to come to the town meeting_ .

5. "Call the Legal Aid Office." Mrs. Peterson told me _to call the Legal Aid Office_ .

6. "Know your rights." Everyone told me _to know my rights_ .

Unit 12 Review and expand

Objectives	Grammar	Vocabulary	Correlations
On-, Pre-, and Higher-level: Expand upon and review unit grammar and life skills	Infinitives and gerunds (*He wants to speak at the meeting. Next week I'll begin working.*) Reported requests (*He told her to stand up.*)	*sign up, take a break* For vocabulary support, see this **Oxford Picture Dictionary** unit: Community	**CASAS:** 0.1.2, 0.1.5, 0.2.1, 4.8.1, 5.6.3, 7.2.6, 7.3.1, 7.3.2, 7.3.3, 7.3.4 **LCPs:** 49.02, 49.16 **SCANS:** Creative thinking, Participates as member of a team, Writing **EFF:** Convey ideas in writing, Listen actively, Read with understanding, Solve problems and make decisions

Warm-up and Review

10–15 minutes (books closed)

1. Review the *Bring It to Life* assignment from Lesson 5.

2. Have students who did the exercise read what they wrote down.

3. Review questions they had about Rosa Parks on the board, and call on volunteers to answer. If no one has the answers, tell them what you know.

Introduction and Presentation

5 minutes

1. Write sentences about Rosa Parks on the board using infinitives and gerunds. *She didn't want to give up her seat to a white man. She continued to fight against discrimination. On the day of her trial, African Americans began boycotting the buses in Montgomery.* Elicit the main verb of each sentence and the form of the second verb. Ask about each gerund/infinitive: *Can we change this to an infinitive/gerund?*

2. Write: *Rosa Parks was sitting in the front of the bus. A white man said, "Stand up. Give me your seat."* Ask students how to change the direct request to a reported request. *He told her to stand up and give him her seat.*

3. State the objective: *Today we're going to review infinitives and gerunds, and reported requests.*

1 Grammar

Guided Practice

40–45 minutes

A Read the example in number 1 aloud. Ask students to work individually to complete the sentences. Ask volunteers to write the completed sentences on the board.

B Read the example in number 1 aloud. Ask students to work individually to complete the sentences. Ask volunteers to read the completed sentences aloud.

C Ask students to work individually to write the answers. Have them take turns asking and answering the questions with a partner.

Multilevel Strategies

For 1C, seat same-level students together.

• **Pre-level** Ask these students the questions, and help them form their answers. Have everyone write an answer before moving onto the next question.

• **On- and Higher-level** While you are working with pre-level students, have these students ask their partners more questions. *What do you hope to do in the future? What did you begin doing recently?* Ask volunteers to write one sentence about their partners on the board.

D Read the example in number 1 aloud. Ask students to work individually to complete the sentences. Ask volunteers to write the completed sentences on the board.

2 Group work

Communicative Practice

20–35 minutes

A 1. Direct students, in groups of three to four, to focus on the picture. Ask: *What are these people doing?* Elicit the specific actions of people in the picture, and write the verbs on the board: *passing out flyers, holding picket signs.*

2. Group students and assign roles: leader, recorder, reporter, and timekeeper. Explain that students work with their groups to write the paragraph.

3. Check comprehension of the roles. Ask: *Who writes the paragraph?* [recorder] *Who will read the paragraph to the class?* [reporter] *Who helps everyone and manages the group?* [leader] *Who tells the group how much time has passed?* [timekeeper] *Who creates the paragraph?* [everyone]

4. Set a time limit (five minutes) to complete the exercise. Circulate and answer any questions.

5. Have a reporter from each group read the group's paragraph to the class.

> ### Multilevel Strategies
>
> For 2A, use mixed-level groups.
>
> • **Pre-level** Assign these students the role of timekeeper.
>
> • **On-level** Assign these students the role of recorder or reporter.
>
> • **Higher-level** Assign these students the role of leader.

B 1. Have students walk around the room to conduct the interviews. To get students moving, tell them to interview three people who were not in their group for 2A.

2. Set a time limit (five minutes) to complete the exercise. Tell students to make a note of their classmates' answers but not to worry about writing complete sentences.

> ### Multilevel Strategies
>
> Adapt the mixer in 2B to the level of your students.
>
> • **Pre-level** Allow these students to ask and answer the questions without writing.
>
> • **Higher-level** Have these students ask two additional questions and write all answers.

C Call on individuals to report what they learned about their classmates. Encourage students to make generalizations. *In most of our communities, people help each other.* Write some of the ways that people help on the board.

PROBLEM SOLVING

15–25 minutes

A 1. Ask: *Have you ever been in a small traffic accident?* Tell students they will read a story about a man who was in a traffic accident. Direct students to read Ruben's story silently.

2. Check comprehension. Ask: *How did the accident happen?* [at a stoplight, another driver hit him from behind] *What does the other driver want to do?* [pay Ruben for the damage]

3. Play the audio. Have the students read along silently.

B 1. Elicit answers to questions 1 and 2. Have the class brainstorm a list of things Ruben can do. Write the list on the board.

2. Have the class vote on Ruben's best course of action.

Evaluation

30–35 minutes

To test students' understanding of the unit grammar and life skills, have them take the Unit 12 Test on the *Step Forward Test Generator CD-ROM* with *ExamView® Assessment Suite.*

> ### Learning Log
>
> To help students record and discuss their progress, use the *Learning Log* on page T-203.

To extend this review: Have students complete **Workbook 3 page 85** and **Multilevel Activity Book 3 page 136**, and the **Unit 12 Exercises** on the **Multilevel Grammar Exercises CD-ROM 3.**

2 Group work

A Work with 2–3 classmates. Write a paragraph about the picture. Share your paragraph with the class.

People in my community are concerned about education.

B Interview 3 classmates. Write their answers.

1. Do people in your community help each other?
2. What rights are most important to you? Why?
3. Why don't some people become involved in community events?

C Talk about the answers with your class.

PROBLEM SOLVING

A Listen and read about Ruben.

Ruben had a traffic accident this morning. At a stoplight, the driver behind him hit his car. Ruben got out of the car to exchange insurance information, but the other driver had a different idea. He didn't want the insurance companies to get involved. He offered to pay Ruben for the damage to his car. It didn't look like there was much damage to the car, but Ruben isn't sure if he should take the man's money or call his insurance company.

B Work with your classmates. Answer the questions. Ruben had a traffic accident, and he doesn't know whether to call his insurance company or take the money the other man offered.

1. What is the problem?
2. What can Ruben do? Make a list and discuss your ideas.

   What is the best thing for Ruben to do?

UNIT 1   Learning Together

Pg. 4   Lesson 1—Exercise 1C

N = Narrator, W = Woman

W: David is a student in an intermediate English class at Central Adult School. He studies hard and learns many things because he has good study skills and habits.

1. W: In class, David always takes notes in his notebook. The teacher asks the class to take notes on the grammar and vocabulary.
   N: take notes
2. W: David spends a lot of time in the library. He can always find a quiet place to study there. It's important to find a quiet place to study.
   N: find a quiet place
3. W: Sometimes David's teacher asks the class to look up information and do research at the library. David likes to do research because he learns many new things.
   N: do research
4. W: David always takes a break every couple of hours. He knows it's important to take a break if he gets tired.
   N: take a break
5. W: When David needs to find information on the Internet, he searches online. He uses the library computers to search online.
   N: search online
6. W: At home, David always organizes his books and papers. He knows it's important to organize materials he uses all the time.
   N: organize materials
7. W: Making a study schedule helps David plan his time. He tries to make a study schedule every week.
   N: make a study schedule
8. W: David memorizes a few new words every day. He likes to memorize words and then use them in conversation.
   N: memorize words
9. W: When David has to write a long story or paper, he makes an outline. He writes the main ideas first and writes the details under each idea to make an outline.
   N: make an outline

Pg. 10   Lesson 3—Exercise 3

1. Shannon isn't studying this afternoon. She's cleaning her apartment.
2. Juan asked his teacher for help and she answered his questions.
3. Mary did research at the library. She didn't do it at home.
4. Franco doesn't organize his study materials very often.
5. We're taking a break before the next chapter.
6. I always take notes in class.

Pg. 11   Lesson 4—Exercise 1A

C = Counselor, T = Tara, Ca = Carlos

C: What kind of career are you thinking about, Tara?
T: I'm just not sure. There are so many choices.
C: What kinds of thing do you like to do?
T: Well, I volunteered at the middle school last year. I enjoyed that. I'm studying many things now. I like my classes and I'm doing well.
C: You should think about a career in education. It's a good field and schools always need good teachers.

C: What kind of career are you thinking about, Carlos?
Ca: I really don't know. There are so many choices.
C: What kinds of thing do you like to do?
Ca: Well, I work part-time in a hotel. I enjoy that. I'm taking a business management class now. I like my class and I'm doing well.
C: You should think about a career in hotel management. It's a good field with plenty of job opportunities.

Pg. 13   Lesson 4—Exercise 4B

N = Narrator, M = Marie, ML = Malik

N: Today we're talking with two students from Freemont High School. Freemont is very different from most high schools. At Freemont, students study the usual subjects like languages, history, math, and science, but they also get real-world experience in the careers of their choice. This is Marie Charles. She's a student at Freemont. Marie, tell us about your high school experience.
M: Well, my family came to this country from Jamaica when I was 12. When it was time for high school, my teachers encouraged me to apply to Freemont. I was so happy when I was accepted. Everyone said I would do well there. I got involved in the school's banking program and I loved it. I knew that a career in banking was right for me. Freemont gave me the chance to practice in the real world and study hard at the same time. Last summer I completed a summer training program at Central Savings Bank. The bank has offered me a full-time job in the Customer Service Department when I graduate next month!
N: Thank you Marie. And good luck with the new job. Our next guest is Malik Emami. Malik graduated from Freemont High School last year. Malik, can you tell us about your time at Freemont and what you're doing these days?
ML: I love making things. My teachers at Freemont encouraged me to do that and they helped me think carefully about what kind of career would make me happy. By my second year at Freemont, I knew I wanted to be a carpenter. So I took all my academic classes and a lot of carpentry classes. In my last year of high school, I worked part-time on a city building project. I helped build an apartment building near the school. It was really exciting to work with real carpenters and learn so much. Now I'm working as a carpenter during the day, and I study drawing and design at nights at the local community college.

N: Thanks Malik. It sounds like you're on your way to a great career.

UNIT 2   Ready for Fun

Pg. 18 Lesson 1—Exercise 1C

N = Narrator, W = Woman

W: Welcome to City Center Recreation Plaza. Thanks for coming to our opening weekend tour. Let me show you around.

1. W: Do you like to buy food straight from the farm? Then come on down to the farmers' market for the freshest fruits and vegetables. The farmers' market is open every weekend.
   N: farmers' market
2. W: This is the theater. You can see wonderful plays performed by the best actors in town every week at our theater.
   N: theater
3. W: For those of you who love excitement, the amusement park is a perfect place to play. There are great rides and games at the amusement park.
   N: amusement park
4. W: If you like dancing to the hottest new sounds, then you'll love the Stardust nightclub. You can dance all night on Fridays and Saturdays at our nightclub.
   N: nightclub
5. W: We are proud to have a state of the art gym at the Plaza. There are low membership rates at our gym.
   N: gym
6. W: Bring the whole family for a whole day of fun at our new zoo. You can see animals from around the world at the zoo.
   N: zoo
7. W: This is our new bowling alley. You can bowl until midnight all weekend at our bowling alley.
   N: bowling alley
8. W: Come visit our playground. The playground is safe, clean, and free! Bring your children to the playground for some great exercise.
   N: playground
9. W: As you can see, the swimming pool is very popular. You can swim from 7 a.m. to 10 p.m., Monday through Saturday at the swimming pool.
   N: swimming pool

Pg. 24 Lesson 3—Exercise 3

1. Sam's going to visit his friends this evening.
2. I'll go to the meeting after work.
3. We're gonna go to the amusement park tomorrow.
4. I think it will rain tomorrow.
5. I'll drive you to class next week.
6. John thinks that he will be a manager at his company in five years.

Pg. 25 Lesson 4—Exercise 1A

M = Man, W = Woman

1. W: Do you want to get together this Wednesday?
   M: Sure. What would you like to do?
   W: Well, on Wednesday night there's a new nightclub that's opening or there's a movie on TV. Take your pick.
   M: I think I'd rather watch a movie. Should I pick you up at 7:00?
   W: Let's play it by ear. I'll call you on Tuesday night.
   M: Sounds good.
2. M: Do you want to get together this Friday?
   W: Sure. What would you like to do?
   M: Well, on Friday night there's a two-for-one special at the bowling alley or there's a sale at the mall. It's up to you.
   W: I think I'd rather go to the mall. Should I pick you up at 6:00?
   M: Let's play it by ear. I'll call you on Thursday night.
   W: Sounds good.

Pg. 27 Lesson 4—Exercise 4B

Happy Independence Day and thank you for calling the Greenville Stadium information line. Here's what's going on this 4th of July holiday weekend.

On Friday, July 4th at 7 p.m., come see Jackie "Funny Man" Nelson live in concert. Jackie's got comedy and laughs for the whole family! Come early for great seats. Great fireworks and music will follow the show.

On Saturday evening, July 5th, come join us for *A Taste of Greenville. A Taste of Greenville* is the popular food festival that we hold on the holiday weekend every year. Restaurants from around the city will be here with samples of their finest food. There's great food, good music, and probably even some dancing under the stars. The festival runs from 5 to 10 p.m. Tickets are $9 for adults and $5 for children ages 6 to 12. Children 5 and under are free.

On Sunday, July 6th, let the games begin! Come out and watch, or come out and play in our youth soccer league from 8 a.m. to noon. Kids from 6 to 17 can play. Each team plays eight games during July and August. The cost to join is $30 per child. That's a great price for a summer full of fun.

UNIT 3   A Job to Do

Pg. 32 Lesson 1—Exercise 1C

M = Man, N = Narrator

M: This is the office where we work. Let me show you around.

1. M: That is Luis. He's a graphic designer. Graphic designers design and prepare art. Most graphic designers work on computers.
   N: graphic designer
2. M: Luis uses a keyboard to do his work. The keyboard is delicate. Take my advice. Never spill water on your keyboard.
   N: keyboard
3. M: Janet is the office manager. The office manager makes sure that everything in the office gets completed on time.
   N: office manager
4. M: Joan is putting pictures on her computer from her digital camera. A digital camera is very important for her job.
   N: digital camera
5. M: Joan is a photographer. She takes pictures and uses her computer to make them look better.
   N: photographer

6. W: Raj sometimes wears a headset. He can listen to things on the computer when he wears his headset.
   N: headset
7. M: That monitor is new. It's larger than the old monitor.
   N: monitor
8. M: The CPU isn't working. They might need to buy a new CPU if Raj can't fix it.
   N: CPU
9. M: Raj is our office's computer technician. A computer technician fixes computer problems.
   N: computer technician

Pg. 38   Lesson 3—Exercise 3

My name is Lin. I'm an office manager for a large insurance company. I usually order all of our office supplies from Office Star or Business Max. For everyday items like paper and file folders, Office Star is usually less expensive than Business Max. For special items like printer ink, Office Star is the most expensive. But, I've noticed that the people who work at Business Max are not as helpful as the people who work at Office Star. The sales people at Office Star are more professional than the salespeople at Business Max. Oh, and I almost forgot! When I order from Office Star, my orders arrive faster than my orders from Business Max. They arrive in 48 hours or less, or they're free!

Pg. 39   Lesson 4—Exercise 1A

C = Ms. Clark, B = Bill, S = Sue
1. C: Bill, can I see you for a moment?
   B: Yes, Ms. Clark? What is it?
   C: You're a good worker, Bill. You're the most creative person in the office, and you're great with customers on the phone.
   B: Thanks, Ms. Clark.
   C: But, Bill, you're very disorganized. You have to be more organized.
   B: I'm sorry, Ms. Clark. You won't have to tell me again.
   C: Thank you, Bill.
2. C: Sue, can I see you for a moment?
   S: Yes, Ms. Clark? What is it?
   C: You're a good worker, Sue. You're the friendliest person in the office, and you're always on time.
   S: Thanks, Ms. Clark.
   C: But, you're always calling and talking to other employees. You have to be more professional.
   S: I'm sorry, Ms. Clark. I promise I'll do better.
   C: Thank you, Sue.
3. C: Now, where is Vicki?

Pg. 40   Lesson 4—Exercise 3B

1. Vicki
2. Becky
3. Fran
4. Brandon
5. Farrah
6. Vera

Pg. 41   Lesson 4—Exercise 4B

J = Mr. Jones, E = Elizabeth, B = Ben 3, H = Habib
1. J: Come in, Elizabeth. Let's talk about your work. I know you're working very hard this year. You're more organized than you were last year. You're the most creative worker in your department, but I'm a little concerned about one thing. I notice you come to work late sometimes. Please try to be on time.
   E: Thanks for the feedback, Mr. Jones. You won't have to tell me again.
2. J: Well, Ben, I've been thinking a lot about your work this year. Customers always tell me that you are the most helpful person in the store. You are very reliable. I know I can always count on you, but I'm a little worried about your paperwork. Please try to be more organized. Let's work on that this year.
   B: Sure thing, Mr. Jones. I didn't know it was a problem. I'm sure I can do better.
3. J: Habib, your work has been very good this year. You're careful and you're confident. I'm really happy about that. But it's part of your job to help new employees. Please try to be more helpful with new workers this year.
   H: Sorry Mr. Jones. Don't worry. I promise to do better.

UNIT 4   Good Work

Pg. 46   Lesson 1—Exercise 1C

N = Narrator, W = Woman
   W: When you are at a job interview, there are a few Interview Do's and Do not do's. First let's look at the things you shouldn't do in an interview.
1. W: If you are late for the interview, the interviewer will think you will be late to work. Don't be late for an interview.
   N: don't be late
2. W: Don't look nervous at an interview. If you talk too fast or can't sit still, the employer might think you look nervous.
   N: don't look nervous
3. W: Don't wear inappropriate clothes at an interview. The employer will think you aren't serious about the job if you dress inappropriately.
   N: don't dress inappropriately
4. W: If you carry a cell phone, turn it off before the interview starts. Don't use your cell phone at an interview.
   N: don't use a cell phone
   W: Now, let's talk about the things you should do at a job interview.
5. W: It's good to arrive on time for an interview. You should leave home a little early. Then you can be sure that you will arrive on time.
   N: arrive on time
6. W: It's important to greet the interviewer. Look the interviewer in the eye, shake hands, and use the interviewer's name. This is the best way to greet the interviewer.
   N: greet the interviewer

7. W: Employers like confident workers. If you stand up straight and make eye contact, you will look confident. Try to look confident.
   N: look confident
8. W: Always dress professionally. For an office job, wear a suit or other conservative clothing. Always wear clean neat clothing. You dress for success when you dress professionally.
   N: dress professionally
9. W: A resume tells the employer that you are organized and serious about the job. It's a good idea to bring your resume to an interview.
   N: bring your resume

Pg. 52   Lesson 3—Exercise 3

My name is Sasha. I work for J & J Shipping Company. I haven't worked here for very long, but I've made some great friends. My best friends at work are named Julie and Jenna. Both Julie and Jenna have worked here for 12 years. They've been in the same department since they started. Jenna helped me learn the company's computer programs and Julie has helped me with all kinds of things. I haven't had a chance to transfer to their department, but I hope I will someday.

Pg. 53   Lesson 4—Exercise 1A

N = Narrator, M = Manager, O = Mrs. Ortiz
N: 2005
M: How long have you been a server at Henri's Restaurant, Ms. Ortiz?
O: I've been a server here since 2003.
M: Why do you think you should be the new assistant chef?
O: I'm a fast learner. I want to learn how to help create delicious food for Henri's customers.
M: Have you ever been an assistant chef before?
O: No, but I know I can do it.
M: That's terrific, Ms. Ortiz.

Pg. 54   Lesson 4—Exercise 3B

1. Is Claudia at home today?
2. Are they going to work this week?
3. Hector sat next to me yesterday.
4. I'm a fast learner and a team player.
5. How many other employees did they interview for the promotion?
6. This store is my family's favorite place to shop.

Pg. 55   Lesson 4—Exercise 4B

I = Interviewer, M = Miguel
I: Tell me about your education, Miguel.
M: Well, I studied accounting and computers at City College for four years. I graduated with honors.
I: Have you worked in a hospital before?
M: Yes, I have. I've worked at Center Street Hospital since February, 2005.
I: Are you working there now?
M: Yes, I am. I work in the billing department. I'm an assistant accounts manager.
I: I see. And why are you looking for a new job?
M: Center Street Hospital is a great place to work, but it's an hour drive from my house. I'd like to work here at Springfield General Hospital because it's an excellent hospital and it's closer to home.

UNIT 5   Community Resources

Pg. 60   Lesson 1—Exercise 1C

M = Man, N = Narrator
M: Thank you for calling the Lakeside City Services hotline. Please listen and select from the following menu.
1. M: City hall is the place where the mayor and city council work. Many other city government offices are also located inside city hall. Press 1 for city hall.
   N: city hall
2. M: Plastic, paper and glass can be recycled at the recycling center seven days a week. Press 2 for the recycling center.
   N: recycling center
3. M: Sign up now at the recreation center for children's and adults' sports classes and teams. Press 3 for the recreation center.
   N: recreation center
4. M: The community clinic offers free and low-cost health services. Clinic hours are Monday through Saturday from 9:00 to 7:00. Press 4 for the community clinic.
   N: community clinic
5. M: The animal shelter is the place to find a lost dog or cat. The animal shelter has a pet adoption day once a week. Press 5 for the animal shelter.
   N: animal shelter
6. M: The Department of Motor Vehicles, or the DMV, is where you go to get a driver's license or to register your car. Press 6 for the DMV.
   N: Department of Motor Vehicles (DMV)
7. M: The senior center offers exercise classes every day. Adults 65 years of age and over can take classes and receive services. Press 7 for the senior center.
   N: senior center
8. M: The employment agency has job listings in the community. Press 8 for the employment agency.
   N: employment agency

Pg. 66   Lesson 3—Exercise 3

M = Man, W = Woman
1. M: Mark hasn't ever been to New York, but he's been to Los Angeles.
2. W: Have you been to the new recreation center yet?
   M: Yes, I've already been three times, but I haven't taken a class there yet.
3. M: Have you gotten a new dog yet?
   W: No, but I'm going to the animal shelter to look this weekend.
4. W: Have Toshi and Roberto started working at the senior center yet?
   M: Toshi hasn't started yet, but Roberto started last weekend.
5. M: Have you ever written a letter to a school board member?
   W: I've never written a letter, but I've gone to three board meetings.
6. W: Have you already gone to the job fair this weekend?
   M: Yes. In fact, I went yesterday afternoon and I went back this morning for more information.

Pg. 67   Lesson 4—Exercise 1A

J = John, S = Ms. Schneider
J: Hi, Ms. Schneider. Did you go to the residents'
    meeting Wednesday night? I didn't see you there.
S: No, I didn't, John. I'm sorry. I had to work.
J: That's OK. By the way, have you signed the petition
    for a new onsite recycling center?
S: No, I haven't. What's it about?
J: The nearest recycling center is 15 miles away.
    We want to have one in the apartment complex.
    We're asking the building owners to put in a
    recycling center.
S: A recycling center in the apartment complex? I don't
    want to sign the petition. There's a recycling center
    on my way to work.

Pg. 68   Lesson 4—Exercise 3B

1. The woman volunteers at the senior center.
2. Check the website for the next job fair.
3. I haven't signed the petition yet.
4. Alex waited in line for two hours yesterday.
5. We've completed the class project already.

Pg. 69   Lesson 4—Exercise 4B

T = Talk show host, L = Dr. Lopez
T: Hello, and welcome to Earth Talk. We're here today
    with Dr. Arturo Lopez to talk about recycling in the
    United States. Dr. Lopez, can you tell us a little
    about the history of recycling?
L: Recycling paper, glass and metal isn't a new idea.
    It's been around for a long time. The first paper
    recycling began just outside of Philadelphia in the
    year 1690. The first recycling center was built in
    New York City in 1897.
T: And tell us, Dr. Lopez, why is recycling so
    important?
L: To say it simply, Sylvia, we produce too much trash!
    The average person in this country throws away
    one thousand six hundred pounds of trash every
    year. Just imagine how much trash that is! And our
    population is still growing.
T: So, I guess the big question is how are we doing?
    Are we recycling enough?
L: Well, in 1970 only 6.5 percent of the people in the
    U.S. were recycling paper, glass, and plastic on a
    regular basis. In the year 2005, that number went up
    to 32 percent. So we're making progress. But we need
    to do much, much more.

UNIT 6   What's Cooking?

Pg. 74   Lesson 1—Exercise 1C

R = Ramon, A = Assistant, J = Josh, N = Narrator
R: Welcome to Ramon's restaurant. I'm Ramon.
    I'm too busy cooking to talk right now, but my
    assistant will tell you what we're doing.
1. A: Welcome to the kitchen. I'm chopping
        vegetables right now. I have to chop the onions
        into very small pieces.
    N: chop
2. A: Ramon, the chef, is pouring broth into his famous
        soup. He must pour only a little bit in at a time.
    N: pour

3. A: He is also stirring his famous soup. He must stir
        this soup every five minutes.
    N: stir
4. A: The chef always uses a large pan for his
        vegetables. He put some oil in the pan first and
        then he added the vegetables to the pan.
    N: pan
5. A: I think that the large pot on the stove is for
        spaghetti. You need just the right pot for pasta.
    N: pot
6. A: It looks like the water for the pasta is boiling.
        Excuse me, Ramon? Do you want the water to
        boil so fast?
    N: boil
7. A: Pardon me. I need to talk to our dishwasher,
        Josh, for a moment… Josh! I need a bowl for
        these onions. Do you have a clean bowl?
    J: Just a minute. I'll bring you a bowl.
    N: bowl
8. A: Oh, Josh…can you bring me a plate too?
    J: The plates are in the sink. I'll clean a plate right
        away.
    N: plate
9. A: Josh works hard. He has to. Ramon makes sure
        that every glass in his restaurant is very clean.
        Josh spends almost 2 minutes washing each glass.
    N: glass
10. A: In the kitchen or in the dish room, you have to
        watch out for knives. Josh usually washes each
        knife separately and lets it dry on the counter.
    J: That way I never cut myself on a knife.
    N: knife
11. J: But forks can be dangerous too! I wash each fork
        carefully.
    N: fork
12. R: Josh! I need some spoons to let everyone taste
        my delicious soup.
    J: OK, Ramon. There's a clean spoon on the counter
        and I'll wash some more spoons right away.
    N: spoon
    R: Here, let me give you each a small bowl of soup
        and a spoon. It's delicious, isn't it?…I thought so.

Pg. 80   Lesson 3—Exercise 3

1. I just can't get over this cold.
2. I'd like a salad, but could you leave out the onions?
3. I need to take out the trash. Tomorrow is trash day.
4. I wrote down the phone number. I'm looking for it now.
5. They'll come over later this afternoon.
6. I got off the bus in front of my house.

Pg. 81   Lesson 4—Exercise 1A

C1 = Customer 1, C2 = Customer 2, S1 = Server 1,
S2 = Server 2
C1: Excuse me. I have a question about the menu. I've
    never heard of a sloppy joe before. What is it?
S1: It's a spicy meat sandwich with tomato sauce.
C1: Sounds good. OK. I'll try it.
S1: Excellent. Ours is the best in town.
C1: Oh, one more thing. Is a sloppy joe salty?
S1: No, it isn't. Our cook doesn't use much salt.
C1: Good. I'm trying to cut down on salt.

C2: Excuse me. I have a question about the menu. I've
    never heard of a chicken pot pie before. What is it?

S2: It's a pie made with chicken, vegetables, and potatoes.
C2: Sounds good. OK. I'll try it.
S2: Excellent. Ours is the best in town.
C2: I'd also like a baked apple. Are yours sweet?
S2: No, they aren't. Our cook doesn't use much sugar.
C2: Good. I'm trying to cut down on sugar.

Pg. 82 Lesson 4—Exercise 3B

M = Man, W = Woman
1. M: Can you help me look for my keys?
   W: I'll help you look for them in a minute.
2. W: Don't forget to turn off the oven.
   M: I'll turn off the oven as soon as the chicken is done.
3. M: Where do you get off the train?
   W: We get off at Grant Street Station.
4. W: Did you turn on the oven before you put the cake in?
   M: Yes, I did. I always remember to turn on the oven.
5. M: I went over to Jimmy's house yesterday afternoon.
   W: You always go over to Jimmy's house before you go over to Larry's house.
6. W: I couldn't get on that elevator because it was too crowded.
   M: That's OK. We'll get on the next one.

Pg. 83 Lesson 4—Exercise 4B

M = Man, W = Woman
M: Well, that was a good lunch.
W: Yes, it was. The kids enjoyed their meals, too. Are you going to pay the bill?
M: First let me check the math. OK, let's see…we had three hamburgers at six dollars each. That's eighteen dollars. And we had 2 turkey burgers at five-fifty each. That's eleven dollars.
W: The service was great. Let's leave a good tip.
M: Just a minute. I'm still doing the math. Then we had three lemonades for the kids, one coffee and a water.
W: How much were the lemonades?
M: Two dollars each. OK. So that's six dollars. This looks right. And coffee is a dollar-fifty. OK.
W: What about the tip. Is the tip included?
M: No, it's not included. OK. Everything looks correct.
W: Leave a good tip.
M: I will.

UNIT 7 Money Wise

Pg. 88 Lesson 1—Exercise 1C

N = Narrator, M = Male customer, T = Female teller,
F1 = Female customer 1, S = Security guard,
F2 = Female customer 2, L = Loan officer,
F3 = Female customer 3, A = Accounts manager
1. M: I need to get a cashier's check because I'm buying a car. Could I please get a cashier's check for seven thousand five hundred dollars?
   N: get a cashier's check
2. T: I'm a teller. Tellers work in banks and help customers with deposits and withdrawals.
   N: teller
3. F1: I started to go to the first teller window near the door but it's closed. It's strange to close a teller window at such a busy time of day.
   N: teller window

4. S: I'm a security guard. I keep the bank safe. I've been a security guard at this bank for 12 years.
   N: security guard
5. F2: I'm Mrs. Ramirez. My husband and I are applying for a loan. We're a little nervous, but it's pretty easy to apply for a loan at State Bank.
   N: apply for a loan
6. L: A loan officer helps people get bank loans or money from the bank so they can buy houses or cars. I'm a loan officer
   N: loan officer
7. A: Welcome to the account services desk. You can open or close your bank accounts at the account services desk.
   N: account services desk
8. F3: I need to open a checking account. How do I open an account with your bank?
   N: open an account
9. A: I'm Mr. Sanchez, the accounts manager. An accounts manager helps new customers with questions about their checking or savings accounts.
   N: accounts manager

Pg. 94 Lesson 3—Exercise 3

1. If you have to get a new car, how will you pay for it?
2. If you have the time to go to the bank, what will you do there?
3. What will you do if the bank is closed?
4. Where will you go if you need new clothes?
5. If I have questions, will the accounts manager help me?
6. If you start saving now, when will you reach your goal?

Pg. 95 Lesson 4—Exercise 1A

M = Min, C = Customer service
M: I'm calling to report a problem on my credit card bill.
C: What seems to be the problem?
M: It says that I spent fifteen hundred dollars in Pacific City, but that's impossible! I've never been to Pacific City.
C: OK. I'll talk to my supervisor and ask him to review it before we send your next bill.
M: So, do I have to pay the fifteen hundred dollar charge this month?
C: Let's wait and see. When you receive your next bill, you'll see your new balance.

Pg. 96 Lesson 4—Exercise 3B

1. Your sister brought her friend. What's her friend's name?
2. Tim will brush his teeth before he goes to bed.
3. He'll go to the bank before he comes home.
4. When he gets his paycheck, Jack will buy a new TV.

Pg. 97 Lesson 4—Exercise 4B

Welcome to State Bank's automated account information system. For savings account information, press one now. For checking account information, press two now. To speak to a customer service representative, press zero now.

Your checking account balance as of 3/15/08 is $625.10. To hear your last five transactions, press one now.

March 7th, 2008: check number 266 in the amount of $44.73.

March 7th, 2008: check number 268 in the amount of $106.50.

March 9th, 2008: check number 267 in the amount of $56.00.

March 9th, 2008: check number 270 in the amount of $27.61.

March 12th, 2008: check number 271 in the amount of $175.90.

UNIT 8   Living Well

Pg. 102   Lesson 1—Exercise 1C

M = Man, W = Woman, N = Narrator

M: The human body is an amazing machine. It's important to keep the parts of this machine healthy and strong. Let's look at what aerobic exercise can do for your body.

1. W: Believe it or not, aerobic exercise is great for your skin. Doing aerobics improves circulation so your skin looks healthy.
   N: skin
2. W: Aerobic exercise is also good for your lungs. Healthy lungs help you breathe more easily.
   N: lungs
3. W: Aerobic exercise, like running or bicycling, makes your heart beat faster, and that makes your heart strong.
   N: heart
4. W: When you do aerobics, you use the major muscle groups in your body. This makes your muscles stronger and healthier.
   N: muscles
5. W: Cycling and other exercise move the blood through the body. This improves your circulation, or blood flow.
   N: blood
   M: Another way to take care of yourself is with good nutrition. Remember, you are what you eat!
6. W: Scientists are learning more about what foods are good for the brain. Fish, eggs and plenty of water all help your brain process or learn new information and stay sharp. These foods are good for your brain.
   N: brain
7. W: Take care of your bones and teeth by getting plenty of calcium in your diet. Cheese, milk and dark green vegetables help make strong bones.
   N: bones
8. W: Pasta and rice, in small amounts, are good for your stomach. This food helps protect your stomach from acid.
   N: stomach

9. W: The intestines are an important part of your digestive system. Whole grain bread, fruit, and dark green vegetables are excellent for your intestines. This food has fiber that helps your intestines work well.
   N: intestines

Pg. 108   Lesson 3—Exercise 3A

1. Livia used to eat white bread, but she doesn't anymore. Now she eats brown bread.
2. Her youngest son, Carlos, didn't used to go to the park, but now he does. He plays in the park every evening.
3. Her oldest son, Tomas, used to spend a lot of money on fast food. Now he cooks healthy dinners at home every night. He saves a lot of money.
4. Her husband, Paulo didn't used to exercise during the week. He used to only exercise on the weekend. Now he exercises four days a week.
5. Elena, their daughter, doesn't play basketball anymore. She used to play all the time, but she hurt her knee. Now she walks for exercise.

Pg. 108   Lesson 3—Exercise 3B

1. When did the kids use to go to bed?
2. Patrick didn't use to stay up all night.
3. John and Gina use to go to bed at nine.
4. Did Gina use to complain about going to bed? I don't remember.
5. They all complain now. We didn't use to have so much stress at bedtime.

Pg. 109   Lesson 4—Exercise 1A

D = Doctor, M = Man, W = Woman

Patient 1

D: I'm a little concerned about your weight, Mr. Ruiz.
M: I've been under a lot of stress recently.
D: Have you been getting enough exercise?
M: Well, I used to jog every day, but it's too cold outside now.
D: Heart problems run in your family, so you need to exercise. Why don't you walk inside the mall to exercise?
M: Good idea. I'll try it.

Patient 2

D: I'm a little concerned about your blood pressure, Mrs. Thompson.
W: I've been under a lot of stress recently.
D: Have you been getting enough exercise?
W: Well, I used to go to the gym, but I moved far away from the gym.
D: High blood pressure runs in your family, so you need to exercise. Why don't you walk in your neighborhood?
W: OK. I can do that. I'll give it a try.

Pg. 111   Lesson 4—Exercise 3B

1. What do most people use to cook vegetables?
2. These days, they use steamers and microwaves.
3. There was a time when people didn't use to eat a lot of vegetables.
4. They didn't use microwaves, because there weren't any!

Pg. 111 Lesson 4—Exercise 4B

D = Donna, K = Katie

D: Welcome to fat-free radio, the radio program that answers your questions about diet and exercise. I'm Donna, your host. Let's take a call. Katie, are you there?

K: Hi Donna. Thanks for taking my call. I'd really like to lose ten pounds. What's the best exercise for me? I'm in good health, but I don't have a lot of time.

D: Great question, Katie. To lose weight, you want to use more calories than you eat. Everything you do uses calories. For example, watching TV uses calories, but only about 60 calories an hour. Cleaning your house uses calories, too! It's great exercise for busy people. You can burn about 225 calories per hour by cleaning the house. So remember, a cleaner house means a leaner you! Another great way to use calories is walking. Experts say that walking is the best way to lose weight. Depending on how fast you walk, you can use about 300 calories per hour. Try walking instead of driving or taking the bus if you want to lose weight. If you have time, swimming burns an average of 425 calories per hour. It's a great way to lose weight and it's easy on the body. If you are in good shape, running might be a good exercise for you. You can burn about 550 calories per hour. Thanks for the call, Katie. Hope you find the exercise that's right for you. Good luck.

UNIT 9   Hit the Road

Pg. 116 Lesson 1—Exercise 1C

R = Ramiro, N = Narrator

R: Hello there. I'm Ramiro. I work at Quick Change and I know a lot about cars. Here are some of the basics you should know.

1. R: Always keep the windshield clean. You can't see the road if the windshield is dirty.
   N: windshield
2. R: The headlights are on the front of the car. They help you see and be seen. Both headlights must work. It's illegal to drive with only one headlight.
   N: headlight
3. R: Check your tires once a month. A low tire or a flat tire can be very dangerous, so check your tires often.
   N: tire
4. R: Many important car parts are under the hood. To check the engine's oil level, open the hood.
   N: hood
5. R: Use the turn signal when you turn left or right. Let other drivers know what you're planning to do and use your turn signal.
   N: turn signal
6. R: Many people forget to keep their gas tanks full. Then they run out of gas. Remember to fill your gas tank. Oh! Don't forget to close the gas tank when you're done.
   N: gas tank
7. R: It's good to have a first aid kit in the trunk. And don't forget a blanket. Put it in the trunk too.
   N: trunk

8. R: You have to have a license plate on your car; it's your car's identification number. It's a good idea to memorize your license plate number.
   N: license plate
9. R: The bumper protects you and your car if you have an accident. There is a bumper on the front and a bumper on the back.
   N: bumper
   R: Well, it's time for me to get back to work. Drive safely.

Pg. 122 Lesson 3—Exercise 3

1. After we called the mechanic, we took the car to the garage.
2. Anna stopped at the gas station before she picked me up.
3. When I stopped the car, I saw my friend on the corner.
4. Before he took his driving test, Mr. Chen was nervous.
5. Before she buys a new car, Susan will sell her old car.
6. When Anthony moves to Los Angeles, he'll learn to drive.
7. After I got an oil change, I went on a trip.
8. After Karla starts the car, she adjusts the rearview mirror.

Pg. 123 Lesson 4—Exercise 1A

D = Car dealer, C = Customer

D: This is a really nice car. It only has 30,000 miles on it, and it has a two-year warranty too.

C: 30,000 miles? That sure is nice. How much is it?

D: It also has a new stereo, and new paint too.

C: Uh-huh. And how much is it?

D: I can sell it to you today for twelve thousand five hundred dollars. It's a great deal.

C: Twelve thousand-five hundred!?!? But the bumper is dented and the windshield has a crack!

D: Uhhh....Let me talk to my manager about the price. We're flexible at Mid-City cars.

Pg. 125 Lesson 4—Exercise 4B

La = Larry, Lo = Lorraine, M = Matt

La: Welcome to Car Time, the radio show that answers all your car questions. I'm Larry.

Lo: And I'm Lorraine. Let's take a call now from Matt in Dallas. Hi, Matt.

La: Hello, Matt.

M: Hi, Larry and Lorraine. I'm getting ready to buy my first car.

Lo: Congratulations, Matt!

M: Thanks. Um, my question is, how much money will I need every month for gas, insurance, and other expenses?

La: Great question, Matt. Now is the right time to be planning for expenses.

Lo: The biggest expense will be car insurance. For most people, that's a monthly expense. You have to get insurance. It's the law! Insurance can be expensive. How much you pay depends on the kind of car you have, your age, your driving record, and where you live.

La: That's right Lorraine. And you should think about gas money. How much will you drive every week? The average person drives about 15,000 miles per year. Look for a car that gets good gas mileage. Anything above 30 miles per gallon is considered good. Some of today's cars can get over 60 miles per gallon.

Lo: In many states, you'll also have to pay taxes on your car every year. How much depends on the price, or value of the car.

La: The last major expense is car maintenance and repairs. This cost will be different for new cars and used cars. With any car, you need to think about how many miles you drive per year, so you can plan for maintenance like oil changes and new tires. You should get an oil change every 5,000 miles. If you have an older car, add money for other problems that might come up.

M: OK. Thanks a lot guys.

Lo: Good luck with that car!

La and Lo: Bye, Matt.

UNIT 10 Crime Doesn't Pay

Pg. 130 Lesson 1—Exercise 1C

K = Kevin, S = Su-Ling, N = Narrator

K: Hi. I'm Kevin, and this is my wife Su-Ling. We had a strange evening recently. We were glad that we knew a lot of neighborhood safety.

S: Here's what happened.

1. S: We went out for a walk. I locked the door. Locking the doors is one of the best ways to keep your home safe. We always lock the doors when we leave home.
   N: lock the doors

2. K: I put my wallet in my jacket pocket. That's a good way to protect your wallet. You should always protect your wallet or purse when you are out in public.
   N: protect your wallet or purse

3. K: We don't walk alone at night. It's not a good idea to walk alone when it's dark out.
   N: don't walk alone at night

4. S: We always walk together in well-lit areas. We walk down streets that have many lights. It's much safer to walk in well-lit areas.
   N: walk in well-lit areas

5. K: So, the other night when we were walking, we saw a young man commit a crime. He was spray-painting the hood of a car! We couldn't believe that someone would commit a crime like that in front of us.
   N: commit a crime

6. S: We were witnessing a crime! At first we weren't sure what to do. Then we remembered that we should call 911. Kevin called 911 on his cell phone and told them that we were witnessing a crime.
   N: witness a crime

7. K: When the police arrived, we reported the crime. It's every person's responsibility to report crimes they see or hear. Be prepared to answer a police officer's questions when you report a crime.
   N: report a crime

8. S: The police found the young man a few blocks away and arrested the suspect. Remember that arresting a suspect is a job for the police. Don't try to stop or arrest a suspect yourself.
   N: arrest a suspect

Pg. 136 Lesson 3—Exercise 3

1. Everyone in the courtroom is listening to the witness.
2. Telling the truth is very important in court.
3. Explaining the rules is the judge's job.
4. The attorneys are asking the witness a lot of questions.
5. The defendant is wearing a suit and tie.
6. Deciding what to do won't be easy for the jury.

Pg. 137 Lesson 4—Exercise 1A

P = Male police officer, W = Witness

P: Police department. How can I direct your call?

W: I'd like to report a crime I witnessed.

P: OK. Please tell me what happened.

W: While I was entering my apartment building, I saw a man in the hallway. First he broke into an apartment. Then he took a TV.

P: What happened after that?

W: I think he saw me because, all of a sudden, he ran away.

P: OK. Hold on. An officer will fill out a complete report. Reporting this was the right thing to do.

W: Thank you.

Pg. 138 Lesson 4—Exercise 3B

1. I called the police. Nobody else had a cell phone.
2. I saw the whole thing officer. They came out of the bank. I saw them. They ran that way.
3. We walk every evening. We never walk in the morning. We're too busy.

Pg. 139 Lesson 4—Exercise 4B

P = Male police officer, A = Ms. Aziz

P: Thank you for holding. This is Officer Wong. What's your name, please?

A: My name is Roya Aziz.

P: Okay, Ms. Aziz. I need to get some information about what you saw. Can you tell me where you were when you witnessed the mugging?

A: Yes. I was sitting on a park bench.

P: Okay. What happened first?

A: I saw a man run by. He was moving fast, but I saw that he was carrying a lady's purse.

P: What did he look like?

W: I didn't get a good look at his face, but he was tall and thin.

P: Okay. What happened next?

A: Next, a woman ran by. She was yelling for the man to stop. She kept saying, "He has my purse! He has my purse!"

P: And what happened after that, Ms. Aziz?

A: Well, I stood up to see what was happening. The man fell and dropped the purse. Then he got up and ran away. The woman picked up her purse and asked me to call the police.

P: Okay, Ms. Aziz. Is the woman there with you now?

A: Yes, she's right here. She says she's fine.

P: A police car should be there in a few minutes. Both of you please wait there until the officers arrive.

UNIT 11 That's Life

Pg. 144 Lesson 1—Exercise 1C

C = Carlos Ortega, N = Narrator
    C: My name is Carlos Ortega, and this is the story of my life.
1. C: I was born on August 22nd. I guess I couldn't wait to get started because I was born 3 weeks early. My mother couldn't wait for me to be born either!
    N: be born
2. C: I graduated from high school at the top of my class when I was 18. My parents were very proud. I'm the first person in my family to graduate from high school.
    N: graduate
3. C: On my first job with ACME Glass, I was promoted from assembly worker to plant manager in only a few years. I remember how excited I was to get a promotion.
    N: get a promotion
4. C: I met Nora, the love of my life, at the factory. We got engaged after only six months. I asked her to marry me at our favorite restaurant. I was so nervous to get engaged.
    N: get engaged
5. C: When we got married, we were both 30 years old. In those days, you didn't get married at that age, but we did.
    N: get married
6. C: We had our first child a year later. We were nervous and excited to have a baby.
    N: have a baby
7. C: Everything was going well at the factory, but I wanted to run my own business—so I started Ortega's Fine Foods. It's a lot of hard work to start a business, but it's worth every minute.
    N: start a business
8. C: Five years ago, I decided it was time to retire. I wanted to travel and spend more time with Nora so I retired.
    N: retire
9. C: Two years ago, I became a grandfather. That's right, Nora and I have a grandson. You feel like a kid again when you become a grandparent!
    N: become a grandparent

Pg. 150 Lesson 3—Exercise 3

1. Smoking is not permitted in the restaurant.
2. A reception is planned immediately after the wedding.
3. Babies born at Glenview Hospital are taken care of by our excellent team of nurses.
4. The party is given by my friends, Tina and Lim.
5. All guests are welcomed by the bride.
6. Birth announcements and death notices are found in Section C of the local paper.

Pg. 151 Lesson 4—Exercise 1A

M = Min, P = Peter
M: Hello, Peter? It's Min. I've got some good news and some bad news.
P: Oh, no. What's the bad news?
M: Well, I had car trouble and I was almost late for my final exam.
P: Oh, no. That's too bad.
M: Yes, but the good news is that I got an A on the test. I'll be able to graduate next month!
P: Terrific! That's the best news I've heard all day. Let's celebrate this weekend.
M: That sounds great. I'll call you Friday.

Pg. 152 Lesson 4—Exercise 3B

1. That's right!
2. That's right.
3. Wait. I can't find my ticket.
4. Wait! I see my friend over there.
5. I got the job! I can start on Wednesday.
6. I got the job….if I want it.

Pg. 153 Lesson 4—Exercise 4B

N = Narrator, W1 = Woman 1, W2 = Woman 2
N: Around the World in 60 Seconds
W1: Do you like to attend weddings? Are you curious about wedding traditions around the world? Maybe you're getting married in the near future? If marriage is on your mind, you'll love today's topic on *Around the World in 60 Seconds*.
W2: That's right. Today we're talking about wedding traditions from around the world. For example, did you know that in Venezuela the bride and groom don't say goodbye to anyone at their wedding reception? It's good luck for them to leave without saying goodbye to their guests.
W1: Yes. And in Greece, dishes are broken for good luck at wedding receptions.
W2: It seems that every culture has their own unique and interesting wedding traditions. Did you know that in Mexico and Panama brides are given 13 gold coins at the wedding ceremony? In China and India, brides often wear red wedding gowns.
W1: And have you ever wondered why rice is often thrown at the bride and groom by wedding guests in the U.S.?
W2: That's right. It's all for good luck.
W1: These are just a few of many traditions from around the world. And the most popular tradition around the world? You guessed it. Almost anywhere you go, the wedding ends with a kiss.

UNIT 12 Doing the Right Thing

Pg. 158 Lesson 1—Exercise 1C

N = Narrator, W = Woman
1. W: The right to vote is a constitutional right of U.S. citizens. Most people think the right to vote is their most important right.
    N: the right to vote
2. W: Everyone in the U.S. has freedom of speech. This first amendment right gives people the right to express their opinions and thoughts. Freedom of speech has played an important role in U.S. history.
    N: freedom of speech
3. W: Freedom of the press means that newspapers and other news sources are free to report the news. The government cannot tell news sources what to say because of freedom of the press.
    N: freedom of the press

4. W: The right to a fair trial guarantees that a judge or a jury will hear both sides of the story. In the United States, anyone accused of a crime has the right to a fair trial.
   N: the right to a fair trial
5. W: In the U.S., people have freedom of peaceful assembly. That means a group of people can get together and protest or voice their opinions in public. Freedom of peaceful assembly is another basic first amendment right.
   N: freedom of peaceful assembly
   W: Carrying a U.S. passport makes traveling in and out of the United States easier. All U.S. citizens have the right to carry a U.S. passport.
   N: the right to carry a U.S. passport

Pg. 164   Lesson 3—Exercise 3

1. The hospital has a great volunteer program. George plans…
2. Lee wanted to help, so he volunteered…
3. Marta likes to speak Spanish with the residents at the senior center. She practices…
4. Jill usually volunteers to clean up after events. She dislikes…
5. Raul is studying to be an attorney. He enjoyed…
6. We were all worried about the future of our city. We decided…

Pg. 165   Lesson 4—Exercise 1A

D = Mrs. Delgado, L1 = Law clerk 1, T = Mr, Tran, L2 = Law clerk 2
D: Hi. I called yesterday. My name is Marta Delgado. The woman on the phone told me to come in.
L1: How can we help you today?
D: Well, I'm not sure what I should do. I've lived in my apartment for eight months. I have a one-year lease. Last week, my landlord told me I have to move.
L1: Do you have any idea why?
D: No. I pay my rent on time and I'm a good tenant. I suspect it's because her brother needs an apartment and the building is full. Can she do that?
L1: No, she can't. I think we can help you keep your apartment.
T: Hello. I called yesterday. I'm Tommy Tran. I'm having a problem with a car I bought last month. The man on the phone told me to come in.
L2: How can we help you today?
T: Well, I don't know what to do. I bought a new car last month. There's a problem with the electrical system. It's been broken three times since I bought it. Now the dealer won't fix it or replace it.
L2: Do you have any idea why?
T: The dealer said there is no lemon law because the car was fine when I bought it. I'm pretty sure they aren't telling the truth. I think it's because they don't want to replace the car. Can they do that?
L2: No, they can't. I think I can help you.

Pg. 166   Lesson 4—Exercise 3B

M = Man, W = Woman
1. W: I get the mail every day.
   M: Pat is a 10-year old male.
2. W: I need to buy some food.
   M: The market is by the bank.
3. W: Tim is a new citizen.
   M: He knew he could pass the exam.
4. W: I'll go to the market.
   M: Apples are in aisle six.

Pg. 167   Lesson 4—Exercise 4B

M1 = Man 1, W1 = Woman 1, M2 = Man 2, W2 = Woman 2, M3 = Man 3, W3 = Woman 3, W4 = Woman 4, M4 = Man 4
M1: The first issue on tonight's agenda is the proposal for the new high school. Let's hear voter comments on that now. Would anyone like to comment?
W1: Yes. I think the new high school is a great idea, but it can't be built on Green Street. The street's too small. Traffic would be terrible.
M2: I agree. There isn't enough parking there for the neighborhood now.
W2: I disagree. Green Street is a great place for a high school. The real problem is the cost of a new high school. The property on Green Street is already owned by the city. It's the best place at the best price.
W3: We don't need a new high school! We should just make Central High School bigger. That would be cheaper.
W4: Cheaper, but not better!
M3: Our taxes are already too high! We don't need a new school!
M4: Order, everyone! Please calm down! Everybody has a right to his or her opinion. Let's give everyone a chance to talk.
M1: Thank you Mr. Kovak. Okay, let me repeat the comments so far. Mrs. Bailey thinks that Green Street is too small for a new high school and the neighborhood is too crowded. Ms. Martinez wants us to build the high school on Green Street because the cost will be less. Ms. Neal prefers making our old high school bigger. Mr. Kovak called for order to give everyone a chance to speak. Who else would like to comment? Yes. First Mrs. Rodriguez, then Mr. Cho.

GRAMMAR CHARTS

THE SIMPLE PRESENT

Statements

I You	work	
He She It	works	every day.
We You They	work	

Negative statements

I You	don't	work	
He She It	doesn't	work	every day.
We You They	don't	work	

Contractions

do not	= don't
does not	= doesn't

Yes/No questions

Do	I you	
Does	he she it	work?
Do	we you they	

Answers

	I you	do.
Yes,	he she it	does.
	we you they	do.

	I you	don't.
No,	he she it	doesn't.
	we you they	don't.

THE PRESENT CONTINUOUS

Statements

I'm You're He's She's It's We're You're They're	working	now.

Negative statements

I'm You're He's She's It's We're You're They're	not working	now.

Contractions

I am	= I'm	I am not	= I'm not
you are	= you're	you are not	= you aren't
he is	= he's	he is not	= he isn't
she is	= she's	she is not	= she isn't
it is	= it's	it is not	= it isn't
we are	= we're	we are not	= we aren't
they are	= they're	they are not	= they aren't

THE SIMPLE PAST

Statements		
I You He She It We You They	worked	last Friday.

Negative statements		
I You He She It We You They	didn't work	last Saturday.

Contractions
did not = didn't

Yes/No questions			
Did	I you he she it we you they	work	last Friday?

Answers						
Yes,	I you he she it we you they	did.	No,	I you he she it we you they	didn't.

PRESENT AND PAST VERB FORMS

	Simple present	Present continuous	Simple past
If verb ends in –y	study, studies	studying	studied
If verb ends in -e	use, uses	using	used
If verb ends in a consonant	walk, walks search, searches	walking searching	walked searched

ADJECTIVES AND ADVERBS

Adjectives without –ly that describe nouns	
close	My car is close.
loud	The music is loud.
quiet	It is a quiet place.

Adverbs with –ly that describe verbs	
closely	He watched closely.
loudly	The band played loudly.
quietly	He spoke quietly.

PREFIXES AND SUFFIXES

Prefix	Meaning	Examples
dis-	not	disorganized, disagree, disobey, dishonest, dislike
un-	not	unclean, unhealthy, unsafe, unhappy, unimportant
re-	do again	refill, reprint, reread, reuse, rewrite

Suffix	What the suffix does	Examples
-ful	Changes some nouns or verbs to an adjective	stressful, careful, beautiful, colorful, helpful, thankful
-tion	Changes some verbs to a noun	description, addition, education, invitation, dictation, production
-al	Changes some nouns to an adjective	personal, accidental, national, musical, professional

THE FUTURE WITH *BE GOING TO* AND *WILL*

Statements		
I'm You're He's She's It's We're You're They're	going to	work next Tuesday.

Negative statements		
I'm You're He's She's It's We're You're They're	not going to	work next Tuesday.

Statements	
I'll You'll He'll She'll It'll We'll You'll They'll	probably work next week.

Negative statements	
I You He She It We You They	probably won't work next week.

Contractions
I will   = I'll you will   = you'll he will   = he'll she will   = she'll it will   = it'll we will   = we'll they will = they'll

COMPARATIVE AND SUPERLATIVE ADJECTIVES

	Comparative form		Superlative form
Add *-er than* to most adjectives with one syllable.	faster than, cheaper than, newer than, smaller than, kinder than, greater than	Add *-est* to most adjectives with one syllable.	fastest, cheapest, newest, smallest, kindest, greatest
In adjectives ending in *-y,* add *-er than* and change the *-y* to *-i.*	heavier than, happier than, angrier than, friendlier than	Add *-est* and change the *-y* to *-i* in adjectives ending in *-y.*	heaviest, happiest, angriest, friendliest
Add *-r than* to adjectives that end in *-e.*	safer than	Add *-st* to adjectives ending in *-e.*	safest
Double the final consonant and add *-er than* in some adjectives.	bigger than, hotter than	Double the final consonant and add *-est* in some adjectives.	biggest, hottest

THE PRESENT PERFECT

Statements

I've You've He's She's It's We've You've They've	worked in a store.

Negative Statements

I You	haven't	worked in a store.
He She It	hasn't	
We You They	haven't	

Contractions

I have	= I've
you have	= you've
he has	= he's
she has	= she's
it has	= it's
we have	= we've
they have	= they've
have not	= haven't
has not	= hasn't

***Yes/No* questions**

Have	I you	worked in a store?
Has	he she it	
Have	we you they	

Answers

Yes,	I you	have.	No,	I you	haven't.
	he she it	has.		he she it	hasn't.
	we you they	have.		we you they	haven't.

Forms of irregular verbs

Base form of verb	Simple past	Past participle
be	was/were	been
do	did	done
drink	drank	drunk
eat	ate	eaten
get	got	gotten
go	went	gone/been
have	had	had

Forms of irregular verbs

Base form of verb	Simple past	Past participle
hear	heard	heard
make	made	made
read	read	read
see	saw	seen
take	took	taken
write	wrote	written

Ever*, *already*, and *yet

ever = at any time; never = not at any time
A: Have you ever worked in a store?
B: No, I haven't. I've never worked in a store.

already = some time before now; Use only with affirmative statements.
A: Have you already eaten lunch?
B: Yes, I have.

yet = any time until now; Use only with negative statements.
A: Have you bought a car yet?
B: No, I haven't.

PHRASAL VERBS

Separable phrasal verbs

bring in	Please **bring** the chair **in** the room.	take out	Now **take** the cake **out**.
chop up	Please **chop** the onion **up**.	turn off	**Turn** the oven **off**.
figure out	I can **figure** the recipe **out**.	turn on	**Turn** the light **on**.
leave out	**Leave** the salt **out** of the soup.	use by	**Use** the milk **by** next week.
pick up	Please **pick** the trash **up**.	write down	**Write** the recipe **down**.
put in	**Put** the cake **in** the oven		

Inseparable phrasal verbs

go over	Will you **go over** to the apartment?	get over	I hope you **get over** your headache.
get off	**Get off** the chair.	look after	Please **look after** the baby.
get on	Don't **get on** the bus.	look for	**Look for** the bus.

POSSESSIVE ADJECTIVES AND PRONOUNS

Possessive adjectives	Possessive pronouns	Note
That is **my** book.	That is **mine**.	*Its* shows possession (*its taste*). *It's* is a contraction for *it is* (*it's spicy*).
How are **your** french fries?	How are **yours**?	
Is **his** chicken soup good?	Is **his** good?	
Her sandwich looks delicious.	**Hers** looks delicious.	
The dog is looking for **its** food.	**Its** food is in the bowl.	
Do you like **our** hamburgers?	Do you like **ours**?	
Is **your** soup too salty?	Is **yours** too salty?	
Is **their** apple pie too sweet?	Is **theirs** too sweet?	

REAL CONDITIONAL STATEMENTS

If clause	Main clause	Main clause	*If* clause
If I go to the bank,	I'll apply for a loan.	I can apply for a loan	if I go to the bank.
If you save money,	you'll buy a TV.	You'll buy a TV	if you save money.
If he buys it,	he'll pay $100.	He can pay $100	if he buys it.
If she wants the car,	she'll buy it.	She'll buy it	if she wants the car.
If it is on sale,	it'll be cheaper.	It'll be cheaper	if it is on sale.
If we find a house,	we'll get a loan.	We'll get a loan	if we find a house.
If you wait,	you'll save money.	You'll save money	if you wait.
If they get jobs,	they'll buy the house.	They'll buy the house if they get jobs.	

USED TO

Statements		
I You He She It We You They	**used to**	eat junk food.

Negative Statements		
I You He She It We You They	**didn't use to**	eat junk food.

Questions			
Did	I you he she it we you they	**use to**	eat junk food?

Answers					
Yes,	I you he she it we you they	did.	No,	I you he she it we you they	didn't.

THE PRESENT PERFECT CONTINUOUS

Statements		
I You	have	
He She It	has	been working for a year.
We You They	have	

Negative Statements		
I You	haven't	
He She It	hasn't	been working for a year.
We You They	haven't	

Questions		
Have	I	
	you	
Has	he	
	she	been feeling well this week?
	it	
Have	we	
	you	
	they	

Answers						
Yes,	I	have.	No,	I	haven't.
	you			you	
	he			he	
	she	has.		she	hasn't.
	it			it	
	we			we	
	you	have.		you	haven't.
	they			they	

DESCRIBING PRESENT, PAST, AND FUTURE EVENTS WITH TIME CLAUSES

Present	When I see a red light, I stop the car.
	I stop the car when I see a red light.
Past	Before I turned left, I used my turn signal.
	I used my turn signal before I turned left.
Future	After I wash the car, I'll drive to the bank.
	I'll drive to the bank after I wash the car.

AND...TOO, AND...NOT EITHER, BUT

and...too	I like to travel. My friend likes to travel.
	I like to travel, **and** my friend does, **too**.
and...not either	The car doesn't need gas. The car doesn't need oil.
	The car doesn't need gas, **and** it **doesn't** need oil **either**.
but	I live in an apartment. My friend lives in a house.
	I live in an apartment, **but** my friend lives in a house.

GERUNDS AND INFINITIVES

Gerund
Driving at night is dangerous.
Locking the car doors is a good idea.
Going out alone at night is not safe.

Infinitive
It is dangerous **to drive** at night.
It is a good idea **to lock** the car doors.
It is not safe **to go** out alone at night.

Notes
• A gerund is a form of a verb that ends in *-ing*.
• An infinitive is *to* + the base form of a verb.

USING GERUNDS AND INFINITIVES WITH VERBS

Verb + Gerund
I enjoy **cleaning** the house.
Ted practiced **playing** the piano.
They continued **studying**.

Verb + Infinitive
Tom volunteered **to clean** the house.
We like **to play** the piano.
Did you continue **to study**?

Notes
• These verbs are often followed by a gerund: *dislike, enjoy, practice*
• These verbs are often followed by an infinitive: *like, begin, continue, want, agree, volunteer, plan, decide, hope, need*
• These verbs are often followed by a gerund or infinitive: *like, begin, continue*

THE PRESENT PASSIVE

The present passive		
I	am	
You	are	
He She It	is	invited to the party.
We You They	are	

Notes
• The present passive uses a form of the verb *be* + the past participle. Lunch **is served**.
• Use *by* + person/thing to say who/what performs the action in a passive sentence. Lunch is served **by Sara**.
• We usually use the active voice in English. Sara serves lunch.

BE ABLE + INFINITIVE (*TO* + VERB) FOR ABILITY

Future	
I you he she it we you they	will be able to go to the party.

Note
In the present, it is more common to use *can* for ability. I can go to the party. In the past, it is more common to use *could* for ability. I could go to the party.

TOLD + PERSON + *TO*

Told + person + infinitive
I **told her to ask** for help.
They **told us to sit**.

Told + person + *not* + infinitive
I **told her not to ask** for help.
They **told us not to sit**.

Notes
• To report an affirmative request, use *told* + person + infinitive. • To report a negative request, use *told* + person + *not* + infinitive.

X,Y,Z

LIFE SKILLS

Consumer Education

Environment and the World

Family and Parenting

Government and Community Resources

Health and Nutrition

Interpersonal Communication

Safety and Security

Transportation and Safety

TOPICS

WORKFORCE SKILLS

Applied Technology

Maintaining Employment

Obtaining Employment

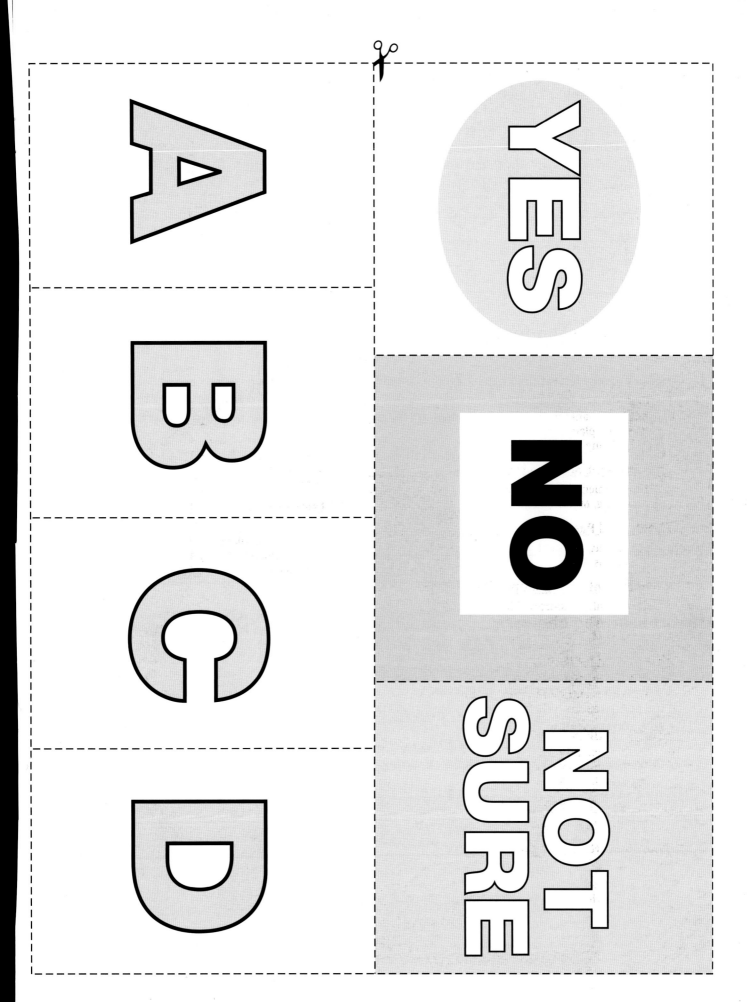

Unit 1 Learning Log for _____ Date: _____

I can

❏ use words for study skills, study habits, and types of schools.
❏ write a journal entry about school.
❏ use present- and past-tense verbs. (*I learn. I'm learning. I learned.*)
❏ answer questions about my career interests.
❏ use adjectives and adverbs to talk about careers.
❏ understand information about library services.

My favorite exercise was _____.

I need to practice _____.

I want to learn more about _____.

Unit 2 Learning Log for _____ Date: _____

I can

❏ use words for recreational places, events, and activities.
❏ write an email invitation.
❏ use the future with *will* and *be going to*. (*I'll be home at 4:00. I'm going to study.*)
❏ talk about my preferences.
❏ understand an article about outdoor activities and health.
❏ use the suffix *-ful* to describe people and places. (*The trees are colorful now.*)

My favorite exercise was _____.

I need to practice _____.

I want to learn more about _____.

Unit 3 Learning Log for _____ Date: _____

I can

❏ use words for computer parts and office workers.
❏ write a memo about classroom policies.
❏ use comparisons. (*The 580 laptop is less expensive than the 680.*)
❏ give and respond to feedback.
❏ use the superlative. (*He is the most efficient worker I know.*)
❏ understand an article about workplace training.

My favorite exercise was _____.

I need to practice _____.

I want to learn more about _____.

Unit 4 Learning Log for _____ Date: _____
(name)

I can

- ❏ use words for job interviews and personal strengths.
- ❏ write a thank-you letter after a job interview.
- ❏ use the present perfect. (*I have worked in an office.*)
- ❏ interview for a promotion.
- ❏ use contractions with the present perfect. (*I've worked here since 2004.*)
- ❏ understand an article about getting a promotion.

My favorite exercise was _____.

I need to practice _____.

I want to learn more about _____.

Unit 5 Learning Log for _____ Date: _____
(name)

I can

- ❏ use words for community resources and services.
- ❏ write a letter about a problem at school or in the community.
- ❏ use *Yes/No* questions in the present perfect. (*Have they fixed the stove?*)
- ❏ give my opinion about a community issues.
- ❏ understand an article about Earth Day.
- ❏ use the prefix *un-* to describe the environment. (*The water is unsafe to drink.*)

My favorite exercise was _____.

I need to practice _____.

I want to learn more about _____.

Unit 6 Learning Log for _____ Date: _____
(name)

I can

- ❏ use words for kitchen items and actions.
- ❏ write a story about a family recipe.
- ❏ use phrasal verbs. (*She wrote down the ingredients.*)
- ❏ order a meal in a restaurant.
- ❏ use possessive pronouns. (*Her dinner was good, but mine was terrible.*)
- ❏ understand an article about food safety.

My favorite exercise was _____.

I need to practice _____.

I want to learn more about _____.

Unit 7 Learning Log for _____ Date: _____
<small>(name)</small>

I can
- ❏ use words for banking.
- ❏ write a story about my financial plan.
- ❏ use the future conditional. (*If I buy it tomorrow, I'll save money.*)
- ❏ report a billing problem or a banking error.
- ❏ use future time clauses (*I'll pay the bill after I get my statement.*)
- ❏ understand an article about identity theft.

My favorite exercise was _____.

I need to practice _____.

I want to learn more about _____.

Unit 8 Learning Log for _____ Date: _____
<small>(name)</small>

I can
- ❏ use words for parts of the body and medical departments.
- ❏ write an outline of a wellness plan.
- ❏ use *used to*. (*I used to eat junk food.*)
- ❏ respond to a doctor's advice.
- ❏ use present-perfect continuous. (*I've been walking to work since April.*)
- ❏ understand an article about using medication safely.

My favorite exercise was _____.

I need to practice _____.

I want to learn more about _____.

Unit 9 Learning Log for _____ Date: _____
<small>(name)</small>

I can
- ❏ use words for car parts.
- ❏ write a story about a trip.
- ❏ use past, present, and future time clauses. (*I stopped for gas before I went home.*)
- ❏ negotiate price.
- ❏ use conjunctions. (*I like the blue car, and she does, too.*)
- ❏ understand an article about lemon laws.

My favorite exercise was _____.

I need to practice _____.

I want to learn more about _____.

Unit 10 Learning Log for _____ Date: _____
(name)

I can

❏ use words for crime prevention and criminal justice.
❏ write an essay about home security.
❏ use gerunds as subjects. (*Locking the doors is important.*)
❏ report a crime to police.
❏ use infinitives and gerunds. (*It isn't safe to walk alone. Walking alone isn't safe.*)
❏ understand an article about careers in public safety.

My favorite exercise was _____.

I need to practice _____.

I want to learn more about _____.

Unit 11 Learning Log for _____ Date: _____
(name)

I can

❏ use words for life events and special occasions.
❏ write a response to an invitation.
❏ use the present passive. (*Dinner is served between 5 p.m. and 7 p.m.*)
❏ talk about good news and bad news.
❏ use *be able to.* (*I won't be able to come to the party.*)
❏ understand an article about renting or buying a home.

My favorite exercise was _____.

I need to practice _____.

I want to learn more about _____.

Unit 12 Learning Log for _____ Date: _____
(name)

I can

❏ use words for civic rights and responsibilities.
❏ write a letter about civic involvement.
❏ use verbs + infinitives or gerunds. (*I decided to go. He dislikes running.*)
❏ describe a legal problem.
❏ report requests with *told.* (*He told me to call him.*)
❏ understand an article about the civil rights movement.

My favorite exercise was _____.

I need to practice _____.

I want to learn more about _____.

MULTILEVEL CLASSROOM TROUBLESHOOTING TIPS

Instructional Challenge	Try this	Read this
Activities seem to run too long and students go off task.	1. Set time limits for most activities. An inexpensive digital timer will keep track of the time and allow you to focus on monitoring your learners' progress. You can always give a time extension if needed. 2. Assign timekeepers in each group, and have them be accountable for managing the time limits.	Donna Moss, "Teaching for Communicative Competence: Interaction in the ESOL Classroom," *Focus on Basics,* http://www.ncsall.net/index.php?id=739 (2006)
There are so many different needs in my classroom, I just don't have time to teach to them all.	1. Use a corners activity to help learners identify shared goals, resulting in more realistic expectations for the group. (See the *Step Forward Professional Development Program* for more information on corners activities.) 2. Encourage learners to identify what they have to do to meet their learning goals. Having learners complete open-ended statements, such as *Good students* _____, creates a forum for a class discussion of the learners' responsibilities in the learning process.	Lenore Balliro, "Ideas for a Multilevel Class," *Focus on Basics,* http://www.ncsall.net/index.php?id=443 (2006)
I'm worried that assigning pre-level learners tasks that are different from the higher-level learners stigmatizes them.	Provide three levels of the same task, and have your learners identify which one they want to tackle. Most pre-level learners appreciate being given tasks that match their abilities in the same way that higher-level learners appreciate being given tasks that match their abilities.	Betsy Parish, *Teaching Adult ESL: A Practical Introduction* (New York: McGraw Hill, 2004), 195.
Students in groups finish tasks at different times and often start speaking in their first language.	1. Supply a follow-up task for every activity. Often a writing task makes a good follow-up. (See the *Multilevel Strategies* throughout this book.) 2. Create a set of self-access materials that students can work on while they wait for other groups to complete the main task—for example, magazine pictures with writing prompts, level-appropriate readings with comprehension questions, grammar worksheets from the *Step Forward Multilevel Grammar Exercises CD-ROM 3, Step Forward Workbook 3,* etc.	Jill Bell, *Teaching Multilevel Classes in ESL,* (San Diego: Dominie Press, 1991), 134–146.
I like the high energy of group interaction, but it's hard to get the groups' attention once they've been engaged in group work.	1. Establish a quiet signal such as a bell, harmonica, train whistle or music to bring the groups back into "whole-class" mode. 2. Give group leaders the job of getting the group quiet once the group timekeeper calls "time."	Peter Papas, "Managing Small Group Learning," *Designs for Learning,* http://www.edteck.com/blocks/2_pages/small.htm (2006).